Wellington and the British Army's Indian Campaigns 1798–1805

Wellington and the British Army's Indian Campaigns 1798–1805

Martin R. Howard

Pen & Sword
MILITARY

An imprint of
Pen & Sword Books Ltd
Yorkshire - Philadelphia

First published in Great Britain in 2020 by
PEN & SWORD MILITARY

An imprint of
Pen & Sword Books Ltd
Yorkshire – Philadelphia

ISBN 978-1-47389-446-4

Typeset in 11/13 point MinionPro

Printed and bound by TJ International

Pen & Sword Books Ltd incorporates the imprints of Pen & Sword Archaeology, Atlas, Aviation,
Battleground, Discovery, Family History, History, Maritime, Military, Naval, Politics, Social
History, Transport, True Crime, Claymore Press,

Frontline Books, Praetorian Press, Seaforth Publishing and White Owl

For a complete list of Pen & Sword titles please contact

PEN & SWORD BOOKS LTD
47 Church Street, Barnsley, South Yorkshire, S70 2AS, England
E-mail: enquiries@pen-and-sword.co.uk
Website: www.pen-and-sword.co.uk

Or

PEN & SWORD BOOKS
1950 Lawrence Rd, Havertown, PA 19083, USA
E-mail: Uspen-and-sword@casematepublishers.com
Website: www.penandswordbooks.com

Contents

List of Illustrations

List of Maps

Preface

The recent 200-year anniversary of Waterloo has highlighted a deep level of interest in the Napoleonic Wars. The British campaigns in the Low Countries and the Iberian Peninsula have been exhaustively studied, with the production of large numbers of secondary works and the reprinting of memoirs. Other campaigns, in what was a global war, have been largely ignored or presented in a limited or clichéd manner. Such is the case for the war in India, which persisted on and off for much of the French Revolutionary and Napoleonic periods and peaked in the years 1798–1805 with the capture of Seringapatam and the campaigns of Arthur Wellesley (the later Duke of Wellington) and Gerard Lake in the Deccan and Hindustan. This was a brutal conflict in which British armies made up of the King's regiments and the mixed native and European troops of the East India Company clashed with the sophisticated forces of the Sultan of Mysore and the Maratha princes. There were dramatic pitched battles such as Assaye, Argaum, Delhi and Laswari, and epic sieges such as Seringapatam, Gawilghur and Bhurtpore. British success was not universal.

Wellington's presence in India is a tangible and fascinating link with the better-known European campaigns of the period, but for him and his fellow officers, and the ordinary soldier, this was a different sort of war with even more extreme climate and terrain and an alien and often unyielding enemy. Despite the daunting challenges, many British soldiers chose to stay in the subcontinent, refusing offers of return to Britain. This was a beguiling war in which Wellington was central, but only a part of a greater story.

With perhaps one exception, previous accounts of the fighting in India have been subsumed into biographies of Wellington, or they appear as relatively inaccessible academic monographs focussing on a specific campaign. Examples of the first genre include the biographies of Elizabeth Longford[1] and Rory Muir.[2] The latter is particularly strong on the Indian years. Inevitably, the biographical emphasis means that events are related through Wellington's eyes, all in which he was not directly involved being relegated to a footnote. Examples of campaign monographs include Randolf Cooper's *The Anglo-Maratha Campaigns and the Contest for India*[3], Anthony Bennell's *The Making of Arthur Wellesley*,[4] and Denys Forrest's *Tiger of Mysore*.[5] All give good, if sometimes dry, coverage of particular actions (in the Anglo-Maratha or Mysore Wars), but none allow the reader a military overview of the whole of Wellington's time in India. Only Jac Weller in his *Wellington in India*[6] seeks to do this, but the text is now dated; Muir dismisses it as being 'unscholarly, simplistic in its analysis and overly partisan in its arguments'[7]. Detailed works on the British military forces in India are not easily accessible, with information mostly limited to parts of more academic texts or in journal articles. None of the above portrays the daily experience of being a British soldier in India (in the manner of Brett-James's *Life in Wellington's Army*[8] for the Peninsula or my own *Death before Glory*[9] for the West Indies) or the lives of the sepoys, the native Indian soldiers in the Company's service.

In summary, there is no well-researched book which both fully acknowledges Wellington's vital role in the Indian campaigns of 1798–1805, but which also properly addresses the nature of the warring armies, the significance of the campaigns of Lake in North India, and which leaves the reader with an understanding of the human experience of war in the region. This work attempts to fill this gap in the literature.

The Anglo-Maratha War, which included the campaigns of 1803, is often referred to as the 'Second Anglo-Maratha War', but as this is not universally accepted I have avoided using this terminology in the text. The presence of two Wellesley brothers – Richard and Arthur – at the centre of the action is a potential cause of confusion. Richard Wellesley is variously referred to by his full name, as Mornington (the Earl of), as the Marquess, or as the Governor-General. Where the surname Wellesley appears in isolation it is Arthur Wellesley, the later Duke of Wellington, who is being referred to. Many place names and some personal names (e.g. the Indian princes) are problematic with multiple different spellings; in general I have chosen the version most widely used in contemporary accounts and learned secondary sources. A glossary is provided to facilitate understanding of the words of Indian origin which appear in the text.

I am much indebted to Rupert Harding for his valuable advice and patience and to Rory Muir for his wise guidance regarding sources and content. Jamie Wilson and Ian Robertson have been supportive of my literary efforts over many years. As always, the staffs of the British Library and National Army Museum in London have given unfailing assistance in my search for archival material.

Martin Howard
Huttons Ambo
2019

I Armies

Chapter 1

The Most Successful Army in the World? The British Forces in India 1798–1805

The British Indian Army, which conquered much of India under the command of George Harris, Gerard Lake and Arthur Wellesley, was an unlikely mix of men. It was an amalgam of the East India Company (EIC) Presidency armies and of King's regiments sent out to the continent from home. The East India Company formed its first sepoy (Indian soldier in British service) companies and battalions in the mid-eighteenth century. European regiments were also first created in Madras and Bengal.[1] The British Government was not keen on sending troops to India, but the first King's regiment, the 39th Foot, arrived in 1754 for the outbreak of the Seven Years' War.[2] At the Battle of Plassey three years later it fought alongside the Company's Bombay, Madras and Bengal European regiments, the first two sepoy battalions, and some artillery companies formed by the Company. This force employed by Clive might be regarded as the first true 'Indian army'.[3]

In the 1780s there was discord between the British Government's Board of Control for India and the EIC's Court of Directors with respect to the number of King's regiments serving in India. The Board was eventually allowed to send these men to India at the Company's expense, but their number was initially restricted to 8,000. At this time, the army in India was composed of these troops in addition to the 12,000 of the Company's Europeans and 112,000 sepoys. It was to be maintained solely for the protection of the Company's interests, the mercantile organisation now itself a major Indian power with full need of its three Presidency armies. This force was equivalent to that of a medium-sized European state, albeit almost devoid of cavalry.[4] The predominance of native troops in the Indian Army was to persist throughout the period under consideration. In 1794 there were 16,000 British operatives to 82,000 Indian and in 1805 there remained a similar proportion of British (24,500) to Indian (130,000) troops.[5] The sepoy regiments were led by officers who were British or from other European countries and they usually operated in concert with British units, although there were isolated examples – for instance, William Monson's detachment of 1804 – where an operation relied entirely on non-European troops.

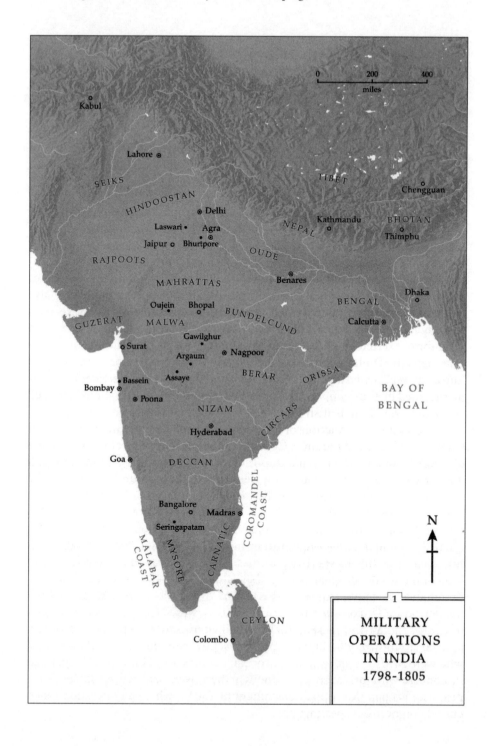

MILITARY
OPERATIONS
IN INDIA
1798-1805

Such a polyglot army was likely to be of uneven quality. British, European and native troops were to be sorely tested by their Indian enemies, but they emerged almost universally successful in the field. Arthur Wellesley, the future Duke of Wellington, extolled the qualities of the British troops before his departure from India. British soldiers, he explained in 1805, were the 'main foundation' of British power in Asia. He acknowledges bravery to be a characteristic of the British Army in all quarters of the globe but nowhere, he believed, was it so striking as in India.[6] John Blakiston, an engineer officer in the Madras Army, agreed with his senior officer. Weakly men soon died off and the regiments' survivors were 'as hard as iron, being proof against sun without and arrack within'.[7]

Lake and Wellesley were convinced of the need of a sizeable core of these seasoned British troops, but in their dispatches they increasingly acknowledge the fighting qualities of the sepoys under their command. It can be argued that, by the end of the eighteenth century, the Company's sepoy battalions were the equal of European soldiers.[8] Another modern historian's assertion that the Indian Army of the period was the 'most successful in the world' may also be contestable, but it reflects the enormous territorial gains made and the control exerted by such a small body of men.[9] This hybrid army of Indian and British and other European troops, commonly supported by irregular Indian allies, allowed a paltry number of military and civil servants to govern 50 million subjects.[10]

More detail of the British forces in India will be provided in Part II, Campaigns, and it is the function of this opening chapter to give an introductory overview of the organisation, scale and functioning parts of the Indian Army between 1798 and 1805. With respect to organisation, the Army was often divided into two wings of roughly equivalent strength. In general, larger independent forces were 'brigaded', each brigade normally consisting of three to four infantry battalions or cavalry regiments. Smaller additional forces were variably referred to as divisions (e.g. Bombay division), subsidiary forces (often of irregular native troops), detachments (e.g. Bundelcund detachment) and corps (e.g. Shepherd's corps).[11]

We will briefly consider Harris's Grand Army in the Mysore campaign of 1799 and both Lake's and Arthur Wellesley's armies of 1803, the year of the major actions against the Marathas, to give an impression of the scale of the British forces. At the outset of the advance to Seringapatam, Harris had organised his army into two wings, both composed of three brigades of infantry. His cavalry was divided into two brigades. The total strength was 21,649 men: cavalry 2,678; artillery 57; European infantry 4,608; native infantry 11,061.[12] Lake's and Wellesley's forces were similarly organised (see Appendix I). The former's 'Grand Army' swelled to around 30,000 men but, as is later described, his effective force for the major battles and sieges of the 1803 campaign was much smaller. In mid-1805, he reported that he had 10,000 men fit for duty under his personal command.[13] For the Battle of Assaye, Wellesley had an army of around 7,000 men, albeit with the extra support of 5,000 native irregular cavalry.[14] At the start of the following year, the general had 12,000 men under his own direction in the field, but he had the wider command of about 60,000 men in the provinces of southern India.[15]

Manpower in India was as much a political as a military issue and was the subject of much wrangling between the Governor-General of India, Arthur Wellesley's elder brother Richard, and the British Government. In 1800, the Governor-General wrote to Henry Dundas, the President of the Board of Control, demanding an increase in the size of the Indian Army. He argued that the King's infantry should increase in proportion to the Company's and that the European infantry should be fixed at twenty-five regiments of 1,200 rank and file, amounting to 30,000 men. Dundas predictably took an opposite view, not least because the resources were sorely needed elsewhere. He calculated the actual strength of the army in India to have grown to more than 100,000 effectives and he countered by suggesting a reduction to 80,000.[16] The politician had made a simple financial decision. Only by curtailing the military establishment could he ensure surplus revenues. He declared himself to be alarmed by the Governor-General's suggestions: 'I consider an overgrown and unwieldy load of Indian debt as our only mortal foe'.[17]

The King's regiments serving in India had more tangible enemies. We will discuss the King's forces first before turning to the EIC armies. The number of King's or Royal soldiers fluctuated during the period. A return dated April 1805 details the state of the King's regiments serving in India at this time (see Appendix II). There were five light dragoon regiments totalling 1,368 troopers and sixteen foot battalions totalling 7,518 infantrymen. Most regiments were significantly below full strength due to sickness.[18]

The King's infantry regiments (designated His Majesty's or HM) were led and organised as in Europe. The battalions were usually commanded by lieutenant-colonels and divided into ten companies, eight central and two flank. The flank companies were the grenadiers on the right and the light company on the left. As each company was nominally composed of 100 men, this gave a full battalion strength of 1,000. The 1805 return indicates that 1,500 of the infantrymen were sick and only two of the battalions were at full strength. The 65th Regiment had only sixty-one men reported present for duty and the majority of units had fewer than 500 combatants.[19]

This was not new. During preparations for the advance on Seringapatam, George Harris wrote to the Governor-General complaining of the state of his King's regiments; '…you may expect both the 12th and the 33rd Foot will be skeletons after one campaign'.[20] The weakened conditions of his King's troops was also a cause of constant worry for Arthur Wellesley. In late 1801, he was forced to replace the unfit 77th Foot with the Swiss *De Meuron* Regiment, which he judged less suitable for jungle warfare.[21] Four years later, he withdrew the 74th Regiment from service in the Deccan as it was reduced to only a few men.[22] Although the King's Foot battalions amounted to only a small proportion of the Indian Army's infantry, any depletion in their ranks had a disproportionate effect on the military effectiveness of the larger force. The European troops were usually selected to lead the line in battle and to storm fortresses.[23]

There was only one King's cavalry regiment in India before 1798, the 19th Light Dragoons, but this increased to four by 1803. These regiments were commanded by lieutenant-colonels and were divided into five squadrons, each two troops. The light dragoon regiments listed in the army return of spring 1805 were the 8th, 19th, 22nd, 27th and 29th. Again there was a significant disparity between the nominal strength of these units (around 600 officers and men) and the number of men actually fit for duty which ranged from 218 to 362.[24]

In Europe, the light dragoons rode smaller horses and were only lightly armed. They were intended mostly for outpost, reconnaissance and skirmishing roles. In India, their performance was uneven, sometimes hampered by a lack of horses. Although defined as 'light' cavalry, the British regular troopers weighed about 17 stone with accoutrements; this was 5 stone heavier than a Maratha cavalryman. They thus lacked some of the agility of their adversaries and were effectively used as 'heavy' cavalry on the battlefield.[25] In 1803, the 29th Light Dragoons in Hindustan were judged to be in a 'state of inefficiency'. Lake organised additional cavalry training during the winter months.[26] Perhaps because of initiatives such as this, the British cavalry was to overcome its shortcomings and play a vital role in the Maratha campaigns. Wellesley was suspicious of the 'cavalry spirit', but he used his mounted arm ably in hunting down insurgents and he later praised the British cavalry in his official despatch after the Battle of Argaum.[27]

There was a very small corps of Royal Engineers serving in India at this time who provided specialist advice to commanders and gave directions to the soldiers of the Royal Military Artificers and Labourers.[28] There were also some Woolwich-trained Royal Artillery officers in the country. However, there were no King's artillery battalions or companies. The artillery and engineering support provided by the East India Company will be discussed later in the chapter.

India was a land of opportunity for the officers of King's regiments. When the 25th Light Dragoons landed at Madras from England in 1796, the commander, Sir John Burgoyne, pointed out that their service was 'not less honourable than lucrative'. As King's officers they were eligible for choice commands and they would have every chance of shaking the 'pagoda tree'. Lieutenant Stapleton Cotton enthused that a Bengal command was a sure fortune in five years. For a general such as John Floyd there was the King's pay, the Company's pay, various allowances and possible prize money.[29] Arthur Wellesley arrived in India in February 1797, a difficult younger son and an impecunious junior colonel of no particular note, his promotion purchased in typical aristocratic fashion. He returned to England a major-general, a wealthy man, and the recipient of the Order of the Bath.[30]

Of course, not all officers had an elder brother who was a Governor-General and such easy access to patronage. Richard Bayly, an ensign in the 12th Regiment, served during the same period but apparently in a different India.

> In no situation of the universe can a King's military officer be so uncomfortably and unprofitably employed. After an arduous service from 20–40 years, he returns to his native country with a broken constitution, unprotected and unnoticed on the half-pay of a Lieut.-Colonel (of £200 per annum): he cannot associate with his equals in worldly knowledge, and is too proud to court the society of those with equal incomes but inferior education…[31]

William Harness was also embittered by his experiences in India. He was appointed to the command of the 74th Regiment in 1800 only to discover that his lieutenant-colonel rank had not been confirmed at home and that his period of command was not acknowledged in his official record of service.[32] It was an example of the poor cohesion between the commander-in-chief in India and the military authorities in England.

Many of the King's officers showed great bravery in the wars of the period, literally leading from the front. The casualty rolls of battles such as Assaye, Delhi and Laswari contain disproportionate numbers of their names.[33] John Blakiston believed his fellow officers, both King's and Company's, to show more 'zeal' than in other parts of the world; 'This must doubtless arise from their peculiar situation, which, as a few among millions, renders their personal exertions more necessary'.[34] It is obvious from Wellesley's despatches that they were often in short supply. As early as 1798, he complains of a shortage of captains in his own regiment, HM 33rd, and five years later, a few weeks before Assaye, he is 'badly off' for officers to command corps.[35]

To function properly, the King's component of the Indian Army needed effective support from the commissariat, intelligence and medical departments. These subjects will be revisited and they will therefore be only briefly alluded to here. The commissariat was designed to meet the logistical needs of the army and it was the responsibility of the quartermaster-general. In India, there were major supply depots in Calcutta, Madras and Bombay and smaller depots elsewhere.[36] In practice, there was much reliance on the local arrangements of successful commanders such as Arthur Wellesley, who was able to exploit local allies and country to continuously supply his men. Massive bullock trains carried these supplies, which were in large part purchased from the native *banjaras*, a nomadic group of traders.[37] The following except from a letter from Wellesley to the secretary of the military board, dated March 1800, is a reminder of the need for local knowledge and the unique nature of campaigning in India.

> I enclose a return of the number, state, & c. of the elephants and camels, the property of the Honourable Company. The camels have been found unhealthy, and in wet weather unable to carry their loads; I do not therefore recommend that they should be retained. The elephants are hardy, and useful for many military purposes besides the carriage of camp equipage, and it is therefore very desirable to retain them in the service.

A stickler for detail, Wellesley continues to explain exactly which elephants he wishes to keep.[38]

There was a limited infrastructure for intelligence gathering and again much dependence on improvisation and the local population. The British recruited *harkarrahs*, local guides, who might pass on useful information. Their use prior to the Battle of Assaye did not prevent a British intelligence failure which was only mitigated by the fighting qualities of Wellesley's army.[39] The medical services were arranged along similar lines to campaigns in Europe and included medical staff officers and the regimental doctors. General hospitals were opened in larger and strategically important towns and cities. Local solutions had to be adopted. The carriage of sick and wounded depended much on the use of *doolies*.[40]

We will now turn to the soldiers of the East India Company who fought in the Presidency armies of Bengal, Madras and Bombay. As has already been described, the native troops of the Company's battalions made up the great majority of the Indian Army. There was no prospect of attracting sufficient European troops to fulfil British expansionist policies and to protect the EIC's interests. In the event, Indians entered the Company's armies in large numbers. They were part of a highly militarised society where the profession of arms was a legitimate option. This was particularly the case in the north. Mercenary soldiers were bound to be attracted by the Company's regular pay, something they would have been much less likely to receive from Indian rulers.[41] The forms of sepoy recruitment are discussed in more detail in Chapter 12.

There were also a small number of European regiments in the EIC's service. In the early days of the eighteenth century the recruits were mostly Dutch, French prisoners of war, and Swiss and Germans from the French service. Towards the end of the century their quality improved; the better recruits being former British regulars discharged when King's regiments were ordered home. These men chose to remain in India, perhaps because of local liaisons or a better quality of life.[42] The Indians referred to them as the 'English' although many were not. In the period 1795–1810, 42% of the Company's British soldiers were Irish, 24% Scots and the rest English or Welsh. In 1792, the Company's Court of Directors debarred men of mixed race from its civil, military and marine services.[43]

The infantry formed the largest part of the Company's three Presidency armies. The basic battalion organisation was similar to that of the King's regiments, the only significant difference being that the EIC units lacked a light company, instead having two grenadier companies. The native Indian soldier was not thought to be a proficient skirmisher.[44] There was a substantial reorganisation of the Presidency armies in 1796, prompted by the suggestions of Lord Cornwallis originally submitted to the Board of Control in 1794. Cornwallis's central recommendation was that all the Company's troops, native and European, should be transferred to the King's service, but that the native troops should form a separate Indian army. It was hoped that this would improve security and reduce antagonism between King's and Company's forces and between the Presidency armies. His plan involved major changes to service conditions and, as we will see, it was vigorously opposed by British officers in the Company's service, especially those of the Bengal Army. When the much diluted reforms appeared in January 1796, the changes were limited to the reorganisation of the infantry into forty regiments each of two battalions, together with new regulations for promotion, leave and pensions.[45]

We will take the Bengal army as our prime example. In 1796, it included twelve double-battalions of native infantry. Each battalion was made up of 800 sepoys (i.e. 1,600 in a regiment) divided into ten companies, giving a total strength of more than 19,000 men.[46] The precise establishments of native infantry and European regiments are detailed in army orders.

Native Infantry

The Battalions of Native Infantry to be formed in Regiments of two Battalions each, with ten Companies in each Battalion, the Regiment to consist of:
1 Colonel
2 Lt.-Colonels

2 Majors
7 Captains
1 Captain-Lt.
22 Lieutenants
10 Ensigns
2 Sergeants
20 *Subidars* [equivalent to captain]
20 *Jemidars* [lieutenant]
100 *Havildars* [sergeant]
100 *Naicks* [corporal]
40 Drums and Fifes
1,600 Privates
20 *Puckallies* [water-carriers]

(Staff: 2 Adjutants, 1 Paymaster, 1 Surgeon, 2 Mates, 1 Sergeant Major, 1 Quartermaster Sergeant, 2 Native doctors, 1 Drum Major, 1 Fife Major, 2 Drill *Havildars*, 2 Drill *Naicks*).

European Infantry

The Battalions on the present establishment to be formed into Regiments of ten Companies each to consist of:

1 Colonel
2 Lt.-Colonels
2 Majors
7 Captains
1 Captain-Lt.
21 Lieutenants
8 Ensigns
40 Sergeants
50 Corporals
22 Drums and Fifes
950 Privates
20 *Puckallies*

(Staff: 1 Adjutant, 1 Quartermaster, 1 Paymaster, 1 Surgeon, 2 Mates, 1 Sergeant Major, 1 Quartermaster Sergeant, 1 Drill Sergeant, 1 Drill Corporal, 1 Drum Major, 1 Fife Major).[47]

This basic structure was little altered until 1852, although the strengths did fluctuate dependant on the threat of war.[48] One consequence of the changes made in the late eighteenth century was an increased European officer presence in native units, even at the company level. This gave rise to an exclusively European chain of command, which reduced the autonomy of the native officers. A *subadar* might command 20–40 sepoys, but any number beyond this would be the responsibility of a European officer.[49]

As would be expected during a period of conflict, the number of infantry regiments in each Presidency army was gradually increased. The *East India Register and Directory* for 1803, the year of Assaye, lists two European and nineteen native infantry regiments in the Bengal Army.[50] Four more regiments were soon raised.[51] The same reorganisations, albeit with minor differences, were enacted in the Madras and Bombay armies. Madras regiments were slightly larger than the Bengal units, 1,800 privates being specified in the 1796 regulations. In 1803, the EIC list shows one European regiment and nineteen native regiments.[52] The Bombay Army was regarded as being too small for purpose. In 1803, it had one European regiment and eight native battalions, each with a normal strength of 1,800 private soldiers.[53]

The Bengal and Madras Presidencies formed cavalry troops in the mid-eighteenth century, but the arm was expensive and its development was slow and interrupted.[54] Regiments were eventually to be organised in a similar manner to the King's cavalry with three squadrons, each of two troops. The 1796 Bengal Army regulations stipulate the following.

Native Cavalry

Each Regiment of six Troops to consist of:
  2 Captains
  1 Captain-Lt.
  6 Lieutenants
  3 Cornets
  2 Sergeants
  6 *Subidars*
  6 *Jemidars*
  18 *Havildars*
  18 *Naicks*
  420 Troopers
  6 *Puckallies*
(Staff: 1 Adjutant, 1 Quartermaster, 1 Paymaster, 1 Surgeon's Mate, 1 Sergeant Major, 1 Quartermaster Sergeant, 1 Drill *Havildar*, 1 Trumpet Major, 6 Pay *Havildars*).[55]

In 1803, there were six regiments of native cavalry in the Bengal Army. The Madras Army, where the organisation was almost identical, had seven regiments.[56] The lack of any Bombay native cavalry in the 1803 EIC Directory reflects the particularly slow formation of cavalry in this Presidency, the first regiment not raised until 1804.[57] Lake and Wellesley had ten native cavalry regiments between them for the war of 1803.[58] Just like the King's troopers, the native cavalrymen played a full role. Lieutenant William Thorn of the 29th Light Dragoons, a veteran campaigner in the north, extolled their efforts in the later struggle against the Maratha chief Holkar; '…the Bengal cavalry, through the campaign, endured trials and hardships almost surpassing conception, and such as astonished even our most active enemies'.[59]

The East India Company's artillery arm lacked firepower compared to its formidable Maratha adversary. At the Battle of Laswari in 1803, Lake complained that each enemy gun had three times the number of men as his own.[60] The EIC's guns were organised as companies, each company consisting of five two-gun units. These were attached to infantry battalions; an artillery company of ten guns was commonly assigned to five battalions operating in concert.[61] Five companies formed an artillery battalion. The 1796 regulations defined the strength for the Bengal Army.

European Artillery

> 1 Colonel
> 1 Lt.-Colonel
> 1 Major
> 5 Captains
> 5 Captain-Lts.
> 10 Lieutenants
> 5 Lieutenant Fireworkers
> 20 Sergeants
> 20 Corporals
> 40 Gunners
> 10 Drums and Fifes
> 280 Matrosses
> 10 *Puckallies*

(Staff: 1 Adjutant, 1 Paymaster, 1 Surgeon, 1 Mate, 1 Sergeant Major, 1 Quartermaster Sergeant, 1 Drill Sergeant, 1 Drill Corporal, 1 Drum Major, 1 Fife Major).

Each company of Lascars for the service of Artillery to consist of:

> 1 *Serang*
> 2 First *Tindals*
> 2 Second *Tindals*
> 56 Lascars
> 1 *Puckally*[62]

The matrosses were the European gunners, often a mix of nationalities and of low quality. In the late eighteenth century, the Company had prohibited the employment of Indians as gunners although this was incompletely enforced.[63] The Indian gun-handlers were variably referred to as *golundas* and lascars.

Efforts were made to strengthen the Presidency armies' artillery on the eve of the Anglo-Maratha War. The Bengal Army of 1803 had a single regiment of twenty-one companies, but it fell short of establishment by fifty-six officers and 820 non-commissioned officers.[64] This in part reflected the reliance on European gunners. In Madras at this time there were two battalions of artillery and in Bombay just a single battalion.[65] The artillery pieces were of Woolwich type, the iron or brass barrels cast in England and the carriages constructed in India. The standard field pieces were 6 and 12-pounders.[66] An ordnance return for Wellesley's army for November 1803 (see Appendix III) shows a predominance of these pieces, but also a smaller number of 18-pounders in addition to 5½-inch and 8-inch howitzers. In all, 2,780 bullocks were needed to pull the artillery and other carts.[67]

The improvised horse artillery of the Company's army proved to be especially useful in the Maratha wars. Earlier experience had proved the utility of attaching horse-drawn artillery pieces to selected cavalry units and, in 1801, every cavalry regiment was armed with two 6-pounders. The idea evolved in the Bengal Army with the creation of an experimental brigade of horse artillery consisting of 3-pounder guns. This 'flying artillery' was effective, terrorising the Maratha cavalry, and it led to the formation of three troops of Bengal Horse Artillery in 1809.[68]

Each Presidency had its own corps of engineers made up entirely of officers. In 1803, the Bengal Army had twenty-eight engineer officers, the chief engineer having the rank of colonel. The Madras and Bombay armies had similar establishments.[69] There was also a department of pioneers which was entrusted with the digging of roads and the building of bridges and earthworks. Their services, often forgotten, were vital in the maintenance of communications in difficult country.[70]

Although efforts were made to standardise the regulations of the three Presidency armies, it is clear that British officers believed the three forces to have their own peculiar characteristics. As discussed in a later chapter dedicated to Indian soldiers, we have very few Indian voices from the wars and we are largely dependent on British sources. John Philippart, a prolific military author who worked in the War Office, appends a description of the native soldier of the Presidency armies to his comprehensive *East India Military Calendar*, first published in 1826. Although entirely Anglo-centric in tone and couched in contemporary language, it contains interesting opinions and some excerpts relating to infantry are worth quoting.

> Bengal Army –…In the Native infantry of Bengal the Hindoos are in the full proportion of three-fourths to the Mahomedans. They consist chiefly of Rajpoots, who are a distinguished race among the Khiteree or military tribe. The standard [height], below which no recruit is taken, is five feet six inches: the great proportion of the grenadiers is six feet and upwards. The Rajpoot is born a soldier: the mother speaks nothing to her infant but deeds of arms, and every sentiment and action of the future man is marked by the first impression that he has received. If he tills the ground (which is the common occupation of this class,) his sword and shield are placed near the furrow, and moved as his labour advances. The frame of the Rajpoot is almost always improved (even if his pursuits are those of civil life) by martial exercises. He is from habit temperate in his diet, of a generous though warm temper, and of good moral conduct. He is, when well treated, obedient, zealous, and faithful.

Philippart continues to acknowledge the Rajput's bravery and apparent lack of fear of death. They were a body of soldiers who had to be managed with care and wisdom 'or that which is our strength may become our danger'.

> Madras Army –…The infantry Sepoy of Madras is rather a small man, but he is of an active make, and capable of undergoing great fatigue upon a very slender diet. We find no man arrive at a greater precision in all his military exercises; his moderation, his sobriety, his patience, give him a steadiness that is almost unknown to Europeans; but although there exists in this body of men a fitness to attain mechanical perfection as soldiers, there are no men whose mind it is of more consequence to study.
>
> Bombay Army –…The men of the infantry of Bombay are of a standard very near that of Madras. The lowest size taken is five feet three inches, and the average is five feet five; but they are robust and hardy, and capable of enduring great fatigue upon very slender diet. The army has, from its origin to the present day, been indiscriminately composed of all classes – Mahomedans, Hindoos, Jews, and some few Christians… It is probably owing to the peculiar composition, and to the local situation of the territories in which they are employed, that the Sepoys at Bombay have at all periods been found ready to embark on foreign service. They are, in fact, familiar to the sea, and only a small proportion of them are incommoded in a voyage by those privations to which others are subject from prejudice of cast. But this is only one of the merits of the Bombay

Native soldier; he is patient, faithful, and brave, and attached in a remarkable degree to his European officers.[71]

The British officers who led the native infantry troops were also a distinct group of men with their own career aspirations and concerns. They were subtly different to the officers of the King's regiments. EIC officers were less aristocratic; they did not purchase their commissions and they were often motivated by financial gain. Many of them were from the middle ranks of society, but it is important not to overgeneralise.[72] When Richard Purvis was commissioned into the Bengal Army at sixteen years of age, his brother officers were a surprisingly diverse group of men. They included younger sons of gentry, sons of officers who could not afford to purchase the King's commission, sons of tradesmen and sons of émigrés who had fled Revolutionary France.[73]

This is not to suggest that EIC officers were much more 'professional' or meritorious than their more privileged peers in the King's regiments.[74] Young men, often fifteen to nineteen years of age, entered the Company's officers' corps as 'cadets'. In the eighteenth century, when EIC military service was still widely regarded as a road to riches, the award of the cadetship was nepotistic, the successful applicants often chosen by self-serving members of the Company's Court of Directors. It was thus a possible refuge for dissipated, profligate and awkward young men whose fathers wanted them out of the country.[75]

Unfortunately, the training the cadets received was unlikely to steer them back on to a virtuous path. In 1796, a few cadetships were created at the Royal Military Academy at Woolwich and, in 1809, the EIC opened a training seminary at Addiscombe, but the great majority were placed with their sepoy corps without any meaningful training. A raw fifteen or sixteen-year-old lad with less than a year's service could be in command of a hundred Indian soldiers about which he knew almost nothing. As the lower age limit was fifteen years and many cadets exaggerated their age, he might even be younger. The situation was exacerbated by their lack of previous proper education; only 5% of the cadets of the Bengal Army had attended the universities or the larger public schools. Some measures were taken to improve training, notably the opening of a special facility at Baraset (sixteen miles north of Calcutta) in 1802. However, despite good intentions, it soon became an ideal venue for the pursuits of an archetypical gentlemen officer; '... – one who drank hard, used foul language, gambled and duelled'.[76]

The EIC's European officers were an increasingly disaffected group. As alluded to, many had joined up with the hope of acquiring fabulous wealth from prize money and the multiple obscure allowances to which they were entitled in India. When the fifteen-year-old John Blakiston became a cadet in 1800, he and his parents were reassured that 'an ample harvest of laurels and lucre was to be reaped'.[77] Richard Purvis believed his cadetship to be an 'honourable' career, but a worldly-wise family friend, writing in his support in 1803, had reservations.

> Respecting my young Friend Richard your Son: he still continues firm in his wishes to go to India but from what I hear on the Military line of Service in India, it is not so good a one as it used to be.[78]

The 1796 proposal for a uniform rate of pay was violently opposed by the EIC's European officers, especially those of the Bengal Army. They were bound to resist the abolition of bazaar money and the dilution of their *batta* and other arcane financial allowances.[79] Their promotion prospects had also receded. This was by seniority, but in the 1790s the logjam was such that, on average, officers had to serve more than thirty years to reach the rank of colonel.[80] Furthermore, the King's officers took precedence over Company officers of equivalent rank. All the Army's generals were from the King's Army and Company officers were regularly superseded by less experienced King's officers newly arrived from Britain.[81] At the start of the nineteenth century, the Company's officers were realising that rather than returning home as 'nabobs' they were to be employed in an 'army of subalterns'.[82] Unsurprisingly, many looked outside their regiments, taking opportunities to transfer into the expanding civilian administration.[83] Junior officers arrived in India to be posted to undermanned EIC regiments officered by their disgruntled seniors.

There was predictable friction between the officers of the King's and Company's armies, each quick to point to the advantages enjoyed by the other. Richard Bayly, the embittered officer of HM 12th Regiment, refers to the wealth of the Company's officers. They were eligible for many 'little pickings' from which the King's men such as himself were excluded.

> The honour and glory of King's officers must hide their diminished heads on comparison with the more fortunate destiny of the enviable situation of those employed in the service of an English company of merchants…[84]

The EIC's officers were equally quick to complain of their poor promotion prospects compared with their King's regiment equivalents. John Blakiston insisted that had he been in the King's service he would have been near the rank of a general officer rather than a simple captain.[85] James Young, a captain-lieutenant in the Bengal Horse Artillery, bemoaned what he perceived to be 'oppressive and cruel' promotion regulations favouring the King's officers.

The option of purchase of rank, only enjoyed by the King's officers, meant that he and his fellow officers were easily superseded by the 'boys' of His Majesty's regiments, whose ages were similar to the periods of Indian service of the Company's officers.[86] Lieutenant Valentine Blacker of the Madras Native Cavalry derided the lack of recognition of the Company's officers in Britain.

> What an advantage it is the King's troops enjoy over us that they can return to their home without prejudice to their military rank whilst the Company's must bid adieu to it west of the Cape.[87]

Amiya Barat, in her superb study of the Bengal Native infantry, argues that the European officers of the Presidency armies were a victim of wider conflicting forces exerted by the ambitious military expansionist policy of the Governor-General and, on the other hand, the cautious, financially dominated considerations of the Board of Control and the Court of Directors. One consequence of their disenchantment was an increasing gap between European officers and the Indian soldiers under their command.[88]

We need only briefly consider the ancillary services to the EIC's armies, as the commissariat responsibilities, the gathering of intelligence, and the provision of medical support were not substantially different from the King's Army. There was no conventional commissariat, but instead a dependence on local bazaars and the itinerant *banjaras*. Transport was usually deficient, the bullocks used for carriage often of low quality and depleted in numbers.[89] Enormous numbers of civilians accompanied the Indian Army; when Lake captured Delhi in 1803 it was estimated that he had five camp followers for each soldier.[90] Intelligence was also heavily dependent on the local population, notably the all-seeing *harkarrahs*. Medical services were much as described in the King's Army; there were separate hospitals for native troops and each native infantry battalion had two native doctors in addition to its complement of three European surgeons.[91]

Other bodies of men supported His Majesty's and the Company's armies in the British assault on India. These were mainly the soldiers of Indian chiefs who chose to make alliances with the British. In the Seringapatam campaign, the Nizam of Hyderabad contributed a sizeable contingent to Harris's army. These were mainly cavalry, but there was also an infantry force including a former French corps now led by native officers. According to John Malcolm, assistant to the Resident at Hyderabad, the infantry were 'cloathed and armed in the European manner'. He was informed by their native leader that that they would be of little use without the reappointment of European officers.[92]

In the Deccan campaign, Arthur Wellesley relied on the assistance of friendly Maratha, Mysore and Mughal forces, although it is clear that he regarded this as an evil necessity. Wellesley had 5,000 irregular horse provided by the Peshwa of Poona and by the Raja of Mysore.[93] The Maratha cavalry came at a price and was unreliable, as Wellesley informed Lieutenant-Colonel Barry Close:

> Bad as they are, and weak as my expectations are from them, I must determine upon keeping them, at least for the present… if they were to go we should be surrounded in our camp and on our marches by *pindaris* [plundering irregular light horse]…[94]

He was more complimentary regarding the Mysore troops. In late 1804, he orders that both the Mysore regular infantry and cavalry should have an essentially supportive role, not entrusted to make any attack in isolation, and to be used chiefly in a defensive capacity.[95]

Lake also used local native troops who had deserted the Maratha service. James Skinner, himself a leader of an irregular cavalry unit, estimated that Lake's Hindustan army contained as many as 20,000 irregular native horse.[96] They were viewed with suspicion by Company officers. James Young noted that they 'made it an invariable rule to desert' if their pay was in arrears.[97] This is understandable as they were mercenaries. There were practical difficulties in the employment of irregular native soldiers. James Welsh, an ensign in the Madras Army, describes British dragoons mistaking allied Maratha cavalry for the enemy and men on each side being killed before the mistake was recognised.[98]

Only one foreign European regiment served with the King's regiments in India at this time. The *Regiment de Meuron* was originally raised at Neuchâtel in 1781. It first fought for the French but it transferred its allegiance to the British cause at the capture of Ceylon in 1795. Its officers received the same rank as the King's service and the regiment was incorporated into the Madras establishment where it saw active service.[99] Wellesley makes a number of references to it in his dispatches, including the following interesting observation in a memorandum of 1805.

> It is a curious fact, but one that has more than once fallen under my observation, that the Natives of India have no fear or respect for the military qualities of the soldiers of any European nation excepting the English [Wellesley commonly used the term 'English' where he clearly means 'British']. I had under my command for some years, the Swiss regiment De Meuron, which, for good conduct, discipline, and other military qualities, was not surpassed by the English regiments. But the Natives heard that they were foreigners, that they had been bought into the service, and they had no confidence in them.[100]

The British rule of India was complex, there being no precedent for the management of such a vast dependency. The most powerful man in India was the Governor-General. He was nominally appointed by the East India Company's Court of Directors but, in reality, he was chosen by the British Government. It was, in many ways, an unenviable situation, the Governor-General exerting influence in Council in India while being answerable to the Court of Directors in Leadenhall Street and the Board of Control in Whitehall, two organisations with different objectives. He might choose to exploit the considerable distance between Calcutta and London to drive a local agenda, but he was ultimately dependant on political support at home. Between 1784 and 1801 this meant that of Henry Dundas, head of the Board of Control. There were governors in Bombay and Madras who were overseen by the Governor-General.[101]

European and native forces were led by the commander-in-chief in India. He was answerable directly to the Governor-General (later to be viceroy) rather than to the commander-in-chief of the British Army or the War Office. The Governor-General exerted much influence over military matters, determining the general nature of any war and having supreme authority over the troops. It was the role of the commander-in-chief to conduct the necessary operations and to ensure the efficient functioning of the soldiers under his command by issuing appropriate general orders.[102]

The men at the top of the hierarchy had a personal and general staff to assist them. For the year 1803, the *East India Register and Directory* shows the Governor-General to have had eleven personal staff including military secretaries and aides de camp. The commander-in-chief, also part of the Bengal establishment, had five: his military secretary, two aides de camp and two surgeons. There were approximately thirty men on the general staff in Bengal ranging in rank from major-general to captain; these included posts such as adjutant-general, quartermaster-general, and judge advocate-general. A number of additional aides de camp were attached to the major-generals. There were similar staffs at Madras and Bombay, although on a smaller scale.[103]

We will conclude this chapter with a brief introduction to three men who were central to Britain's effort in India at the end of the eighteenth century and the early years of the nineteenth. Richard Wellesley (the Earl of Mornington until 1799, when he became Marquess Wellesley) was the third Governor-General of India. He divided opinion at the time and still does. He was a man of supreme self-confidence, sharp intellect and moral courage, who paid fastidious attention to detail. He fully exploited his distance from London – 'all this dreadful space of half the convex world' – to further his own expansionist policies. To his detractors, he was arrogant and immovable, convinced of his own intellectual and moral superiority. He left little to chance, his iron control extending to regulation of the Indian press. He was in truth very much a product of the aristocratic class of the time. He viewed his period in India in an almost evangelical light, making it his mission to bring 'civilising' Anglo-Saxon values to the country. He was also determined that it should be the platform for a successful political career at home.[104]

Richard Wellesley's objectives never entirely matched those of the British Government and the Company's directors. Dundas believed him to be too bent on conquest, actually contravening the Government's policy, which declared wars of aggression in the country to be injurious to British honour. The Company's directors were jealous of his grasp on power and concerned at the cost of his wars.[105] His favoured strategy was that of the 'subsidiary alliance' system. This was designed to first support British expansion in India, and then to exert the necessary control. In return for a defensive guarantee, the East India Company posted troops in the native state. These men were paid for by the local power, but were available to be used as determined by the EIC. It was a bargain in which the protected state gained some security, but lost its right to an independent foreign policy. If followed relentlessly, it was a strategy that was bound to result in British domination.[106] P.E. Roberts has produced the most thorough review of Richard Wellesley's Governor-Generalship. Written more than fifty years ago, this may be judged to be too adulatory.

> …within seven years [he] worked a wonderful transformation. The kingdom of Mysore was swept away; the Nizam's French trained battalions were broken up; the Company took over the complete control of the Carnatic, Tanjore and Surat; Oudh was shorn of her valuable north-western provinces; the Peishwa was bound in subsidiary alliance to the British power; Sindhia and Berar [Maratha princes] were vanquished in brilliant campaigns and mulcted of important territories. Then came the only errors and failures of this breathless but triumphant administration – the early disasters of the war with Holkar [Maratha prince]. They were already being more than retrieved when Wellesley, on his brother Arthur's perhaps too precipitate advice, and yielding to the resentment of the Court of Directors, who had for long been regarding the Governor-General's victorious progress with feelings about equally compounded of astonishment and dislike, resigned his office.[107]

Gerard Lake was commander-in-chief in India at this time. A veteran of the Seven Years War, he was now sixty years old, but still energetic enough to rise at 2am to lead his men on the march. He personally commanded the British Army in the Hindustan campaign of 1803 and in the later actions against Holkar. Rather as for the Governor-General, he divides opinion. He was tremendously brave and straightforward. Some have dismissed him as a 'fox-hunting general' who charged at the enemy with everything he had. Certainly, he was impetuous and, at times, over-optimistic as to his military options. That he preferred action to meticulous preparation is obvious from his favourite maxim: 'Damn your writing! Mind your fighting!'[108]

We need mention only one other British soldier at this point. Arthur Wellesley is a dominant figure in the pages of this book. Arriving in India in 1796 as colonel of the 33rd Foot, his rapid rise was no doubt in part due to his aristocratic lineage, his purchase of rank and having an elder brother who was Governor-General. He was to lead the British army in the Deccan campaigns of 1803. Richard and Arthur were not particularly close, especially after their first two years together in India.[109] The younger brother had the temerity to criticise the elder's Indian policy. Richard's continued support of Arthur might be regarded as nepotistic, but it is also obvious that he recognised his considerable talents and that he valued his ability to operate autonomously.[110] They were a powerful team.

> …from the combination of the elder brother's roaring imagination and comprehensive grasp in the realm of political idealism, and the younger's magnificent common sense and sanity in the world of reality, there was forged a superbly efficient instrument for the task of governing men.[111]

After initial ambivalence, Arthur grew to like India.[112]

Chapter 2

A House of Cards: Britain's Enemies in India 1798–1805

Britain and the East India Company had numerous enemies in India, but during the period under consideration only two powers were capable of sustaining significant armies in the field. At the end of the eighteenth century, these were the Mysore forces of Tipu Sultan and, in the first few years of the nineteenth century, the diverse group of regular and irregular soldiers commanded by the Maratha princes. The campaigns fought by these men are detailed chronologically in following chapters and the intention of this chapter is to give an introductory overview of the sizeable armies which opposed Harris, Lake and Wellesley. We will also briefly consider smaller insurgent forces which pursued 'little wars' against British-led troops.

In the course of the eighteenth century, Mysore had proved to be Britain's most implacable enemy in India. Three wars had been fought, the most recent in 1790–92, in which the British were eventually victorious, with the Mysore ruler, Tipu Sultan, forced to cede half his dominions and to pay an enormous indemnity. Tipu remained hostile and he laboriously rebuilt his realm and army.[1]

> He began to add to the fortifications of his capital [Seringapatam] – to remount his cavalry – to recruit and discipline his infantry – to punish his refractory tributaries – and to encourage the cultivation of his country, which was soon restored to its former prosperity.[2]

Although antagonistic to all Europeans, Tipu was a pragmatist and the modernisation of his army involved significant westernisation. He employed French mercenaries – in 1798, eighty-five joined his forces – and he was also prepared to use South Asian and British soldiers who had gained western military knowledge in the EIC's service. European prisoners of war might be given the option of fighting in his army to avoid incarceration with hard labour. In this way, he merged European, predominantly French, influences with more traditional Mughal and Afghan techniques. He did not seek to simply copy a European army. Indeed, his suspicion of Europeans was central to all his actions and European officers were not routinely given command of regiments.[3] The European auxiliaries in the Mysore Army probably never amounted to more than a few hundred.[4]

Tipu's character will be further analysed in the next chapter, not least in the context of the labyrinthine negotiations with the Governor-General which ultimately led to war. As a soldier, he was perhaps Mysore's 'Duke of York', a man capable of constructing a capable military machine, but less able to lead it in the field. In his early years, he had shown vigour and bravery on the battlefield. By the late 1790s, he was still physically courageous but lacking in mental energy.[5] At Seringapatam, '...he fell in the defence of his capital; but, he fell performing the duties of a common soldier, not of a general'.[6]

Tipu was not well served by his senior officers, at least some of whom were of dubious loyalty. In early 1799, the Governor-General wrote to General George Harris informing him of the disaffection in the Sultan's senior command. Not only his subjects, but also his 'principal officers' were judged by the British to be 'inclined to throw off [Tipu's] authority' with the real prospect that they would put themselves under the protection of the Company.'[7] Tipu brutally punished any infraction of discipline among his men and, when victorious, they were rewarded by the traditional presentations of jewellery. The irregular cavalry plundered freely in times of war. Selected Mysore soldiers were dedicated to their ruler; the *janbaz* troops were a form of suicide corps.[8]

When Tipu inherited control of the Mysore Army on the death of his father, Haidar Ali, in 1783, it numbered 144,000 regular soldiers and 180,000 militia, many of them volunteers.[9] However, the number of effectives he was able to bring into the field against the British Army at any given time was considerably less. In 1799, the year of the fall of Seringapatam, John Malcolm, the Assistant Resident at Hyderabad, gives the following estimate of Mysore strength. We are often reliant on British sources for the characterisation of native Indian armies.

Abstract of Real Strength [of Mysore Army]

Regular Horse	6,000
Irregular Horse	7,000
Regular Infantry	30,000
Guards & c.	4,000
Pikemen	15,000
Carnatic Peons	8,000
Pioneers	6,000

This excluded battery guns, field pieces and rockets. Malcolm assumed that Tipu was carrying as many of these as he could transport with his elephants, camels, mules and draught cattle. Malcolm also mentions Tipu's 'European or French force', sometimes referred to as Lally's Corps, which numbered around 450 men, of whom only a hundred were actually Europeans.[10] A more detailed return for Tipu's army at the commencement of the 1799 campaign is appended to a letter of Arthur Wellesley to Lieutenant-Colonel Arthur St Leger (see Appendix IV).[11]

The Mysore Army was arguably the best equipped and disciplined of an Indian state at this time.[12] This was the common view of British officers. Arthur Wellesley is quick to praise Mysorean troops. In the communication to St Leger, he writes:

> …we did not lose anything to signify during our whole march, not-withstanding the efforts of the enemy's light troops who constantly attended us, and who are certainly the best troops of that kind I have ever seen.[13]

Elsewhere, he pays a similar compliment to Tipu's cavalry.[14] Against this testimony, must be weighed the apparent poor performance of Mysorean forces in pitched battle, for instance at Malavelly in March 1799 where the British triumphed with minimal casualties. Malcolm informs us that Mysore morale was low during parts of the Seringapatam campaign, the troops demoralised by the nature of Tipu's defensive strategy and their arrears in pay.[15]

The structure of Tipu's army was much influenced by French practices of the late eighteenth century. Under his father, the infantry was organised into *risala* (equivalent to battalions) of 1,000 men.[16] The best concise explanation of the reorganisation undertaken by Tipu is provided by Kaushik Roy.

> … the Westernised infantry was organised in *kushuns* (equivalent to brigades). Five *kushuns* constituted a *kutcheri* (equivalent to a division). Each *kushun* comprised 5,000 men commanded by a *sipahdar*. The *sipahdar* was assisted by four *risaladars* (equivalent to colonels) and a *naqib* (adjutant). Each *risaladar* had under him 10 *jowkdars* (equivalent to captains). Each *jowkdar* commanded a *jowk* i.e. a body of 100 men (equivalent to [a] company). Each *jowk-dar* had under him two *sur kheil*, 10 *jemadars* and 10 *dufadars*.[17]

Chroniclers acknowledge the smart appearance of these regular infantry units. The soldiers wore woollen or cotton tunics of a 'tiger pattern', with or without short trousers. They were armed with muskets and practised western-style drill.[18]

Tipu's cavalry was of three types. The regular household cavalry, the *siladari* cavalry and the *kazzaks*. The latter two types were irregular horse unfamiliar with Western discipline. The regular cavalry was organised into *kutcheries*, each *kutcheri* made up of six *mokubs* which were equivalent to a European cavalry regiment. The 376 troopers of each *mokub* were armed with *tulwars*.[19] It was very likely the destructive power of these sabres which Richard Bayly witnessed at the battle of Malavelly; '...I have only to mention that the barrel of one of the men's muskets was completely cut in two by one stroke'. The mutilated musket was preserved as a souvenir.[20]

The *siladar* rode his own horse while the *kazzaks* were very similar to the plundering *pindari* horsemen of the Marathas.[21] The British sometimes referred to the latter as 'looties'. Irregular cavalry also provided their own arms and their efforts were predictably erratic, more likely to devastate the country-side than an enemy army. Lieutenant Patrick Brown witnessed them in action.

> Tippoo's Horse are the same as the Nizam's, without any discipline or uniform. Everyone arms himself and dresses as he chooses. They are generally armed with a sword and target, some have spears and others carbines, few have pistols, but all in general are well mounted and are excellent horsemen but the most part of them, great cowards, and in short are only formidable by their numbers.

He describes the 'looties' tracking the British Army, taking any opportunity to kill stragglers and plunder baggage.[22]

Each *kushun* had a corps of artillery of one to five guns.[23] Tipu had a consistent advantage over the British in this arm. When Seringapatam was captured, the Mysoreans were found to have ten times the number of cannon as the attacking force.[24] These field pieces, mostly locally cast under French supervision, were of larger bore and longer range than the Company's artil-lery. The largest brass cannon were 42-pounders. These massive guns were the hangover of Mughal practices. Anything of 26 pounds or greater was mainly used for siege-work and Tipu increasingly manufactured lighter field guns. The highly diverse armament of cannon, mortars and howitzers, and Tipu's predilection to experiment, meant that his artillery's effectiveness was com-promised by a lack of standardisation.[25]

A *jowk* of rocket men was also attached to each *kushun*.[26] The rocket had been used in India since times of antiquity. They were similar to fireworks, but usually had a tube of iron fixed to a long bamboo. An explosive charge or blade might be attached to the front of the missile. The rockets had a range of around 1,000 yards. Many contemporary observers are dismissive, but in skilled hands and employed against bodies of troops they could be a fearsome weapon.[27] Richard Bayly saw them in action at Seringapatam.

> Every illumination of blue lights was accompanied by a shower of rockets, some of which entered the head of the column, passing through to its rear, causing death, wounds, and dreadful lacera-tions from the long bamboos of twenty or thirty feet, which are

invariably attached to them. The instant a rocket passes through a man's body it resumes its original impetus of force, and will thus destroy ten or twenty until the combustible matter with which it is charged becomes expended. The shrieks of our men from these unusual weapons were terrific; thighs, legs, and arms left fleshless, with bone protruding in a shattered state from every part of the body, were the sad effects of these diabolical weapons of destruction.[28]

Ensign George Rowley of the Madras Engineers also saw rockets creating havoc. They bounced along the ground constantly changing direction and were impossible to avoid.[29]

The Mysorean commissariat and transport arrangements were not radically different to those of other Indian armies on the move. Haidar Ali transported his military stores with 10,000 bullocks, 100 elephants and 800 camels. A similar organisation was maintained under Tipu, animals being bred under the supervision of the government. The cattle were the best in South India. These resources were fully tested by the scale of the Mysore artillery; a single 24-pounder gun required seventy bullocks to pull it.[30]

Most contemporary commentators concluded that the failure of the Mysorean Army in the Seringapatam campaign of 1798–99 was attributable to wrong strategy rather than to any inherent weakness of forces. Arthur Wellesley wrote to the Governor-General after the battle of Malavelly:

If Tippoo had had sense and spirit sufficient to use his cavalry and infantry as he might have done, I have no hesitation in saying that we should not now be here, [two miles west of Seringapatam] and probably should not be out of the jungles near Bangalore.[31]

Tipu has been criticised for reducing his cavalry numbers while strengthening his infantry. The argument, made by several historians, is that with a dominant force of light cavalry he would have been able to execute a more effective scorched earth policy and threaten the lines of communication of his adversary. The British advance might have been slowed until the onset of the monsoon.[32]

The Marathas are a Hindu people of west and central India, their lands centred on the Deccan plateau.[33] They were the last indigenous Empire builders of India, rising to sudden prominence in the early seventeenth century. Their fortunes fluctuated; in 1794 they recovered from earlier setbacks to crush the Nizam and revitalise their power. This new ascendency was to be short-lived. In the words of Surendra Nah Sen:

Hardly eight years elapsed before the Peshwa became a feudatory of the British Government in India, the grand armies of Daulat Rao Sindhia and Raghuji Bhonsla were defeated and destroyed by Lake and Wellesley, and the Maratha Empire collapsed like a house of cards. If their rise was sudden and swift, the fall of the Marathas was no less sudden and spectacular. The Empire was apparently at the zenith of its power, it had reached its greatest extent, its man-power was almost unlimited, yet it was destroyed by a foreign power with a small army after a brief campaign of fifteen weeks.[34]

There were five main Maratha protagonists in their unsuccessful confrontation with the Company: the Peshwa and four northern chiefs. We will briefly introduce these men who make frequent appearances in the following pages. The Peshwa, equivalent to a hereditary prime minister, was nominally the most senior figure with the power to make policy for the whole Maratha Confederation. However, by the 1790s the influence of the Peshwa was in decline; the young Baji Rao II ruled over lands around Poona and in the south, but he was weak and increasingly dominated by his own ministers and Sindia.[35] In stark contrast, the Sindias were now the most powerful of the northern chieftains. Daulat Rao Sindia used his large army, partly officered by Europeans, to exert control in extensive parts of Hindustan. He was a cosmopolitan man who had grown away from his Maratha roots and he had become more than an equal member of the Confederation. Arthur Wellesley judged him to be 'very weak in intellect', although the British resident at his court differed, believing him 'more deficient in application than ability'.[36]

Raghuji Bhonsle, the Raja of Berar, held his court at Nagpur and controlled the eastern part of the Maratha country to the Carnatic coast. Bhonsle was a conscientious ruler who made efforts to remain aloof from the feuding of the Confederation. He was inclined to accommodate the British, but the strategic importance of his lands was always going to bring him into conflict with an expansionist European power.[37] Anud Rao, the Gaikwar of Baroda, was the least influential of the Maratha chieftains, his dominions being in the northwest beyond Bombay. He was feeble and he subjugated himself to the British in a subsidiary alliance.[38]

Jaswant Rao Holkar, a young man in his twenties, was from a different class of Marathas, a soldier who had risen from the lower ranks. Compared with Sindia and Bhonsle, men more fortunate in their birth, he had much experience but was less cultured. The British chose to view him as a marauding barbarian. Wellesley describes him as 'chief of all the freebooters and vagrants'.[39] He was a dangerous guerrilla leader, a Maratha warrior who was intelligent, cruel and determined to expand his limited territories.[40]

Most of the Maratha chiefs would have routinely received practical military training as part of their wider education. Sen argues that they were not worse commanders than soldiers of other nationalities.[41] However, the leadership of the Maratha Confederation was undermined by infighting between the main players. Sindia and Holkar were the mainstays of the Maratha Empire in the north, but their frequent disagreements culminated in open hostility. Bhonsle stood back when the threat of a foreign enemy demanded active cooperation; he has been accused of cowardice. Policy disagreements and personal quarrels denied the Maratha chiefs the unity of command enjoyed by the British.[42] There were feudal chiefs at different levels of the Confederation and the dissension continued within their domains. Sindia's court was particularly affected by a power struggle between native and European factions.[43]

A great Maratha statesman might have risen above all this to give cohesion and leadership but, fortunately for the British, none of the Maratha power-brokers were of this calibre. Their failings were both political and military, as Major Thomas Munro of the Madras Army explained to the Governor-General:

> It is not that they want resources, that they have not men and horses, but that there is no one amongst them possessed of those superior talents which are necessary to direct them to advantage.[44]

None of the Maratha chieftains had sufficient military ability to consistently challenge the Company's armies in a traditional form of warfare. Sindia and Bhonsle were inexperienced and indecisive in the field.[45] Holkar's abilities were undoubted, but he was more of a plunderer than a great leader. A skilful Maratha officer class might have filled the vacuum in competence and leadership but, in Sen's words, they 'began their military careers too early, were much too tied to the time-honoured system to learn anything new and generally died early'.[46] They failed to match their European adversaries in battle. We will return to the European officers who acted as mercenaries in the armies of Sindia and Holkar.

The strengths of the Maratha forces are described for individual actions in the Campaigns section, but it is convenient to give an overview of the substance and nature of their armies here. The information is largely from European contemporary sources and the figures must all be regarded as estimates. Major Lewis Ferdinand Smith gives the following strengths for the Marathas on the eve of war with the British.

Sindhia

	Battalions	Guns	Cavalry
Perron's Brigades	39	225	5,000
Filoze's Brigade	8	45	500
Sombre's Brigade	6	35	500
Shepherd's Brigade	5	25	500
Umbajee's [Ambaji Inglia's] Army	10	40	10,000

Holkar

Vicker's Brigade	6	30	500
Armstrong's Brigade	4	20	200
Dodd's Brigade	4	20	200
Under Native Commanders	10	130	30,000

Bhonsla

Under Native Commanders	15	60	30,000

The Peshwa's army was less substantial, containing only two battalions of regulars.[47]

In his excellent study of the Anglo-Maratha War, modern historian John Pemble has combed the available literature to give more information pertaining to the size of these armies. The force of the French mercenary Perron was made up of four brigades of infantry and one of cavalry.

> Each infantry brigade consisted of 4,800 sepoys (eight battalions of 600 men), with 360 gunners and 51 pieces of artillery (of which 15 were siege guns) and 200 cavalry. The separate brigade of cavalry contained 3,000 men at the most. The full strength of Perron's army was thus something like 200 guns and 24,500 fighting men, making, with Ambaji's [Sindia's minister Ambaji Inglia] troops, 280 guns and 30,000 men.[48]

Estimates of effective numbers are further complicated by the mix of regular and irregular troops and the dispersal of forces in the north and south. Perron's and Ambaji's men were regarded as 'regulars' as they had been trained by Europeans. The force at Perron's disposal in the north would have been less than that quoted, as two of the battalions were with Sindia in the Deccan. In addition to these brigades, Sindia had the weaker corps commanded by the European mercenaries Browning and Filoze. Pemble calculates the probable effective strength of Sindia's army to be 36,000 men (29,000 infantry, 2,500 artillery, 4,500 cavalry) and 330 guns. The chief also had assistance from the female military leader, the Begum Somru, and the tens of thousands of irregular Maratha cavalry which were mostly in the Deccan.[49]

Bhonsle's army, which was officered only by Indians, was composed of two brigades of infantry. Their strength was estimated to be 10–12,000 men in the 1790s, but it is likely that he only brought 6,000 infantry into the field in the summer of 1803.[50] Quantification of Holkar's forces is especially problematic as there was no British resident at his court to gather intelligence. The historian of the Marathas, James Grant Duff, estimates that the Maratha chief had 26,000 infantry and 199 guns when he invaded Hindustan in 1804.[51] A statement from the Wellesley papers dated February 1803 gives the total strength of Holkar's forces as 56,000 cavalry, 15,900 infantry and 157 guns of different calibres.[52] The Marathas had a significant but not overwhelming numerical superiority in the years 1803–1805, mobilising 56,000 regular troops compared with British forces of 21,000 in the Deccan and 16,000 in Hindustan and Orissa.[53]

Whatever the precise numbers, most 'Maratha' soldiers were not true Marathas. In the late eighteenth century, the Maratha armies were increasingly denationalised. The Marathas were not keen to be away from their homes for long periods and there was no tradition of joining a regular army. The influx of foreigners particularly affected the foot battalions. Sindia's regular infantry forces were composed entirely of non-Marathas.[54] He instead recruited *Parbias* or easterners from Oudh, the Doab and Rohilkhand. In the Peshwa's army, Arabs and other foreigners outnumbered the natives; in Bhonle's army there were Arabs, Rajputs, and Pathans; in Holkar's army *pindaris* of various ethnic backgrounds predominated.[55] The quality of these Indian mercenaries varied enormously. The Arabs enjoyed the greatest reputation for valour, while others, for instance Christian recruits from Goa, had a poor reputation.[56]

Sindia's regular infantry was the best commanded by an Indian prince of the period. These were the men who were to impress Lake and Wellesley at Laswari and Assaye. They benefitted from European training, especially in the hands of two French adventurers, Benoit de Boigne and Perron. Many of these European adventurers were mediocrities, but de Boigne is acknowledged to have been an able soldier and leader. He had a talent for organisation and was almost solely responsible for the army which gave Sindia his supremacy in the Confederation.[57] When he retired due to ill health in 1796, he was effectively succeeded by Pierre Cuillier, commonly known as Perron. The son of a cloth maker, Perron was a less attractive character then de Boigne, but he was a competent commander and Sindia had allowed him to attain almost regal status, receiving tributes, holding trade monopolies and coining money. On the eve of the war, his power was waning and he had little appetite for a fight with the British, preferring to take his fortune back to France.[58]

The regular battalions led by de Boigne and Perron were in many ways comparable to contemporary European armies. Each battalion of 6–700 men was organised with companies and had approximately forty native officers and a much smaller number of Europeans.[59] The battalions were named after famous cities or forts such as Delhi and Agra.[60] The soldiers' uniform, arms and drill were all heavily influenced by European practices. A British observer in 1802 describes Sindia's infantry regulars:

> The uniforms of the sepoys are the same as the Company's. So are
> the accoutrements with the exception that they carry a sword as

well as a bayonet and musket. The band which was in full tune, as they marched by my little camp, played nothing but English tunes, perfectly in the European style.[61]

The muskets and bayonets were manufactured at Agra.[62] Selected Maratha sharpshooters carried the more accurate long-barrelled matchlocks.[63] The men were disciplined using the British regulations originally issued in 1780 and still in force in the British Army.[64] In December 1804, near Deig, James Young saw enemy infantry practising 'platoon and file firing and the formation of columns and lines'.[65] Each regular battalion had five pieces of field artillery, three battery guns and two mortars.[66]

Sindia's regular infantry provided stern opposition to the British. This is apparent from the eyewitness accounts of the ferocity of fighting in the major battles. Arthur Wellesley rated Sindia's regulars more highly than Tipu's infantry[67] and Indian old hands, such as William Thorn, were quick to correct those at home who were dismissive of Indian armies. The British public were;

> ...uninformed in regard to the changes that have taken place among the warlike tribes of India, through the introduction of European tactics and French discipline, which combined with their natural courage often bordering on enthusiastic frenzy, and their numerical superiority, has rendered our conflicts with them sanguinary in the extreme.[68]

There was also a British view that European officers remained vital to the cohesion of Sindia's army. George Carnegie, who fought as a mercenary for Sindia, thought them to be essential; 'For it has, I believe, generally been found both in the Company's service and in ours, that if a European will lead, a native will follow'.[69] Bhonsle did not employ European officers, but Holkar emulated Sindia, some of his battalions commanded by French (Dudrenec, Plumet) and British officers (Vickers, Gardner, Armstrong).[70]

The Maratha irregular infantry was not subject to European discipline and was heterogeneous. It was poorly equipped and badly led. Some irregular infantrymen carried muskets and matchlocks, but others went into battle with weapons 'handed down from the early stone age'. These primitive weapons included bows and arrows, spears and stones.[71]

There were four different types of cavalry in Maratha service. The elite were the *bargirs*, the private cavalry of the Peshwa. They were armed, equipped and paid for by the state but their numbers were small.[72] The second group, the *silahdars*, were regarded as state cavalry but were more irregular. They might receive pay or depend more on the spoils of war. The term *silahdar* implied that the cavalryman was an 'equipment holder'. They rode their own horses and if the horse was killed or wounded the soldier would lose both his animal and his allowance.[73] The third class of horsemen were the *ekas* or *ekandas* who were single volunteers who joined the camp with their own horses and accoutrements. They were variably armed with muskets and matchlocks, spears, lances, daggers, clubs, and bows and arrows.[74]

The fourth class were the predatory hordes of the *pindaris* (*pendharis*). They were not soldiers but 'trained robbers' who could easily be encouraged to harass an enemy.[75] An anonymous observer of 1819 describes their methods:

> The climate and hardy habits of these plunderers render tents or baggage an unnecessary encumbrance; each person carries a few days' provision for himself and for his horse; and they march for weeks together, at the rate of thirty and forty miles a day over roads and countries impassable for a regular army. They exhibit a striking resemblance to the Cossacks…[76]

John Shipp, a sergeant in HM 22nd Regiment, saw *pindaris* riding at full speed with one child in front and another behind. Their wives were excellent horsewomen.[77] Often well-armed with lances and swords, the *pindaris'* objective was plunder, not fighting. If they came under attack they would disperse and reassemble elsewhere.[78]

The Maratha princes had access to enormous numbers of horsemen. George Carnegie, writing in 1801, believed that the four great chiefs could furnish 500,000 cavalry in two or three months.[79] This may have been an exaggeration, but each of the major princes had tens of thousands of horsemen in addition to the innumerable hordes of *pindaris* who attached themselves to their armies. These forces were more a product of the Maratha way of life than a state creation. The Marathas were natural horsemen and horse breeding was essential to their economy. Many of their cavalrymen were mounted on home-reared '*Deccanis*'.[80] The horses were graded as being first, second or third class, and useless.[81]

The Maratha cavalry was less effective as a shock force than in performing light cavalry functions such as reconnaissance, pursuit and protection of the flanks of the army. Their toughness, lightness and small mounts ideally equipped them for these duties.[82] Carnegie noted that the bulk of the Maratha cavalry was 'almost entirely unacquainted with Order or Discipline'. They could endure great hardships, but they were, he says, 'not able to oppose Regular troops in the proportion of one to ten'.[83] The *silahdar* was bound to carefully protect his horse and arms and there was little reason for him to take undue risks in battle.

Elephants had been used by Indian armies since ancient times but they were not a prominent part of the Maratha army. Their employment in offensive operations was limited as they were easily frightened by firearms and liable to cause confusion in their own ranks.[84]

The Maratha artillery was a mixture of iron and brass guns. The former were generally of European manufacture, whereas the latter were mostly cast and bored in India.[85] In his meticulous review of the Maratha military machine, Surendra Nath Sen is disparaging of the artillery's performance.

> Their artillery among other things ensured the supremacy of the English in India. To the Marathas it afforded little or no advantage in their final struggle for the empire. The weapon was not ineffective. It had a great future and its possibilities had not yet been exhausted. But the Marathas had borrowed a scientific weapon without mastering its science and unintelligent imitation seldom leads to success.[86]

Pemble argues that the opposite was true, the Marathas regularly having the advantage in firepower.[87] British accounts of the larger battles of the Anglo-Maratha War suggest that the Maratha artillery was a formidable destructive force. At Laswari, Lake attributed his heavy losses to his enemy's 'immense artillery'; the hundred cannon, many of large calibre, generated as heavy a fire as he had ever witnessed.[88] At Assaye, Wellesley was similarly impressed by the heat of the Maratha fire. The enemy's artillery, he informed Colonel James Stevenson, was excellent, the ordnance so good and well equipped that it would serve for British use.[89] Engineer John Blakiston agreed.

> Nothing could surpass the skill or bravery displayed by their golum-dauze, as our loss fully testified. When taken, their guns were all found laid a few degrees below the point-blank, just what they ought to be for a discharge of grape or canister at short distance; while, so rapid was their fire that the officers left behind with the baggage, and were out of sound of small arms, could not compare the report of the guns to anything less than the rolling of musquetry. The pieces, which were cast under the direction of Europeans, were all of the best kind and equipped in the most efficient manner.[90]

The artillery captured after the Battle of Delhi was also considered to be at least as good as the British arm.[91] The number of guns taken after major battles reflects the scale of the Maratha artillery; for instance, sixty-eight at Delhi and ninety-eight at Assaye.[92] The Marathas had rockets which were usually carried by camels.[93] It seems that they were not very widely used, although Arthur Wellesley describes Bhonsle's troops 'throwing great numbers of rockets' in a skirmish in November 1803.[94]

Maratha fortifications and siege-work were judged to be rudimentary by Europeans. An eyewitness account of the Marathas desultory attempts to besiege the fortress of Dharwar in 1791 is typical.

> A gun is loaded, and the whole of the people in the battery sit down, talk and smoke for half an hour, when it is fired and if it knocks up a great dust it is thought sufficient; it is reloaded, and the parties resume their smoking and conversation.[95]

Although larger fortresses, notably, Gawilghur and Bhurtpore, were significant obstacles to the British, the great majority of Maratha forts were primitive in their design and armaments. Many had defences made of a mixture of mud and rubble rather than stone.[96] The garrisons were largely composed of foreigners, mainly Arabs and non-Maratha Indians.[97]

When on the march, the Maratha Army was often divided into three parts. The vanguard included all the infantry, the centre division formed a body of reserve, and the grand park and all the baggage was at the rear.[98] The soldiers were accompanied by vast numbers of male and female non-combatants and also animals. Bhonsle had a personal staff of five clerks and 181 attendants. His cavalry regiment had nine stirrup holders, five farriers, eight camel drivers, four *khijmatgars* (waiters), three musicians, two scouts, five store keepers, two wardrobe keepers, thirteen palanquin bearers, two saddlers, one washerman, two macebearers, one leather worker, one sweeper, two drummers, four messengers, one torchbearer, one barber, one tailor, seven water-carriers, two sunshade bearers, two trumpeters, four elephant drivers, one *potdar* (treasurer) and ninety-nine grooms.[99]

The camp-followers had their own horses, usually numbering several thousand. Camels, asses and bullocks were used to carry the tents and baggage. The camp bazaar or market-place which sprung up at the end of a march required 20,000 bullocks to carry the shopkeepers' goods.[100] George Carnegie witnessed these gatherings.

> A Mahratta (or any Indian camp) has much the appearance of a Country Fair in England, cloth, corn and every product of the country selling, and Jewellers and other Mecanicks at work the same as in a City, and equally at their ease as in times of profound Peace or tranquillity.[101]

There was no formal commissary department in the Maratha armies. There was instead an entire dependence on their foragers and the *banjaras* and *pindaris*. The latter pillaged the stores of local villages and sold the items at the Maratha camp. This unsupervised supply chain meant periods of both plenty and hardship and the Maratha soldier was necessarily adept at subsisting on little food and fodder.[102] Intelligence gathering was also mostly opportunistic, the Maratha chiefs employing scouts (*jasuds*) who had a deep knowledge of the country and who often travelled in disguise. These men did not form a separate department but it was common for a number of them to be attached to each army.[103]

The Maratha Army failed to match the British in battle and there are divergent views as to the main reason for their failure. The favoured contemporary opinion was that they had partly abandoned traditional methods of warfare much dependant on mobility and the use of cavalry in favour of regular infantry and artillery. The adoption of a westernised approach led them to fight when flight would have been more judicious.[104] Maratha commanders were trapped between two alien systems of waging war. Sen is a proponent of this theory.

> When they began to adopt the new tactics with which they had become familiar in their warfare against the Europeans, they did not reject the traditional system of fighting. The two methods were found in practice to be irreconcilable but they persisted in their useless efforts at hybridisation in a way that invariably led to disaster.[105]

Contemporary supporters of this view included intelligent observers such as Arthur Wellesley and Thomas Munro. Wellesley wrote to John Malcolm in November 1803:

> Scindia's armies had actually been brought to a very favourable state of discipline by the exertions of the European officers in their service; but I think it is much to be doubted whether his power, or rather that of the Marhatta nation, would not have been more formidable, at least to the British government, if they had never had an European, as an infantry soldier, in their service, and had carried on their operations, in the manner of the original Marhattas, only by means of cavalry. I have no doubt whatever but that the military spirit of the nation has been destroyed by their establishment of infantry and artillery...[106]

Munro agreed, believing that 'by coming forward with regular infantry' the Marathas had handed every advantage to the British.[107]

John Pemble vigorously rejects this theory of Maratha 'strategic error', arguing that it is formed in isolation. It particularly fails to take into account improvements in the Company's arms which neutralised the Maratha cavalry threat.

> The Marathas' attempt to fight the British with their own weapons was not the error of idle vanity; it was the only strategy that offered a chance of success.[108]

Pemble points to a tendency for contemporaries and later historians to underestimate the performance of Sindia's regular infantry in battle. Although on the losing side, they had fought bravely and inflicted significant numbers of casualties. Wellesley may have had second thoughts as to the Marathas' optimal strategy, writing to Colonel Murray in September 1804 that the Maratha cavalry had been ineffective; 'The infantry is the strength of Holkar's, as it is of every other army'.[109]

It is less contentious to state that poor leadership was a factor in Maratha defeat. There are ample instances of mediocre generalship by the Maratha princes and, unlike their predecessors, they failed to instil unquestioning loyalty in their Indian officers. Their reliance on Europeans was bound to be a weakness when their armies confronted a European power. The European officers and non-commissioned officers in Maratha service were a mixture of nationalities, mostly British, French and Eurasian. The British were largely adventurers, deserters or cashiered officers; the French the descendants of French garrisons; the Eurasians the product of liaisons of Indian women with the British.[110] As a group, they were judged to be of poor quality. Many of them had no military training. The French were despised more than most. Perron's men were 'raised from cooks, bakers, and barbers, to be the Majors and Colonels, absurdly entrusted with the command of brigades...'. This was a British verdict and there was discord between British and French officers in Maratha ranks.[111]

Contrary to the common view, British and Eurasian officers outnumbered the French in Sindia's and Holkar's armies at the outbreak of war. At least some of the British were reputable men. Among them was George Carnegie, who gives us glimpses of life in the service of an Indian prince.

> The European Officers in this Service [Sindia's] certainly suffer many inconveniences, I may say, hardships, little known and seldom felt by the Company's Military servants. The Fudal system of Government is the cause of unnecessary War. Between the Princes and their powerful rebellious Chiefs, this keeps our Troops constantly marching, I must say, on Active Service at least nine months of the Year... We are frequently (as in our present encampment [50 miles from Delhi, July 1802]) at too great a distance from any of the Company's settlements to get supplys of Wine, and other European Articles. But young men in health can bear fatigue and want of Wine. A few years soon pass away, and hope, 'all chearing hope,' points to the happy season, when we shall again taste life, enjoy the Society of our Friends, and fair Country women, and all the comforts that can flow from a contented mind and honest independence. Meantime we are not without our advantages. Our pay is better and our promotion quicker than in the King's or Company's Service. We lead an active and a sober life (having frequently nothing to drink will account for

that), no temptation to spend half a Crown out of six pence a day. Being deprived of the Society of our Country women, we are also excused the expences of Balls, Plays, Fruit and Glove Shops, which ruin one third of the Company's Officers.[112]

When hostilities became inevitable, men such as Carnegie mostly moved across to the British ranks. The Governor-General facilitated this defection by issuing a 'proclamation' in the summer of 1803 which promised attractive employment and pensions.[113] While some were probably enticed by this offer, many will have abandoned their Maratha employers for less mercenary reasons. For the British, there was an inevitable aversion to fighting their own countrymen and they also perceived that Perron discriminated against them, favouring their French peers.[114] Three English mercenaries in Holkar's service preferred execution rather than taking up arms against their homeland.[115]

Even allowing for their mixed quality, the sudden defection of these European officers must have had an impact on Sindia's and Holkar's armies. Pemble argues that the damage was limited by the resourcefulness of the sepoys and native officers. Maratha armies were still able to offer stiff resistance in battle and had some success without any European officer support, for instance Holkar's pursuit of Monson in 1804.[116] Historian Randolf Cooper believes the effects to have been more deeply felt; the collapse of the European officer corps destroying Sindia's command function, depriving him of officer leadership in battle, and leading to a catastrophic loss of intelligence.[117] With respect to the latter, it appears that at least some officers displayed a residual loyalty to their Maratha employers. George Carnegie enjoyed the benefits outlined in the proclamation, but he was unwilling to hand over any of Sindia's secrets.

> I either did not or would not know anything, considering that I had done my duty to my Country in leaving poor Dowlet Row when he most wanted my Services... I did not feel myself authorized (even in this just and necessary War!!!) to assist personally in the destruction of an Army, in which almost every individual was known to me.[118]

To conclude this brief review of Britain's enemies in India we should mention the *polygars* and also those men loosely referred to as 'freebooters'. The *polygars* were the subordinate feudal chiefs of the south who, as we will see, were frustrating opponents for the British, stubbornly defending their hill forts and adept in an elusive form of jungle warfare. Ensign James Welsh, who is the best eyewitness of the Polygar Wars, believed the *polygar* soldiers to be of variable quality. Some were simple villagers attracted by the spoils of war. Such men might have firearms, and even artillery and rockets, but Welsh says that they made a great noise but 'did little execution'.[119] Others, notably the men from Panjalumcoorchy, had been forced to take up arms and were more formidable foes: '…it is my serious opinion, that twenty thousand Panjalum-coorcheans, would have been invincible in his [Murdoo's] country'.[120]

The British were consistently harassed by the *pindaris* and other irregular elements. The term 'freebooters' was often used to describe the hordes of bandits and adventures who shunned formal warfare but were quick to exploit it. These men were as likely to pillage friends as foes.[121] On occasion, a deter-mined adventurer attracted enough followers to become a threat to British control and required individual attention. One example is Dhoondiah Waugh, a desperado who had escaped the dungeons of Seringapatam and who had enough ambition and guile to draw men around his flag. His 'army' was a ragbag of Maratha soldiers seeking their fortune, troops dispersed from Tipu's army, and peasants who had little to lose.[122] A mass of freebooters was no threat in a pitched battle but, as Arthur Wellesley was to discover, they were quick-moving and it was a challenge to bring them to a decisive action. The *pindaris* of the north, under the leadership of men such as Ameer Khan, were equally destructive, as is testified by William Thorn.

> Contemptible as they may seem in a military point of view, they are far more pernicious to the country, and infinitely more difficult of suppression, than a regular force, better known by the impression they leave than their actual presence.[123]

II Campaigns

Chapter 3

Dangerous Consequences: Mysore 1799

At the start of the eighteenth century, the British and French traders who established their stations on the coast of India must have seemed little threat to a warrior nation which had a quarter of a million men in arms. These early settlers, at first in thrall to the provincial native princes, were soon flexing their muscles, exploiting their European military prowess to the full. By the middle of the century it was clear to the native rulers not only that there was a new form of warfare on the continent, but also that an alliance with one of the European powers was the surest path to the domination of their local rivals. In theory, the British and French might have cooperated in this expanding Western sphere of influence, but their longstanding mutual antagonism was such that only one could prosper. By the second half of the century it was apparent that this was to be the British.[1]

At the time of the first landing of Richard Wellesley, Lord Mornington, in India in May 1798, his country's possessions were essentially in three parts around each of the East India Company (EIC) presidencies described in the opening chapter: Bengal, Bombay and Madras. As Roberts points out, the three presidencies were not only geographically distinct, but also self-contained and close to being independent; more like friendly states than constituent parts of a larger government.[2] Relations between the presidencies were mostly harmonious, which was more than could be said for the native princes. Their potential political and military power has been described (see Chapter 2) but their suspicion of the British was matched by their disunity. The Nizam of Hyderabad had been weakened by his defeat at the hands of the Marathas in 1795 and he was likely to be a supplicant to the British or to be subsumed by other more powerful native states. The larger Maratha Confederation was itself in disorder. The Peshwa at Poona was its nominal leader, but in reality he was overshadowed by his compatriots Sindia, Holkar and Bhonsle. The most influential of these, Sindia, was himself vulnerable to the French officers who increasingly trained and commanded his Indian troops. Mysore, to the south and west, remained especially resentful of the British presence following its defeat by Cornwallis in 1792, the so-called Second Mysore War. It was here, in the last year of the eighteenth century, that war would be catalysed. The neutrality was fractured by a combination of the complacency of the native ruler, Tipu Sultan, British perceptions of a resurgence of French influence following Bonaparte's expedition to Egypt and, perhaps above all, the arrival of a new Governor-General with expansionist ambitions.[3]

Tipu was a contradictory character. Devoid of any Eastern conservatism, he was industrious and innovatory, embracing concepts of Western science and philosophy. Few subjects escaped his attention. Conversely, he was tyrannical and cruel to his enemies. Historian Sir Penderel Moon judged him to be Britain's most formidable and determined enemy in India. A more contemporary observer, Wilkes, thought him a poor soldier who was too easily led astray and discouraged.

> He was unable to grasp the plan of a campaign or the conduct of a war; although he gave some examples of skill in marshalling a battle…
> Tipoo was intoxicated with success and desponding in adversity.[4]

He often dabbled in something without fully mastering it and his undoubted knowledge was not translated into good judgement. His political and military reforms were 'the strange aberrations of untutored intellect'. He was a man who was 'perpetually deceived'.[5]

It was Tipu's naivety and reluctance to take counsel from his advisors which led to the absurd attempted collaboration with the French which would ultimately lead to his demise. Determined that France would help him drive the British out of India, he had made several approaches to Britain's enemy in the last decade of the eighteenth century. The most recent and hopeless of these initiatives involved a Monsieur Malartic, the French governor of Mauritius, who promised Tipu's envoys a French expedition, but who eventually landed ninety-nine hapless volunteers at Mangalore two days after Mornington's arrival at Madras. An instinctive ruler would have sensed the need for damage limitation and stealth, but the Sultan, surrounded by rogues, failed to disown Malartic, or send the small band back whence they came or, most crucially, to keep his machinations a secret from the British.[6]

Malartic's proclamation, a call to French arms 'to serve under the banners of Tipoo', was soon in Mornington's hands. For a Governor-General who was a Francophobe and already primed to take strong action, this was an incendiary document, almost signing Tipu's death warrant. Mornington's instinct was to use the proclamation to justify a pre-emptive strike against Mysore. The inference was that if the British did not attack Tipu, he would soon attack them. In reality, it was not clear that Tipu's feeble attempt to enrol French help was of any immediate threat to Britain.[7] Mornington's typically labyrinthine assertion that, '…neither the measure of his hostility, nor of our right to restrain it, nor of our danger from it, are to be estimated by the amount of the force which he has actually obtained', was not universally accepted by his political and military peers in Madras and Bengal. Accordingly, he reluctantly decided to defer any action against Mysore, informing Secretary of State Henry Dundas in early July 1798 that he had first called upon Tipu to explain his attitude to the British and also the nature of the force landed at Mangalore. In the event, this letter was not sent.

Two of the men counselling caution in the summer of 1798 were to feature prominently in the coming campaign against Seringapatam, the chief city and fortress of Mysore. Lieutenant-General George Harris, Commander-in-Chief of the Madras Army, warned that his troops were not ready to take the field. He was also concerned that military action had not been properly thought through; perhaps Tipu should be allowed to think again rather than 'avail[ing] ourselves of the error he had run in to'. Mornington replied to Harris accepting the impossibility of an immediate campaign against Tipu, but insisting that the reduction of Mysore was 'warranted by principles of justice and demanded by those of policy'. The Governor-General's brother, Arthur Wellesley, at this period colonel of the 33rd Regiment serving in Bengal, echoed Harris's reservations, suggesting that Tipu would be 'glad of an opportunity of getting out of the scrape'.[8] Other senior men on the spot in Bengal, Adjutant-General Barry Close, Secretary to the Government Josiah Webbe and Lieutenant-General Alured Clarke, a former governor of Madras, all rubbished the prospect of an imminent attack. Money was short, the monsoon would make the roads impassable and neither the Nizam nor Peshwa would provide support.[9]

Momentarily frustrated by the unpreparedness of his armies and the opinions of his political and military advisors, Mornington turned his attention to diplomacy. Instructions were sent to the British residents at the courts of the Peshwa, Sindia and the Nizam to make the case for the marginalisation of Tipu. The subsidiary treaty subsequently concluded with the Nizam by the British resident at Hyderabad, Captain James Kirkpatrick, proved to be a considerable success for the Governor-General. In return for 6,000 native troops and some European artillery provided by the British, the Nizam would pay a subsidy and disband the 'French force' which had been originally assembled in his dominions by François Raymond.[10] The French infantry mutinied, but they were incapable of much resistance. The bloodless transfer of force in late October 1798 is best described by Colonel George Roberts, who led a detachment of around 6,000 men of the Madras and Bengal native infantry assisted by 2,000 of the Nizam's horse.

> I moved down with the four Madras battalions, and artillery attached, about noon on the 22nd, sending the necessary orders to Lieutenant-Colonel Hyndman who was encamped at a short distance in rear of the French lines, to support me with the Bengal detachment should circumstances render it necessary. About three in the afternoon I reached and occupied the heights immediately in front of the French lines, within musket shot, which they

permitted me to do without offering the least opposition, and soon after surrendered themselves, and laid down their arms. By seven o'clock that evening my troops were in complete possession of every part of the extensive lines, their guns, and arms and all their military stores to a considerable amount. Upwards of 12,000 stand of arms and 27 pieces of cannon mounted have already been collected. Their force consisted of 13,000 men.[11]

The Governor-General had neutralised a potential enemy, gained extra troops for the coming campaign and considerably boosted his own credibility. The reduction of the French force would, he informed Dundas, be '…highly favourable to your political interests in the Peninsula of India'.[12] Alexander Beatson, an aide-de-camp in the Madras Army, was one of many applauding the coup:

No one suspected so grand and masterly a stroke as the total annihilation of the French faction at Hyderabad. It is easier therefore to imagine than to describe the joy and satisfaction which the intelligence of this important event excited when it reached Calcutta and Madras.[13]

Other initiatives were less productive. The Peshwa in Poona was embroiled in Maratha politics and he was not to be drawn into a subsidiary alliance. Sindia discouraged the Peshwa's links with the British and also played his own double game. Any British success attracted his 'abundant congratulations', while he missed no chance to bolster Tipu's resistance.[14] This was, however, purely by political means and the Marathas were to remain militarily neutral in the forthcoming war with Mysore.[15]

Mornington's subsequent correspondence with Tipu was protracted and remarkable only for the profound insincerity shown by both men. The Governor-General must have well understood that the terms he was determined to impose on Tipu – the expulsion of all Frenchmen from his dominions, the reception of an allied resident at Seringapatam and the cession of coastal territory below the Ghats – were an anathema to a proud ruler who had not, as yet, been defeated in battle. On his part, Tipu had underestimated his protagonist's determination to wage war and he adopted an evasive and dilatory style of diplomacy, apparently believing that the adoption of a tone of strained cordiality and persistent stalling would suffice to keep the English army outside his borders.[16]

A few of the many letters can be briefly quoted to capture the flavour of the exchanges. At the outset, in the summer of 1798, Tipu greets Mornington effusively; the news of the Governor-General's arrival in India '…reached me at the happiest of times and afforded me a degree of pleasure and satisfaction that cannot be adequately expressed upon paper'.[17] By November, Mornington had moved beyond pleasantries and had started to make allusions to Tipu's contacts with the French. He had little sense of humour, but he surely must have smiled as he informed his adversary of Nelson's victory at the Battle of the Nile:

> ...confident from the union and attachment subsisting between us that this intelligence will afford you sincere satisfaction, I could not deny myself the pleasure of communicating it.

A proposal was made that a British commissary should attend Tipu's court but again there was procrastination: '...I will let you know what time and place it will be convenient for me to receive Major Doveton'.[18]

Tipu also made half-hearted attempts to explain away the Mauritius debacle, referring to the 'vice and deceit' of the French. He encouraged the Governor-General to 'continue to rejoice me with happy letters'. He was to be disappointed. By January 1799, Mornington's tone was more accusatory, with some drops of acid, one long epistle concluding with the cryptic threat that 'dangerous consequences result from the delay of arduous affairs'.[19] Tipu's distracted reply – 'Being frequently disposed to make excursions and hunt, I am accordingly on a hunting excursion' – meant that even his acceptance of Doveton's mission was now too late to save him. Mornington ordered Harris to move towards Mysore in early February.[20] That this had always been his objective, and that his negotiations with Tipu were a charade, is confirmed by his comment to Dundas that he had succeeded completely in 'drawing the Beast of the Jungle into the toils'.[21] Tipu's frame of mind at this stage can only be guessed at; Robert's view that he was plunged into 'a hopeless and fatalistic despair' is redolent of Greek tragedy and probably true.[22]

Mornington was exultant and optimistic, but his senior soldiers had mixed feelings regarding the rationale for war and the chances of success in a campaign which must ultimately capture Seringapatam. In a private letter of late February, Harris admitted to having at first been daunted by the nature of his command, but he drew succour from the Governor-General's confidence; '...Lord Mornington's plans seem everywhere to succeed... Tis true we still have our struggles though most things are so favourable'.[23] Arthur Wellesley was less sanguine, still despondent that a diplomatic solution had been scorned and anxious that Seringapatam could not be seized in a single campaign. In a letter to his younger brother Henry, he lists his concerns in methodical style: a shortage of grain and money; the possibility that the Nizam's force from Hyderabad would not be able to join the main army; the unpreparedness of the Bombay Army to simultaneously invade Mysore from the west; and, most controversially, the lack of a competent general. The younger officer had perhaps sensed Harris's lack of confidence and he was to openly criticise his senior in his correspondence and also lecture him when he saw fit.[24]

The slow military preparations by the Madras Presidency had been a cause of considerable frustration to Mornington. The machinery for war was bureaucratic and ponderous. The initial estimate that it would take six months to equip an army enraged him; if this was the case, what use was it for the defence of the Presidency against sudden attack?[25] Harris, still apparently surprised to have the onerous command, wrote to Captain George Robinson: 'Wonderful exertions have been made to fit out the army which Dame Fortune, in her freaks, has placed me at the head of'. The difficulties had indeed been overcome and the commander believed his force 'to be appointed beyond every expectation'.[26] The Governor-General was persuaded by his brother Arthur not to accompany the army in person. This at least gave Harris the opportunity of exerting his authority.[27]

The British army assembled had claim to be the best-equipped force ever seen in India. Harris's main army at Vellore was more than 21,000 strong. This was made up of two King's regiments (19th and 25th Light Dragoons) and four native regiments of cavalry (2,678 men); six regiments of European infantry (His Majesty's (HM) 12th, HM 33rd, HM 73rd, HM 74th, HM Scotch Brigade and de Meuron's Swiss regiment) (4,608) and eleven battalions of native infantry (11,061); and two corps of Bengal artillery and two battalions of Madras artillery (576). This gave a total of 18,923 fighting men of whom 5,520 were European. The final strength of 21,649 men was reached by adding the number of lascars and pioneers (see Appendix V). The army was divided into left and right wings, the cavalry into two brigades and the infantry into six.[28]

This force would be joined on 20 February by the 'Hyderabad Contingent', made up of six battalions of the Company's sepoys gifted to the Nizam as part of the recent alliance, four battalions of the disbanded French units and the Nizam's cavalry. The French troops were 'turbulent and disobedient' and now under the command of British officers.[29] In all, the contingent was composed of around 10,000 infantry and 6,000 cavalry and was supported by two companies of Bengal and Madras artillery.[30] It was under the command of the Nizam's principal minister, Meer Allum, but Harris decided to strengthen it with the 33rd Foot and he also appointed Colonel Arthur Wellesley to accompany the force. Wellesley's precise role is interpreted differently by historians, many asserting that he was in command of the whole corps. Strictly, this was still Meer Allum's role, but Wellesley was probably the 'virtual commander'. This appointment inevitably attracted charges of nepotism, but Meer Allum had specifically requested Wellesley and the decision was to prove propitious. Harris was probably relieved to have a little distance between himself and this highly competent but unusually assertive junior officer.[31]

The third part of the British force for the invasion of Mysore was the Army of Bombay, assembled at Cannanore (see map 2) under the command of

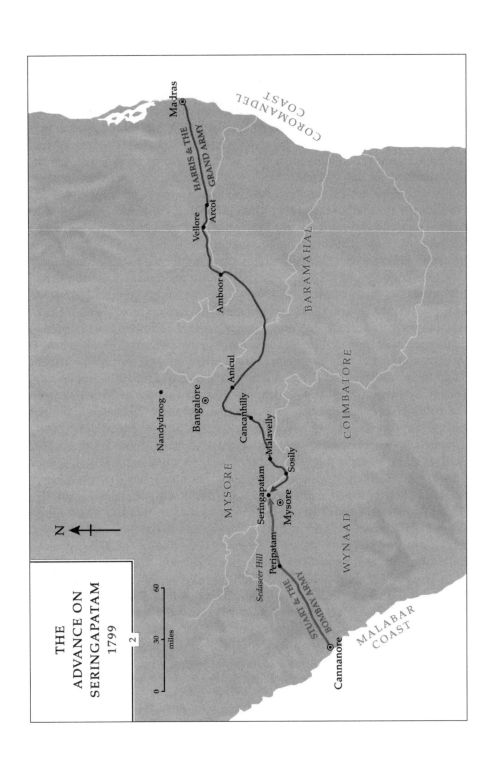

THE
ADVANCE ON
SERINGAPATAM
1799

N

0   30   60
miles

MYSORE

BARAMAHAL

COIMBATORE

WYNAAD

MALABAR COAST

COROMANDEL COAST

Madras

Vellore
Arcot

Amboor

Anicul

Nandydroog

Bangalore

Cancanhilly

Malavelly
Sosily

Seringapatam
Mysore

Sedaser Hill

Peripatam

Cannanore

HARRIS & THE GRAND ARMY

STUART & THE BOMBAY ARMY

Lieutenant General James Stuart. This army was 6,400 strong including more than 5,000 infantry. Two King's regiments (HM 74th, HM 77th), one EIC Bombay European Regiment (103rd), and six native battalions were organised into three brigades, the centre composed entirely of European troops.[32]

Tipu's forces are more difficult to calculate. Captain John Malcolm was instructed to gain intelligence of the enemy and he estimated the Mysore Army to number around 47,000 fighting men including 23,000 regular infantry, the remainder made up of regular and irregular cavalry and smaller numbers of armed militia, rocket men and peons. There were probably an additional 20,000 men attached to the army as non-combatants and also around 30,000 troops manning various forts (see Appendix IV).[33] A later strength quoted by Captain Alexander Beatson differs in detail, but he also concludes that Tipu had approximately 48,000 effectives at his disposal for the coming campaign.[34]

Harris commenced his march on 3 February and reached the frontier of Mysore at Ambour on 4 March. A letter penned by Mornington and passed on by the general to Tipu on the 5th was effectively a declaration of war.[35] The British plan was straightforward. Harris's Grand Army, including the Hyderabad contingent, was to march on Seringapatam, in all, 270 miles. Smaller British forces to the south in the Baramahal and Coimbatore, each numbering around 5,000 men, would escort supplies and join the main army at Seringapatam. Stuart's Bombay Army, supported by the Raja of Coorg, would march from Cannanore via Sedaseer to attack Mysore from the west.[36] Tipu's plan was more difficult to decipher and he was later to be criticised for his conduct of the war. He knew that he was slightly outnumbered by the combined forces of his enemy and he most likely hoped to combine a policy of scorched earth against the bulk of British arms, with surprise attacks on more isolated detachments.[37]

Tipu's pre-emptive strike against Stuart's army suggests that this was his strategy. Stuart had moved from Cannanore and ascended the Ghats. Good camping ground was difficult to find in the forests and the General had posted John Montresor's sepoy brigade on a high hill named Sedaseer. This was seven miles from Peripatam and 50 miles from Seringapatam. James Dunlop's European brigade was eight miles distant and John Wiseman's brigade was about four miles to the rear. This was a potentially dangerous dispersal of forces by Stuart; in his later report to Harris he attributes this to the difficult nature of the terrain and the need to maintain signal contact with Harris's army.[38] Tipu's force, marching via Peripatam, was probably made up of 12,000 of his best troops divided into four columns. Beatson tells us that the right column was commanded by Syed Ghoffar; the centre by the Binky Nabob; the left by Bubber Jung; and the reserve by Tipu in person. This arrangement is confirmed by a wounded prisoner taken in the battle who also stated that there were no Europeans in the Sultan's army.[39]

On the morning of 5 March, British observers on Sedaseer Hill saw an extensive enemy encampment forming by the fort of Peripatam. They were able to count 3–4,000 tents and among them was one of a green colour apparently denoting the presence of Tipu. Other intelligence was against this but Stuart was anxious enough to reinforce Montresor's brigade with an additional native battalion.[40]

On the following day, Major-General Hartley was sent forward to reconnoitre, but he could see little through the woods and mist. By nine o'clock it was evident that the enemy were attacking the British line. Major David Price was at Stuart's headquarters when the first news of the enemy movement arrived a little before noon.

> The attack opened as usual, with a discharge of rockets along the front of the post; the enemy, in numbers vastly superior, and with a daringness not always expected, advancing within 20 or 30 yards of our bayonets.[41]

The assault was on both the front and rear of Montresor's right brigade. Only three native battalions (1st/2nd Bombay Native Infantry (BNI), 1st/3rd BNI, 1st/4th BNI) were in action as the fourth was prevented from making a junction by a 5,000-strong column of the enemy. Montresor's outnumbered battalions held out for six hours until Stuart, who had received intelligence of the crisis from Hartley, brought up reinforcements. The denouement of the battle is best told in Stuart's own words.

> ...I moved to their assistance with the two flank companies of his Majesty's 75th Regiment and the whole of the 77th. I arrived about half past two in sight of the division of the enemy, who had penetrated into the rear, and possessed themselves of the great road leading to Sedaseer. The engagement lasted nearly half an hour, when after a smart fire of musketry on both sides, the enemy were completely routed and fled with precipitation through the jungles...[42]

Stuart times the retreat as occurring at twenty minutes past three. According to Price, the fleeing troops were 'tumbled headlong in masses, under the bayonets of the soldiers, into the ravines...'[43] Stuart found Montresor at his post, his men exhausted and their ammunition almost expended.

It had been a close call but ultimately a brilliant day for the Bombay Army. As its historian, Sir Patrick Cadell, points out, the battle was one of the most considerable ever fought by Indian troops in the Company's service, with no European assistance beyond that of their own European officers and the detachment of artillery.[44] British reported losses were much less than might have been expected, around 140 men.[45] Tipu's losses are variably quoted as being between 1,500 and 2,000. Stuart admitted that they were 'impossible to ascertain', adding that they must have been heavy because of the volleys of grapeshot and musketry they received. The Sultan retreated from Peripatam to Seringapatam. His surprise attack might have annihilated Montresor's brigade had he not chosen to pitch an ostentatious tent.[46]

Having crossed the border into Mysore, Harris destroyed two key forts and camped near Bangalore on 14 March (see map 2). The army had so far marched in two parallel columns, the Grand Army on the right and the Nizam's contingent on the left, with cavalry at front and rear. Between them marched the vast horde that was an Indian army, up to 100,000 camp followers and as many bullocks and other animals. A considerable battering train and arsenal contributed to a total column that was six miles across and eighteen miles square.[47] As the General entered deeper into Mysore territory, his army had to negotiate some narrow defiles and he arranged his force into three divisions; the cavalry and left wing were in advance, the right wing in the centre, and Wellesley's division in the rear.

Failure was more likely to result from logistical meltdown than from a lost battle. The animals needed forage and its supply was fragile. An officer of the 25th Light Dragoons saw Tipu's agents at work.

> The enemy, observing the same inhuman policy as in the last war [Cornwallis, 1791] were extremely active all that day and during the whole march to Seringapatam, burning the villages and forage for several miles around, and many of our followers, who had strayed too far from camp in search of straw, were either killed or wounded by their Cooties.

The same officer witnessed the near disintegration of the Grand Army's bullock train; '…on the 14th of March about 1,000 cattle, most of them belonging to the public departments, were left dead on the road, and between 5000 and 6000 shot dropped…'[48]

Harris was in despair, but more food was found for the starving bullocks, the situation slightly improved and the army moved on, albeit with frequent halts. By the 21st it had reached Cancanhilly, having covered 25 miles in the previous five days. There was to be no improvement in this slow rate of march.[49] The River Maddoor was crossed three days later and by the 26th the entire force was encamped five miles east of the village of Malavelly.[50] Tipu had so far scorned opportunities to oppose Harris's ponderous progress. His failure to dispute the crossing of the Maddoor was judged to be 'unaccountable' by one British observer.[51] Another officer believed that the adjacent hills meant that he could easily have impeded the British advance for a 'considerable time'.[52] Arthur Wellesley was by now feeling more optimistic about the campaign.

He admitted to his elder brother that he was exhausted, but believed that there was no doubt that Seringapatam would fall.[53] The news of Stuart's victory at Sedaseer had reached Harris on the 25th and provided a valuable boost to British morale. From the camp near Malavelly, the enemy's advanced outposts and some elephants were spotted on a distant ridge and an action on the following day was suddenly likely. Harris did not need a battle – he well understood that only the seizure of Seringapatam would defeat Tipu – but he was now to have the chance to test his arms.

Early on the morning of the 27th, the army marched three miles. The whole of the Mysorean force appeared regularly drawn out in order of battle in two distinct lines, covering the country beyond Malavelly as far as the eye could reach. The ruins of a fort were occupied by a British advance guard and at ten o'clock Tipu opened a cannonade from several heavy guns. At first, Harris paid this little attention, as the guns were distant, but when the shot started to fall into his line and his piquets and advance cavalry were menaced by enemy horse he ordered forward Wellesley's division on the left and further to the right the infantry brigades of Roberts, Baird and Gowdie. The British advance over uneven ground brought on a general action (see map 3).[54]

The great historian of the British Army, John Fortescue, portrays Wellesley's push as being highly regular ('in echelons of battalions with the left refused')[55] but the account of a credible eyewitness, Captain Colin Mackenzie of the Madras Engineers, suggests that it was more improvised.

> Colonel Wellesley, wishing to avail himself of the favourable moment when the enemy in front of us seemed to be in confusion, moved on his own corps and ordered the Bengal and other corps on the left to advance each as fast as they could be formed.[56]

Mackenzie describes the 33rd climbing the hill with 'great spirit'. A body of Mysorean infantry, estimated as 10,000 strong by Fortescue and 2,000 by Beatson, were at first repelled and then cut to pieces by General John Floyd's First Brigade of cavalry.[57]

Closer to the centre, General David Baird's brigade, and particularly the 74th Foot, came under attack from another body of Mysorean infantry and also from an enemy unit of cavalry emerging from the jungle. Baird steadied the 74th and then, as is related by Richard Bayly of the 12th Foot, Bayly's own regiment and the Scotch Brigade intervened with decisive effect.

> A large body of cavalry was in the act of charging our Light Infantry, who were skirmishing in front, but now running with headlong speed to rejoin the British line. This wedge-like column of horse, at the nearest angle, was led on by two enormous elephants, having

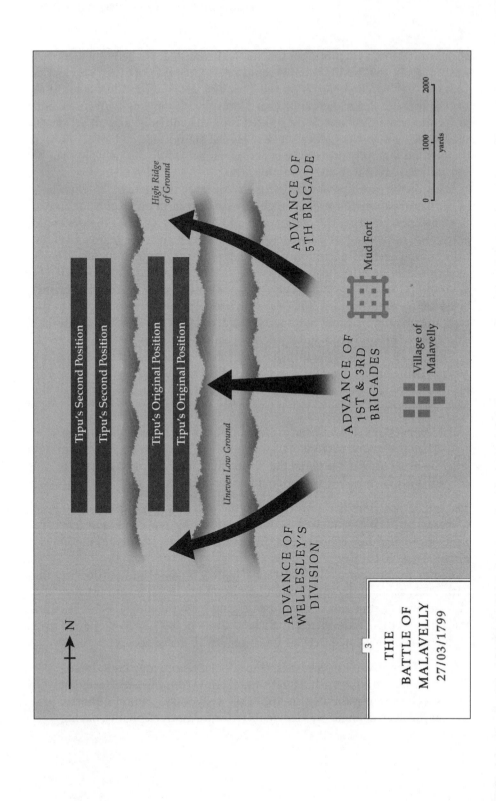

N

Tipu's Second Position

Tipu's Second Position

Tipu's Original Position

Tipu's Original Position

High Ridge
of Ground

Uneven Low Ground

ADVANCE OF
5TH BRIGADE

Mud Fort

ADVANCE OF
1ST & 3RD
BRIGADES

Village of
Malavelly

ADVANCE OF
WELLESLEY'S
DIVISION

0   1000   2000

yards

3

THE
BATTLE OF
MALAVELLY
27/03/1799

huge chains hanging on their probosci, which they whirled about on both sides, a blow from which would have destroyed ten or twelve men at once. At first we mistook these men for the Nizam's troops but as they rapidly approached towards an interval between the right of our corps and a battalion of Sepoys, we were soon convinced of their intention of passing through and attacking the rear of the 12th. Fortunately, at this momentous crisis, a detachment of the Native cavalry of our army suddenly rode up and filled the interval, when the enemy made direct to the front of the old 12th Regiment. General Harris rode up to the rear, crying, 'Fire, 12th! fire!'[58]

As the smoke cleared, many enemy men and horses lay on the ground and the elephants were making off, maddened with pain. Tipu, who was present at Malavelly, must by now have realised that he was facing the full might of the Grand Army and he retreated at about one o'clock. Harris had originally intended to camp upon the field, but due to a shortage of water he returned to his original position.[59]

Fortescue's account of Malavelly implies a significant battle, but the minimal British losses – sixty-six men killed, wounded or missing – are at odds with this. His vision of 'Ten thousand [Mysorean] infantry, supported by cavalry, marching boldly upon the Thirty-third'[60] is hardly consistent with the British regiment suffering no fatalities and having only four men wounded. We must presume either some exaggeration of the Mysorean forces, or that they were hopelessly ineffectual in an open field. Ensign George Rowley witnessed the action and his comments of the moment are prescient:

> The Official Account of it will appear as regular as those of Marlborough or Frederick where every circumstance appears to have been foreseen, known and provided for... Our loss is so trifling as to render our victory not worth gazetting.[61]

To be fair to Harris, his report of the battle to Mornington was short and unassuming. Tipu's losses are estimated at between 700 and 4,000 by British eyewitnesses and historians, but there is no evidence to support any of these figures.[62] The real damage was to Mysorean morale; in Beatson's words, the reverse 'appeared from subsequent events to have made a deep impression on the Sultaun's mind'.[63] Historian Denys Forrest raises the possibility that Tipu had been drawn into the damaging action at Malavelly by the collusion of his senior officers with the British, a theme that was to re-emerge later in the campaign.[64]

It was approximately 25 miles from Malavelly to Seringapatam and Harris had a surprise planned for his adversary. Instead of following the main road west to the capital he turned to the left and crossed the River Cauvery using a ford at Sosily. The crossing was uncontested and the entire army was encamped on the south bank of the river by the afternoon of 30 March. This manoeuvre had a number of advantages; it facilitated the union with Stuart's army, brought the army closer to the supplies being shepherded from Baramahal via the Pass of Caveriporam, and, most vitally, gave access to better forage. The anonymous officer of the 25th Light Dragoons noted the sudden and striking contrast in the surrounding country compared with what he had seen before, '...this part having escaped the general desolation, from the Sultan having so fully expected our taking the other route'.[65] The army's progress continued to be slow at five to six miles per day and Seringapatam was finally reached on 5 April. This was twenty-five days later than Harris had planned in his original instructions to Stuart. However, the siege train and ammunition was intact, there was an immediate adequacy of food and the major logistical challenge of the march had been overcome.[66]

Seringapatam was Tipu's great capital and fortress. Since the fighting of 1792, the Sultan had made efforts to reinforce the defensive works. Most of the strengthening of the walls and entrenchments was concentrated at the east of the fort. The southern part of the citadel, close to the other arm of the Cauvery, was already strong and a new brick bastion had been constructed at the north-west angle. All forts had some weakness and at Seringapatam this new bastion had not fully addressed the vulnerability of this part of the defences, which were open to both to destructive enfilading fire from the north side of the river and the fire of breaching batteries from the southwest.[67] A return later obtained from one of Tipu's officers suggests that the Mysore ruler had 14,000 men inside the fort, 8,000 in the entrenchments outside, and 14,000 troops operating in the surrounding country. The latter were mainly horse. There was a small group of French troops in the garrison, in all about 120 with commissioners from the French Government.[68]

The British army took up a strong position about two miles from the west face of the fort. The right was on high ground, the rear protected by deep ravines and the left by the Cauvery. An aqueduct gave additional protection to the front (see map 4).[69] Harris was to rely on his infantry and artillery for the siege and subsequent assault. Following the planned junction with Stuart's force, he had at his disposal seven King's regiments, a Swiss regiment (de Meuron's), a Bombay regiment of European infantry, five battalions of Bengal Native Infantry, six battalions of Bombay Native Infantry, twelve battalions of Madras Native Infantry, and artillery, engineer and pioneer corps from the EIC presidencies.[70] Harris encouraged his men in a General Order, promising that their perseverance would place British colours on the walls of Seringapatam. Arthur Wellesley remained upbeat, writing to his brother Mornington

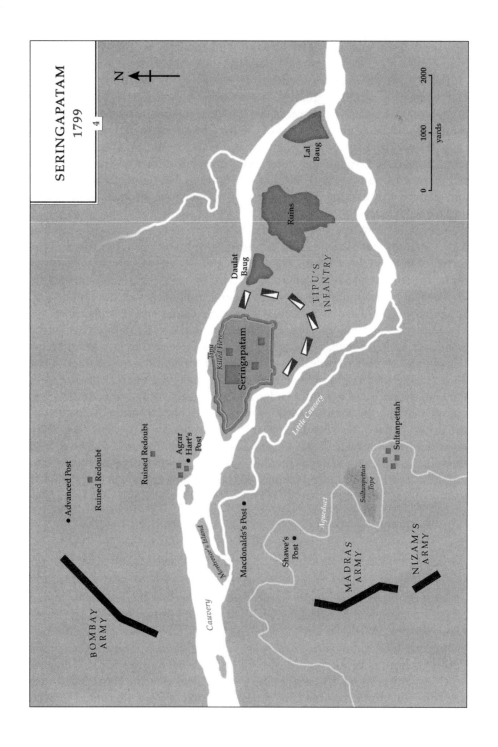

SERINGAPATAM
1799

4

N

Bombay Army

Advanced Post
Ruined Redoubt

Ruined Redoubt

Agrar
Hart's Post

Montresor's Island

Cauvery

Macdonald's Post

Shawe's Post

MADRAS ARMY

Aqueduct

Sultanpettah Tope

Sultanpettah

NIZAM'S ARMY

Little Cauvery

Tipu Killed Here

Seringapatam

Daulat Baug

TIPU'S INFANTRY

Ruins

Lal Baug

0   1000   2000
                yards

that the fort was only strong by its natural position and that it was unlikely to hold out for more than a few days once the siege guns were in place.[71]

The British plan for the capture of Seringapatam was hotly debated by Harris and his senior engineers. It was eventually decided that while the army would work its way towards the Cauvery's southern stretches, the final assault would be against the west of the fort. Storming troops would have to cross the southern arm of the Cauvery, but Harris's scouts had seen men and animals wading through the water without much difficulty. The walls were to be bombarded from both sides of the river, by Harris's army to the south and Stuart's to the north. This approach nullified the stronger eastern and southern defences.[72]

Before the formal siege works could begin it was necessary to clear some of Tipu's infantry and rocket men from uneven ground between the army and the fortress. On the night of 5 April, HM 12th Regiment and two battalions of sepoys under the command of Colonel Robert Shawe, and HM 33rd Regiment and the 2nd Bengal Native Infantry Regiment under Arthur Wellesley, were ordered to seize the ruined village of Sultanpettah, a water course and the adjacent grove of cocoa trees and mangos ('tope').[73] A night attack a few days earlier in the same area by Baird had almost led to the small force getting lost, but it seems that no lessons had been learnt. Wellesley led forward five companies of the 33rd, leaving a reserve in his rear, and was soon met with a fierce crossfire from the enemy concealed behind a hedge and in houses. At first, momentum was maintained and the Mysorean troops were driven back from the hedge, but as the British entered the trees they became disorientated and Wellesley was soon detached from his men. The Colonel failed to engage the reserve as he missed them in the dark and, realising that he could achieve little more, he returned to report to Harris who briefly documented the unhappy episode in his journal.

> Near twelve, Colonel Wellesley came in to my tent in a good deal of agitation to say he had not carried the Tope. It proved that the 33rd, with which he attacked, got into confusion, and could not be formed, which was a great pity, as it must be particularly unpleasant to him.[74]

Most of the men eventually found their way back to the reserve or joined Shawe's detachment but a few were killed, around forty wounded and some taken prisoner. Wellesley's emotional reaction to the setback has been much elaborated by authors. Ensign Rowley, writing contemporaneously, simply describes him as being 'mad at this ill success' but Ensign Richard Bayley, writing many years later, describes the young officer entering Harris's marquee and throwing himself on the table repeatedly exclaiming 'I am ruined forever' and behaving like a 'madman'.[75]

Harris ruefully noted in his journal, '...no wonder night attacks so often fail'. This raises the question as to why he ordered the assault in the first place. Witnesses describe the night as being 'pitch black' and the ground had not been well reconnoitred. The target of the raid, the 'Tope', was not well defined. Harris must take some of the blame but Wellesley did not escape disapprobation, his critics, including fellow officers such as Bayley and Captain George Elers, inferring that only his influential connections saved his career.[76] This appears jaundiced and Rory Muir's conclusion that it was only Wellesley's prominence and subsequent fame that made the trivial military reverse newsworthy is surely closer to the mark. The episode is a footnote in the siege of Seringapatam and it is only raised to the main text by Wellesley's presence. The post was easily occupied the next day.[77]

Harris also scribbled in his journal the words 'anxious times'. The General was confident that his army could batter down the walls of the city; the problem was feeding his soldiers. Theft and fraud had caused a sudden rice shortage. Fortunately, fresh supplies were brought up by Colonel Alexander Read and some of the corruption was undone, allowing the besieging force to continue its operations.[78] These now involved the Bombay Army under Stuart, which had arrived on 14 April.

On the 17th, final orders were issued confirming that the northwest angle was to be the principal point of attack. On the same day, the Bombay Army, on the north bank of the Cauvery, seized the village of Agrar where a battery was dug at 'Hart's Post' to enfilade the northwest angle. On the south bank, the besiegers drove the enemy back from the Little Cauvery, establishing a foothold at 'Macdonald's Post', which was linked by a communication trench to 'Shawe's Post'. The defenders were forced back to a third line where they dug in along the south bank of the river. The British engineers were divided into four 'brigades', one with the Bombay Army on the north bank while the other three were with the Madras Army. A battery was placed near Sultanpettah to enfilade the trenches along the river bank. Also raked from guns at Hart's Post across the river, the Mysoreans had to evacuate a powder mill on their right which was promptly incorporated into the British position by a parallel.[79]

The net was gradually closing, with an increasing number of British batteries being brought into action against the north and west faces of the fortress. These included six 18-pounders near the captured mill. In the early hours of 22 April, Tipu launched a desperate assault against the Bombay Army. Stuart's troops were attacked by about 6,000 Mysorean infantry and Lalley's corps of Frenchmen. The French led the attack on the right and, according to Beatson, they 'behaved with great spirit and some of them fell within the entrenchment upon our bayonets and others were killed close to it'. After obstinate fighting, the attempt was beaten off with enemy losses of perhaps 6–700 men.[80]

The zigzags had brought the besiegers within 200 yards of the enemy's entrenchments on the west bank of the Cauvery and several more batteries were in place. The entrenchments were attacked on 26 and 27 April, Wellesley leading one of these parties. The British suffered significant losses, around 300 killed, wounded and missing, but the ground gained allowed the establishment of the first breaching battery of 18-pounders against the western face of the northwest angle.[81] By the evening of 3 May, this battery and others – a total of twenty-nine guns and six howitzers – had made a 'large and extensive' breach and the enemy guns were mostly silenced.[82] The breach's practicability was formally assessed by two engineers making a brave reconnaissance across the river. It was felt in some quarters that Harris later undervalued the service of his engineers and artillery at Seringapatam. The historian of the Madras Engineers, Henry Meredith Vibart, points out that the siege works commenced on the evening of 17 April and on 2 May the second breaching battery was completed and opened fire.

> In these fifteen days, three batteries were made north of the river, and seven batteries south, not including the 'Headquarter batteries' which were commenced and abandoned. Besides this, about a mile and a quarter of approaches were made and a considerable amount of labour was expended in strengthening the various posts taken from time to time.[83]

While this work was proceeding, there had been further communication between Harris and Tipu. The Sultan was offered peace terms but only if he assented to these unconditionally and agreed to surrender his sons as hostages. Unsurprisingly, these discussions had fizzled out by 29 April.[84] Having created the breach, Harris decided to storm the fortress immediately. This was in part because there was only two days' food left in the camp. His army had to triumph or it would starve.[85]

The troops assembled for the assault were two European flank companies. HM 12th, 33rd, 73rd, 74th Regiments, three corps of grenadier sepoys from the Presidency's armies and 200 of the Nizam's men. The whole, under the command of General David Baird, was divided into two parts. The first, intended to move to the right from the breach under Colonel John Sherbrooke, was made up of a sergeant's party, the forlorn hope, supported by a subaltern's party of thirty commanded by Lieutenant Vesey Hill and conducted by Lieutenant John Lalor of the 73rd. Behind them would be half of the European flank companies, followed by the engineers and pioneers and the remaining half of troops. The second detachment, under Colonel James Dunlop, was to turn to the left, its forlorn hope and subaltern's party under Lieutenant Alexander Lawrence of the 77th and guided by Lieutenant James Farquhar of the 74th.

It was completed by the flank companies of the Bombay European Regiments, engineers and pioneers and the remaining men. Lalor and Farquhar had both previously examined the ford. Part of the Swiss regiment, de Meuron's, and three battalions of native infantry, under the command of Arthur Wellesley, remained in the trenches to support the attack as necessary.[86]

Harris was determined to make the effort in the heat of the day to gain an element of surprise. After gaining the breach, the two parts of the divided force were to move in their prescribed directions to clear the ramparts and reunite on the eastern side of the fort. Baird strained to make the plan explicit.

> Colonels Sherbrooke and Dunlop were directed on no account to quit the inner rampart previous to their junction, for any other object but that of seizing on the cavaliers [fortifications built within the larger fort; often a gun platform] in the neighbourhood of their respective attacks, and to lose no time in regaining their situation on the ramparts as soon as that object should be attained, and every cavalier or post on the rampart, which it might be deemed essential to secure, were immediately to be occupied by a battalion company or companies from the supporting European regiments, so that the whole of the ground once captured might be secured, and the flankers on their junction be in full force to follow up their success, by an attack on any of the cavaliers which had not fallen in their way, or by an assault on the body of the town and the palace of the Sultaun.[87]

According to Ensign Rowley, the hungry troops were in low spirits despite the issue of drams and biscuit. Their leaders were edgy. 'The trenches were crowded with officers who were making their arrangements for the ensuing service and passed and repassed with hasty steps and anxious looks.'[88] All were, however, steeled by stories of Tipu's cruel treatment of prisoners. They had an inspired commander. At 1pm on the 4th, Baird went to the head of the column, climbed to the reverse of the trenches, and drew his sword.

> 'Men, are you all ready?' He was answered in the affirmative. 'Then, forward, my lads.' Now setting up a loud huzza they rushed into the river.[89]

The crossing was treacherous because of the heavy fire of musketry and rockets from the ramparts and the river's rocky bed and variable depth. The breach itself was less of an obstacle due to the ditch being largely filled with rubble and, within seven minutes, British colours were on the summit. David Price, watching from the trenches in a state of intense anxiety, saw the acclivity of the breach 'covered in a cloud of crimson'. He could then see the files of men moving rapidly to the left and right along the walls.[90]

Rowley, who has left the best eyewitness account, was with Dunlop's party, which turned left. After intense hand-to-hand fighting around the breach and a number of casualties sustained from the enemy's musketry, this column first cleared the northwest bastion and then the faussebraye (a second rampart exterior, parallel to, and lower than the main rampart) beneath, before advancing along the northern rampart.

> …a heavy fire of musketry was directed against them [the left column] from the inner rampart, between which and that on which we were passing was a deep wet ditch. We were relieved from this annoyance by a very small party of the 12th Regt., headed by an officer, before whom the enemy fled without resistance. About two or three hundred yards from the breach the column met with a check in front from a large body of the enemy, headed as we afterwards found by the Sultaun in person: they were posted behind the traverses [parapets thrown across to prevent enfilading fire] which crossed the rampart, and gave so steady a fire that our Europeans were staggered. Most of the leading officers were killed and wounded on the breach and in the river. The grenadiers complained that their ammunition was wetted in crossing the river. Farquhar of the 74th with reproaches and persuasion at length made them follow him towards the enemy, and was instantly shot through the heart in advancing. More officers and men, however, had now come up, and the column carried all before them. The enemy, armed and unarmed, were shot and bayoneted without mercy. Some leaped over the parapet into the outer ditch or faussebraye, and were either killed by the fall, or shot from the rampart above: others plunged into the inner wet ditch and were drowned. Those who attempted to escape into the inner fort, or town, by the Delhi gate in the north face, were met in the arch by those who were driven out by the troops which had entered the place. Here the Sultaun himself was killed, and overwhelmed by the bodies of his subjects. As the two parties approached each other, the crowds of the unhappy Mysoreans thickened, and were slain in heaps; for no quarter was give.[91]

Sherbrooke's men had met with less resistance. Another spectator, Alexander Beatson, could easily see the unfolding of events to the right of the breach; 'Here, the enemy retreated the moment our men advanced upon them with the bayonet'.[92] Three cavaliers on the southern face described by Beatson as being 'stupendous works' were not defended and in less than an hour the right column had arrived at the eastern face of the fort. When the heads of the two columns spotted each other there was a loud triumphant shout. All real opposition had evaporated and what was left was panic and slaughter. Some of the garrison escaped through the Bangalore gate, but this was soon forced shut and then, to add to the misery of Serigapatam's defenders and populace, it caught fire.[93] Rowley admits that women and children were also killed. 'Many particular scenes of horror could not but meet the eye during the heat of the assault'.[94] After another two hours, the palace and the sons of Tipu surrendered to Baird. It was now half past five in the afternoon. Tipu's body lay under the arch of the Delhi gateway with many others. It was eventually found by a search party which included Arthur Wellesley. The corpse had three bayonet wounds in the body and a musket wound in the temple where the ball had entered a little above the right ear and lodged in the cheek.[95]

The Sultan's army had suffered terribly. Twenty-four principal officers were killed and seven wounded besides a great number of inferior rank. A hospital was opened in the great mosque for the many enemy wounded. The total Mysorean losses are a matter of conjecture. Rowley immediately estimated the number killed in the storm as being near to 10,000, Vibart concluded 8–10,000 killed, whereas a modern Indian historian suggests around 8,000 casualties.[96] Considering the severe nature of the task and the importance of the goal, British casualties were relatively light; just under 900 Europeans and 640 native troops were killed, wounded or missing. The corps most affected was the King's 74th Regiment with twenty-one killed and ninety-nine wounded. The distribution of casualties reflected the prominent role played by the King's regiments in the assault.[97]

The prize was considerable. Almost 1,000 pieces of ordnance fell into British hands: 373 brass guns; sixty mortars; eleven howitzers; 400 iron guns; twelve mortars. The captured arms and ammunition included 400,000 rounds of shot, 500,000lb of powder and 100,000 muskets. The victorious British soldiers and sepoys were more interested in the city's treasures, estimated to be worth at least 2,500,000 pagodas or nearly £900,000 sterling.[98]

Beatson's assertion that 'all violence ceased with the conflict' is contradicted by other eyewitnesses. Lieutenant Patrick Brown tells us that soldiers were running amok in the streets with drawn sabres and lighted torches, many dressed in the silk clothes they had plundered from the terrified inhabitants. Wellesley reported to Harris on the 5th that the situation in the fallen city was improving but 'still very bad'. He believed that order and safety could only be restored by a provost's order to execute some of the miscreants.[99] Harris had directed Wellesley to take command of Seringapatam because Baird, exhausted by his role in the fighting, had asked to be relieved. When Wellesley was subsequently made permanent governor of the place, Baird complained that he had been superseded by a junior officer '...before the sweat was dry on my brow'.[100] Harris's choices were logical. Headstrong Baird was the man to lead the storm and the more methodical Wellesley the man to restore calm. By the 6th, the new governor was able to report that 'plunder has stopped, the fires are extinguished. I am now employed in burying the dead'.[101] The arrival of General Floyd with the detachments of lieutenant colonels Read and Brown and a large convoy of cattle and sheep on 13 May finally resolved Harris's victualling problems.[102]

The contemporary British view was that Tipu had overestimated the strength of the fortifications of Seringapatam and had not properly employed his infantry and cavalry. Beatson believed him to 'have laboured under the infatuation that Seringapatam was impregnable'.[103] Harris thought that the conquest of Mysore in one campaign would have been impossible if his adversary had used his horse to ravage the hinterlands.[104] As alluded to in the previous chapter, Wellesley agreed that the Sultan had adopted the wrong tactics.[105] Tipu had not fully exploited British vulnerability in the battle for forage and supplies. He had failed because, in Fortescue's words, he had put 'more faith in bastions than bullocks'.[106] He was not helped by his leading advisors, who were both ignorant and sycophantic. Forrest explores the accusation that they were also in league with the British, but he finds the charges of treachery unproven.[107]

The settlement of the conquered territories was to be decided by a 'Peace Commission'. This small group of able men, including Harris and Wellesley, had to divide the spoils of victory and determine the future government of Mysore. Their solution was ingenious and successful. To have simply divided up Tipu's kingdom between the Company and the Nizam would have been legitimate, but would have risked antagonising the Marathas and overly empowering the Nizam. Instead, some territories were annexed – the province of Canara and the districts of Coimbatore and Wynaad went to the Company, and a substantial area to the northeast of Mysore to the Nizam – but the central kingdom of Mysore was retained under the rule of a five-year-old child, the representative of a former Hindu dynasty in the region. This arrangement was designed to appear magnanimous but, in reality, the realm of the child Raja, with the Brahmin Purneah as his chief minister, was British in all but name. There was expansion of the Company's lands and influence. Eventually, the ageing Nizam would yield even more territory to his British protectors.[108]

For British soldiers, the sudden acquisition of Seringapatam and Mysore was an awe-inspiring achievement. Major Lachlan Macquarie of the Bombay Army simply put three exclamation marks against the date of 4 May in his journal.[109] Captain John Malcolm was more eloquent:

> This day will ever be celebrated in India for the accomplishment of one of the grandest and most important achievements whether

considered in a military or political point of view that has ever occurred.[110]

There was an understandable perception that the capture of Mysore had wider implications and that this was much more than an acquisition of land. Malcolm believed that British power and influence was now secured in the Deccan. The Governor-General, writing to Lord Grenville eight days after the fall of Seringapatam, admitted that the campaign had exceeded his expectations: '…I shall use no disguise, but inform you plainly that the manner in which I have conducted the war has been received with exultation'.[111] He too was optimistic of wider gains, informing Dundas later in the year that Bengal and the provinces were tranquil.

> …the effect of our success in Mysore has utterly annihilated the spirit of insubordination which for some time past has been gaining ground among our Mahommedan subjects.[112]

The new regimen in Mysore was indeed stable and popular in some circles but, in retrospect, Mornington's words appear complacent. Outside Seringapatam and the small enclaves of East India Company power around hubs of trade, soldiers and officers, there was a constant threat of anarchy and insurgent violence.[113]

Chapter 4

Little Wars: Dhoondiah Waugh, the Polygar Uprisings and the Restoration of the Peshwa 1799–1803

The period between the fall of Mysore and the campaigns against the Marathas was marked by a series of smaller conflicts against discontented factions in Southern India. Fortescue warns us that the relation of these 'petty operations' might be tedious to the general reader, but he also stresses that they must be chronicled as they form a vital part of the history of the British Army and of British India. Since his account, penned in 1915, these little wars have been almost entirely ignored, excepting those parts where Arthur Wellesley was directly involved. This is an unfortunate omission as, whatever its legitimacy, the pacification of South India was bloody and heroic, and ultimate success was crucial to British ambitions in the wider subcontinent.[1]

On 15 June 1799, Harris wrote to Mornington from his camp at Milgottah, a few miles from Seringapatam, alerting him that he was receiving reports from the northwest that the country was being overrun by a 'formidable banditti' named Dhoondiah Waugh, who had escaped from captivity in Seringapatam in the confusion of the assault.[2] Dhoondiah is generally portrayed as a simple 'freebooter' but the historian of the Marathas, Govind Sakharam Sardesai, judges him to have been extraordinarily resourceful and bold, a man who had served several powerful masters in the late eighteenth century. He also had a predilection for plunder and extreme cruelty and, following his escape from Tipu's dungeons, he had soon assembled a sizeable number of like-minded followers and captured several forts in the Bednore district. Acquiring arms and money, the newly titled 'King of the Two Worlds' was poised to take Chitteldroog and Harris ordered his headquarters northward and launched two field attachments of native cavalry, infantry and artillery under Colonel John Pater and Lieutenant-Colonel James Dalrymple.[3]

The coming campaign was to be limited, but challenging. William Harness, Lieutenant-Colonel of HM 74th Regiment, describes Dhoondiah's mode of operations.

> They set out in a large body and set fire to every village they came to, took away all the money in it, and all the horses and cattle and forced

away with them all the men. If they met with any opposition they killed all the old men, and all the women and children, in a way that would almost make you cry to read… These people knew all the strong places in the country and all the roads, and travelled so secretly that we could not sometimes tell whereabouts they were; for they would sometimes separate and go in small parties and, as they were dressed like the country people, we did not know them; so that we marched many hundred miles at one time, hearing of Towns being burnt by him in one place, at other times cruelties committed in others.[4]

Dalrymple occupied Chitteldroog (see map 5) on 6 July without opposition and, reinforced by more cavalry and Bengal sepoys, he marched forty miles in twenty-four hours to destroy a party of 200 horse and 400 foot. Forty prisoners were executed as punishment for the depredations committed. The forts of Goondair, Chengherry, Shimooga, Honelly, Hurryhur and Hoolal were then captured. In the course of these operations, Colonel Pater was relieved by Colonel James Stevenson and the force further strengthened by the arrival of a battalion of Bengal Native Volunteers and the flank companies of HM 73rd and 74th regiments under Colonel William Wallace.

The short campaign was brought to an end when, early on the morning of 17 August, Dalrymple defeated Dhoondiah's force of 1,200 horse and 300 infantry posted under the walls of the fort of Shikarpoor in Nuggur. Dhoondiah's men were formed behind a small river much swelled by recent rains. Dalrymple's regiments of native cavalry charged and drove their foe into the water with the loss of 600 men. British infantry seized the fort and the *killedars* were hanged on the walls in sight of the enemy, who, according to Harris, 'fled in the utmost disorder'. Dhoondiah was pursued to Maratha country and his camp was attacked by a fellow chief and officer of the Peshwa, Dhoondiah Punt Gokla, who dispersed his remaining followers and captured his elephants, camels, bullocks and guns. Bednore was reoccupied by British troops and it was thought that the threat had been eradicated.[5]

Two other areas of operations can be described before we necessarily return to Dhoondiah Waugh. The Peshwa had rejected British conditions attached to the offer of Soonda, a small district above the Western Ghats, and Mornington ordered Wellesley to acquire the place for the Maharajah of Mysore. Wellesley wrote a placatory letter to the local Maratha chief asking him to evacuate and simultaneously ordered a small force of native cavalry, infantry and artillery under Lieutenant Colonel Arthur St Leger to take possession. The only credible opposition was met at the barricaded village of Sambranee on 29 September 1799, but this fell after an action of two hours and most of the 300-strong garrison were killed. British losses were trifling. Wellesley thanked St Leger in Division Orders for having 'brought forward, with incredible expedition, his troops and guns through jungles, over swamps, by the worst roads I have seen in India'.

He was less convinced that the new British dependency was worth the manpower to maintain it, '…there is little in it to govern but trees and wild beasts'.[6]

Wellesley also had to deal with Kistnapah Naik, the Raja of Bullum, who had taken possession of a vital route leading from Mysore into Canara, interrupting British communications with Mangalore. He had collected 3–4,000 adherents who were attacking supply convoys. On 22 March 1800, Wellesley instructed Lieutenant Colonel Edward Tolfrey to enter the territory of Bullum with thirteen companies of sepoys, some Mysore troops and two guns: '…you will immediately attack the people at Eygoor: you will burn that place, and you will hang all the people that you may find in arms'.[7] After destroying Eygoor, Tolfrey advanced on Arrakaira, a strong stockaded position in thick forest. The attack on the fort on 2 April was repulsed with the loss of forty-seven men killed and wounded. Reinforcements, including flank companies of HM 73rd and 77th regiments, arrived at the end of the month under Colonel John Montresor, and the place was carried by storm after stiff resistance. In his report, the Colonel applauded the gallantry of his men in the almost impenetrable terrain. They 'overcame a continued range of obstacles and resistance for near a mile and a half through a most intricate country'. The assault had cost 140 casualties but the recalcitrant chief and his followers had been suppressed. Wellesley was determined that there should be no repeat, emphasising to Montresor that every deserted village must be burnt and every armed man killed.[8]

Dhoondiah Waugh was proving to be an even more resilient enemy. After his earlier reverse, he had soon collected not only his scattered followers, but also a large body of Tipu's cavalry and disaffected factions from Hyderabad and elsewhere. Consolidating his hold over lands in southern Maratha country, he was now threatening to re-enter Mysore. Reports, probably exaggerated, suggested that the adventurer was at the head of 40,000 armed men. Arthur Wellesley was instructed to tackle this emerging threat in what was to be his first campaign as an independent commander. He would have the advantage of Maratha cooperation and the objective was unambiguous, Josiah Webbe writing to him from Madras on 24 May 1800: 'You are to pursue Dhoondiah Waugh wherever you may find him, and to hang him on the first tree'.[9]

Wellesley's broad strategy was to seize all the fortified places in Dhoondiah's hands and, presuming that he still remained in arms, to gradually drive him eastwards into one of the narrow angles formed by the Kistna, Toombuddra and other rivers before destroying him. It was the monsoon season and crossing rivers would be problematic, particularly if the constant movements gave little time to build boats.[10] This was to be a campaign of few certainties, Wellesley later writing to his cavalry commander, Colonel James Stevenson:

> It is difficult, if not impossible, to give detailed instructions regard-
> ing the pursuit of a flying enemy as what may be perfectly proper

this day may be otherwise to-morrow by a change in the situation of the enemy.[11]

The British force was assembled at Chitteldroog and, having crossed the Toombuddra River near Hurryhur, it reached Bednore on 27 June (see map 5). The small army was made up of two brigades of cavalry consisting of HM 19th and 25th Light Dragoons and 1st, 2nd and 4th Madras Native Cavalry; three brigades of infantry consisting of HM 73rd and 77th in addition to 1st, 8th, 12th and 2/4th Madras Native Infantry and 2/2nd and 2/4th Bombay Native Infantry. The force was completed by a detachment of Madras artillery and a body of pioneers and was to be supported by the Hyderabad Subsidiary Force.[12]

The tortuous twists and turns of the ten-week campaign need not be related in detail. It was a rollercoaster for the young commander, with notable successes, including the capture of hill forts and the destruction of parts of his enemy's forces, offset by the elusiveness of Dhoondiah. Wellesley's variable mood is well captured by his copious correspondence. Initially, he is positive and aggressive. On 11 July, at Savanoor, he assures Colonel Close that if Dhoondiah came too close, he would 'dash at him immediately'.[13] A week later, he informs Colonel John Sartorius that he has a moral ascendency in the field. 'It is very evident from what has passed, not only that I am superior to him, but that he knows it'.[14] Elsewhere, after the capture of the fort at Dummul, he applauds the troops for their exertions. On 1 August, he believes the war to be nearly at an end; 'another blow... will probably bring it to a close'. Dhoondiah's followers were deserting him and the chief was not finding 'the amusement very gratifying'.[15]

Wellesley had his own problems. One of his Maratha allies, Ghokla, had been routed by Dhoondiah at the end of June. The rains were heavy, the rivers swollen and there were the inevitable logistical problems, the bullocks dying in large numbers.[16] It was proving difficult to land that final blow. On 30 July, a detachment of Dhoondiah's force had been driven into the River Malpurba at Manoli, but the enemy leader escaped. That Wellesley's initial optimism was ebbing away is clear from his letters of 8 and 9 August to Close and James Kirkpatrick. 'The war will literally have no objective nor end if we are to follow a single man with a few horsemen to the end of the world'.[17] He admitted that Dhoondiah had slipped away into the 'jungles' and he was ignorant as to where his adversary would go next. On the 17th he discloses to Close that he will give Dhoondiah 'one more run' but that he believed that he would never catch him.[18]

This pessimism proved to be misplaced. Dhoondiah and his remaining followers were in a bad way. Men were starving and there were numerous desertions.[19] There was still the possibility of trapping him in the fork of the Kistna and Toombuddra rivers. On 8 September, Dhoondiah broke camp at Mudgheri and moved towards the Kistna. Sighting Stevenson's force, he

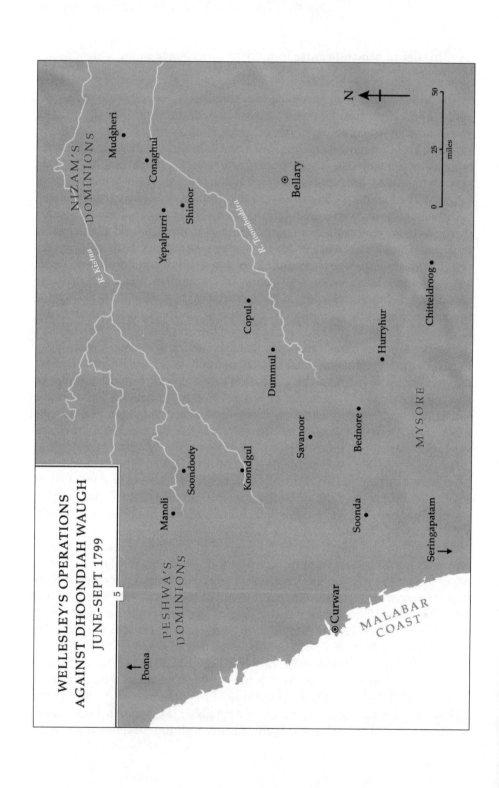

WELLESLEY'S OPERATIONS
AGAINST DHOONDIAH WAUGH
JUNE–SEPT 1799

5

PESHWA'S
DOMINIONS

Poona

NIZAM'S
DOMINIONS

R. Kistna

Mudgheri

Conaghul

Shinoor

Yepalpurri

Bellary

R. Toombuddra

Copul

Dummul

Chitteldroog

Hurryhur

Manoli

Soondooty

Koondgul

Savanoor

Bednore

MYSORE

Soonda

Seringapatam

Curwar

MALABAR
COAST

N

0   25   50
miles

turned south again and encamped three miles from Conaghul and nine miles from Wellesley at Yepalpurri.[20] The chief had wrongly believed his pursuer to be at Shinoor. The clash of arms at Conaghul is described by Wellesley in his despatch of 10 September.

> He [Dhoondiah] had only a large body of cavalry, apparently 5000, which I immediately attacked with the 19th and 25th dragoons and 1st and 2nd regiments of cavalry. The enemy was strongly posted, with his rear and left flank covered by the village and rock of Conahgull, and stood for some time with apparent firmness; but such was the rapidity and determination of the charge made by those 4 regiments, which I was obliged to form in one line, in order at all to equalise in length that of the enemy, that the whole gave way, and were pursued by my cavalry for many miles. Many, among others Dhoondiah, were killed; and the whole body dispersed, and were scattered in small parties over the face of the country.[21]

Dhoondiah's irregular force had been routed and his death ended the campaign. There had been very few British casualties. British and Indian historians have detailed the lessons learnt, by both Arthur Wellesley and the British authorities in India. Muir notes that Wellesley was already displaying the seminal characteristics – an 'unremitting aggression' and keen eye for logistics – that would underpin his subsequent campaigning in India.[22] Fortescue concludes that while the young officer had gained little experience of fighting, he now even more fully understood the value of rapid movement and flexible transport and supply.[23] Sardesai emphasises the importance of the contact with his Indian allies; 'Colonel Wellesley thus gained a close acquaintance with the Maratha character, their government, their leaders, the calibre and methods of their troops.'[24] It was a rehearsal for the greater Maratha campaigns to come. In a wider context, the Dhoondiah episode was a reminder to the British that conquest, in this case that of Mysore, brought its own problems with the potential for disbanded enemy elements to reappear elsewhere.[25]

Augmentation of British territory in India remained against official Government policy but the capture of Mysore had given Mornington, now Marquess Wellesley, an insatiable appetite. In a letter to a friend, he revealed his intention to 'heap kingdoms upon kingdoms, victory upon victory, revenue upon revenue'.[26] As this policy was inherently anti-French, Government officers such as Henry Dundas acquiesced and, between the years 1799 and 1801, the kingdoms of Tanjore, Surat, the Carnatic and Oude were all brought under the Company's control. The assimilation of Oude meant the gain of Rohilkhand and the lower Doab, an extremely rich region which was known henceforth as the 'ceded provinces'. It was an area of strategic significance, Arthur Wellesley judging that, in military terms, the land was 'all gain and strength without the smallest degree of disadvantage or weakness'.[27] These 'peaceful acquisitions by coercion' resulted from the Marquess's autocratic and bullying style of diplomacy. His exceptionally malign treatment of the Nawab of Oude attracted criticism from the Company's Board of Directors. The negotiations, they said, were 'painful to peruse'. In London, the Secretary of the Board of Control was reluctant to publish the treaty papers, concerned that 'the manner in which it was extorted from the Nabob' might leave the Government open to attack and provide propaganda material for the French.[28] The Marquess would no doubt have claimed that the Nawab's subjects would be happier under the Company's jurisdiction than under corrupt local rule. Whatever the moral objections and the political reservations at home, the newly acquired lands remained in the Company's hands; in Robert's words, '…the objectives achieved were far better than the means employed to attain them'.[29]

Britain's most obdurate enemies in South India were the *polygars*. 'These Polygar wars are terrible', Wellesley informed a fellow officer, 'we lose in them our best men and officers… and neither the public nor individuals derive from them the slightest advantage'.[30] The Southern Indian feudal chiefs (the word *polygar* means literally the head of a military camp) had been suppressed in 1792, but by 1799 the *polygars* of Madura and Tinnevelly were making inroads into the district of Ramnad and the Company's territory, allegedly burning villages and murdering the inhabitants. The Governor-General appointed Major John Bannerman to the command of a detachment composed of 400 men of HM 19th Foot in addition to Madras native infantry and cavalry, and Bengal artillery. He proceeded immediately against Cataboma Naig, the Polygar of Panjalamcoorchy, a fort 26 miles northeast of Palamcottah (see map 6). After some inconclusive negotiations, Bannerman attacked the fort with six companies of Madras native infantry on 5 September 1799. The gate was blown open with a 6-pounder but the storming party was forced back, with the loss of ninety-three men and six European officers. The native commissioned and non-commissioned officers were judged to have performed badly and Harris recommended their dismissal. It was a temporary setback, and the arrival of the 19th Foot on the following day led to the enemy evacuating the fort and retreating to the north. The short war ended in mid-October with the capture and execution of the *polygar* chief. Forty-four forts were demolished, arms were given up and land forfeited. Some efforts were made to mollify the defeated *polygars* as they were from this time relieved of the obligations of military service and police duties.[31]

Wellesley was himself planning a campaign against the Psyche Rajah who was resisting the Company's authority in Wynaad. In the event, he was called to Ceylon and he instead instructed Colonel James Stevenson, who

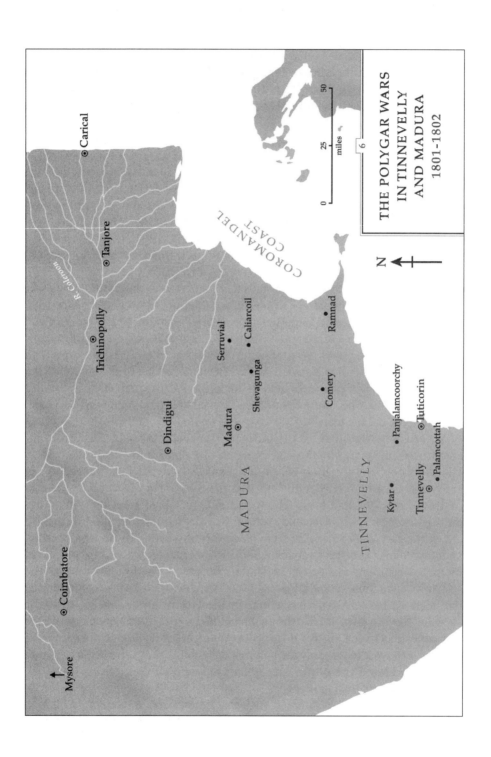

THE POLYGAR WARS
IN TINNEVELLY
AND MADURA
1801-1802

entered the Wynaad in January 1801 with a small force including the 19th Light Dragoons, companies of HM 12th and 77th regiments, Bombay native infantry and cavalry, and artillery. There was little resistance and the province was soon under British control, the Rajah escaping into the hill country of Travancore.[32]

Another short successful campaign in early 1801 was conducted against refractory *polygars* in the region of Dindigul. Colonel James Innes arrived at Pylney in the middle of March with a force of Madras native infantry, a Malay corps, pioneers and artillery. Having subsequently received reinforcements, including a detachment of HM 12th Foot, he commenced operations against Gopal Naigue, Polygar of Veerapatchy, the principal of the enemy chiefs. Several strongholds were taken, culminating in a futile last stand by the *polygars* at Jelliputty in late April. By the following month, Innes was able to reassure Government that civil power had been re-established.[33]

These minor operations were a sideshow to the more serious and costly war fought against the *polygars* of Tinnevelly and Madura between February 1801 and March 1802. Mostly forgotten now, a brief account of the conflict can be constructed from Lieutenant-Colonel William Wilson's masterful history of the Madras Army and the graphic eyewitness account of James Welsh, an ensign in the 3rd Madras Native Infantry. The insurrection broke out following the escape of *polygar* prisoners held in the fort at Palamcottah since the earlier uprising of 1799. They were soon joined by 4,000 armed men who had been alerted to the escape plan.[34]

Major Colin Macaulay, commander in Tinnevelly, assembled all his available troops at Kytar, nineteen miles north of Palamcottah, and marched on Panjalamcoorchy (see map 6). Fending off *polygar* attacks, he eventually arrived at Panjalamcoorchy to find that the fort, reported to be completely destroyed in 1799, had been rebuilt with a determined garrison within and outside the new walls. Macaulay retired to Palamcottah, deciding to instead attack the fort at Cadulgoody. This place was also found to be well guarded and, forced into another strategic withdrawal, Macaulay was publicly rebuked by the government authorities in Madras for overly dividing his forces: 'The system of detachments, at all times exceptionable, the Governor in Council considers to be peculiarly hazardous in the face of an enemy so avowedly superior to your own force'. The British suffered a further setback when the fort of Tuticorin fell to the insurgents. Wilson's acknowledgement that the *polygars* behaved 'reasonably well on this occasion' – they returned a captured British officer and the postmaster unharmed with all their effects – may be regarded as an understatement.[35]

Macaulay had been reinforced such that he now had a force of 2,800 men (two companies of HM 24th Regiment, a complete battalion and eighteen companies of Madras native infantry, one native cavalry troop and Bengal and Madras artillery) and he drove the *polygars* back before attacking Panjalamcoorchy on 31 March 1801. The fort was an irregular oblong about 500ft in length and 300ft broad with walls and bastions at a height of 12 to 15ft. Following the creation of a practicable breach at the northwest angle, the storming party, including the two companies of the 74th and all the native grenadiers, moved forward covered by the fire of the remainder of the force. Welsh witnessed the outcome.

> They advanced with alacrity, under the heaviest fire imaginable, from the curtains and five or six bastions, the defences of which we had not been able to demolish; our men fell rapidly, but nothing impeded their approach; even the hedge was speedily passed, and repeated attempts were made to surmount the breach, but all in vain. Every man who succeeded in reaching the summit was instantly thrown back, pierced with wounds from both pikes and musquetry, and no footing could be gained. At length a retreat was ordered, and a truly dismal scene of horror succeeded, all our killed, and many of the wounded being left at the foot of the breach, over which the enemy immediately sprung, and pursued the rear, while others pierced the bodies both of the dying and the dead.[36]

The bastions were hollow, allowing no footing to the assailants, the defenders well used their 20-foot pikes and the breach was too narrow. Macaulay applauded the bravery of his men, of whom he had lost 317, killed or wounded.[37]

Following the arrival of Lieutenant-Colonel Patrick Agnew on 21 May with additional forces including HM 77th Regiment, it was resolved to make a second attempt. This occurred at one o'clock in the afternoon of the 24th, the storming party including men of the 74th, 77th, native grenadiers and Malay troops. Again stubborn resistance was met. In Welsh's words:

> the defenders shrunk not from their duty, but received our brave fellows with renewed vigour, and the breach was so stoutly defended that, although the hedge was passed in a few minutes, it was nearly half an hour before a man of our's could stand upon the summit: while bodies of the enemy, not only fired on our storming party from the broken bastions on both flanks, but others sallied round and attacked them in the space within the hedge. At length, after a struggle of fifteen minutes in this position, the whole of the enemy in the breach being killed by hand-grenades, and heavy shot thrown over among them, our grenadiers succeeded in mounting the breach, and the resistance afterwards was of no avail.[38]

Around 3,000 *polygars* evacuated the fort and were pursued by British cavalry, their losses estimated as 1,000. The attackers had suffered 186 casualties, the 77th Regiment afflicted the most with fourteen men killed and thirty-nine wounded.[39] Wellesley, writing to Baird from Seringapatam, implies that Macaulay's native infantry had performed badly earlier in the campaign, but he reports that they 'behaved well' in the second attack on Panjalamcoorchy.[40]

A new phase of the struggle now ensued, operations being commenced against the Murdoos, chiefs in the region of Shevagunga who had refused to give up men fleeing from Panjalamcoorchy. Welsh had some sympathy for the insurgents at Panjalamcoorchy, who 'had been driven to take up arms as their only resource', but he believed the Murdoos to have no real grievances.[41] Colonel Agnew first relieved the fort at Comery, which had been invested by the enemy, and then marched on Ramnad. Short of provisions, he returned to Madura in July. Minor skirmishes culminated in an effort to reach the fort at Caliarcoil, the chief stronghold of the rebels about five miles south of the village of Serruvial. A road was dug through the jungle by pioneers and local woodcutters but Agnew admitted that the attempt was futile.

> Covered by banks and entrenchments against which the troops cannot advance from the thickness of the jungle, the enemy has baffled every attempt which has been made to penetrate further: the pioneers being unable to work under the fire brought against them by the rebels from situations of perfect security. Repeated failures have dispirited the troops…

His men were also falling sick with many officers unfit for duty.[42]

At the end of August, there was sharp reversal of fortune, Agnew receiving intelligence of a hitherto unknown jungle path connecting the newly created road with Caliarcoil. After the tortuous struggle, the denouement was surprisingly quick. A 1,000-strong force, including HM 77th Regiment and the 2nd battalion of the 6th Regiment of Madras Native Infantry, reached and captured the rebel stronghold on 1 October, the defenders dispersing into the surrounding countryside. By the end of the month, the Murdoos and Panjalamcoorchy chiefs had been deported to Prince of Wales Island. The destruction of the enemy forts and disarming of the local population was completed by March 1802. Welsh and his comrades were much relieved; '… we were not a little weary of such a tedious and unprofitable warfare'.[43] Total British killed and wounded for the whole insurgency was probably close to 1,000 men.[44]

At the end of October 1801, Arthur Wellesley wrote to Lieutenant-General James Stuart proposing an attack on the non-compliant Rajah of Bullum, who had reoccupied his position at Arrakaira following the departure of Montresor's detachment in June 1800.[45] Wellesley concluded that the seizure of Arrakaira should 'settle the business' and, in January 1802, he marched from Seringapatam with a force of 300 men of HM 77th, 240 of de Meuron's, four native battalions, 500 pioneers, ten guns and four mortars. He was subsequently joined by the 19th Light Dragoons and the 5th Madras Native Infantry and he was also supported by troops of the Rajah of Mysore.[46] Upon reaching Arrakaira, he divided his infantry into three parts for his planned attack on the stockaded posts in the forest. The outcome is narrated in Wellesley's laconic style, so familiar from his later dispatches of more substantial and famous victories;

> on the 16th, in the morning, [I] made the attacks as soon as the fog had cleared away. Two of the divisions which attacked from entirely opposite sides of the forest arrived in the village of Arrekeery at the same moment, and the third, commanded by Colonel A. Cuppage, was at no great distance. The Rajah's [of Mysore] troops...attacked the forest likewise near the great attack made by our troops, and were of essential service in covering our right flank. The cavalry (Company's and Rajah's) occupied all the open ground to cut off the fugitives. The forest was everywhere strongly fortified in the Polygar style, but particularly at the place which I attacked, being the same which Tolfrey and Montresor attacked before. However, we have lost but few men, no officer touched; one European of de Meuron is killed, and but few wounded, and that slightly.[47]

All the posts were carried and Wellesley proceeded to destroy other strongholds. The Rajah of Bullum was captured on 9 February and executed, allowing the British commander to break up his detachment and return to Seringapatam. In April he was promoted to major-general and placed on the staff in India.[48]

There was constant unrest in the south and any instance of British complacency was likely to lead to rebellion and bloodshed. On 11 October 1802, the small post at Panamurtha Cottah in Wynaad was surprised by 300 natives. Wellesley later attributed the outbreak of violence to a previous murder and riot, the attack on the British being opportunistic. The aggressors, he informed the Adjutant-General, '...had [not] a firelock or matchlock among them, but were armed with Nair's knives and bows and arrows'.[49] They had the element of surprise and two British officers and twenty-four sepoys were killed, the barracks and officers' houses set alight. The local major in command, nine miles distant, showed little initiative and Wellesley felt the need to rouse his officers by writing to the commander of the Bombay troops in Malabar.

> I beg that you will urge the officers to active measures. Let them put their troops in camp forthwith, excepting the number of men

that may be absolutely necessary for the defence of the small posts against surprise. If the rebels are really in force, let a junction be formed, and then not a moment lost in dashing at them, whatever may be their force.[50]

Captain Thomas Gurnell was ordered to enter the region with Madras and Bombay forces and he quickly suppressed the insurrection. Wellesley was able to report that the troops 'behaved remarkably well'.[51] There was a tendency for such disturbances to spread to neighbouring areas and Colonel John Montresor had to quell an uprising in Malabar in early 1803. Wellesley admitted that the inhabitants were encouraged by the increasing prospect of British soldiers being drawn away to Maratha territory.[52]

We will complete this review of 'little wars' with a reference to the fighting in Gujarat. The rights of the new local Gaekwar, Anandrao, were disputed by family members. To support him, the British funnelled a mixture of King's troops (detachments of HM 75th, 80th, 86th and 88th Regiments) and Bombay army forces into the area under the leadership of Major Alexander Walker. Early actions in March 1802 were inconclusive and further reinforcements meant that by the end of April the British army, now under Sir William Clarke, amounted to 5–6,000 men, of whom more than 2,000 were Europeans. Clarke captured entrenched enemy positions at the end of the month and the fort of Kadi fell on 5 May. The Gaekwar's general conceded that the British forces were brave: 'I do not suppose anybody in the world can fight like them'. The campaign effectively ended in December 1802 with the capture of the town of Baroda by Colonel Henry Woodington. The formidable garrison of 2,000 Arab mercenaries surrendered after a siege of ten days with 120 British troops killed or wounded. It was 'a thoroughly creditable campaign of which too little has been heard'.[53]

Europe must have appeared a very distant prospect to soldiers fighting in these obscure jungle wars, but events there directly influenced the military and political climate in India. The Treaty of Amiens allowed both Britain and France respite to further their global strategic objectives. Bonaparte was still determined to see the Tricolour flying above Indian fortresses. The treaty permitted the French to reoccupy the colony of Pondicherry in the Carnatic and the First Consul promptly sent a contingent of 2,000 soldiers under the command of General Charles Decaen who had confided to his master that he hated the English. Decaen, and other French agents, were given the murkier objective of coordinating any actions with General Perron, the influential French commander in Sindia's army. They were also to collect information on the strength and location of British forces and the mood among the local inhabitants. The British had their own underhand designs. They were determined to block the legitimate return of Pondicherry. Decaen's mission ended in dismal failure but Mornington, who was aware of Perron's correspondence with the French Directory, was bound to view France as his most deadly enemy in the subcontinent.[54]

Following years of infighting, the Maratha Confederacy was fractured and unstable. Daulat Rao Sindia and Jaswant Rao Holkar were in a desperate struggle to control the Peshwa, the feeble Baji Rao. At first, Sindia prevailed, Baji Rao no more than a state prisoner in his grasp. The old power of the Peshwa, only maintained for so long by the astute diplomacy of the Brahmin minister, had been extinguished. Soon, Sindia's power was in turn usurped, Holkar's remarkable recrudescence confirmed by his victory over the combined armies of the Peshwa and Sindia at Poona on 23 October 1802. The Peshwa was no friend of the British, but he had already opened tentative negotiations for a defensive treaty of alliance and military defeat forced him to flee to Bassein under British protection. Holkar entered Poona and installed the son of Amrit Rao, Vinayakrao, on the throne. The situation remained precarious; Holkar's own men were threatening to sack the city and Sindia, Raghuji Bhonsle (Rajah of Berar) and the Peshwa's *jagirdars* were all hostile to him.[55]

The Marquess Wellesley sensed an opportunity to intervene decisively in the Maratha polity and achieve the ultimate goal of his Governor-Generalship. He wanted a pacified Maratha Confederation that recognised British supremacy.[56] The immediate means to this end was the subsidiary alliance encapsulated in the Treaty of Bassein signed by the British resident at Poona, Barry Close, and Baji Rao on the last day of 1802. In essence, the British would restore the Peshwa to his throne and station a substantial force at Poona to protect him. The Peshwa would surrender much of his sovereignty to the British. The treaty had five key provisions. The subsidiary force of five battalions was to remain in the Peshwa's territories in perpetuity. Various territories were to be surrendered to provide revenues to support this force. The Company was to control the Peswa's relations with other states and act as an arbitrator in any dispute. The Peshwa was to take no Europeans into his service without British Government approval. Finally, the subsidiary force was to be ready at all times to intervene in any local disturbance. This force was not, however, allowed to act 'against any of the principle branches of the Maratha Empire'. The net effect of this unique and unequal agreement was that, at least in theory, the Company was committed to control not just a single state but a federation of states.[57]

The Marquess had other options open to him, but there were objections to alternative strategies. He might have followed a policy of non-intervention, but this was contrary to his instincts and war may still have resulted with the British in a less favourable strategic position. He could have supported Holkar's candidature, but he would have been a fragile ally with little popular support and no stable military or political power. The third alternative was to make any support of the Peshwa against Holkar dependent on the cooperation of other powerful Maratha factions including Sindia and Bhonsle. This would have embroiled the British in complex and potentially endless diplomacy. Mornington justified his policy on the basis that it not only fulfilled his broader objective of cementing British influence in Maratha affairs, but also that all the key Maratha players had appealed to the British Government for help;

> the Peshwa for help to recover his throne; Sindhia for British co-operation in carrying out the restoration; Holkar, that we would recognise the *status quo*; Berrar [Bhonsle], that we would not forget his reversionary claim to the rajaship of Satara.[58]

The treaty has been subject to much historical perusal. The essential conclusions are that it fundamentally changed the British situation in India and increased the likelihood of war with the Marathas. British responsibilities in the country were suddenly much increased: 'Previously there existed a British Empire *in* India; the Treaty gave the Company the Empire *of* India'. The Governor-General's subsidiary forces were now camped in the capitals of all four great Indian powers: Mysore, Hyderabad, Lucknow and Poona.[59] In historian Arthur Bennell's words, the 'setting for the British contest with the Marathas had been created'.[60] Penderel Moon goes further, stating that the Treaty of Bassein was the 'real cause' of the Maratha War.[61] Sardesai also believed that the agreement pre-empted hostilities and he accuses the British of duplicity: 'Baji Rao engaged British help to put down his antagonists Amitrao and Holkar. Instead of doing this they put down his friends Sindia and Bhonsle'.[62]

The most notable British contemporary criticism of the alliance was written by Lord Castlereagh and sent to the Marquess Wellesley in early 1804. The minister argued that there was no need to seek an alliance with the Marathas as British power was sufficient in itself and there was no immediate prospect of any Maratha alliance with the French. This was too late to influence events, but the Marquess asked his brother to draft an answer. Arthur Wellesley had himself been sceptical of the treaty; he believed that interfering in the Peshwa's affairs might unite Holkar and Sindia.[63] After the subsequent operations to restore the Peshwa, he suggested that the alliance should be broken unless it could be entirely revised. Despite his contemporary doubts, he gave a robust response to Castlereagh's objections, emphasising the minister's limited knowledge of Indian affairs, his underestimation of the French threat, and the dangers of passivity: 'In all military operations, but particularly in India, time is everything...'.[64]

Military preparations for intervention in Maratha affairs were underway well before the signing of the Treaty of Bassein. Wellesley was instructed to suspend any minor initiatives and to concentrate his forces while awaiting further guidance from the Marquess. In mid-November 1802, the General had written to Major Macleod from Seringapatam.

> You will have heard of the terrible defeats sustained by the Peshwa and Scindiah in their contest with Holkar; in consequence thereof we are preparing to interfere in force, and every disposable soldier in Mysore will be marched to the Mahratta frontier. This is between ourselves.[65]

In early 1803, there was optimism that the restoration of the Peshwa would be achieved by peaceful means. However, there was no guarantee of this and it was necessary to assemble a British force capable of defeating Holkar or Sindia or both together. This would be part of the Madras Army of which General James Stuart was now commander-in-chief. On 3 March, Stuart received a directive from Madras that the detachment should be 7,000 strong and that it was to be commanded by Arthur Wellesley. Rory Muir describes this order as being 'remarkable'.[66] Stuart was an able commander and Wellesley, now a major-general, was his inferior in rank and thirty years younger. It is likely that the award of the onerous operation to Wellesley was not intended as a snub to Stuart, but was simply an acknowledgment that the younger man, with his acute knowledge of Maratha affairs, was ideally suited for the task. Wellesley's ascendency owed more to pragmatism than nepotism.

The British force at Hurryhur had a total strength of 10,617 men. Wellesley describes it to Barry Close in a letter of 8 March.

> I shall proceed with my march tomorrow. I have with me the 19th light dragoons, 4th, 5th, and 7th regiments of [Madras native] cavalry, under Colonel [Thomas] Dallas; the 74th and Scotch brigade, and 6 complete battalions of [Madras] native infantry; 4 iron 12 pounders, 2 brass 12 pounders, sixteen 6 pounders, 4 galloper 6 pounders, besides the guns attached to the cavalry.[67]

He was disappointed not to have been joined by his own regiment, the 33rd, but he did have the support of around 2,500 of the Rajah of Mysore's irregular Indian cavalry. Wellesley's detachment was to operate in conjunction with the Hyderabad contingent, approximately 8,000 strong, under the command of Colonel James Stevenson. The Scotch Brigade was to be transferred to this latter force to stiffen it such that it could fend off Sindia or Holkar as necessary.[68]

There was still hope that the Peshwa could be restored without the eruption of hostilities. Wellesley was informed by Stuart that 'the principle of his Excellency the Governor General's policy is to avoid a war'. More specifically,

Wellesley was instructed to move rapidly, to placate the southern *jagirdars*, to link up with the Hyderabad contingent without undue delay and to make a junction with the Peshwa or his representatives before proceeding to Poona to complete the restoration. He was necessarily allowed a degree of autonomy: 'The means of accomplishing these objectives must be regulated by your own judgment in conforming to circumstances.'[69]

Wellesley crossed into Maratha territory on 11 March. He was optimistic, writing to his elder brother, 'all your plans will be carried into execution.'[70] As the British force moved north, Holkar's men fell back. Wellesley's dispatches reveal his increasingly characteristic attention to detail and a growing understanding of the logistical and political aspects of his mission. The natural obstacles of extreme heat, drought, crop failure and a shortage of forage were all to be overcome by meticulous planning. He particularly stresses the importance of the maintenance of the bullock train and the need to pay for everything; on 5 April, he assures Stevenson, 'We have got on by these precautions.'[71]

Ten days later, the British forces were in communication with each other at Ecklaus on the River Neera. Holkar was at Chandore to the north of Poona. He had left Amrit Rao, another claimant to the Maratha crown, in the city with 1,500 men.[72] Wellesley later recalled the events of 18–20 April to Stuart.

> I continued my march towards this place [Poona] by the road of Baramootty: I received different intimations from Lieut. Col. Close that it was Amrut Rao's intention to stay in this neighbourhood till I should approach with the British troops, and then to burn the city... I determined to march to Poonah in the night of the 19th, with the cavalry and a battalion of Native infantry. Accordingly, I arrived here yesterday about 3 o'clock, having been detained about 6 hours in the Bhore ghaut, and found the city in safety. Amrut Rao heard of this movement in the morning, and marched off with some precipitation.[73]

Wellesley's march was a considerable feat; following the usual daily march of twenty miles, the cavalry and a single battalion of infantry set off at nightfall and marched until midday, the cavalry then negotiating the ghat to arrive in the early afternoon. John Malcolm was with the party:

> there is every reason to believe [that Poona] was saved from total destruction by a rapid movement of the cavalry under the General's command who actually marched near sixty miles in thirty two hours to its relief.[74]

Baji Rao entered Poona as Peshwa on 13 May. He had made a dilatory journey from Bassein and he was a disappointment to his British collaborators.

Malcolm noted that, because of his weakness and depravity, 'we have no child's play in hand and must devise means of directing his councils or of rendering ourselves independent of their operation'.[75] The timid and non-compliant Peshwa had lost not only the confidence of the British, but also any authority over the other Maratha princes. His bloodless restoration did not have the sense of an endgame. There was the prospect of the three great Maratha chiefs – Sindia, Bhonsle and Holkar – settling their differences and marching through the territories of the Nizam of Hyderabad north of the Godavery River towards Poona. On the day following the Peshwa's return to the city, Wellesley wrote to his younger brother Henry:

> I have got a fine army, in excellent order; and I think that this combination or confederacy, with which we are threatened, will find that we can march as well as fight.[76]

Chapter 5

The Greatest Gamble: War in the Deccan 1803; Ahmednuggar and Assaye

The occupation of Poona was followed by negotiations between the British and the Marathas which dragged on through the months of June and July 1803. The key players were the chieftains Sindia and Bhonsle, Colonel John Collins, the British resident at Sindia's court, and Arthur Wellesley, who had been granted considerable autonomy by his elder brother. The British were frustrated by Sindia's insistence that he should meet separately with Bhonsle to discuss the prospects of peace or war, and also alarmed that this junction was to be on the edge of the Nizam's dominions in the presence of a sizeable Maratha force.[1] Major William Thorn, a participant in the subsequent campaigns in the north, well expresses the British position in his history of the Anglo-Maratha War, published in 1818.

> Major-General Wellesley, whose particular influence among the Mahrattas, and general acquaintance with the affairs of India, qualified him in an eminent degree for such a trust, was empowered to enter into negotiations with the principal confederated chiefs, Scindiah and the Bhonslah, apprising them of the pacific intentions of our government, and requiring, as a proof of their sincerity, the separation and return of their respective armies. The answers to this reasonable demand were marked in equal proportions of cunning and ignorance, of deception and insolence; the chieftains offering to retire from their present position on the same day that the British troops should have reached the stations of Bombay, Seringapatam and Madras; a compliance with which absurd proposition would have had the effect of disbanding our army, and placing the principal part of it at a distance of above one thousand miles, while the united forces of Scindiah and the Rajah [Bhonsle] remained within fifty miles of the Nizam's frontier, to take advantage of his weakness and our credulity…The lapse of time sustained by useless negotiation would consequently have increased the confidence and resources of the Mahratta chieftains now in the field, and have

added to their numbers; while to ourselves it would have had the effect of dispiriting an army prepared for action, and have weakened the trust which the friendly powers had in the superiority of our arms, and the vigour of our resolutions.[2]

In early July, Collins informed the Governor-General that he had warned Sindia that the British could no longer be held responsible for any outbreak of hostilities. He had agreed to wait 'a few days longer' for a promised Maratha proposal.[3]

The Maratha perspective was entirely different. In truth, they had few strong cards in their hands and a policy of procrastination was logical as they wanted neither peace nor war. They could ignominiously climb down and assent to British superiority, or escalate to military operations in which they were likely to be defeated. Delay brought some hope; perhaps of British distraction by unrest elsewhere, reconciliation with Holkar, or at least the approaching end of the rainy season which would allow them greater mobility in the field.[4] Holkar proved to be less reliable than the weather. The Marquess Wellesley had forwarded to the Maratha chief a captured letter from Sindia addressed to Baji Rao. In it, Sindia promised to 'wreak full vengeance' on Holkar once the war was over. Unsurprisingly, Holkar now gave up all thoughts of joining a coalition and fell back on Malwa.[5]

The correspondence became increasingly bellicose. On 10 July, Barry Close, one of Wellesley's closest confederates, wrote to him complaining of Sindia's 'systematic course of deceit and treachery'.[6] Four days later, Wellesley warns Sindia that unless he immediately withdraws his troops, he would assume hostile intent and exploit 'the advantageous position of the Company's Armies'.[7] On the 17th, he decries the further delay to Close, stressing that there is no time to lose.[8]

Did the Governor-General really expect to avoid bloodshed? He reassured General Lake that the Marathas would 'vanish' upon the appearance of the British forces[9] and he was slow to admit that war was likely, only acknowledging the failure of diplomacy on 1 August, two days before Collins left Sindia's camp.[10] Arthur Bennell, who has meticulously dissected the political dimensions of the episode, asserts that the war was in part a failure of British strategy. There were no meaningful negotiations with Sindia and Bhonsle. The Marquess, under political pressure from Whitehall, was impatient to impose his own restructuring of Maratha polity with the objective of destroying the military power of either or both of the chiefs. By delegating the decision of peace or war to Arthur Wellesley, a soldier who was likely to prefer the quicker arbitration of war to indefinite diplomacy, he must have known that he was 'transferring the contest from the *durbar* negotiating tent to the battlefield'.[11] On their part, the Maratha princes had risked war by political infighting and by indulging in brinkmanship, refusing to withdraw their forces at the critical moment.[12] In March, John Malcolm had written to General Stuart; 'A political agent is never so likely to succeed as when he negotiates at the head of an army'.[13] If this was success, it was also war.

There were two major theatres in the coming conflict, with intense fighting in both during 1803. To the north, Sindia would be attacked by the army of General Gerard Lake assembled in Oudh. This campaign and the subsequent actions against Holkar will be recounted in chapters 7 and 8. In the current and following chapter we will follow events in the Deccan, where Arthur Wellesley might be judged to have the greater immediate military challenge, pitted against a Maratha enemy better organised, officered and commanded than the French-dominated forces in Hindustan. Both Lake and Wellesley were given extensive political and military powers. There were also two more minor centres of operations. In the west, Colonel John Murray was to attack Sindia's holdings in Gujarat and, in the east, Orissa and Bhonsle's possessions were to be seized by forces under the command of Lieutenant-Colonel George Harcourt.[14]

On 6 August, Wellesley wrote to Sindia; 'I offered you peace on terms of equality, and honourable to all parties: you have chosen war, and are responsible for all consequences'.[15] This may not have been entirely true, but it served as a declaration of war. If the 34-year-old general was daunted by his command, he gave little indication of this in his correspondence. He had earlier informed Colonel Stevenson that he wanted nothing more than an end to the procrastination:

> Either peace or war will relieve my distresses: peace as it will enable me to approach my supplies at Poonah; war as it will give me an opportunity of attacking Ahmednuggur, in which place I shall find plenty.[16]

The delays had at least given him the chance to cement alliances with local chieftains and make military preparations. Sardesai notes that he approached 'every Maratha chief, small or great, from the Tunghabadra to the Namada' to try and undermine any Maratha confederacy.[17] Supplies, as always, were central to his planning. He needed a functional bullock train, a reliable commissariat and pontoons to cross the rivers. The failure to form a large depot near Bombay, caused by local ineptitude, underlined the importance of an advanced location for provisions.[18]

On 29 July, Wellesley revealed his intentions to Lake.

> My plan of operations…is to attack Ahmednuggur with my own corps, by the possession of which place I shall secure the

communication with Poonah and Bombay, and keep the Nizam's army on the defensive upon his Highness' frontier. When I shall have finished that operation, and have crossed the Godavery, I shall then, if possible, bring the enemy to action.[19]

Thus Wellesley's first move would secure the vital supply base. The broader objectives of the southern, and more defensive, of the two major British fronts were to seize Sindia's park of artillery, all armaments of European construction and general military stores. The capture of Sindia and Bhonsle was, the Governor-General informed Wellesley, 'highly desirable' but, short of this, military action 'pursued to the utmost extremity' should culminate in the acquisition of extensive Maratha territories.[20]

Some in the British camp believed that their foe would rely heavily on their marauding horsemen, but Wellesley was dismissive.

> The Marathas have long boasted that they would carry on a predatory war against us; they will find that mode of warfare not very practicable at the present…a system of predatory war must have some foundation in strength of some kind or other.[21]

He was convinced that the real contest of the war would be with the regular infantry and artillery of Sindia and Bhonsle. He remained impatient to commence hostilities while the rivers were still full. He promised Collins that he would fill Ahmednuggar with provisions: 'when this is completed, all the Marathas in India will not be able to chase me from my position.'[22] By 3 August he was encamped at Walkee, six miles from the fort.[23]

To achieve his objectives, Wellesley had a force of just over 11,000 King's and Company troops under his personal command (see Appendix VI). His cavalry (1,731 strong) was made up of the HM 19th Light Dragoons and three regiments of Madras native cavalry, and his infantry (6,999) of HM 74th and 78th, and six battalions of Madras native infantry. The force was completed by approximately 1,000 artillery and pioneer personnel and about thirty-four guns. He was supported by 2,000 horse of the Rajah of Mysore, which he described to Lake as being 'excellent', and 3,000 'bad' Maratha cavalry under two reluctant local chieftains. The combined detachment amounted to around 15,000 combatants with 1,600 of them European.

In addition, there was the smaller force of Colonel James Stevenson stationed on the northern frontier of the Nizam's dominions at Aurangabad. This detachment of more than 9,000 men was composed of the two Madras native cavalry regiments (909 strong), an infantry contingent made up of HM Scotch Brigade and five native battalions (6,891) and around 500 artillerymen and pioneers and about twenty guns. The force contained 900

European troops. There were also infantry and cavalry units of the Nizam of doubtful quality and affiliation. A reserve for Wellesley had originally consisted of 8,000 men under General Stuart at Moodgul, south of the River Kistna, but this was subsequently weakened, losing both Stuart and part of its strength, sent to the Carnatic. It was eventually only 4,000 strong, including 1,200 Europeans.[24]

These armies faced the combined forces of Sindia and Bhonsle in the Deccan. British intelligence reported Sindia and the bulk of his troops to be at Julgong in the rear of the Adjunta Pass near the Nizam's territories. Bhonsle was encamped just to his left.[25] The best information we have for the Maratha armies is the memorandum sent by Collins to Wellesley at the end of July.

Sinde

Under the command of Colonel Pohlman; 500 Hindustani horse, 7 sepoy battalions [each battalion estimated as 700 strong so 4,900 regular infantry in total], 500 matchlock men, 8 heavy guns and 4 field pieces.

Under the command of Colonel Saleur and in the pay of the Begum Sumru; 4 sepoy battalions [2,800], 2 heavy guns and 30 field pieces.

Under different native sirdars; 12,000 Hindustani horse and 2,000 Deccani horse.

Under the command of Bapoji Sindhia 4,000 Hindustani horse.

Park of artillery; 25 heavy guns and 100 field pieces.

Raja of Berar [Bhonsle]

Under the command of different native sirdars 20,000 Hindustani horse.

Under the command of Beni Singh 6,000 infantry and 35 field pieces.

500 camels carrying rockets and 500 carrying shutarnals.[26]

Sindia had sent 4–5,000 of his regular infantry north to reinforce his army in Hindustan.[27] Holkar's army was believed to be north of the River Taplee with his troops 'in the greatest distress'; there remained no likelihood of him joining the war.[28]

Wellesley needed to capture Ahmednuggar quickly to consolidate his supplies, to discourage any Maratha thrust on Poona, and to allow him to advance towards Stevenson so that their combined forces could bring the Maratha princes to a decisive battle. He was determined to be aggressive just as he had been in his earlier campaign against Dhoondiah Waugh.[29] He arrived at his first objective on 8 August (see map 7).

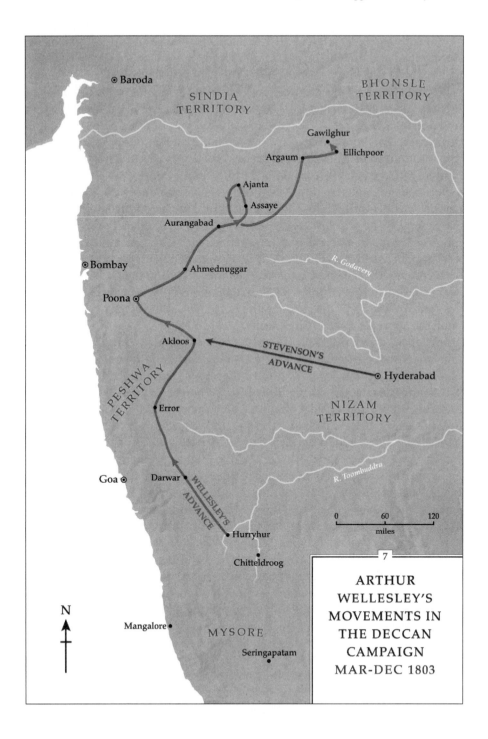

N

7

**ARTHUR
WELLESLEY'S
MOVEMENTS IN
THE DECCAN
CAMPAIGN
MAR-DEC 1803**

Ahmednuggar is strategically located on the route from Poona to Aurangabad and the north. The formidable fort was outside a village or *pettah* which would have to be captured first. The British had detailed, albeit incomplete, knowledge of the defences and garrison. A memorandum penned by Wellesley in June describes the *pettah* as having mud walls ten feet high with twelve gates and no ditch. There were forty bastions or round towers, eight of them larger and containing guns, the remainder having only loopholes. The fort was a gunshot to the east of the *pettah*. It was round with twenty-four bastions, a large gate, three small sally ports and a considerable ditch. It had a glacis but no covered way. Much of the construction of the rampart and parapet was of stone and brick. The bastions contained guns, perhaps up to 200 in total.[30] The *pettah* was garrisoned by 1,000 Arab mercenaries who were renowned as marksmen and had a reputation for defending fortifications. They were supported by a battalion of Sindia's regular infantry who had initially been encamped in an open space between the *pettah* and the fort. The garrison of the fort was believed to be 3,000 strong, the men armed with matchlocks or firelocks. The 3,000 enemy Maratha horsemen in the vicinity melted away upon the approach of the British army.[31]

Wellesley issued orders for the assault of the *pettah* on 7 August, but heavy rain meant that the operation was postponed until the following day. His offer of surrender to the *killedar* of Ahmednuggar was summarily dismissed. The plan was for an attack by escalade on different parts of the *pettah* walls by three mutually supporting assault columns. Contemporary accounts are a little confused as to the prioritisation of these attacks, which are only tersely related in Wellesley's dispatch. It appears that the first attack on the left of the main gateway was made by the pickets of the day. This detachment was formed of a half company from each of the King's regiments and from each battalion of the Madras native infantry, making in total one company of Europeans and two and a half companies of sepoys. It would be supported by the flank companies of HM 78th under the command of Colonel William Harness. The second column, led by Lieutenant-Colonel William Wallace, was to take a gun forward to blow away the main gate. It was formed of battalion companies of HM 74th supported by the 1/8th Madras Native Infantry. The third column, consisting of 1/3rd Madras Native Infantry and the flank companies of HM 74th had the task of assailing the walls to the right of the gate. It was commanded by Captain Poole Hick Vesey.[32]

Wellesley makes no reference to a feint, but Captain John Blakiston of the Madras Engineers states that Harness's column was to make the principal attack and that Vesey's third column was sent forward 'more as a feint than a real attack'.[33] Conversely, Lieutenant-Colonel Alexander Adams of the 78th insists that the central column was 'principally intended as a feint and to keep the garrison of the fort in check'. He adds that the guns of the cavalry were ordered to cannonade the walls and that further feints to distract the enemy were made by two regiments of native infantry.[34]

Whatever the precise plan, there was a vital gap in British intelligence. The *pettah* walls had no rampart.[35] This meant that when the assailing troops placed their ladders and climbed to the top there was no place to step onto but only a sheer drop to the earth on the other side. The column on the left moved off just before 10am and was the first to reach the walls, as recounted by Adams.

> The wall is a simple mud one without ramparts, but with small round towers at different distances. Some fortified houses in the inside command the wall at certain places and in no part except the towers is there any footing on the inside [of] the wall after having ascended the ladders. I will not pretend to say how it happened, but it certainly was the case, that the attack on which our regiment was employed was made directly in the face of one of these houses, and [we were] ordered to escalade three towers which formed a re-entering angle. By the hurry of the native pioneers, the ladders were placed altogether on the left one of the three towers, and upon the curtain directly in front of the fortified house. The grenadiers headed by poor Humberstone, and the light infantry by poor Grant, proceeded in the most gallant manner to ascend the ladders, but the cross fire was so heavy, and fired with such cool aim, and there being no footing for those that got up to jump down on the defending party after getting to the top, that I believe not above four or five men that once set foot on the ladders came down unhurt. Humberstone and Grant were shot dead at the top of their respective ladders; Anderson was mortally wounded in two places as he set his foot on the ladder; Larkin was knocked down by a stone as he got near the top; Grant falling across Campbell and preventing him getting higher saved him, and the ladder breaking under Captain Fraser caused his escape. The ladders were again manned, but the success continued as bad, and the slaughter was so great that the retreat was ordered...[36]

After about ten minutes, Harness was forced to withdraw his men, leaving the ladders against the wall and the dead at the foot of it.

On the right, Vesey's men prepared to make their attack. James Welsh was a veteran of the Polygar wars, but this was the first time he had seen the face of an enemy. The walls of the *pettah* and fort were lined with men, their arms

glittering in the sun. A gun elephant ran amok, causing confusion and delay-
ing the British advance. The right column faced the same problem as the left
but, due to astute judgement or good fortune, their ladders were placed by one
of the *pettah's* bastions, thereby allowing an easier passage inside the walls.
Welsh is the best witness.

> Being furnished with two scaling ladders only, we reached the
> curtain and placed them at the very re-entering angle, formed by
> a small bastion, the enemy playing some heavy guns on us, from
> the fort. Such a rush was made at first, that one ladder broke down,
> with our gallant leader and several men, and we were forced to
> work hard with the other. Captain Vesey was then a very stout
> heavy man; but what impediment, short of death, can arrest a
> soldier at such a crisis? He was soon on the bastion, surrounded
> by men, determined to carry every thing before them. Our two
> European companies had all scrambled up, and about one hun-
> dred and fifty, or two hundred of the 3rd [Madras Native Infantry],
> when a cannon-shot smashed our last ladder, and broke the thigh
> of my Subadar. We were now a party of three hundred men, left
> solely to our own resources, and dashing down we scoured all the
> streets near the wall, the enemy only once making a stand, and
> suffering accordingly.[37]

Colonel Wallace blew the main gate at the same time as the sepoys of the
1/3rd were opening it from the inside, causing several men to suffer burns
and also a friendly fire death.[38] The defenders made some resistance; Captain
James Frazer of the 78th, writing two days after the action, entered the village
where the right column had penetrated the walls.

> [I] entered into the body of the place [*pettah*], and shortly after
> met with a numerous body of Arabs, who seemed as well-disposed
> for the attack as myself, and both parties closed in a moment. The
> contest was short, several were bayonetted, who fell on the spot, and
> a vast many very badly wounded…[39]

The momentum was now with the British, the *pettah* in their grasp by 3pm.
The fleeing defenders were prevented from reaching the fort by British and
allied cavalry. Wellesley acknowledged the loss of 'some brave officers and
soldiers'.[40]

There remained the significant task of the reduction of the fort. On the
evening of the 9th, Lieutenant-Colonel Wallace led five companies of HM
74th Regiment and 2/12th Madras Native Infantry to seize a position within
400 yards of it, thus allowing the construction of a battery of four guns to create

the breach.[41] The bombardment commenced the following day and the fort's *killadar* soon sought a ceasefire to start negotiations. Wellesley replied that he would not stop firing until the fort was taken or it surrendered and the place promptly capitulated, the garrison of 1,400 men, mainly Arabs, marching out on the 12th. The surrender was timely as the besiegers were running short of ammunition and their scaling ladders were too short to be used from the fort's ditch. Various Maratha sources claim that the fort's precipitate downfall was facilitated by bribes and treachery.[42]

The capture of Ahmednuggar fort may have had a trifling human cost, but this was not true of the three-pronged assault on the *pettah*. The official British return for the period 8–11 August lists twenty-two killed and ninety-seven wounded; these are divided into seventy European and forty-nine native casualties.[43] Welsh believed 160 men to have been killed or wounded in the action.[44] Adams, another participant, details the losses of his own regiment, the 78th Highlanders, to be four officers and ten rank and file killed and two officers and thirty-nine rank and file wounded.[45] As was almost inevitably the case following the British capture of a fort during this period, some of the victorious survivors indulged in rape and looting. According to Welsh, two native soldiers were hanged at a gateway, the Europeans escaping punishment.[46] Another eyewitness admitted that the measure created some disgust, but added that it was justified in view of the need to establish discipline and to give an indication of British 'justice and good faith'.[47]

After a few days in Ahmednuggar, Wellesley headed north towards Stevenson, crossing the River Godavery to reach Aurangabad. His first objective was to prevent the Marathas striking southwards into Hyderabad, where they could plunder the land and force the British to chase them. He had to block their path and impose a battle they did not want. This was not straightforward and he would need the inspiration of the volume of Caesar's *Commentaries* that he carried with him.[48] His decision to keep his forces divided was criticised by some of his fellow officers, who stressed the problems of communication and the risk of the two armies being defeated in piecemeal fashion. Certainly, Wellesley felt the need to energise the nervous Stevenson: 'Dash at the first fellows who make their appearance and the campaign will be our own'.[49] Following reports of Maratha movements to the southeast, Wellesley was forced to make a dash himself, first to the north bank of the Godavery and then eastward to Rackisbaum, Hasnapoor and Kurka, which he reached on 6 September. Stevenson was at Jalna, which he had taken by force, and Sindia's forces were at Purtoor. The British commander had succeeded in placing his men between the Marathas and Hyderabad.[50]

On the same day, Wellesley reported to John Malcolm that his army was in excellent 'marching trim'.[51] This was a testament to his determination and attention to logistical detail as the campaign was unfolding in a wasteland. Colonel Harness, writing on 27 August, believed that there 'never was a country producing the finest crops, almost without cultivation, so wretched, so distracted'.[52] The populace of the fortified villages of Maharashtra was so desperate to protect their meagre food supplies that they resisted the looting *pindaris*. Despite Wellesley's best efforts, morale among the sepoys of the Madras army had suffered due to a combination of an unfamiliar diet – the rice was not of the preferred white variety – and the unyielding nature of the campaign. He was forced to conduct a number of courts martial for desertion.[53] His Maratha cavalrymen were threatening to withdraw their support and he had to personally meet their demands for pay:

> I must determine upon keeping them, at least for the present… if they were to go, we should be surrounded in our camp and on our marches by *pindaris* and we should lose even the name of a body of cavalry….[54]

On the evening of 6 September, Sindia, harried by Stevenson, withdrew northwards toward the Ajanta hills. The chiefs had also given instruction to their infantry and artillery to move south through the Adjunta gap, allowing the junction of the Maratha forces. Wellesley's *harkarrahs* reported this concentration to be at Bokarden. There were rumours that Sindia and Bhonsle were divided, unable to agree on their best strategy. The former favoured the employment of his regular infantry, while the latter preferred to use his horse in a 'predatory war'. James Grant Duff, the British historian of the Marathas, accuses them of being 'feeble in the extreme'.[55] Wellesley now moved north and, by 21 September, the two British armies were camped within a mile of each other at Budnapoor. Their commanders consulted and it was decided to keep their forces separate before uniting to tackle the Marathas at Bokarden on the 24th.[56] The Maratha Army was estimated by *harkarrahs* to be composed of 40,000 cavalry, 20,000 regular infantry and 100 cannon. Wellesley's decision to maintain the division of his troops remained controversial; he later justified it to Thomas Munro:

> I have to observe, that this separation was necessary; first because both corps could not pass through the same defiles in one day; secondly, because it was to be apprehended that, if we left upon one of the roads through these hills, the enemy might have passed to the southward while we were going to the northward, and then the action would have been delayed, or probably avoided altogether.[57]

His strategy was based on the premise that either British force was capable of defeating the Marathas.[58]

Wellesley was to get his battle and sooner than he expected. The prelude to the battle of Assaye was marked by a significant failure of British intelligence. This was not unpredictable. The shortcomings in the means for collecting information were understood by Wellesley himself and also Mountstuart Elphinstone, a military secretary whose role extended to being an interpreter and EIC intelligence gatherer. The numerous enemy horse meant that their position could not be reconnoitred by any European officer.[59] The *harkarrahs* the British had brought with them from Mysore were also too conspicuous to be effective spies, while the local *harkarrahs* were unreliable. Elphinstone complains that they were selected for their 'stupidity'.[60] At about eleven o'clock on 23 September, two captured *banjaras* claimed that the Maratha army was not just at Bokarden, but spread over an area to the east along the north bank of the Kaitna River towards the village of Assaye. This was startling news as it meant that the Marathas were five miles nearer to Wellesley than he had thought, while Stevenson was still ten miles distant from him at Hussainabad.[61]

The British general advanced his army, only leaving the 1/2nd Madras Native Infantry to guard the baggage train. When he reached some high ground he saw that the *banjaras* were in part correct. The Maratha army was much closer than he had thought. However, this was not a peripheral part of his enemy's force, but the entire Maratha host: the combined armies of Sindia and Bhonsle. It was possible to discern the separate camps of Sindia's cavalry to the west, Bhonsle's forces around the village of Assaye and Sindia's regular infantry brigades stretched along the north bank of the Kaitna River (see map 8). The Marathas were both united and in a strong position of their own choosing. He had not caught them on the move as he would have preferred.[62]

This was the extreme test of Wellesley's oft-stated conviction that aggression – 'dashing' at the enemy – was the only way to wage war in India. Retreat was an anathema, surrendering the initiative and giving the Maratha horsemen an easy target to harass and demoralise. He decided to attack. The Marathas, on their part, underestimated the aggression of their enemy. Well aware of the proximity of Wellesley's force, and also of the location of Stevenson, they had presumed that the British would delay any offensive until their armies were combined. According to Welsh:

> Some of the [Maratha] prisoners said it was generally understood that when Colonel Stevenson's and our force had united, we intended to offer them battle; but when they first discovered only one body advancing, they thought them actually mad, as it was their own intention to have attacked our little camp the same day.[63]

Assaye was a battle into which both sides blundered, but in which only one side had the crucial element of surprise.

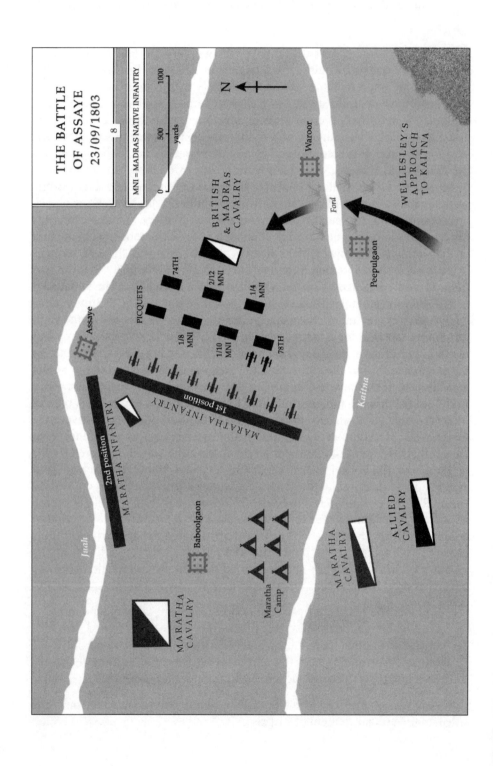

THE BATTLE
OF ASSAYE
23/09/1803

8

MNI = MADRAS NATIVE INFANTRY

0   500   1000
      yards

N

Waroor

BRITISH
& MADRAS
CAVALRY

74TH

PICQUETS

2/12
MNI

1/4
MNI

1/8
MNI

1/10
MNI

78TH

Ford

Peepulgaon

WELLESLEY'S
APPROACH
TO KAITNA

Assaye

Kaitna

Juah

2nd position

MARATHA INFANTRY

MARATHA INFANTRY
1st position

Baboolgaon

Maratha
Camp

MARATHA
CAVALRY

MARATHA
CAVALRY

ALLIED
CAVALRY

The regular force available to Wellesley amounted to around 7,000 men. The infantry (5,170 strong) was made up of two King's battalions (HM 74th and 78th) and five battalions of Madras native infantry. His cavalry (1,731) consisted of the 19th Light Dragoons and three regiments of Madras native cavalry. He had a battalion of pioneers, around 500 artillerymen and twenty-two cannon, the latter including the 'galloper guns' with the cavalry regiments. The 5,400 native cavalry of Mysore and Maratha origin would be used mainly to deter the attentions of *pindaris*.[64]

The Maratha army at Assaye is often described as being 50,000 strong. The mass of men swarming in the peninsula between the Juah and Kaitna rivers was almost certainly much greater than this, possibly as many as 200,000, but this included many irregular troops and camp followers who were unlikely to act against a well formed enemy. More precise estimates of Maratha strength vary between different sources. Extrapolating from earlier British intelligence reports and information subsequently available to Wellesley, it seems that there were more than 10,000 regular Maratha infantry in sixteen battalions, 20–30,000 cavalry and 250 cannon. Sindia's infantry was made up of Colonel Pohlmann's brigades of 6,000 men, that of Dupont of 2,500 and a further 2,000 men of the Begum Somru (commanded by Colonel Saleur). Wellesley later concluded that these were the infantry brigades primarily engaged in the battle. It appears that Bhonsle's infantry and Sindia's more irregular foot soldiers were mostly superfluous.[65]

The initial situation of the Maratha camp in the tongue between the two rivers was the key factor in Wellesley's plan. His first objective had to be the complete defeat of Sindia's regular battalions, but his enemy was too strong to allow a frontal assault. He later explained his logic to his elder brother.

> Although I came first in front of their right, I determined to attack their left as the defeat of their corps of infantry was most likely to be effectual: accordingly I marched around to their left flank, covering the march of the column of infantry by the British cavalry in the rear, and by the Marhatta and Mysore cavalry on the right flank.[66]

The success of this plan required a crossing point on the Kaitna River. Wellesley noted the two villages of Peepulgaon and Waroor on each side of the Kaitna. His local guides denied any knowledge of a crossing, but Wellesley's instinct, finely honed by his now considerable experience of Indian campaigning, was that there was almost certainly a routine communication between the two places. He set his force in motion on the diagonal to the presumed ford; the order of march was firstly the pickets of the day, HM 74th Foot, 2/12th Madras Native Infantry (MNI), 1/4th MNI, 1/8th MNI, 1/10th MNI, and lastly HM 78th Regiment. Two large bodies of Maratha horse had come across to the south side but they were to be kept at a distance by Wellesley's own cavalry screen.[67]

When the Marathas saw their foe approaching the river they commenced a long-range fire, as is related by Mountstuart Elphinstone, who was with the general's staff.

> The shot fell pretty thick round, but did scarce any damage, on account of the distance. However, it bounded off the ground, and made the people duck and one shot some-how or other hit Mr. Campbell, Brigade-Major to General Wellesley, in the heel, and brought him off. We kept moving on, and got among ravines, when they cannonaded hotly but still ineffectually…[68]

Unsurprisingly, the eyewitness accounts are not entirely consistent. Sergeant Thomas Swarbrook of the 19th Light Dragoons reports that, despite some protection from the undulations of the land, the Maratha fire 'made many fall besides a greater many of our horses'.[69] When asked if the fire was 'hot', Wellesley was dismissive; 'Well they are making a great noise', he told his military secretary, 'but I do not see any one hit'.[70]

The advancing soldiers also held their composure. John Blakiston was impressed by the steady movement of the column of infantry, 'so unlike the usual order of march… not a whisper was heard through the ranks'.[71] The river was less than three feet deep and the crossing was not fiercely contested. This was perhaps a vital omission. A solitary enemy battery was brought up, the result of which is graphically described by Blakiston.

> No sooner, however, did the head of the column begin to ascend the opposite bank, than it was met by a shower of shot from a battery advanced near the bank of the river for that purpose, which continuing without intermission, caused us severe loss. At this time the General's orderly dragoon had the top of his head carried off by a cannon ball, but the body being kept in its seat by the valise, holsters, and other appendages of a cavalry saddle, it was some time before the terrified horse could rid itself of the ghastly burden, in the endeavour to effect which he kicked and plunged, and dashed the poor man's brains in our faces, to our no small danger and annoyance. This was a rather ugly beginning I thought.[72]

With the infantry across the river, Wellesley ordered Colonel Patrick Maxwell to bring across his regular cavalry to form in their right rear. His Maratha and Mysore horsemen were to remain on the south side. The timeline for the early phase of the battle is imprecisely documented: Wellesley probably arrived in front of the Maratha camp in the early afternoon, around one o'clock, and it is unlikely that it took him more than two hours to complete the river crossing.[73] Captain James Frazer of the 78th states that the British force was on the north bank before 3pm and that these troops reformed immediately.[74]

Wellesley drew up his men in three lines. From left to right, the first line was composed of HM 78th Regiment, 1/10th MNI, 1/8th MNI, and the pickets; the second line the 1/4th MNI, 2/12th MNI, and HM 74th Regiment; the third line was the cavalry held in reserve.[75] The British general was hopeful of falling onto the Maratha left flank, but now something unexpected occurred. Blakiston, who had been sent forward to reconnoitre, is the best witness.

> On gaining the top of the high ground between the two rivers, I observed the enemy's infantry in the act of changing their front, and taking up a new position, with their right on the river Kailna and their left on the village of Assaye. This manoeuvre they were performing in the most steady manner possible, though not exactly according to Dundas [the author of the standard British drill manual]; for each battalion came up into the new alignment in line, the whole body thus executing a kind of echellon movement on a large scale.[76]

Blakiston reported back to Wellesley, who was evidently taken aback that his enemy was disciplined and well drilled enough to alter their formation while under threat of immediate attack. Sindia and Bhonsle were at the other end of the encampment and Colonel Pohlmann was in command of Sindia's regular infantry.[77]

The most immediate result of the change in the Maratha line to a north-south orientation was that the British flanks were now vulnerable. Wellesley accordingly started to extend his front by merging his two infantry lines into one. This involved issuing personal instructions to the battalion commanders. On the far right the 74th were to line up on the right side of the pickets. Explicit orders were given to Colonel William Orrok, the commander of the pickets, and to Major Samuel Swinton of the 74th, not to approach too close to the village of Assaye. To the left of the pickets were the two native battalions, the 2/12th MNI and 1/4th MNI, and to their left their fellow sepoys of the 1/8th MNI and 1/10th MNI. Wellesley positioned himself with the 78th Regiment on the extreme left of the new line.[78]

While these movements were underway, the Maratha line advanced and opened fire from their 9 and 12-pounders. The British 6-pounders, now across the river, were outgunned and all eyewitnesses agree that the Maratha artillery barrage was now murderous. Lieutenant Colin Campbell recalls that the casualties began to mount and that the British artillery response was largely ineffectual.

> During these formations we lost numbers of officers and men as the enemy fired mostly grape and chain-shot... The line was ordered to

advance. The piquets at this period had nearly lost a third of their number and most of the gun bullocks were killed; some of the corps, I think, waited too long, wishing to bring forward their guns, which could be of no service.[79]

The centre of the British line, the sepoy battalions, received the most intense fire.

The advance was enforced. No troops could endure such an artillery pounding for long and there was an urgent need to capture the Maratha guns. The men moved forward with the bayonet before the merge into a single line had been completed, Wellesley ordering the battalions of the second line to move to their allocated places on the march.[80] He directed that the guns be left behind. This activity induced an even more ferocious response from the Maratha artillerymen, who were determined to man their guns to the last. Blakiston describes the result: 'In the space of less than a mile, 100 guns, worked with skill and rapidity, vomited forth death into our feeble ranks'.[81]

With an evolving formation and subjected to destructive artillery fire, there was a danger of the British advance becoming uncoordinated and a problem soon occurred on the right extremity. Wellesley was forming the line to the left himself and Elphinstone describes him 'impatiently' sending several messages to the right.[82] Orrok had been ordered to angle towards Assaye, but then to turn half left to avoid the village and bring his infantry in alignment with the southern part of the line. For whatever reason – Fortescue suggests that he might have been confused by the intensity of enemy fire and that he lacked confidence that his men could manage the corrective manoeuvre[83] – he instead continued to march off to the right directly towards Assaye, the 74th obediently following the pickets. The British advance was now split into two parts; the 74th and the pickets in the north, and the 78th and the Maratha native infantry in the south.[84] It was a critical moment in the battle and Wellesley was later to mercilessly attribute blame.

> Desperate as the action was, our loss would not have exceeded one half of its actual amount if it had not been for a mistake in the officer who led the piquets which were on the right of the first line. When the enemy changed their position, they threw their left to Assaye, in which village they soon had some infantry, and it was surrounded by cannon. As soon as I saw that, I directed the officer commanding the piquets to keep out of shot from that village: instead of that, he led directly upon it…[85]

On the field, Wellesley was as yet unaware of the crisis unfolding around Assaye. In the south, where he could personally direct events, the attack was delivered slightly en echelon. The 78th Regiment was the first to enter the action, advancing in determined fashion. Eyewitnesses describe Sindia's battalions ceding ground, two of them on the right eventually breaking. According to Campbell:

> The line moved forward rapidly (I may say without firing two rounds) and took possession of the first line of guns, where many of the enemy were killed. They then moved on in equally good order and resolution to the second line of guns, from which they very soon drove the enemy; but many of the artillery, who pretended to be dead when we passed on to the second line of guns, turned the guns we had taken upon us, which obliged us to return and again to drive them from them.[86]

Blakiston saw many of the *golumdauze* (artillerymen) bayonetted in the act of loading their guns. He admits that some of the sepoys of the Madras native infantry took cover in the undulating terrain or were reluctant to move forward, but insists that the main body 'continued to advance rapidly in good order'.[87] Captain Frazer also observed that the ground was 'very bad' but that the troops 'managed to keep always a good line and pressed the enemy'.[88]

In the face of repeated volleys of fire from the Highlanders and the battalions of Madras sepoys the Maratha infantry were forced back towards their secondary position, a line running east-west on the south bank of the River Juah, with their left flank on Assaye (see map 8). There was a transient danger of the Madras native infantry troops being carried away with their success and recklessly pursuing their foe, thus bringing the prowling Maratha horsemen into play. In the event, the 78th redeployed into column of companies, presenting a solid wall to the enemy cavalry, and the Madras native infantry officers had time to rally their men and restore order.[89]

Wellesley now rode to the north, where the sound of gunfire emanated from Assaye. Here the situation was becoming serious for the isolated British units. There were perhaps 20,000 enemy infantry and twenty cannon in the village and the pickets and the 74th were caught in a lethal hail of fire.[90] Lieutenant Campbell concedes that 'things at this period did not go so well on our right'.

> [This was] owing to some mistake of the piquets in having, when ordered to advance, inclined to their right, which brought the 74th regiment into the first line. Major Swinton went to the piquets, and asked them why they did not move on? On his return to his regiment he found that numbers of his officers and men had fallen. He immediately moved forward. At this period the cannonade was truly tremendous. A milk-hedge in their front, which they had to

pass to come at the enemy's guns, threw them into a little confusion; but they still pushed forward and had taken possession of many of their guns, when the second line, which opened on them, obliged them to retire from what they had so dearly purchased. The numbers of the 74th regiment remaining at this period were small...[91]

Waiting anxiously in the ranks of the 19th Light Dragoons, Thomas Swarbrook had a close view of the effects of enemy musketry and round and grape shot.

> The Right Brigade charged but was forced to retreat for they were nearly all killed or wounded. The brave 74th Regiment displayed their bravery to the last moment. For the Regiment had only 63 men left....The enemy then charged our infantry on their retreat and advancing in front of their own [artillery] Park gave no quarter to any of our wounded then only cutting and shooting them as they came up with them.[92]

Almost all the officers were killed or wounded and the remnant of the pickets and 74th made an improvised square under constant attack from Maratha cavalry and some of Pohlmann's infantry battalions near to Assaye.

Wellesley would have preferred to hold back his own cavalry until later in the battle to 'cut up' a defeated enemy.[93] Now, faced with the imminent destruction of the 74th and the pickets, he had little choice but to order Maxwell to charge and disperse the rampant Maratha horsemen and infantry. The 19th Light Dragoons and 4th and 5th Madras Native Cavalry were soon in the maelstrom, as is well related by Swarbrook in exciting but ungrammatical prose.

> Our brave general [Wellesley] made up saying now Maxwell you must make the best of your cavalry or we shall be done. Our gallant commander of the Cavalry then gave the word 19th spare nobody – 3 cheers – on the 3rd cheer we dashed forwards with our brave general with us exclaiming death and victory riding over our poor wounded men as they lay bleeding with their wounds. We cut our Roads [?] to their guns and took 100 pieces and killed their French general...[94]

The sight of British cavalry in action enervated the watching infantry to the south, Blakiston hearing a 'shout of triumph' from the whole line. The charge was 'like a torrent that had burst its banks'.[95] The British horse was larger and better disciplined than their adversaries and they soon saw off the Maratha cavalry, which joined its infantry and artillery in flight across the Juah River. Inflicting heavy casualties, the exultant cavalrymen crossed the river and, in a common scenario for the British army of the period, were soon in danger of losing their own cohesion. Fortunately, Maxwell succeeded in re-forming his charges who, having successfully retrieved the situation around Assaye, splashed their way back across the Juah to the south bank.[96]

With the right flank apparently secured, Wellesley turned his attention to the centre of the field where the troops were caught in crossfire. Retreating Maratha infantry had paused to reopen musketry fire and, as related by Campbell, Maratha artillerymen left for dead during the first infantry advance had sprung to life and turned their guns on the backs of the British infantry. The latter event caused the men much 'annoyance' and Wellesley quickly took control, ordering the four re-formed Madras native infantry battalions to observe the large body of Maratha irregular cavalry on their left flank.[97] The remaining two sepoy units were to oppose the resisting Maratha infantry and the 78th were to retake the re-manned Maratha guns, on this occasion from the west. He then personally led back the 7th Madras Native Cavalry, the only fresh cavalry regiment, in preparation for their own attack on the Maratha gunners, whose spears and half-pikes proved to be little protection against a combined British infantry and cavalry assault. In Captain Frazer's words, 'the fellows that had got round to them [guns] were soon obliged to forego the fancied recovery they had made thus for *our* own attack was successful'.[98] Wellesley had his horse, Diomed, killed under him, but was soon remounted on his third horse of the day and issuing orders to the 7th Madras Native Cavalry to protect the line of the recaptured guns.[99]

Having safeguarded his rear, the British general was now able to re-form his infantry into a single line and march them northwards to attack the Maratha fall-back position along the Juah. The plan was for this infantry assault to coincide with a second Maxwell-led cavalry charge, this time on the left flank of Pohlmann's line. The Maratha infantry was strongly placed and at least three of the battalions had not previously been engaged. However, compared with at the outset of the battle, Pohlmann's artillery arm was depleted, with perhaps as few as fifteen cannon.[100]

Maxwell had rallied 600 of his cavalrymen and he formed up with the 19th Light Dragoons in the centre and the 4th and 5th Madras Native Cavalry on the flanks. His problem was that he was attacking the enemy line obliquely, at an angle of 45 rather than 90 degrees. This presented an easy target, as is related by Blakiston, who had opportunistically joined the charge;

> seizing a sword which the General's horsekeeper had picked up on the field, I fell in among the files of the 19th dragoons. We were not long in coming up with the enemy, who, having formed with their left to the Jouah, steadily awaited our approach. The charge was sounded: we advanced with rapidity, amidst a shower of musquetry and grape,

which latter I could actually hear rattling among our ranks, and had already got almost within the bayonets of the enemy, who still gallantly stood their ground, when, instead of dashing among their ranks, I suddenly found my horse swept round, as it were by an eddy torrent. Away we galloped, right shoulders forward, along the whole of the enemy's line, receiving their fire as we passed...

Blakiston later describes the British cavalrymen 'glancing' off the Maratha infantry line. Maxwell was killed by canister and the effort was ended by a trumpet call, all 'in complete disorder, dragoons and native cavalry pell-mell'.[101]

The failure of the second British cavalry charge of the battle was not to much delay the victory. Wellesley placed himself to the right of the 78th Foot and led forward the British line in determined fashion. Without waiting for the anticipated impact, the Maratha infantry melted away, some directly north across the river and others to the west. Whether this followed an order to retreat given by Pohlmann, or was a collapse of Maratha morale, is uncertain.[102] It was an unequivocal retreat but not necessarily a rout; Blakiston describes the Maratha troops moving off in 'tolerable order'.[103] The only potential for further resistance was in Assaye itself, but the village was soon evacuated, Bhonsle's infantry following Sindia's men. Campbell states that the action was not over until near six o'clock.

It was unfortunate that the cavalry were obliged to be introduced into the action as it rendered them unfit for pursuing the enemy... We were all greatly fatigued, having marched by the perambulator that day twenty-four miles to the first nullah.[104]

A Maratha chronicle describes Sindia's army as being unable to withstand the 'incessant fire of the English'. His soldiers were 'scattered like the stars of the constellation Bear and their formation was broken up'.[105] The magnitude of Maratha losses in the battle is uncertain. Most historians follow Wellesley, whose correspondence states 1,200 killed in the action and perhaps four times that number wounded. He believed that many had deserted. The Marathas lost around 100 cannon.[106] The British casualty numbers are discrepant in different sources, but their losses were undoubtedly very heavy for a British-led force fighting in India. One oft-quoted return suggests a total of 1,584 men: 428 killed, 1,138 wounded and eighteen missing. This was between a quarter and a third of the troops engaged in the fighting. As the wounds were largely inflicted by artillery, many of them were severe. The 74th Regiment had been terribly mauled, losing eleven officers and 113 men killed, and six officers and 271 men wounded. The Madras native infantry to the right of the British line and the 19th Light Dragoons had also paid a considerable price.[107]

The exhausted British army spent the night on the ghastly field. Regimental parties were sent out to collect the wounded and a field hospital was established at Ajanta.[108] On learning of the victory, the Governor-General heaped praise on his brother. However, he felt obliged to mention the heavy cost in human life.

> Your battle of the 23rd (of which I have seen plans) is equal in skill and fortitude to any of which the account exists in history. Your loss certainly was dreadful (if not exaggerated to me) – the result must I think reduce the enemy either to peace, or to the condition of mere freebooters; accompanied as your success is by such a crowd of victories [an allusion to Lake's actions in Hindustan], as, I believe, never before were condensed in so small a space of time. You may be assured, that your reputation is of the first lustre and magnitude; and splendid, matchless, as was your victory of the 23rd, it was not more than was expected of you…[109]

Contemporary and modern historians have picked over the details of Assaye, distributing praise and blame. Reasons given for the Marathas losing the battle include their misjudgement of their enemy's intentions, the troops' poor morale, and feeble leadership. Their failure to anticipate Wellesley's impulsive attack meant that they fought the entire battle on the back foot, surrendering any initiative. They were so taken by surprise that some of the bullocks of the artillery team had been put out to graze. Maratha sources suggest that Sindia's whole army was 'unprepared', his officers of doubtful loyalty and his men unpaid and hungry.[110] The Maratha princes perhaps mismanaged their forces. The four battalions under Colonel Saleur were left guarding the baggage; an unnecessary weakening of combat strength when the enemy had insufficient cavalry to threaten the Maratha camp.[111] The failure to occupy the ford across the Kaitna was an elementary tactical mistake. Sindia is credited with a display of bravery, personally leading a cavalry charge, but he was an inexperienced leader and his ally, Bhonsle, left the field early in the action.[112]

Contemporary British commentators are especially critical of the Maratha cavalry. Campbell is typical.

> I can assure you, till our troops got orders to advance, the fate of the day remained doubtful; and if the numerous cavalry of the enemy had done their duty, I hardly think it possible that we could have succeeded.[113]

Elphinstone describes them as 'behaving very ill', often threatening but only charging once to cut up the 74th.[114] Fortescue agrees that this was a factor in the Maratha defeat but, as is argued cogently by Cooper, this was unsurprising.

The *pindaris* were never intended for formal combat; their role was to harass convoys and threaten lines of communication. By carefully guarding their baggage the British had neutralised them.[115]

Wellesley has not escaped censure for his role in the Assaye campaign. Much of the adverse comment relates to his decisions to first divide his forces before the battle and then to risk his own army in what might be interpreted to be an opportunistic and unplanned attack. Some of this criticism was contemporary. Army veteran Thomas Munro wrote to the General questioning his decision to split from Stevenson and chiding him for the scale of the losses; 'I hope you will not have occasion to purchase any more victories at so high a price.'[116] East India Company official Edward Strachey, writing in his letter book in early October, opined that Wellesley's attack was 'hazardous', the possibility of defeat making it 'extremely rash and injudicious.'[117] Historians including James Mill and John Fortescue have made similar judgements and, in more recent years, Wellesley's conduct at Assaye has again been questioned.[118] Enid Fuhr accuses him of exaggerating the resistance of the Maratha infantry and of mishandling his opening attack to gain a 'pyrrhic' victory.[119] Huw Davies agrees that 'certain elements of the battle had been botched', intelligence misread and orders poorly conveyed.[120] Edward Ingram dismisses the British tactics as being 'primitive' compared to those of their opponents.[121]

There is, of course, another side to this well-worn coin. Even Wellesley's keenest detractors allow that his leadership carried the day. Munro doubted the decision to fight, but he thought that the conduct of the battle was faultless.[122] Strachey believed that only Wellesley would have attempted it and that 'no man in India but himself could have executed it'.[123] In his history of the Indian Army, Philip Mason describes Assaye as a 'general's battle' where Wellesley displayed 'courage, resolution and dash'.[124] Wellington's biographer, Rory Muir, makes an eloquent case for Assaye being his young subject's first great victory, comparable to Napoleon's successes at Marengo or Jena. The British general had seized the initiative and formulated an excellent plan. The execution was imperfect, but this was true of almost all battles and Wellesley could not be everywhere at once.[125] As P.E. Roberts notes, he had fulfilled his duty to defeat the enemy and had done it 'swiftly, brilliantly and completely'.[126] Sindia's army had been dispersed and demoralised and much of his artillery was in British hands.

No historian has questioned Wellesley's bravery on the field. That he led from the front is well documented in a number of memoirs. Elphinstone, who had only known the commander for six weeks, was impressed.

> The General will doubtless get great credit for this; I am sure he
> deserves it... he exposed himself on all occasions and behaved with
> perfect indifference in the hottest fire...[127]

Campbell also saw Wellesley in the thick of the action: 'No man could have shown a better example to the troops than he did… I never saw a man so cool and collected as he was the whole time'.[128]

After the battle, Wellesley was physically and emotionally exhausted. For much of the following night, he sat on the ground with his head bent down between his knees, talking to no one. He was surrounded by dead and wounded officers, many of whom were his friends.[129] His correspondence of the time reveals a man who believed that he had underestimated his enemy, particularly the artillery and the French-trained regular infantry who were the main protagonists in 'furious' fighting.

> Sciandiah's French infantry were far better than Tippoo's, his artil-
> lery excellent, and his ordnance so good, and so well equipped that
> it answers for our own service…[130]

He was mortified by the human cost of his victory, writing to Stevenson on 12 October that, 'I should not like to see again such a loss as I sustained on the 23rd Sept., even if attended by such a gain'.[131] His instructions to his subordinate are suddenly more cautious; 'I have only to warn you against having any thing to do with them if you should find them very strong in guns'.[132] Elsewhere, Stevenson is told not to attack the enemy in an entrenched position, 'because they always take up such as are confoundedly strong and difficult of access…'.[133]

Wellesley was slowly coming to terms with the magnitude of the risk he had taken. It was arguably his greatest ever gamble. He was fully aware of the disastrous consequences that would have followed defeat at Assaye. He raised the subject in later conversation with Elphinstone.

> He said one morning that 'so-and-so would have happened if we
> had been beat, and then I should just have made a gallows of my
> ridge-pole and hanged myself'.[134]

Chapter 6

Marching to Victory: War in the Deccan 1803; Argaum and Gawilghur

After the defeat of Sindia, Wellesley targeted the homelands of Bhonsle, the Maratha prince whom he seems to have most disliked. The victor of Assaye remained unsettled. Supplies and money were in short supply, he was constantly troubled by the squabbling between soldiers and administrators in Gujarat, and his allies, the Nizam and Peshwa, were unreliable; 'deplorably weak on every point'.[1] He also complained of the 'total want of defence in this country', his bullock trains under threat and the local dignitaries conspiring with his enemies. Unless matters improved, particularly with respect to the Nizam's government, he protested that he would be limited to defensive operations. Despite the apparent pessimism of his correspondence, Wellesley was determined to take Gawilghur, Bhonsle's great mountain fortress in Berar.[2]

On their part, the Maratha princes had a number of military options open to them after the significant reverse at Assaye. They might risk a second direct confrontation, move south to threaten the Nizam's territories, or intercept British supply lines from Surat to the west. Between them they still had significant numbers of infantry and tens of thousands of horsemen at their disposal. Some artillery had been retrieved from the battlefield.[3] Once again, they failed either to formulate a decisive plan of campaign or even to agree. In early October, Wellesley, debilitated by a fever, was encouraged by the reports of his *harkarrahs*.

> The enemy appear to be in the utmost distress and confusion and not to know what step to take. It is said that they have quarrelled and that Scindiah has gone by one road and Ragojee [Bhonsle] by another, both towards Berar. Nothing can be more fortunate than this if it be true.[4]

Immediately after Assaye, the British commander kept his own and Stevenson's forces separated in a period of manoeuvring and acquisition. Wellesley initially made for Ajanta on 30 September but then moved south-westwards to protect Poona before returning to Ajanta on 8 October. Stevenson's men were fresher and they had pursued Sindia towards Ajanta within thirty-six hours of the battle. They captured Burhampoor on the 16th. Wellesley still feared a Maratha raid in the south. By the 11th, he was halfway to Aurangabad when he received the gratifying news of the discord in the enemy camp. Sindia was thought to have retired westwards, possibly with a view to attacking the territories of the Peshwa and Nizam, while Bhonsle was approaching Burhampoor, although of little threat to Stevenson.[5]

Wellesley needed a supply base to the north – something similar to Ahmednuggar – and he ordered Stevenson to capture Asseerghur. This fortress was the last of Sindia's strongholds in the area and its fall would give the British dominance in the corridor between the Deccan and North India.[6] Stevenson, who was struggling with illness, was doubtful of the feasibility of a direct attack and his siege train was inadequate.[7] As is clear from Wellesley's account of the episode to the Governor-General, the morale of the garrison was poor and there was a deal to be done.

> On the 19th [October] all the preparations were made for carrying on the siege; and 2 batteries were ready to open at two o'clock in the afternoon of the 20th; one to breach the upper wall, and another, of 4 brass 12-pounders, to destroy the defences of the lower wall. On the 18th Col. Stevenson had sent a flag of truce to the killadar to summon him to surrender the fort, to which message he did not receive a decided answer. The communication was continued; but Col. Stevenson did not relax his operations against the fort, as there was reason to believe that the negotiation was carried on only to give time to Dowlut Rao Scindiah to come to its relief. Before opening his batteries, Col. Stevenson apprised the killadar of the terms on which he should surrender the fort; which were, that the garrison should march out with their private property, and be allowed to go where they might think proper, and that their arrears should be paid to the amount of 20,000 rupees. After the batteries had opened about an hour, a white flag was shown from the walls of the fort...[8]

The fort was found to contain a considerable amount of treasure, necessitating the appointment of four prize fund managers. Wellesley instructed that a garrison of 800 men and well stocked granaries be established in the town.[9]

Stevenson had achieved his immediate objective and his role in the combined operation was now to observe Sindia's movements and to prepare for the siege of Gawilghur. Wellesley continued to move in the country to the south and by 25 October, four days after the fall of Asseerghur, he was back at Ajanta.

> Since the battle of Assaye I have been like a man who fights with one hand and defends himself with the other. With Colonel Stevenson's

corps I have acted offensively, and have taken Asseerghur; and with
my own, I have covered his operations, and defended the territories
of the Nizam and the Peshwa. In doing this, I have made some terrible marches…[10]

Achieving thirty miles a day, Wellesley reached Chicoli on 10 November.
Sindia, no doubt discouraged by the incoming news of General Lake's triumph
at Delhi, now made tentative overtures for a suspension of hostilities by sending a *vakil* to the British camp. Wellesley, who was to justify the arrangement
in a long letter to the Governor-General, sensed an opportunity to divide the
Maratha chiefs. The armistice would not apply to Bhonsle: 'It is impossible
that the Rajah of Berar can ever hereafter have any confidence in Scindiah,
and it may be considered that the confederacy is dissolved.'[11] Indeed, Wellesley
believed the agreement 'so favourable to us and so little so for Scindiah' that
he doubted his enemy ratifying it.[12] In essence, this is what happened, Sindia
quickly reneging on his commitment to withdraw to the east of Ellichpoor
by remaining in the field and by drawing his cavalry near to a large force of
Bhonsle's regular infantry. Wellesley had continued to move north and on the
morning of 29 October his column was marching to make a rendezvous with
Stevenson at the village of Paterly, 50 miles southwest of Gawilghur.

Bhonsle sent a messenger to inform Wellesley of the proximity of the
Maratha army, only a few miles to the north at Argaum (see map 7).[13] According
to Welsh, Wellesley did not stop to receive the *vakil*, but conversed with him.

> He told the General that his master's army was encamped at
> Putheilee, about ten miles in our front, and entreated him to halt
> short of that place, which the General refused. He then asked seri-
> ously, 'Whether, if he came up with their army, he would attack
> them?' to which he replied, 'Most undoubtedly'…[14]

A cloud of dust to the left of Wellesley's left flank was indicative of the
nearness of Stevenson's detachment and the entire British force was soon
encamped around Paterly. There was no expectation of an imminent battle, but when Wellesley climbed an old tower in the village he could see a
'confused mass' of men about two miles beyond the neighbouring village
of Sirsoni; he presumed this to be the combined armies of Bhonsle and Sindia. Perhaps the close scrape at Assaye was still much in his mind, as his
first instinct was to hold off and preserve his men. However, events quickly
prompted him to more characteristic action.

> The troops had made a great distance on a very hot day, and I there-
> fore did not think it proper to pursue them; but, shortly after our

arrival here [Paterly], bodies of horse appeared in our front, with which the Mysore cavalry skirmished during a part of the day; and when I went out to push forward the piquets of the infantry to support the Mysore cavalry, and to take up the ground of our encampment, I could perceive distinctly a long line of infantry, cavalry, and artillery, regularly drawn up on the plains of Argaum, immediately in front of that village, and about 6 miles from this place, at which I intended to encamp. Although late in the day, I immediately determined to attack this army.[15]

Blakiston believed the Maratha show of force to be 'a piece of braggadocio which the General could not stand...'[16] Wellesley marched on in a single column, his cavalry leading. It was three o'clock in the afternoon. The troops, deprived of their partly cooked dinners, moved through fields of high grain and for the first few miles up to the village of Sirsoni little could be seen.[17]

The exact strength of Wellesley's army at Argaum is unclear. Most historians do not quote a figure and others give differing estimates; we might accept Fortescue's suggestion that the entire British force numbered 'from ten to eleven thousand men'.[18] They faced a typically diverse Maratha foe. Bhonsle's infantry, under the command of his brother, Munnoo Bappoo, were supported by his own cavalry and artillery and Sindia's horsemen. The regular infantry was perhaps 10,000 strong and whole host probably consisted of 30–40,000 men.[19] Brigadier K.G. Pitre, whose erratic account of the war includes an unusual number of Maratha sources, quotes a total Maratha strength of 30–35,000 troops. He asserts that Maratha records show that neither Sindia nor Bhonsle were on the battlefield and that there was little unity of command.[20]

As Wellesley's men entered Sirsoni they could suddenly see the Maratha army across the open plain which had replaced the cultivated fields (see map 9). The village was the only feasible entry to the plain and the Marathas were quick to train their artillery, almost fifty guns, on the emerging British battalions which were attempting to deploy in line. This induced panic, particularly in two EIC units. The sepoys had fresh memories of the destruction wreaked by the Maratha guns at Assaye and they ran and took refuge behind the village.[21] Blakiston was deeply impressed by Wellesley's innovative reaction to the crisis.

The General, who was then close to the spot under a tree giving orders to the brigadiers, perceiving what had happened, immediately stepped out in front, hoping by his presence to restore the confidence of the troops; but, seeing that this did not produce the desired effect, he mounted his horse, and rode up to the retreating battalions; when, instead of losing his temper, upbraiding them, and endeavouring to force them back to the spot from which they had

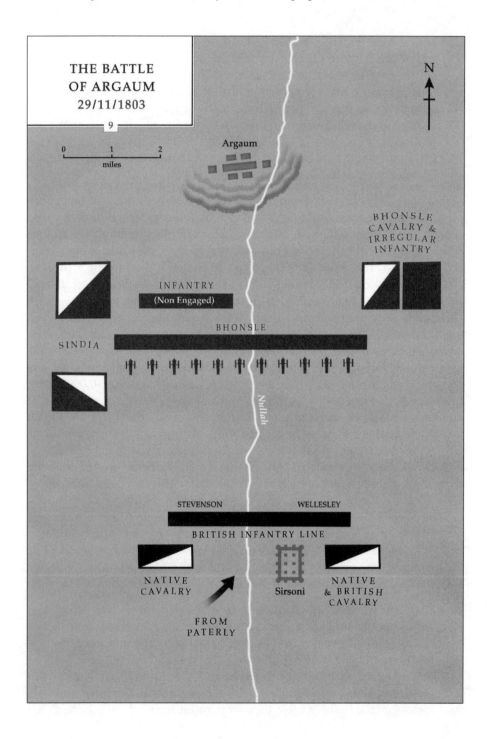

THE BATTLE
OF ARGAUM
29/11/1803

9

0   1   2
miles

N

Argaum

BHONSLE
CAVALRY &
IRREGULAR
INFANTRY

INFANTRY
(Non Engaged)

BHONSLE

SINDIA

Nullah

STEVENSON   WELLESLEY

BRITISH INFANTRY LINE

NATIVE
CAVALRY

Sirsoni

NATIVE
& BRITISH
CAVALRY

FROM
PATERLY

fled, as most people would have done, he quietly ordered the officers to lead their men under cover of the village, and then to rally and get them in order as quickly as possible. This being done, he put the column again in motion, and leading these very same runaways round the other side of the village, formed them on the very spot he originally intended them to occupy, the remainder of the column following, and prolonging the line to the right... As fast as each battalion came into line, the General ordered the men to lie down...

Blakiston, whose memoirs were first published in 1829, believed the episode to be an early sign of the 'genius' of Wellesley.[22]

British guns were brought into action on each side of the village as the troops were deploying, but they were a poor match for the enemy artillery. Wellesley's order that his men lie down was partly designed to protect them from enemy fire, but also to discourage them from any further flight to the rear.[23] The single infantry line was drawn up from left to right as follows: the six EIC native battalions of Stevenson's force; the Scotch Brigade; four EIC native battalions of Wellesley's army; the 74th Regiment; the 78th Regiment; then four further EIC native battalions and the advanced guard or piquets.[24] Stevenson remained debilitated by illness and he led his men from a *howdah* on the back of an elephant.[25]

The Maratha infantry had formed a considerable line, 5,000 men under Beni Singh in the centre and as many as 2,000 Arab troops on Bhonsle's flank. The ethnicity of many of these men is uncertain. Various authors describe the different factions as Arabs, Persians, Ghosseins and Rajputs. There was a smaller body of foot to the rear and fifty pieces of artillery. Sindia's cavalry, light troops and *pindaris* were divided into two large groups to the right of the infantry line and Bhonsle's horsemen were formed on the left.[26] This was not the strongest army that Wellesley would ever face, but it must have had a formidable appearance, the whole mass of men extending for five miles in front of the gardens and enclosures of Argaum.[27]

By half past four, the Maratha artillery fire had become intolerable and the British advance was ordered.[28] Stevenson's force had just formed up on the left of the line. As the infantry moved forward in good order, Wellesley personally rode over to the cavalry regiments and, putting himself at their head, he advanced to within 600 yards of the enemy.[29] Drummer Roderick Innes of the 78th recalls the cavalrymen shouting to the infantry, 'Now my lads, lather them, and we'll shave them'.[30] The British horsemen came under some mostly ineffective fire from a Maratha rocket corps mounted on camels before the British gallopers commenced their own fire with a plan to charge once sufficient damage had been inflicted.[31]

The infantry advance was uneven and the centre, composed of the two King's line regiments and the native battalions to their left, was soon in front of the rest of the line. The Maratha attempts to repel the British attack were ill coordinated. Welsh gives the best account of their futile counter thrusts.

> It was a splendid sight to see such a line advancing, as on a field day; but the pause when the enemy's guns ceased firing, and they advanced in front of them, was an awful one. The Arabs, a very imposing body [described by Blakiston as a thousand men of a Persian battalion wielding swords], singled out our two European regiments; and when we arrived within about sixty yards, after a round of grape, which knocked down ten of our men [3rd Madras Native Infantry], and about as many in each of the European regiments, they advanced and charged us, with tremendous shouts. Our three corps were at this time considerably in front of the rest of the line, and a struggle ensued, in which we killed and wounded about six hundred of these Arabs, and our corps alone took eight standards. While this was acting, nearly in the centre, I observed Benee Syng's Ghosains, dressed like beef-eaters, bearing down to turn our flank; but the Arabs once routed, and the rest of our line coming up, there was little more to do, and it was soon a perfect rout. The enemy's cavalry made two feeble attempts to charge our two flank corps, under Captains Maitland and Vernon, but were repulsed by steady fire from each.[32]

The whole Maratha army now melted way in disorder. According to Innes; 'No sooner had the rout began than our cavalry thundered down on the flying wretches, pursuing and slaying them as long as the light enabled them to see their victims and aim the stroke'.[33] The pursuit continued for several miles. Many elephants and camels and much enemy baggage was captured. Mughal and Mysore cavalry joined in and, according to Wellesley, inflicted 'great misery' on the enemy.[34] Nightfall saved the defeated army from annihilation, but their losses in men and equipment had been heavy. Wellesley makes no estimate of enemy casualties in his dispatch. Pitre suggests close to 5,000 Maratha losses.[35] Mountstuart Elphinstone, walking on the field, saw the ground where the 74th and 78th charged covered with enemy dead.

> They are all Mussulmans, dressed in blue. They have long beards and fine countenances. There are many old men among them.

Where the British cavalry had attacked, he saw enemy dead with horrific wounds including decapitation.[36] Thirty eight pieces of cannon and large amounts of ammunition were captured.[37]

In contrast, the British losses were relatively small, reflecting the fragile nature of the Maratha forces. The official return lists forty-six men killed, 308 wounded, and seven missing.[38] No European officer was killed but the losses were disproportionally greater in the British line regiments, the 74th losing fifty-two men, the 78th, forty-seven and the Scotch Brigade, forty-one.[39] As was the case at Assaye, many of the wounds suffered by the British were severe; Welsh acknowledges that few of his comrades were killed on the field but he adds with some understatement that 'cannon-shot wounds are no joke in general'.[40]

Wellesley had achieved his objective of effectively destroying Bhonsle's infantry arm. Although overshadowed by Assaye, Argaum further demonstrated his considerable talents. He had shown confidence in himself and his fatigued troops in making the attack, coolness in rallying his men, and skill in manoeuvring his infantry and artillery on the ground. The Marathas can be criticised for poor leadership and tactical naivety. Their cavalry were again mostly passive observers, the transient opportunity to exploit the British embarrassment in Sirsoni squandered. However, the major cause of their failure at Argaum was the poor quality of the troops. The Maratha artillery was destructive, but Bhonsle's legions were not of the calibre of Sindia's trained infantry. Blakiston expressed astonishment that Bhonsle had had the temerity to seek a battle.[41]

The campaign in the Deccan was now entering its final phase. Wellesley was able to turn his attention to his final objective, Bhonsle's fortress at Gawilghur, where some of his surviving infantry had taken refuge. Its reduction was necessary to complete the neutralisation of Bhonsle's military capacity and to cement British control in the region. Wellesley was determined to waste no time.[42] On the day after the battle, Stevenson, still very ill, marched in pursuit of the enemy. Wellesley moved off a day later and the two divisions met at Ellichpoor on 5 December where they rested for 48 hours. Having established a hospital in the dilapidated town, the united force made the final 32-mile advance to the neighbourhood of Gawilghur. Stevenson's force, now commanded by Colonel John Haliburton, moved round to the opposite side of the range of mountains as the fortress was thought to be more accessible from the south.[43]

When Roderick Innes first saw Gawilghur in the distance, he thought that anyone who tried to storm it would need wings.[44] The fort was vital in the control of a historic route between the Deccan and Hindustan and the nature of its construction and the impressive exploitation of the surrounding terrain reflected its strategic importance.[45] The immense works rose to 3,500 feet above sea level.[46] Wellesley's description of the place to the Marquess is detailed and it well sets the scene for the subsequent operations.

The fort of Gawilghur is situated in a range of mountains between the sources of the rivers Poorna and Taptee. It stands on a lofty mountain in this range, and consists of one complete inner fort, which fronts to the south, where the rock is most steep; and an outer fort, which covers the inner to the north-west and north. This outer fort has a third wall, which covers the approach to it from the north, by the village of Labada. All these walls are strongly built, and fortified by ramparts and towers. The communications with the fort are through 3 gates; one to the south with the inner fort; one to the north-west with the outer fort; and one to the fort with the third wall. The ascent to the first is very long and steep, and is practicable only for men; that to the second is by a road used for the common communications of the garrison with the countries to the southward; but the road passes round the west side of the fort, and is exposed for a great distance to its fire: it is so narrow as to make it impracticable to approach regularly by it, and the road is scarped on each side. This road also leads no farther than to the gate. The communication with the northern gate is direct from the village of Labada, and here the ground is level with that of the fort; but the road to Labada leads through the mountains for about 30 miles from Ellichpoor; and it was obvious that the difficulty and labor of moving ordnance and stores to Labada would be very great. However, after making inquiry at Ellichpoor, it appeared, both to Col. Stevenson and me, that this point of attack [i.e. the north] was, upon the whole, the most advantageous, and we accordingly adopted it.[47]

The normal garrison of Gawilghur was of 200–400 men under the command of a Rajput *killedar*. It had been strengthened by the infantry of Beny Singh, which had fled from Argaum, and by an influx of men from surrounding outposts. It transpired that the defenders were well armed with new muskets and bayonets. The permanent garrison had their families with them and there was also a sizeable resident civilian population.[48]

As Stevenson's force had been equipped for siege-work while at Asseerghur, it was entrusted with the principal attack from the north via Labada. Wellesley would cover Stevenson's operations with his own division and cavalry and would assist as much as possible by making attacks from the south and west.[49] Blakiston, who had reconnoitred the fort, believed that Wellesley's efforts would be little more than a diversion.[50] Despite the daunting nature of the fort itself, and the severe logistical challenge of even getting close to it, Wellesley was bullish, informing Lieutenant-Colonel Barry Close on 6 December that he hoped that Gawilghur would be taken 'with ease'.[51] On the following day,

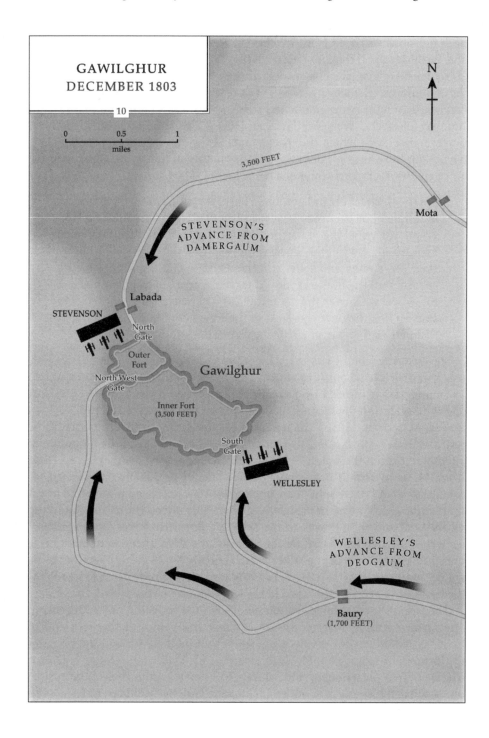

GAWILGHUR
DECEMBER 1803

N

10

0   0.5   1
miles

3,500 FEET

Mota

STEVENSON'S
ADVANCE FROM
DAMERGAUM

Labada

STEVENSON

North
Gate

Outer
Fort

Gawilghur

North West
Gate

Inner Fort
(3,500 FEET)

South
Gate

WELLESLEY

WELLESLEY'S
ADVANCE FROM
DEOGAUM

Baury
(1,700 FEET)

both divisions marched from Ellichpoor, Stevenson making for Damergaum and Wellesley for Deogaum (see map 10).[52]

To reach Labada, Stevenson's detachment marched the thirty miles through the mountains. The siege equipment and stores had to be dragged over the heights, through ravines and along roads previously dug by the Madras and Bombay pioneers. Wellesley later applauded the 'utmost cheerfulness and perseverance' with which the troops tackled the almost unprecedented challenge.[53] Elphinstone describes the arduous nature of this work, albeit with the air of an observer rather than of a participant.

> We then passed on and got into a narrow valley, where the road was infamous, but the place shady and pretty. Here we found an iron 12-pounder sticking. It had got into such a position, that if it moved forward the nave of the wheel came against a tree. The people, however, put stones under the wheel, so that when the sepoys gave a general pull the bullocks moved forward, and the elephant pushed, the wheel rose over the stones and the carriage leant to the other side, so that the nave was clear of the tree. I could not have thought that getting a gun over a stone was so interesting.[54]

Stevenson reached Labada on the 12th and, on the same night, two batteries were erected against the north face of the fort. The first, formed of two 18-pounders and three 12-pounders, was designed to breach the outer fort and third wall, and the second, made up of two 12-pounders and two 5½-inch howitzers, was to destroy the defences on the point of attack. At the same time, Wellesley constructed a battery of four 12-pounders on the mountain to attempt to breach the wall near the south gate, or at least distract the garrison from the main assault in the north. The General personally encouraged his exhausted men but, despite their great exertions, it proved impossible to get up the iron guns.[55] The four brass guns had little effect, the shot rebounding off the wall and rolling back to the muzzles. Fortunately, Stevenson's batteries were more effectual and, by the night of the 14th, there were practicable breaches in the wall of the outer fort.[56] During these siege operations, the enemy maintained artillery fire, but this was more annoying than deadly as the besiegers were well sheltered in the surrounding terrain.[57]

The assault was planned for ten o'clock on the morning of 15 December. The main storming party consisted of flank companies of the 94th and of native corps in Stevenson's division, supported by the 94th and the brigades of Lieutenant-Colonel John Haliburton and Lieutenant-Colonel Hector Maclean. Two diversionary attacks were to be made from the southern side; one against the south gate under Lieutenant-Colonel William Wallace, with five companies of the 78th and the 1/8th Madras Native Infantry, and the other against the northwest gate under Lieutenant-Colonel John Chalmers, with five companies of the 78th and the 1/10th Madras Native Infantry.[58]

Wellesley's own account of the fall of Gawilghur is very brief, but it seems that the operation was complicated by the uneven nature of the ground and incomplete intelligence of the fortifications. Stevenson's men were soon in the outer fort and the fleeing enemy were met by Chalmers's force entering at the north-western gate. The British had control of the outer fort, but they quickly realised, with consternation, that the citadel was situated on a hill on the far side of a deep gorge. Lieutenant-Colonel William Kenny of the 11th Madras Native Infantry found a track and he bravely led the men of his regiment across and over an intermediate wall. There was now a narrow road leading to the wall and gate of the main fort. Apparently inaccessible, this wall was eventually escaladed by the light company of the Scotch Brigade. Entering the stronghold, they opened the gate and admitted the storming party who routed the remaining defenders.[59]

Of the eyewitness accounts, Elphinstone's is the most explicit and is supportive of the above version of events. He joined the 94th Regiment as part of the main storming party.

> We drew our swords, stuck pistols in our belts or handkerchiefs tied round our middle, and passing in rear of the batteries, marched on to the breach. Colonel Kenny led the whole... Then followed the 94th Regiment. Our advance was silent, deliberate, and even solemn. Everybody expected the place to be well defended. As we got near, we saw a number of people running on the rampart, near the breach. Colonel Kenny said they were manning the works. I asked him if they were not flying? He said, 'No! no! They won't fly yet awhile.' We went and got close to the works, to a wide hedge, where Johnson [Captain John Johnson of the Bombay Engineers] had been during the night. I was amazed that they did not fire; our cannon fired over our heads. We got to the breach, where we halted, and let the forlorn hope, a sergeant's party, run up; then we followed, ran along, and dashed up the second breach and huzzaed.

Elphinstone continues his incomplete journal account in a letter to Edward Strachey;

> [we] leaped down into the place. Such of the enemy as stood, were put to the bayonet; but most of them ran off to the right, and down a narrow valley which led to a gate. Here they met Colonel Chalmers's coming on with half the 78th (he had been sent round by the General to attack this gate). The 94th pressed behind, firing from above,

and a terrible slaughter took place. After this, we endeavoured to push on, when to our astonishment we discovered that we had only gained a separate hill, and that the fort lay behind a deep valley, beyond which appeared a double wall and strong gates... the troops halted, and the officers endeavoured to form them... Colonel Kenny, almost alone, had run straight on to the gate where he was now perceived. The Europeans found the road down, and crowded after him. The first wall joined to a steep hill, and the Europeans began slowly and with difficulty to climb up one by one. Beyond the first wall was a narrow, rocky road, overtopped by a steep rock, and another wall and gate, over which those who climbed the first wall would have to go, which the steepness and height of the wall made impossible. While the Europeans were clambering over, the enemy kept up a fire from their works; in the meantime our people poured in at the breach, and covered the hill opposite to the enemy. They fired on the enemy, and the valley was filled with such a roar of musketry as can hardly be conceived. The sight cannot be described. At last our men got over, and opened the first gate. Scaling-ladders were brought, got up the hill, and applied to the second wall. The enemy fled from their works; we rushed over the wall, and the fort was ours. I forgot to mention that at the first breach all ran where they liked, without order.[60]

John Blakiston admits that the troops 'moderation after victory was not equal to their valour'. Plunder, rape and murder were fuelled by drink. In one incident, witnessed by the engineer, men of the Scotch Brigade invited concealed enemy troops to run from a house before callously shooting them 'like basket-hares'. When he tried to restrain soldiers who were robbing and abusing the inhabitants, he narrowly escaped with his own life.[61] In desperation, many of the defenders cast themselves over the ramparts, falling on to the rocks below. To compound this scene of horror, the clothes of the dead had caught fire from their matchlocks and powder. Several hundred corpses were ablaze and the smell was so disagreeable that European troops were ordered to leave the area. It was, Roderick Innes reflected, enough 'to melt even the most hard hearted man in the whole regiment'.[62]

Maratha losses were heavy; at least several thousand must have perished. Wellelsey simply states that 'vast numbers' were killed, particularly around the gates. A large amount of ordnance was captured; fifty-two guns, 2,000 muskets and a variety of local arms.[63] British losses were only fourteen killed and 112 wounded, the European losses (sixty-seven) slightly exceeding those of the sepoys (fifty-nine).[64] The relatively small scale of the casualties suggests that the defenders failed to fully exploit the strength of their mountain fortress.

While Wellesley's operations were in progress, the campaign against Bhonsle's territories in Cuttack had been brought to a successful conclusion. Due to the illness of Lieutenant-Colonel Campbell, the British force was placed under the command of Lieutenant-Colonel Harcourt of the 12th Regiment. He had close to 3,000 men; 500 European infantry (of the 22nd Foot and 102nd Foot (Madras European Regiment)), 2,200 native infantry (two battalions of Madras and one battalion of Bengal native infantry), a small detachment of Madras native cavalry, and Bengal and Madras artillery. The bulk of the troops left Ganjam on 8 September and occupied Juggernaut on the 18th. Subsequent operations were delayed more by flooding than by enemy opposition. The town of Cuttack was entered on 10 October and the adjoining fort of Barabutty was successfully stormed four days later. The province of 1,200,000 inhabitants now capitulated in a further disastrous setback to Bhonsle. Harcourt's losses had been minimal, only six men killed and forty-seven wounded.[65]

The fall of Gawilghur was the last battle of the Deccan campaign and Wellesley's last serious action in India. At the end of 1803, Sindia and Bhonsle were both weakened and demoralised. This was in large part due to the military defeat inflicted on Sindia by the army of General Gerard Lake. It is to the north and the fighting in Hindustan that we must now turn.

Chapter 7

A River of Blood: War in Hindustan 1803; Delhi and Laswari

At the end of July 1803, the Military Secretary James Armstrong wrote to the Marquess Wellesley informing him of the strength of British forces in Hindustan. In all there were 20,000 men, just over half under the personal command of General Gerard Lake and the remainder divided into smaller detachments in Bundelcund, Gohud and Tonk.[1] The coming campaign was to be spearheaded by the Commander-in-Chief's force and, on 7 August, Lake moved up the Ganges from his headquarters at Cawnpore to Kanoge. Here, in the luxurious ambience of the Indian camp, the army was reinforced such that there were 15,000 combatants. This total included nine regiments of cavalry and fourteen of infantry arranged into brigades as follows (see Appendix I):

Cavalry

1st Brigade (Lt Col Vandeleur): HM 8th Light Dragoons; 1st and 3rd Bengal Native Cavalry
2nd Brigade (Col St Leger): HM 27th Light Dragoons; 2nd and 6th Bengal Native Cavalry
3rd Brigade (Col Macan): HM 29th Light Dragoons; 4th Bengal Native Cavalry

Infantry

1st Brigade (Lt Col Monson): HM 76th Regiment; 1/4th and 2/4th Bengal Native Infantry; 4 companies 17th Bengal Native Infantry
2nd Brigade (Col Clarke): 2/8th; 2/9th; 1/12th; 6 companies 16th Bengal Native Infantry
3rd Brigade (Col Macdonald): 2/12th; 1/15th and 2/15th Bengal Native Infantry
4th Brigade (Lt Col Powell): 1/2nd and 2/2nd; 1/14th Bengal Native Infantry

Artillery

1 Brigade Horse Artillery (six guns)
12-pounders (four)
6-pounders (nine)
5½-inch howitzers (three)
Galloper guns with each regiment of cavalry (eighteen) and battalion
guns with each battalion of infantry (twenty-eight)

In addition to these fighting men there was, of course, the innumerable host of camp-followers and animals.[2]

Sindia's army was commanded by General Perron. Maratha headquarters were at Coel, fifty miles north of Agra. Calculation of the strength of Perron's force is complicated by its dispersion and the transit of reinforcements from the Deccan (see Chapter 2). Thorn appends a complex tabulation based upon the intelligence of a British officer recently in Sindia's service (Appendix VII). This suggests that Perron had a total of 40,000 regular infantry at his disposal, but only a minority of these were available for the immediate conflict with Lake.[3] Duff's estimate that Perron's Hindustan army amounted to 16–17,000 regular infantry and 15–20,000 horse, of which 4–5,000 were regular cavalry, is probably close to the truth.[4] Fortescue provides similar figures.[5]

The Governor-General's instructions to his Commander-in-Chief were explicit. The major military objectives for North India were the seizure of Sindia's territories between the Gunga and Tamuna rivers, the release of the Mughal Emperor from Maratha custody, the creation of alliances with the Rajputs and other states to the west of Delhi, and the control of Bundelcund.[6] Beyond this detail, the overwhelming priority was to destroy Perron's conventional forces. Lake and the Marquess had a sound working relationship which was not seriously tested by the latter's tendency to interfere in purely military matters. A memorandum written by Lake in the summer of 1803 is annotated in the margins by the Marquess rather as a teacher might mark homework. Both men were in full agreement as to the primary objective. They concurred that Perron's defeat would in all probability bring the campaign to a decisive conclusion. Lake was determined to move against his principal adversary as quickly as possible. Once Perron was overthrown and expelled from the Doab, the British could undertake the sieges of Agra and other key strongholds 'without inconvenience'.[7]

It should be noted that the British had already been involved in low-level conflict in the north. Only a very brief allusion needs to be made to the so-called 'mud war' fought against insurgents in the Doab in the winter months of 1802–3. This little remembered war, which derived its name from the local mud forts, reflected longstanding discontent in the region. The brutal

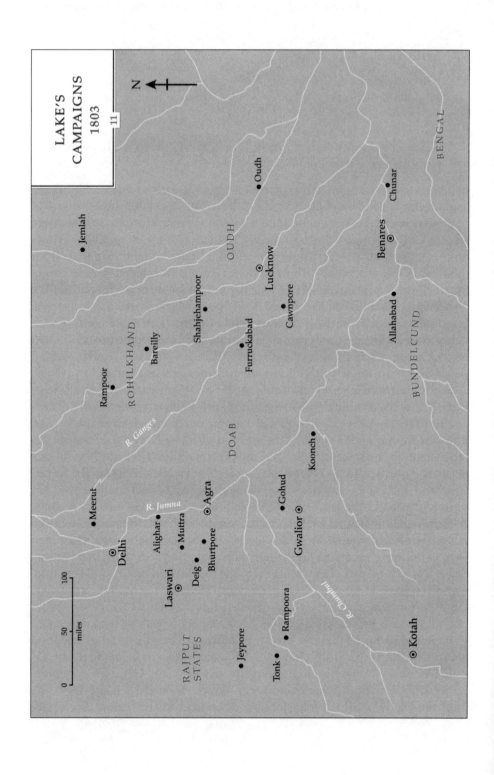

LAKE'S
CAMPAIGNS
1803

11

N

extermination of the enemy following a series of short sieges foreshadowed Lake's much more extensive operations of the Maratha War.[8]

On 26 August, Lake marched his forces into Maratha territory. Two days later he was camped within sight of the mosque in the town of Coel, where Perron was well posted with the men under his personal command. At four o'clock the next morning Lake left his baggage under the protection of sepoys and some artillery and set off with the intent of attacking Perron near to the fortress of Alighar (see map 11). John Pester, an ensign in the 2nd Bengal Native Infantry, describes the army's march in his journal. It moved in one column, the cavalry leading the line.[9] At around 7am the British came up with the enemy, who immediately struck their tents. The whole of their horse, amounting to about 20,000, of which a quarter was regular cavalry, drew up in a strong position on the plain. Their right extended to the fort of Alighar and their left was protected by the lie of the land and some villages. A huge morass, made even more impenetrable by recent monsoon rains, shielded their front (see map 12).[10]

Lake elected to attack the enemy's left flank, a plan which meant moving his cavalry in an extensive detour around the right side of the swamp. The Commander-in-Chief took personal command of his mounted troops and, having gained the necessary ground and driven in the Maratha skirmishers, he formed the cavalry from column of regiments into two lines and attacked, supported by four lines of infantry.[11] As the two opposing armies closed, the British could easily see the bright red uniforms of Perron's bodyguard.[12] Pester admits that the retaliation from enemy matchlocks was 'hot', particularly from a village to the British right which was soon cleared by a native battalion.[13] The British moved on, supported by the covering fire of the cavalry's gallopers, which also dispersed a threatening column of enemy cavalry. The advance was now inexorable, the Maratha foe forced to retreat, their cavalry abandoning the field in a cloud of dust and their remaining infantry funnelling back towards the fort.[14] Cornet George Isaac Call of the 27th Light Dragoons witnessed the denouement;

> we charged in line after them till within a few yards of Alighar but they got in time within the walls; and finding ourselves so near we marched off to the left by troops – the dust being by this time pretty well dispersed, the fort played on us and a spent 4-pounder killed the Dragoon's horse next to me. We now retired in a trot to get out of reach of their cannon shot. The fort then fired a few shots at our Infantry but without doing much mischief. His Excellency [Lake] was almost foremost and much enraged at the 50,000 chosen few flying having been threatened to be slaughtered by General Perron's body.[15]

Lake may well have been frustrated by his failure to force a more general action, but the driving of the Marathas from the field while suffering only a handful of casualties was a psychological blow at the start of the campaign. He believed that his day's work had had 'a most wonderful effect on the minds of the natives'. Perron's aura of invincibility had been punctured and six of his European officers came across to the British side.[16] Lake's men had marched for seven hours in extreme heat, the thermometer topping 100 degrees; soldiers quenched their thirst in muddy pools and some fainted.[17] The General now took possession of Coel, his army encamped to the north of the place. Perron, whose infantry barracks and mansion were in the town, had withdrawn to Agra leaving Colonel Pedron in command of Alighar.[18]

The fortress was formidable. Built on a rectangular plan, it had circular bastions. The rampart was covered by a *fausse-brai* with a wide *terreplain* and was surrounded by a ditch over 100 feet wide filled with ten feet of water. There were close to 100 guns of various calibres, 180 wall-pieces, and an abundant supply of ammunition.[19] Perron, safely off the scene, left instructions for his deputy. Pedron was to hold out to the last: 'Do your duty, and defend the fort while one stone remains upon another. Once more remember your nation. The eyes of millions are fixed upon you'.[20] There were rumours of dissension in the Maratha camp and Lake hoped to achieve his objectives by bribery. He was soon to be disappointed by the prevarication of the French commander and, not wanting to undertake a formal siege which would take at least a month, he reluctantly resolved to attempt a *coup de main*. The plan was to use artillery to blow the gates and allow the European elite troops to enter.[21]

The main gateway, the only means of crossing the ditch, was selected as the point of assault and a cross-fire against the outworks of the gate was commenced on the night of 3 September. The storming party was composed of four companies of HM 76th Regiment under Major William MacLeod, the 1/4th Bengal Native Infantry under Lieutenant-Colonel George Browne, and four companies of the 17th Bengal Native Infantry under Captain Robert Bagshaw. It would eventually be reinforced by the 2/4th Bengal Native Infantry. The daunting task of leadership was given to Lieutenant-Colonel William Monson, a man who was to have mixed fortunes in the war. He was assisted by a Mr Lucan, a British officer of Irish descent, who had recently defected from Sindia's service and who would act as a guide.[22]

The men left camp at 3am on the 4th, marching in a circular route to the gateway. They halted 400 yards from their objective. There was a transient hope that that they might exploit the presence of sixty or seventy Marathas 'smoaking under a tree' in front of the gateway, to create confusion and gain easy entry as the surprised enemy retreated through the open gate. Unfortunately, the men despatched from the 76th were too efficient, killing all the Marathas

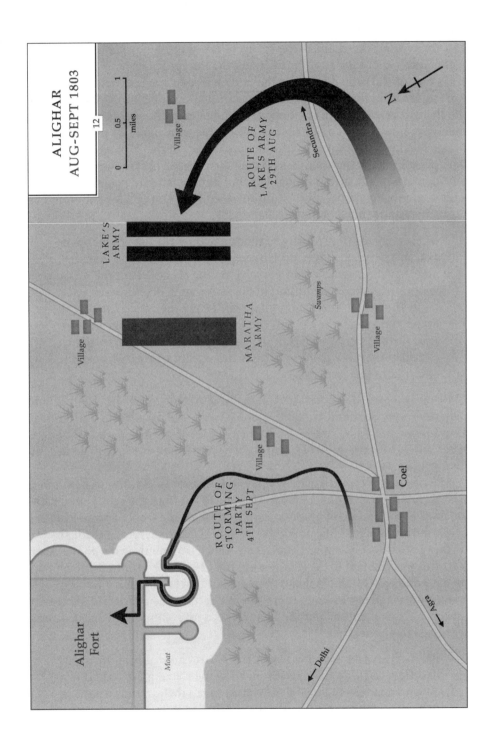

ALIGHAR
AUG-SEPT 1803

12

0   0.5   1
        miles

Village

ROUTE OF
LAKE'S ARMY
29TH AUG

Secundra

N

LAKE'S
ARMY

Village

MARATHA
ARMY

Swamps

Village

Village

Coel

ROUTE OF
STORMING
PARTY
4TH SEPT

Agra

Alighar
Fort

Moat

Delhi

128 Wellington and the British Army's Indian Campaigns 1798–1805

and thus losing the chance. The firing of the morning gun announced the commencement of the attack proper and the intrepid party were soon within 100 yards of the gate, displacing the enemy from a traverse before they had time to fire from three 6-pounders. Again, any hope of entering the fort with the flying garrison was disappointed, the targeted gate firmly shut. Monson's men were now receiving destructive fire from enemy batteries and outworks. Major MacLeod attempted to lead the grenadiers of the 76th up scaling ladders placed against the walls before they were forced back down by a row of pikemen. A 6-pounder was brought up, but its blast failed to penetrate the gate and, in increasing desperation, Monson called for a 12-pounder.[23] John Pester was at the centre of the bloody exchanges;

> the whole face of the fort was illuminated by the fire of their cannon and musketry. Our covering batteries opened at the same time, and their fire, as we could perceive by the slaughter on the walls, was well directed. In addition to the heavy guns which played upon us in the sortie, the enemy had also heavy mortars loaded with grape and canister shot, and the leading twelve-pounder of ours, was, in the hurry to carry it up to the gate, thrown into a trench [a collapsed mine gallery], which the enemy had made near the entrance of the sortie.[24]

By now, some defenders had actually climbed down the scaling ladders and were in hand-to-hand combat with the assailants. The crucial 12-pounder had to be dragged over the bodies of the killed and wounded. After around twenty minutes, and four or five rounds of fire, the gate was finally flung open.[25]

Monson had received a pike wound and officer casualties were mounting. His men charged along the circular road which led from the gate. Continually harassed by a cross-fire of musketry and grape from the loopholes and bastions of the surrounding fortifications, the troops successfully broke through two further gates before reaching a fourth gate, which communicated with the inner fort. This was resistant to the attentions of the 12-pounder painfully brought up by the wounded Captain William Shipton, but MacLeod found a way through a small door and led his men up to the ramparts.[26] The attack had gained an unstoppable momentum and the fighting became even more frenzied, as was witnessed by Cornet Call;

> the 'Gallant Heroes' now began their parts and rushing forwards like Tigresses who have been robbed of their young, brought down all who opposed them. A few escaped to tell their friends what was to be expected by resisting the 'British Indian Armies'…[27]

Thorn estimates that the Marathas lost 2,000 killed, the fort's ditch full of corpses.[28] Fortescue attributes the slaughter after the fall of Alighar to the enemy's 'refusal to surrender', but there were contemporary reservations.[29] Pester remonstrated with a soldier who was casually shooting men swimming in the ditch, while Lieutenant Charles Stuart of the 3rd Bengal Native Cavalry was critical of the widespread killing of unarmed men.[30] Call confirms that his dragoon regiment was ordered to 'cut up' those who were running away.[31]

The British had also suffered, albeit on a much smaller scale. Total casualties amounted to fifty-nine killed and 212 wounded of all ranks.[32] Lake had anticipated heavy losses, not least among his officer corps, of whom several were casualties. In his letter to the Marquess, written on the evening of the 4th, he honestly describes his mixed emotions.

> I feel happy at having gained the fort, which stood out for more than an hour. A more anxious time I never experienced… I have wrote more than I intended, and must beg you will pardon me for being so prolix, but really my mind is so much agitated from the loss of so many excellent men, that I hardly know what I do.[33]

Lake accepted the surrender from Pedron, a tired old man dressed in a green jacket and epaulettes who, in all likelihood, had been forced into the vigorous defence by the Maratha *sardar* Bali Rao.[34] Despite the significant losses, the capture of the fortress was a considerable achievement. The British had quickly acquired a logistical objective, thus potentially shortening the war. Arthur Wellesley believed Lake's capture of Alighar to be 'one of the most extraordinary feats that I have heard of in this country'.[35] A Maratha account describes the place falling 'in a twinkle of an eye'.[36] Many of the locals believed a violent earthquake on 1 September to have foreboded the disaster.[37]

Immediately after the capture of Alighar, Lake received news which served as a reminder that the British presence in North India was tenuous. A French mercenary in Sindia's service, Monsieur Fleury, had led 5,000 Maratha horsemen against the remote but apparently secure British outpost at Shikohabad on the frontier of Etauch. The post's commander, Lieutenant-Colonel Daniel Coningham, had five companies of 1/11th Bengal Native Infantry and one gun under his command. This brave garrison resisted the repeated Maratha cavalry charges from four in the morning until two in the afternoon, but they finally capitulated on the following day. Coningham undertook that his men would not serve against Sindia for the remainder of the war in return for safe passage and the retention of their personal weapons and gun. The cantonment was subsequently burnt and pillaged, although it should be acknowledged that, compared with the scenes of retribution at Alighar, Fleury's actions were restrained. Lake despatched Richard Macan's brigade of cavalry to chase the

Frenchman, but after forced marches as far as the village of Firozabad about twenty-four miles east of Agra he abandoned the pursuit.[38]

Having left a native battalion to garrison Alighar, Lake marched on Delhi on 7 September. On the same evening, he received a letter from Perron asking for permission to proceed with his family to Lucknow. The defection of Perron, whose intention was to leave India, deprived Sindia of his most skilled and influential mercenary leader, and it was a hammer blow to the Maratha cause.[39] No doubt delighted at this turn of events, Lake pushed on and took the abandoned fort at Khurja, an acquisition which further undermined Sindia's prestige and logistical power. By the 10th, the Grand Army was eighteen miles beyond Surajepoor. It was understood that Louis Bourquin, Perron's deputy, had assumed command of the Maratha forces and that he had crossed the River Jumna in the night.[40] John Pester was still assiduously keeping his journal.

> 10 September… Dined today with Dyer; at dinner I received a private note from Wemyss telling me that it was the opinion of all at headquarters that we should have an action certainly tomorrow or the next day. Scindiah's troops were said to be at this moment drawn up on the banks of the Jumnah, in order of battle, and ready to engage us. This position said to be a very strong one, supported by a numerous and formidable train of excellent artillery. We drank an extra bottle of claret upon this intelligence, and without much discussion or reflection on the fate of a battle enjoyed ourselves till near nine o'clock.[41]

The troops, much fatigued, reached their camp about six miles from Delhi at eleven o'clock the next day (11 September). Although expecting a battle, it seems that the British were unaware of the proximity of the enemy. According to Pester, the men were sitting in the shade of the trees drinking water: 'At this period we did not know that the enemy line was within a mile and a half of us, nor had they the smallest idea of our being within fifteen miles of them'.[42] As more Maratha forces appeared, the grand guard and advanced piquets turned out and Lake took his three regiments of cavalry to personally reconnoitre the enemy position. Bourquin was at the head of a force of sixteen battalions of regular infantry, 6,000 cavalry and a large train of ordnance. His total strength probably amounted to 19,000 combatants.[43] Lake's view was impeded by jungle, and his escort came under fire, but it was obvious that the Maratha entrenched position was strong. They were drawn up on high ground in front of the Jumna, each flank covered by a swamp. The infantry was in the front line with cavalry behind and the whole was protected by seventy guns (see map 13).[44]

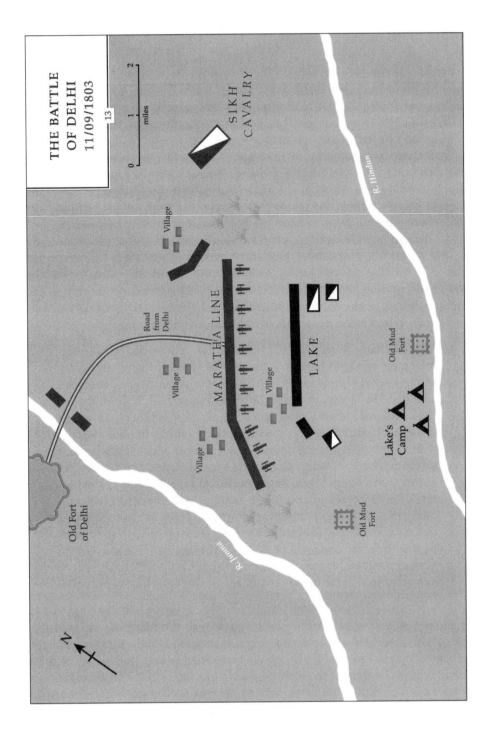

THE BATTLE
OF DELHI
11/09/1803

13

0   1   2
miles

SIKH
CAVALRY

R. Hindun

Village

Road
from
Delhi

MARATHA LINE

Village

Village

Village

Village

LAKE

Old Mud
Fort

Lake's
Camp

Old Mud
Fort

R. Jumna

Old Fort
of Delhi

N

The British had little alternative but to attack the enemy front. Allowing for the absence of detachments for other services, Lake had around 4,500 men available for the coming action. These were the 76th Regiment on the right and the following sepoy infantry battalions: 1/4th, 2/12th, 1 and 2/15th, 1 and 2/2nd and 1/14th Bengal Native Infantry. His cavalry force was made up of HM 27th Light Dragoons and the 2nd and 3rd Regiments of the Bengal native cavalry, and he had some supporting artillery.[45]

Lake had been taken by surprise and it was a full hour before the infantry came up to join his cavalry, which had advanced two miles to the front. Most traditional accounts of the battle suggest that the gradual retreat of the British cavalry, which was taking heavy casualties from enemy artillery, was a deliberate lure or feint to draw the Marathas out of their entrenchments.[46] Lake showed great leadership qualities and coolness at Delhi. He had already had a horse shot from under him and a cavalry officer gives him credit for his 'slow walking' of the cavalry retreat, giving his infantry time to join the fray and avoiding panic.[47] However, Cornet Call's convincing account of the opening phase of the battle suggests that the Commander-in-Chief's actions were improvised rather than part of a preconceived plan.

> We remained quietly till 11, when to our astonishment, we were informed by the Adjutant of the Day of Cavalry that a large body of the Enemy's horse was advancing towards our camp – The bugle sounded 'To Horse', the brigade consisting of HM 27th Dragoons, the 2 and 3rd Native Cavalry soon advanced upon them, on which, the enemy retired by degrees till we were within the full range of their guns which opened upon us most warmly and being kept up in salvos at length forced us to retreat a short distance where we halted in line – this caused their guns which had been hidden by the high grass, to be advanced and for an hour played on us so much that both men and horses were mown down like grass; our gallopers were of little use and the Tumbril of the 27th blew up early in the action; by this time, the [infantry of the] Right Wing had just reached the encampment and marched under General [Charles]Ware directly to our support, we, retiring towards them and drawing the enemy's guns from out of the hollows and long grass, nearer to ours.[48]

Believing their adversary to be in full retreat, the Marathas charged forward with their light artillery 'shouting and exulting as if the victory had been already secured'.[49] As the British horsemen wheeled away to both flanks, Sindia's men were shocked to see the British infantry in a single line with the remaining cavalry in a second about forty yards to the rear of the right wing. A party of the latter was detailed to deter some Sikh cavalry which threatened the British flank and rear. The left of the British infantry line was covered by the 1/2nd Bengal Native Infantry with four guns. With Lake personally leading the 76th on the right of the line the whole force moved forward. The battle remained in the balance as the troops were advancing into a maelstrom of Maratha round, grape and chain-shot.[50] In his later despatch, the Commander-in-Chief praised all his men; 'the steadiness and gallantry of the whole corps, both Europeans and natives, under a formidable fire of artillery, does them infinite honour'. Well led by their chief and officers and demonstrating exemplary bravery and discipline, the entire line advanced to within 100 yards of the enemy without taking their firelocks from their shoulders before firing a volley and charging with the bayonet.[51]

John Pester was, as usual, in the middle of the action, having his horse shot from under him and one of his pistols shattered by grape shot. He saw the enemy turn and run.[52] In a bloody *coup de grâce*, Lake ordered the victorious battalions to form column of companies, thereby allowing the cavalry to charge through the intervals to pursue the fugitives to the Jumna. While the cavalry were thus engaged to the front and right, the infantry, under Lake's supervision, wheeled to the left and chased the enemy in that direction among the ravines and broken ground.[53]

It was now a rout. Call says that an 'immense number' of Marathas were killed;

> [they] were dispersed, slaughtered and pursued many miles, at last drawn to the banks of the Jumna and, no resource left, they plunged in and endeavoured to swim across; our gallopers raked with grape some hundreds and many were drowned attempting to get across the rapid stream which represented a red river...[54]

According to Pester, the water 'boiled' with British grape.[55] At least some officers believed that the legitimate pursuit of a defeated foe had descended into a gratuitous massacre. Charles Stuart accuses Call's regiment, the 27th Light Dragoons, of unnecessary cruelty: 'whenever an unhappy wretch showed his head above the water a dozen pistols were levelled at it'. He describes the butchery of old men, children and camp followers. Stuart was with the baggage train and therefore his information was second-hand, obtained from his brother officers in the 3rd Bengal Native Cavalry who had apparently stood back from the worst of the excesses.[56]

The action ended at seven in the evening. Maratha losses are generally estimated to have been around 3,000, although Call makes an elaborate calculation based on regimental returns of enemies killed and arrives at a larger figure of 4,500.[57] As always, all these figures are at best approximate; Charles Stuart notes that much of the Maratha infantry had been 'dispersed' rather than killed.[58] British losses, inflicted mostly by artillery fire, were 485 killed, wounded and missing (197 Europeans and 288 natives).[59] Lake lists two British officers as having 'died of the sun' rather than in action, well demonstrating the harsh conditions in which the battle was fought.[60] Sixty-eight Maratha guns were captured.[61]

The battle of Delhi is sometimes compared with Assaye, fought only two weeks later. Lake manoeuvred little at Delhi. The enemy's well secured flanks and the limited size of his force meant that a turning movement was not feasible. Crucially, he was able to keep his cavalry intact, not afflicted by the error that hindered Wellesley's right at Assaye. Both generals had shown impressive leadership qualities on the field; the *sang froid* with which Lake gradually withdrew his exposed mounted troops might also be compared with Wellesley's rallying of his shaken native infantry at Argaum. From a Maratha perspective, there is evidence that several of their battalions were less than fully committed to the fight.[62] A contemporary Maratha account admits that Bourquin had been decisively defeated.[63]

After halting for three days, Lake crossed to the western side of the Jumna. Here he accepted the surrender of Bourquin and his French officers. Call describes their poor appearance; they spoke low French and were of 'mean extraction'.[64] Their troops had evacuated the city and fort of Delhi. Of greater strategic significance was Lake's subsequent entry into the city and meeting with Shah Alam, the elderly, blind and impotent Mughal emperor. Seated under a small tattered canopy, the Commander-in-Chief promised him British protection. The Governor-General was overjoyed at Lake's victory and pleased by the wider political consequences. The Mughal emperor, he wrote, 'has never been an important or dangerous instrument in the hands of the Marathas, but... [he] might have become a powerful aid to the cause of France under the direction of French agents.'[65]

Leaving Lieutenant-Colonel David Ochterlony in charge of the Delhi garrison, Lake marched for Agra on 24 September. He intended to use some of the captured Maratha ordnance for the siege of the city, a vital garrison and weapons production centre. While the guns and heavy stores were carried on boats down the Jumna, the army trudged along the banks. Their progress was disrupted by the constant harassment and looting of the Gujars. Pester comments that these brigands frequently mutilated or put to death the unfortunates in their grasp.[66] Mathura (or Muttra) was reached on 2 October. Lake was joined by the 8th and 29th Light Dragoons, two native regiments of cavalry, and three and a half native infantry battalions. The General must also have been heartened by the ratification of a formal alliance with the powerful Jat leader, the Rajah of Bhurtpore, and the defection of more of Sindia's French officers into his camp.[67] The latter, including Chevalier Dudrenec, were willing to give the British some approximate intelligence of the state and location of Sindia's forces. Alerted to the proximity of enemy battalions, Lake was reluctant to halt for too long in Mathura but, mindful of the need to maintain the soldiers' morale, he did allow some of his Hindu sepoys to make religious observance in the place. By the 4th, the army was encamped on the south side of Agra.[68]

Lake had previously written to the Marquess expressing the view that the city 'must fall upon our approach'.[69] However, his summons to the garrison to surrender was not answered. There was confusion among the defenders with discord between the Marathas and their European officers. That the enemy was determined to make some resistance was confirmed by the presence of several of their regular infantry battalions with artillery support positioned on the glacis, in the town including the main mosque, and in the ravines to the south and west of the city. These forces would have to be removed before any formal siege could start. There was little time to lose as it was feared that the garrison might be imminently relieved by Sindia's battalions sent from the Deccan.[70] Lake's bold plan, which evolved as he gathered more intelligence, was to make a two-pronged assault. On the morning of the 10th, Colonel Edward Clarke attacked from the west, particularly targeting Maratha forces in the town and mosque. Simultaneously, British forces advanced from the east, their objective to drive the enemy from the ravines and glacis and to seize their artillery. The attacks were made entirely by native infantry, Lake later explaining to the Governor-General that he could not 'spare Europeans'.[71]

Clarke's brigade of 2/9th, 1/12th and five companies of the 16th Bengal Native Infantry met stiff resistance in the town, but eventually the enemy was forced to evacuate. There was similar hard-fought success in the ravines, where the three sepoy battalions (1/14th, 2 and 3/15th Bengal Native Infantry) came under sustained artillery and musketry fire. Within 48 hours, 2,500 Maratha troops posted outside the walls surrendered. The attack had caused 600 enemy casualties and captured twenty-six fine brass guns. This was at a cost. The official British return lists 228 killed and wounded including nine British officers.[72]

Lake was now able to lay siege to the inner fort. There were desultory negotiations involving two European officers in Maratha service, Colonel Hugh Sutherland and Colonel George William Hessing, acting as intermediaries. The truce was short-lived, and on the 17th the British grand battery consisting of eight 18-pounders and four howitzers began a destructive fire on the south-east bastion, the weakest point. Its fire, supported by further artillery to the left and right, was well enough directed to take chunks out of the red sandstone walls. A practicable breach was imminent and the garrison of 5–6,000 Maratha troops surrendered on the following day.[73]

Livesey and myself [Pester] rode down to a hill in front, and knew
nothing of the surrender till we saw the garrison marching out…
Our regiment was ordered into garrison and I had the inexpressible
satisfaction with my own hands to haul down Scindiah's colours,
and plant the British Standard in its stead on the ramparts.[74]

An enormous amount of ordnance and treasure was taken. The former
included the famous 'Great gun of Agra' weighing nearly 1,500 pounds.[75] The
capture of Agra was a weighty success for Lake. He had possession of the 'key
to Hindustan':

The gaining of this place has relieved my mind exceedingly, as it
liberates my army so completely. The effect this will have upon the
minds of the natives is beyond all description as they imagine this
fort could have held out a long time.[76]

Notwithstanding Lake's and Arthur Wellesley's notable successes, Sindia's
regular infantry remained a formidable foe. Fifteen regular battalions had been
detached north from the Deccan and they had been joined by two battalions
which had not been engaged at the Battle of Delhi. This force had a potentially
competent general in Ambaji Inglia and was well supported by a detachment
of horse and a numerous train of artillery. During the siege of Agra it was
positioned within 30 miles of the city. It remained a threat to British political
ambitions and arms, and to Delhi in particular. Lake resolved to disperse it
and accordingly marched westwards from Agra on 27 October. A torrential
downpour forced the army to halt at Karowly. Lake, opting for speed, left his
baggage and siege guns at Futtehpore and, by the 31st, the Maratha forces were
close enough to persuade the General to pursue them with his cavalry. Setting
out at eleven o'clock at night with all eight regiments of mounted troops, he
made 25 miles in six hours and came up with what appeared to be Maratha
infantry in confused retreat at sunrise on 1 November. His own infantry had
been ordered to follow on at three in the morning.[77]

Lake believed that he had taken his adversary by surprise and, as he was
later to inform the Marquess, he was tempted to make an attack with his
cavalry alone. He was determined to prevent a retreat and to seize Sindia's
artillery. However, as he also admitted, his view of the Maratha army was
obscured by clouds of dust.[78] In reality, the Marathas were formed in a strong
position. They had taken the precaution of cutting the embankment of a large
tank of water, thus rendering the road very difficult for the passage of the
British cavalry. Their right was partly protected by a deep ravine in front of the
village of Laswari (now Naswari, 20 miles east of Alawar city), while their left
rested on the fortified village of Mahalpur (now Hasanpur). To their rear was

a deep rivulet and their entire front was hidden by high grass and protected by a line of seventy-five cannon (see map 14).[79] The total Maratha force was around 5,000 regular infantry, Sindia's 'Deccan invincibles', in addition to 4–5,000 cavalry, and the ample artillery pieces. Only a minority of these men were actually of Maratha origin; most were Purbias (from Avadh), Rajputs and Jats, with a few Muslims and lower caste Christians.[80] It is unlikely that Lake would have had the temerity to launch an isolated cavalry attack if he had understood the strength and resolute nature of his enemy.

As Randolf Cooper points out in his fine account, the few available eye-witness descriptions of the Battle of Laswari are incomplete and conflicting.[81] Perhaps the best overview is by William Thorn of the 29th Light Dragoons, who was with a galloper crew and was himself wounded at the end of the action by grape shot which fractured his jaw. Thorn describes Lake ordering the advance guard and the first brigade of cavalry to move upon a point where the enemy had last been spotted in motion; this was the left of their new position. The two remaining brigades were to support this initial attack once they had crossed the stream. Having navigated the water, the advance guard under Major Watkin Griffith of the 29th Light Dragoons and the first brigade led by Colonel Thomas Pakenham Vandeleur of the 8th Regiment of Light Dragoons impetuously charged the Maratha line. The Maratha artillerymen were driven from their guns and the British cavalry penetrated into the village of Mahalpur, but Vandeleur was mortally wounded and the squadrons ultimately withdrew leaving the targeted artillery in enemy hands.[82] The second and third brigades made equally valiant but futile attacks, as is dramatically narrated by Thorn.

> The third brigade under the command of Colonel Macan, which was next in succession, consisting of the twenty-ninth regiment of dragoons, and the fourth regiment of native cavalry, attracted particular notice on this occasion… Having received orders to turn the right flank of the enemy, this brigade came up with them at a gallop, across the Nullah, under a heavy fire from their batteries; then forming instantly into line, and moving on with the same steadiness as if it had been a review, our men charged the foe in the face of a tremendous shower, which scattered death in every direction, from all their artillery and musketry. To the former were fastened chains running from one battery to another, for the purpose of impeding the progress of assailants; while, to make the execution the more deadly, the enemy reserved their fire till our cavalry came within the distance of twenty yards of the muzzles of the guns, which being concealed by the high grass jungle, became perceptible only when a

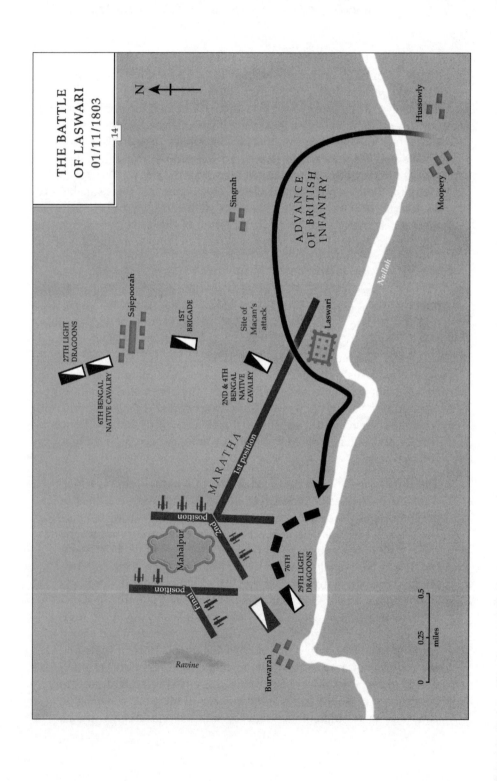

THE BATTLE
OF LASWARI
01/11/1803

14

N

27TH LIGHT
DRAGOONS

6TH BENGAL
NATIVE CAVALRY

Sajepoorah

1ST
BRIGADE

Site of
Macan's
attack

2ND & 4TH
BENGAL
NATIVE CAVALRY

Singrah

ADVANCE
OF BRITISH
INFANTRY

Hussowly

Moopery

Nullah

MARATHA
1st position

Laswari

2nd
position

Mahalpur

Final
position

76TH

29TH LIGHT
DRAGOONS

Burwarah

Ravine

0   0.25   0.5
miles

frightful discharge of grape and double-headed shot mowed down whole divisions, as the sweeping storm of hail levels the growing crop of grain to the earth.[83]

Macan's men pierced the enemy line and charged forwards and backwards three times. They were subjected to a galling fire from two sides from both artillery and musketry and all eyewitnesses agree that the troops suffered heavy casualties. Only two guns had been captured due to the lack of infantry and draught bullocks to retrieve them.[84] Lake was forced to restrain Macan from making a fourth charge and the cavalry brigades were recalled to await the arrival of the infantry.[85] An anonymous major relates the General's proximity to the cavalry charges and his 'wonderful escapes': two horses killed under him and six or seven musket ball holes in his hat and uniform.[86]

After an eight-hour march of 24 miles, the infantry reached the banks of the stream at eleven o'clock. Fortescue describes four native infantry battalions accompanying the 76th, but other sources suggest that there were six battalions of Bengal sepoys.[87] The new arrivals were fatigued and Lake allowed them some time to rest and eat. During this period, Ambaji, presumably chastened by the appearance of the infantry battalions, made an offer to surrender his guns upon certain conditions. Lake acquiesced and allowed the Maratha general an hour to decide. Both sides used this brief suspension of hostilities to prepare. Ambaji reorganised his force on the ground, throwing back his right wing to take up a new position. His infantry was now in two lines, the first covering the front or east and the second in the rear or west of Mahalpur, while the cavalry extended beyond the village almost to the stream (see map 14).[88] Lake, meanwhile, organised several columns for the attack. In his own words:

> The infantry formed in two columns upon the left: the first, composed of the right wing under the command of Major-General Ware, was destined to gain the enemy's right flank, which he had thrown back since the morning, leaving a considerable space between it and the rivulet, and to assault the village of Lasswary; the second, composed of the left wing, under Major-General [Frederick] St. John, was to support the first column. The third brigade of cavalry under Colonel Macan was to support the infantry; the second brigade under Lieut.-Colonel [John] Vandeleur was detained to the right, to be ready to take advantage of any confusion in the enemy's line, and to attack him upon his retreat.[89]

Colonel George Gordon commanded the reserve formed behind the second and third brigades and the advance was to be bolstered by four batteries formed of the gallopers and as many field pieces as could be brought up.[90]

After the short truce expired, the British infantry moved forward along the northern bank of the stream, initially concealed by broken ground and high grass. They were soon discovered and, understanding his right flank to be threatened, Ambaji further withdrew his right wing; this precise movement meant that the Maratha forces were now arranged in the shape of a letter L with an obtuse rather than a right angle at the junction of the two lines (see map 14). The British batteries were fully employed, but they were far inferior to the Maratha artillery, which was pouring a devastating mix of heavy calibre gunfire and grape from mortars into the right flank of the advancing infantry column.[91]

Lake had put himself at the head of the grenadiers of the 76th Regiment and he spurred them on, reminding them of the 'invincibility' of British soldiers. Three cheers rang out, echoed by the native troops at the front of the column (2/12th and 5 companies of the 16th Bengal Native Infantry).[92] It was soon obvious that the 76th was suffering severely, being the main target of the relentless enemy cannonade. The remainder of the infantry column had not properly formed, but Lake judged it better to hasten the attack with the available three corps rather than halting in the shower of well-directed fire.[93] As the casualties mounted, the 76th remained steady, the Commander-in-Chief exhorting them to slow their pace as they became detached from the following battalions.[94] The intrepid regiment was now also receiving attention from the Maratha cavalry. An initial charge was repulsed by musketry fire, but the enemy horse was rallying at a short distance and a second charge was imminent. Perceiving the threat, Lake brought up the 29th Light Dragoons, which had been posted in files in a hollow to the north of the stream behind the British guns.

The cavalrymen were relieved at the order, as they had been only partly screened from the Maratha artillery, which was ploughing up the ground amongst them.[95] Thorn charged with his regiment and he gives the most personal and probably most accurate version of the culmination of the battle. His historical work is now little remembered, but his better passages of prose are reminiscent of William Napier's descriptions of the Peninsular War.

> On forming up on the outer flank of the seventy-sixth regiment the cavalry were greeted with three cheers, which gratulatory sound was as heartily re-echoed by the dragoons, on whose sudden appearance the enemy's horse, after having advanced to charge our infantry, made a precipitate retreat. An awful pause of breathless expectation now ensued; the numerous artillery of the enemy seemed to watch an opportune moment to frustrate the meditated attack, by pouring destruction upon their assailants. The affecting

interest of the scene was heightened by the narrow escape of the commander-in-chief, whose charger having been shot under him, his gallant son, Major George Lake, while in the act of tendering his own horse to the general was wounded by his side. This touching incident had a sympathetic effect upon the minds of all that witnessed it, and diffused an enthusiastic fervour among the troops, who appeared to be inspired by it with more than an ordinary portion of heroic ardour. The cavalry trumpet now sounded to the charge: and though it was instantly followed by the thundering roar of a hundred pieces of cannon, which drowned every other call but the instinctive sense of duty, the whole animated with one spirit, rushed into the thickest of the battle. The twenty-ninth, now the twenty-fifth regiment of dragoons [the 29th were renumbered as the 25th in 1804], pierced with the impetuosity of lightning through both lines of the enemy's infantry, in the face of a most tremendous fire of grape shot, and a general volley of musketry. This advantage was followed up instantly by our veteran chief, who, at the head of the seventy-sixth regiment, supported by the twelfth, fifteenth, and a detachment of the sixteenth regiment of native infantry, seized the guns from which the enemy had just been driven. The twenty-ninth dragoons, after this achievement, made a wheel to the left to charge the enemy's horse, who had assumed a menacing posture; and after completely routing and pursuing them to the pass through the hills, our cavalry fell upon the rear of the main body, and entirely cut off their retreat. During these rapid operations, the infantry still continuing to press forward, routed the enemy against whom they were opposed, and succeeded in driving them towards a small mosque in the rear of the village [Mahalpur], about which they were met, and charged by the British cavalry in various directions. The remainder of the first column of our infantry came up just in time to join in the attack of the reserve of the enemy, which was formed in the rear of their first line.[96]

The 29th Dragoons' original commander, Major Watkin Griffith, had been killed by a cannon shot and the charge was led by Captain Henry Wade. The infantry column was also under fresh command, Colonel John Macdonald replacing Major General Ware who had been fatally wounded by artillery fire, his head 'being carried off'.[97]

Although a British victory was now inevitable, eyewitnesses acknowledge that the Maratha forces continued to put up stiff resistance. Thorn describes enemy soldiers 'defending their position to the last, contending every point inch by inch' as their left wing tried to retreat in good order. It was their misfortune that the British cavalry regiments were still mostly intact and the 6th Regiment of Bengal Native Cavalry and the 27th Light Dragoons led by Lieutenant-Colonel John Vandeleur broke into the column.[98] Little quarter was given by the troopers;

> after an action of nearly three hours' duration, the severest perhaps that ever was fought in any quarter of the world, [the enemy] were most miserably mangled by our enraged Dragoons, who cut up the flying wretches without mercy or a particle of pity, the whole plain for several miles in extent being strewed with human bodies.[99]

The 8th Light Dragoons were rendered 'almost frantic and uncontrollable' by the loss of Vandeleur.[100] Thorn estimates that there were 7,000 enemy dead and 2,000 prisoners, while George Isaac Call believed only 2,000 of the enemy to have survived;[101]

> 72 pieces of cannon and 36 standards of colour were taken besides a great quantity of baggage, camels, elephants and bullocks etc etc – in short nothing escaped except their horse which fled early in the action.[102]

Lake's account confirms the 2,000 prisoners (later mostly released), but he stopped short of any numerical estimate of enemy losses, simply noting that few could have survived the 'general slaughter'.[103]

British total losses were 172 killed and 652 wounded. The heaviest infantry losses were predictably taken by the three units at the head of the advancing column. The 76th Regiment suffered forty-three killed and 170 wounded, the 2/12th Bengal Native Infantry twenty-one killed and eighty wounded, and the five companies of the 16th Bengal Native Infantry seventeen killed and seventy wounded. Among the cavalry regiments, the 29th Light Dragoons (eighteen killed, forty-three wounded) and the 8th Light Dragoons (eighteen killed, thirty-six wounded) had similar casualty numbers. Thirteen British officers were buried on the field.[104]

A week later, on 8 November, the Grand Army marched away from Laswari towards Agra. The key objective of the destruction of seventeen Maratha infantry battalions had been achieved. Undoubtedly, the valour of the European and native troops in British service had contributed sizeably to the victory. Fortescue applauds the conduct of the 76th Regiment as ranking 'with the very highest that has ever been recorded in the British Army'.[105] The men had also shown remarkable resilience. The cavalry had entered the action after covering 42 miles in less than 24 hours, and the infantry had marched 65 miles in 48 hours.[106] Lake admitted that the Maratha soldiers had also shown great bravery: 'These fellows fought like devils, or rather heroes...'.[107] The Maratha army was, as Lake also freely acknowledged, very well appointed.

> [These battalions]... have a most numerous artillery, as well served as they can possibly be, the gunners standing to their guns until killed by the bayonet, all the sepoys of the enemy behaved exceedingly well and if they had been commanded by French officers, the event would have been, I fear, extremely doubtful.[108]

Although individual units maintained their discipline, it was perhaps the lack of inspirational leadership which contributed most to the calamitous Maratha defeat. Ambaji Inglia displayed none of the personal characteristics of Lake and was quick to flee the field, exchanging his elephant for a fast horse.[109] As implied by Lake, the loss of the European officer corps who had trained the troops was sorely felt (see Chapter 2).

During December, the Grand Army rested and reorganised. Reinforcements were received, but there was no likelihood of them being imminently used. The political repercussions of Laswari were such that prominent local chieftains and Rajas were now keen to form defensive pacts with the British.[110] On 10 December, the officers of the British Indian Army presented their Commander-in-Chief with a silver service valued at £4,000 as an expression of their 'attachment and esteem'.[111]

To conclude this account of the Indian campaigns of 1803 we should briefly mention two of the more obscure operations. In August, a field force under the command of Lieutenant-Colonel Henry Woodington was sent to Gujarat to capture Sindia's possessions in the region. On the 21st, Woodington marched from Baroda against the fortress of Baroach. A breach was quickly made and the place was stormed on the 29th, with only seventy-nine of the assailants killed or wounded. The British promptly took control of the populous and fertile region.[112] The conquest of Bundelcund was also achieved with celerity. Thorn describes the mountainous area as the 'Switzerland of India'. It was a desirable target for the British in view of its proximity to their own territories and its potential use as an invasion route for the Marathas or other enemies. A detachment of British troops under the command of Lieutenant-Colonel Peregrine Powell was supported by a friendly local chief, Rajah Himmut Behauder, at the head of irregular infantry and horse. The united force crossed the rivers Jumna and Cane and defeated the army of the resistant chief, Shumsheer Behauder, near Capsah on 13 October. The battle was one sided, Powell's force losing only a few men, and, following the reduction of the town of Calpee, the British were masters of the province by December.[113]

Faced with defeat on all sides, Sindia and Bhonsle had no alternative to suing for peace. At the close of 1803, both Maratha princes were forced to make considerable territorial concessions. The treaty with Bhonsle was ratified on 17 December, three days after the fall of Gawilghur. He ceded to the Company his eastern province of Cuttack and all of his land west of the River Wardha. He resisted a subsidiary force but had to agree to the Company's mediation in all disputes with the Peshwa or Nizam and to only employ Europeans with British consent. The treaty with Sindia, concluded on the 30th, also included the latter two provisions. He gave up to the Company Baroach and some possessions in Gujarat, the region in the Deccan between the Ajanta Hills and the Godavery and, in the north, the country in the Doab between the Jumna and Ganges rivers including Delhi and Agra. Unlike Bhonsle, he accepted a subsidiary force on the frontier of his territories.[114]

The seat of war in 1803 extended over much of the continent of India. In the short period of four months, there had been four large battles and eight general sieges, 'in all of which, British valour prevailed over accumulated obstacles, the combination of formidable powers, and every advantage arising from local position, military means and numerical strength'.[115] The East India Company had acquired immense new territories and a commanding position, albeit with some political anxiety as to the ultimate direction and expense of the conflict. Arthur Wellesley was knighted and Lake made a peer. There was great acclaim at home. Many on the scene, including Wellesley, believed the Maratha War to be at an end.[116] The usually level-headed Thomas Munro enthused, 'We are now complete Masters of India, and nothing can shake our power...'.[117] In the event, the subjugation of Sindia and Bhonsle was to be only the first phase of the war. The British had still to face their most ruthless adversary.

Chapter 8

An Elusive Enemy:
The War against Holkar 1804–1805

The strategically important fort of Gwalior is situated just less than 100 miles south of the River Jumna (see map 15). In negotiations at the end of 1803 with Ambaji Inglia, widely regarded by the Marathas as the representative of Sindia in Hindustan, it was agreed that the Company should take possession of the fort and town. Accordingly, a corps under the command of Lieutenant-Colonel Henry White was despatched at the end of December. On arrival, the fort's commandant refused to surrender the place, an action that it subsequently became clear was ordered by the duplicitous Ambaji. The British detachment was reinforced with men and siege artillery and a practicable breach was achieved on 4 February 1804, leading to the surrender of the 4,000-strong garrison. John Pester, as was his habit, planted the British colours on the ramparts of the 'renowned and hitherto almost impregnable fortress'.[1]

Gwalior was a great depot for Sindia's artillery, ammunition and military stores in Hindustan and its capture was another part of the Governor-General's grand plan. However, there remained the unresolved issue of the third great Maratha chieftain, Jaswant Rao Holkar, who had so far stood aloof from the war. It was the Marquess's hope that Holkar would agree to a peace that was mutually beneficial but, in P.E. Robert's words, '..he was making the common mistake of supposing that an Indian chief would necessarily be guided by a policy that was reasonable and in accordance with his own best interests'.[2]

It is understandable that Holkar was suspicious of British intent. It is possible that he interpreted his immunity to date as proof of fear of his power and his negotiating style was hubristic, a mixture of demands and thinly veiled threats.[3] If his requests were not met by the British, he informed Arthur Wellesley, then 'countries of many hundred *coss* [local unit of measurement, often around 2 miles] should be overrun plundered and burnt'. Furthermore, Lake would not be given a moment's respite by Holkar's army, which would overwhelm him 'like the waves of the sea'. The Commander-in-Chief was unimpressed by the threats, but he was also aware that the British did not hold all the cards, as he admitted to the Governor-General.

> I was never so plagued as I am now with this devil. We are obliged
> to remain in the field at an enormous cost. If we retire, Holkar

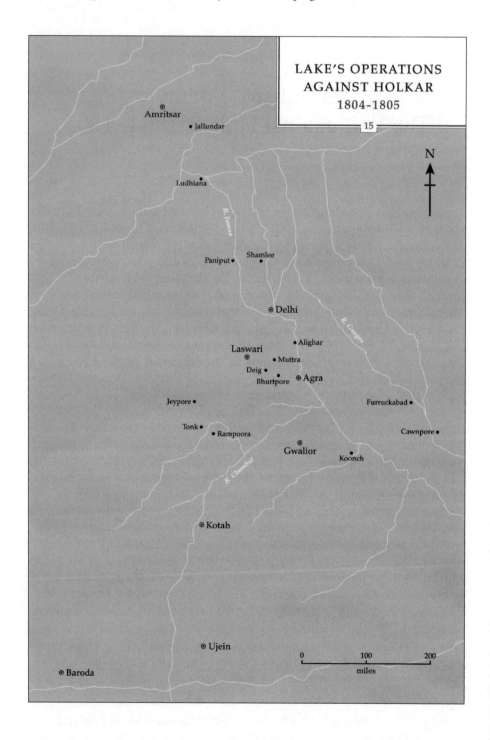

will come down upon [the Raja of] Jaipur and extract a crore [ten million rupees] from him and thus make his army more formidable than ever. If I advance and leave an opening, he will give me the slip, get into our territories and burn and destroy.[4]

By mid-April 1804, it was clear that hostilities were inevitable and the Governor-General commanded Lake and Wellesley to commence a war against Holkar both in Hindustan and in the Deccan. Unless he was stopped, Holkar would continue to plunder petty states under the protection of the Company, and his uninterrupted presence in the field would act as a magnet for irregular and turbulent factions. The reduction of his predatory power was judged to be justified by both political and economic considerations.[5] The broad British strategy involved Lake pursuing Holkar from Delhi in the north while Wellesley chased him from the Deccan in the south, and Colonel John Murray cleared Gujarat. It was hoped that an army provided by Sindia would approach from the east and collaborate with Murray. In the event, this plan misfired. As for Holkar, his war aims were perhaps predicated on survival rather than any expectation of clear victory over the British. He would pursue a guerrilla-style war hoping to avoid pitched battles while devastating the Company's territories.[6]

Arthur Wellesley spent much of the early part of 1804 encamped around Ahmednuggar launching expeditions against local unruly elements referred to as 'freebooters'. One of his dispatches, written at Munkaiseer in early February, gives a flavour of the arduous nature of these operations.

> They [the freebooters] were at the distance of 80 miles from my camp, and there was some reason to hope that I might surprise them by making forced marches. I began my march on the 4th, in the morning, with the British cavalry, the 74th regt., the 1st batt. 8th regt., and 500 men belonging to the other Native corps in my camp, and the Mysore and Mahratta cavalry. On my arrival at Sailgaon, near Perinda, after a march of 20 miles, I learnt that the enemy had broken up from their camp at Vyerag, and were come nearer Perinda, and that at that time they were not farther from me than 24 miles. I therefore marched again last night with an intention to attack their camp at daylight this morning. Unfortunately, the road was very bad, and we did not arrive here till 9 in the morning.[7]

Wellesley continued his pursuit with his cavalry alone and he ultimately caught and defeated the formidable band of freebooters. The obscure expedition was, in his own words, 'short but active' and he later remarked that this was the greatest march that he ever made.[8]

Wellesley was not an enthusiastic supporter of the war against Holkar. There were a number of strategic objections to the conflict, including Lake's relative unpreparedness in Hindustan, the imminent heat and rains, the employment of Sindia as a reluctant and weakened ally, and the distance of Wellesley and his army in the Deccan from Holkar's possessions. He may have, inadvertently, increased the chance of war by his casual dismissal of Holkar's military prowess, informing his elder brother in January that the chieftain was only a freebooter and that to crush him 'cannot be called a war in the present state of the Company's power'.[9] Later, he was less confident, stressing the need for an energetic strategy in a letter to Josiah Webbe of 20 April.

> The General's [Lake's] intention not to quit Hindustan, and not to follow Holkar, will be fatal. He ought to leave a corps in Hindustan for its security, and move with a light body in pursuit of Holkar, whose force will fritter away daily, whether he retreats after fighting or without fighting.[10]

A defensive war might be lost.

Upon receiving official news of the commencement of hostilities in early May, Wellesley wrote to Murray, instructing him to take the field in Gujarat. His force consisted of at least two European and four native battalions in addition to the native cavalry of the Gaekwar of Baroda. Murray was informed that he had 'a great game in his hands'. Wellesley could not be explicit as he was unaware of the detail of Lake's plans, but he intimated that Ujein was the most likely point of march.[11] Wellesley himself prepared to move northwards but, by the start of June, heavy rains and regional famine made this impossible. He was to be a mere spectator of the campaign against Holkar, soon recalled to Bengal from the Deccan in the first stage of his long journey home.[12]

Lake made his first move by marching on Jeypore on 18 April; the town was already held by three battalions under the command of Colonel William Monson. Holkar fled to the south, his moves monitored by parties of irregular horse under European officers. It was reported that Holkar's men were in a 'miserable' state. Nevertheless, they moved rapidly and had soon distanced Monson's detachment which was in advance of Lake's main body. After a halt at Tonga, Lake reached Nowai, about 40 miles south of Jeypore, on 8 May.[13]

Attempts by Holkar to renew negotiations had been rejected and, on the 10th, Lake instructed Lieutenant-Colonel Patrick Don to seize the fortified town of Rampoora (see map 15). Don judiciously camped outside the place on the opposite side of his intended point of attack. At two o'clock in the morning of the 15th, the Colonel marched off with the flank and four battalion companies of the 2/8th and the flank companies of the 2/21st Bengal Native Infantry. A 12-pounder at the head of the column was to blow in the gates and another in the rear was to deter a body of the enemy approaching from Tonk. The rear was also protected by a detachment of troops under Captain George Raban of the artillery. Don's men were within 100 yards before a brisk fire commenced from the ramparts. Three of the four gates were soon blown – the fourth was in disrepair and open – allowing the British to enter the town. The panicked garrison was hunted down by the 3rd Regiment of Bengal Native Cavalry commanded by Major Richard Doveton.[14]

Lake now made the fateful decision to abandon the pursuit of Holkar by his main army and to withdraw the bulk of his forces in to cantonments at Cawnpore, at least until after the monsoon. Some historians have criticised the Commander-in-Chief for his failure to actively press on himself, one describing this as an act of 'unaccountable imprudence'.[15] Lake believed that Holkar had gained too great a start to be caught and also his own army was suffering terribly. The thermometer had regularly stood at 130 degrees in the shade and in the last four days of marching fifty European troops had succumbed to heat and dehydration. Even the sepoys and camp-followers were perishing. It was therefore with some relief that the main army marched into Cawnpore on 20 June.

Monson was ordered to occupy the passes of Bundi and Lacheri to the south of Rampoora and north of Kotah to prevent Holkar's return from that direction. Lake was confident of the security of the British position. He understood Holkar's forces to be spent and he anticipated both that British forces in Gujarat under Colonel Murray could intervene as necessary, and that Sindia would actively cooperate from Malwa. The Commander-in-Chief had overestimated the command abilities of Monson and Murray and the compliance of Sindia, and had underestimated the toughness of Holkar. In fairness to Lake, the decision to remove his main force from the field was strongly supported by the Governor-General, the redeployment being also motivated by economic factors.[16]

With the principal army in cantonments, the fighting was left to scattered detachments and the British suffered a series of setbacks. Because of the illness and death of Colonel John Powell, the overall command of British forces in Bundelcund devolved upon Lieutenant-Colonel W.D. Fawcett. In search of forage, he sent a small party of seven companies of sepoys and some guns under a Captain Smith to take a small fort about five miles from his position at Koonch. The *killedar* of the fort offered to surrender the next morning in return for a ceasefire, while treacherously appealing for help from the *pindari* leader Ameer Khan, who was in the vicinity with 7–8,000 horse. Smith had ill-advisedly divided his paltry force and on the next day, 22 May, the Maratha horde fell upon two companies of sepoys and fifty artillerymen in the trenches.[17] We have a Maratha view of the denouement in Ameer Khan's own memoirs, translated from the original Persian.

> He [Ameer] then divided his party into three bodies... and so prepared for attack of the British battalions. The [British] men who

were old soldiers and well disciplined, formed square and beat off the Afreedees and Dukhunees of the Ameer's left wing. The horsemen, indeed, unable to support their fire, went behind the wall of [the fort of] Mulaya for cover, and there brought up. The Ameer, who had been studying how best to make the attack, turned now his standard elephant right towards the enemy and boldly advanced. Just at this time, the men of the left wing who had gone behind the wall referred to for protection, found a way under guidance of the people of the fort between it and the bazaar, or town, and so making an attack in support of the Ameer's charge from a different direction, succeeded in slaying by the point of the spear, and by the edge of the sword, a great many of the enemy...[18]

The British party was cut to pieces with loss of the guns. Fawcett rode out to relieve Smith and belatedly found him with his remaining five companies, his troop of horse and galloper gun intact. There was no evidence that Smith had attempted to rescue his two companies when firing had first been heard in the village. Ameer Khan continued to devastate the land before being roughly handled at Koonch in late May by a body of irregular troops lately in the service of Ambaji Inglia.[19]

The loss of personnel had been small, but there was mortification at the damage to British prestige and morale. The Marquess wrote to Lake on 8 June.

> It is difficult to calculate the extent of the evil consequences which may result from this unparalleled accident. The least mischief which can be expected is the encouragement of Holkar, Ameer Khan, and the whole horde of freebooters and professional robbers in Hindostan and the Deccan...[20]

Worse was to follow. Holkar had continued to retreat to the south and Monson, now reinforced by Don to a total strength of five native battalions (2/2nd, 2/8th, 1 and 2/12th, 2/21st Bengal Native Infantry) and 3,000 irregular horse, followed him, reaching Kotah at the beginning of June.[21] The British commander continued his southward progress to the Pass of Mokundra, eventually arriving near the fortress of Hinglaisgurh on 1 July (see map 16). Holkar was understood to be camped with his entire army 40 or 50 miles to the southwest on the opposite bank of the River Chumbul. After capturing Hinglaisgurh with slight loss of life, Monson took up a position 50 miles south of the Mokundra Pass, where he hoped to open communications with Murray, who was presumed to have marched upon Ujein.[22]

Unfortunately, Monson's assertiveness was matched by Murray's indecision. Arthur Wellesley strained to dispel Murray's misgivings and tried to spur him into action, writing to him on 28 June.

Richard Wellesley

1 WELLINGTON AND THE BRITISH ARMY'S INDIAN CAMPAIGNS 1798–1805

Arthur Wellesley

Madras Native Infantry

Bengal Native Infantry

Sindia

Holkar

Maratha foot soldier, 1813

Maratha horseman

George Harris

Storming of Seringapatam

Death of Tipu Sultan

Battle of Assaye

Maratha artillery at Assaye

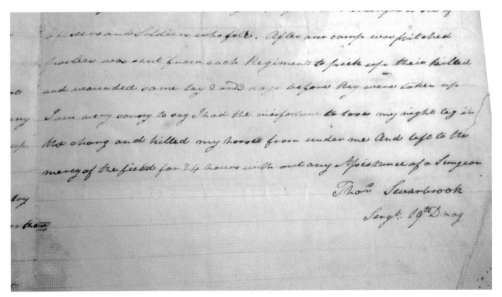

Thomas Swarbrook's letter describing the loss of his leg at Assaye (Courtesy of the Council of the National Army Museum)

Gerard Lake

Lake and his son at Laswari. Lake's horse has just been shot from under him

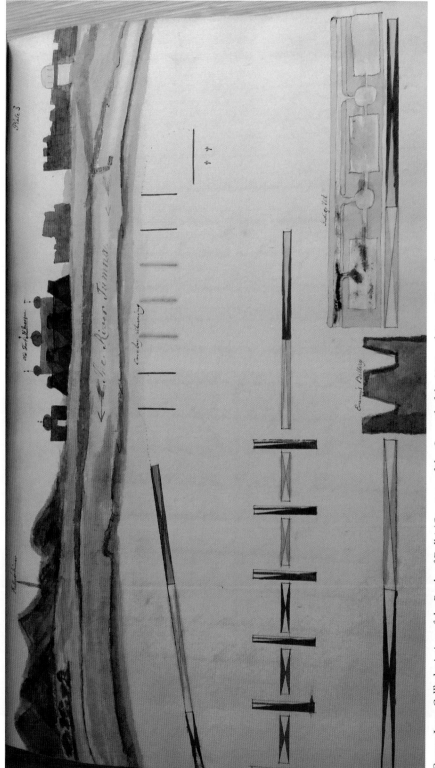

George Isaac Call's depiction of the Battle of Delhi (Courtesy of the Council of the National Army Museum)

George Isaac Call's view of the operations around Deig (Courtesy of the Council of the National Army Museum)

An East Indiaman, 1779

MADRAS. LANDING.

Landing at Madras, 1837

View of a British resident's camp from a Maratha camp, 1813

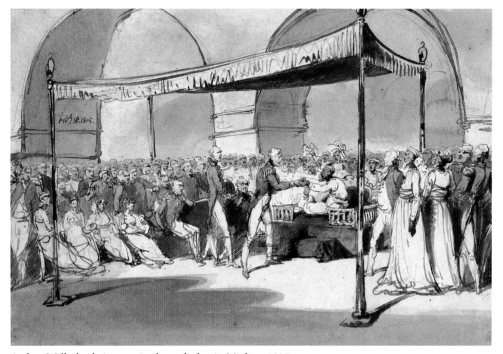

Arthur Wellesley being received at a *durbar* in Madras, 1805

Captain William Sandys of the 5th Bengal Native Infantry
(Courtesy of the Council of the National Army Museum)

A British officer sketching

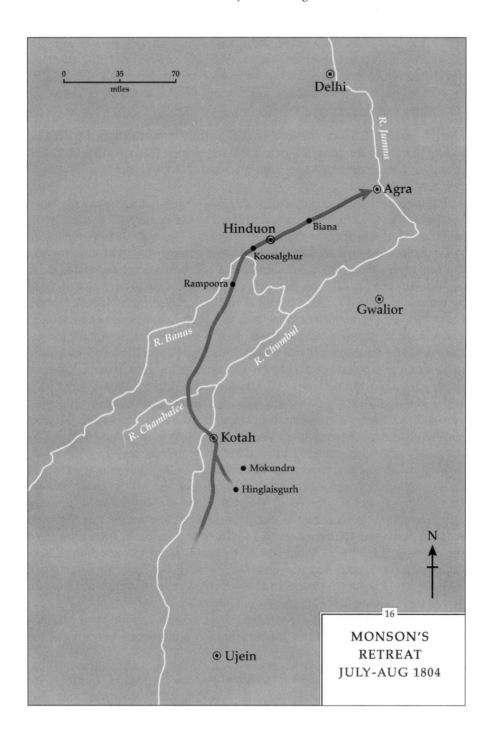

Delhi

R. Jumna

0   35   70
miles

Agra

Hinduon
Biana

Koosalghur

Rampoora

Gwalior

R. Banas

R. Chumbul

R. Chambalee

Kotah

Mokundra

Hinglaisgurh

N

Ujein

16

MONSON'S
RETREAT
JULY–AUG 1804

> I am concerned to hear of the sickness of your Europeans; and
> particularly so, as there does not appear any prospect of being able
> to increase your force in Europeans, or in cavalry... You have a
> larger body of Europeans than the Commander in Chief, or than
> I have ever had...[23]

Murray was no Lake or Wellesley. After further prevarication, he decided
to retreat behind the River Myhee, justifying this on the basis that he risked
losing his detachment. His subsequent advance back to Ujein was too late to
rescue Monson.[24]

The latter, who had already advanced dangerously far, was suddenly faced
by Holkar's whole army, which had crossed to the north side of the Chumbul. Instead of grasping the nettle and attacking – an approach we have seen
to be much advocated by Wellesley – Monson decided to retreat, at least to
the Mokundra Pass. The resulting debacle can only be briefly related here.
Monson moved his infantry first, leaving the irregular cavalry commanded
by Bapoji Sindia and Captain Lucan of the 74th Regiment to oppose Holkar.
On 4 July, 40,000 Maratha troops attacked them, causing losses of around
2,000 killed or missing. Ameer Khan asserts that Holkar personally cut off
Lucan's head.[25] Monson was still within 10 miles of a Maratha army estimated
to have nineteen battalions of infantry and close to 200 guns. After a desperate
march, already running short of provisions, the British infantry were back
at the Mokundra Pass within a day. Having refused an offer to surrender his
guns and repulsing an attack on his camp, Monson then reached Kotah after
another interrupted march of 22 hours. The British were refused supplies by
the Rajah, who no doubt sensed the sudden shift in local power.

By mid-July, the party had reached a tributary of the Chumbul, the artillery
by now abandoned, and Rampoora was entered on the last day of the month.
Here, Monson was reinforced by two battalions of Bengal Native Infantry
sent from Agra. Within two weeks, Holkar was close to the city. Monson
remained reluctant to make a stand and the final stage of the retreat involved
the crossing of the Banas River, where Holkar's infantry, cavalry and artillery
inflicted heavy casualties on the remaining detachment. Suffering desertion of
local allies and sepoys, Monson and his surviving men straggled into Agra on
31 August. Close to half of the sepoy battalions were lost.[26]

There are few eyewitness accounts of the retreat, but Captain Henry Anderson of the 12th Bengal Native Infantry has left a harrowing narrative of the
crossing of the Banas.

> Colonel Monson thought it expedient to cross the troops, the river
> being now fordable up to a man's neck, at 4pm having got every body
> over except the 2nd Bt. 2nd Regiment and the picquets who were

left as a rear guard the enemy got up some guns and opened upon them on which Major [James] Sinclair commanding the 2nd Bt. 2nd perceiving that he could not cross under such a fire, in conjunction with the picquets faced about and charged them – He succeeded in getting possession of eleven of their guns, but unfortunately just as the gallant Sinclair was with his own hands planting the British colours on one of them he received a shot in the knee which brought him and the colours to the ground, which the enemy perceiving, they made a last effort and charged sword in hand in such numbers that our men being faint and weary from the length of the fight and broken by the inequality of the ground which was among ravines, from the great inequality of numbers, were obliged to give way and were at last pushed into the river where most of our men perished either by the water or the weapons of the enemy who followed them into the river… it was truly shocking to see our friends cut to pieces in that manner without being able to render them the smallest assistance.[27]

A Maratha account of the River Banas skirmish states that Holkar's cavalry was at first repulsed, and that some of his guns were captured, but that the action started to turn the Marathas' way when they were able to cross the river and fight on both banks. Holkar himself 'applied the match to the touch hole [of a gun] and drove back the charging British sepoys, slew many of them and recovered his own lost guns'.[28]

After such a disaster, there had to be an inquest. Writing to the Governor-General, Lake bemoaned the loss of men, 'the flower of the army, and how they are to be replaced at this day, God only knows'.[29] Arthur Wellesley was more analytical, criticising both Monson's original advance and subsequent retreat: 'I do not think that the Commander-in-Chief and I have carried on war so well by our deputies as we did ourselves'. He believed the episode to be 'the most disgraceful to our military character of any that have ever occurred'.[30] To their credit, neither Lake nor Wellesley indulged in public recriminations. Lake was keen to take some of the blame upon his own shoulders, which was apposite as both Monson and Murray had been placed in awkward situations with insufficient forces to counter a determined and numerous enemy.[31]

Holkar returned to Hindustan, revelling in his victory. Lake marched out of Cawnpore in heavy rain on 3 September, crossing to the south bank of the Jumna on the 22nd. His force, assembled at Secundra a few days later, was as follows:

Cavalry (Colonel Richard Macan)

1st Brigade (Lt Col John Ormsby Vandeleur): HM 8th Light Dragoons; 2nd, 3rd and 6th Bengal Native Cavalry

2nd Brigade (Lt Col Thomas Browne): HM 27th and 29th Light
Dragoons; 1st and 4th Bengal Native Cavalry
European Horse Artillery

Infantry (Major General John Henry Fraser)

1st Brigade (Lt Col William Monson): HM 76th Regiment; 1/2nd
and 1/4th Bengal Native Infantry
2nd Brigade (Lt Col George Browne): 1 and 2/15th and 1/21st
Bengal Native Infantry
3rd Brigade (Lt Col George Ball): 1/8th and 2/12th Bengal Native
Infantry
Reserve (Lt Col Patrick Don): HM 22nd Regiment; 1 and 2/12th
and 2/21st Bengal Native Infantry[32]

Holkar's forces are more difficult to enumerate. Duff follows John Malcolm
in his estimate of 60,000 horse, 15,000 infantry and 152 guns.[33] Despite the
Monson disaster, British high command remained dismissive of their chief
opponent, Lake informing the Governor-General that Holkar's men were
dissatisfied and prone to desertion: 'They are a most despicable set, and will,
I think be an easy conquest'.[34] Malcolm believed his compatriots to have
underestimated the effectiveness of Holkar and to have placed too much trust
in 'petty Rajput chiefs'.[35] Intelligent officers such as James Young of the Bengal
Horse Artillery understood that the British did not hold all the cards.

> I wish we may not be going on a goose-chase after this man… if
> he betakes him to the direction of the Punjaub, where the water
> is almost as scarce, as in the desert of Egypt, and as he leaves an
> encampment, poisons or fills up the few wells there are, we shall be
> in a most awkward predicament.[36]

The Maratha horse fell back in the face of the advancing Grand Army and
Lake reoccupied Muttra on 3 October. He was, however, unable to bring Holkar to a significant action. Thorn's account of the manoeuvres on the 10th well
captures the nature of the impasse and British frustration.

> Our cavalry, formed in two lines, moved in columns of half regi-
> ments at regular intervals. In this order, we swept clear the whole
> plain where the enemy were encamped [a few miles from Muttra],
> at a full gallop; but we could not succeed in our endeavour to charge
> them, for they scampered off in all directions, dispersing as usual.
> When we halted, they did the same, rallied, and stood gazing at us;
> and when we turned our backs, to return home, they dashed on,

attacking our rear and flanks, firing long shots with their match-locks, while those who were armed with spears and tolwars, flour-ished their weapons, making, at the same time, a noise like jackals, by way of bravado.[37]

By mid-October, Lake was able to relieve Delhi, which had been besieged. The resident, Massachusetts-born Colonel David Ochterlony, had made a brave defence against Holkar's forces, his small garrison of a battalion and a half of sepoys and local levies holding out for nine days.[38] The stalwart resist-ance was all the more creditable as the fortifications were crumbling. George Carnegie, at this time attached to an independent corps, related the events in a letter home;

> there did not remain above 2500 Men of every description to defend seventeen Gates and an old Wall seven Miles in extent… We suf-fered much from fatigue, being constantly on duty day and night. What the Enemy breached by Day, we contrived to rebuild or cut off by Night, and every attempt to scale the Wall was defeated… on the morning of the 15th to our great Joy, we found the Enemy had marched off in the Night.[39]

Denied the capture of Delhi, Holkar sent his infantry back towards Deig and moved his cavalry up the Jumna towards Paniput, where he crossed the river determined to inflict harm on the Doab. Lake responded by dividing his army, the main part of his infantry, two regiments of native cavalry and the field artillery entrusted to the command of Major-General John Fraser, who was instructed to observe the enemy force at Deig. The Commander-in-Chief led the remainder of the King's cavalry (8th, 27th, 29th Light Dragoons), the horse artillery, the 1st, 4th and 6th Regiments of Bengal Native Cavalry and the reserve brigade of infantry, in a further pursuit of Holkar across the Jumna.[40] On 3 November, Lake's men were able to relieve the small ruined fort at Shamlee, 60 miles north of Delhi, where Colonel William Burn's famished garrison had held out against Holkar's marauding horse.[41] What followed was a chase south through the Doab: 'continued at the rate of twenty miles a day, through clusters of mischievous little forts and luckless burning villages'. We need not relate every step of the way, but by mid-November Lake had arrived at Aligunge in Rohilkhand, another village recently ransacked by Holkar. Here, the British general received intelligence that his elusive enemy was at Furruckabad, 36 miles to the east (see map 15).[42]

At nine o'clock in the evening, Lake set out with the British cavalry.[43] Holkar was complacent. According to his contemporary biographer, the chief was engaged in 'pleasure and repose' and he dismissed warnings of a British night attack, believing his foe to be too far away.[44] George Isaac Call describes the massacre at dawn.

> The moon was up ere we marched – the night mild and pleas-
> ant – everyone in high spirits (at the idea of coming up with our
> Friends) singing the whole way – as the morning gun fired at
> Futtighur – we arrived close to the enemy's camp and Hicarrahs
> were arriving to accompany us to the spot when unfortunately a
> tumbril blew up and gave the alarm; a few seconds elapsed ere
> our gallopers opened on their camp (with Grape) which put
> them into the utmost confusion; the cavalry then charged them
> thro' and thro' – the Pursuit and Slaughter continued for some
> hours – the strength of their force are said to have been nearly
> 10,000 – between 2,000 and 3,000 of the enemy were left dead on
> the field – The action lasted till 10 o'clock.[45]

Holkar, who managed to escape over the River Kali, had suffered a chas-
tening reverse. James Young says that the fruits of the chief's plunder were
also taken: 'Holkar's own elephant, twenty or thirty camels loaded with grain,
tents etc., etc., bullocks and buffaloes, horses and tattoos innumerable besides
twenty hackeries loaded with grain'.[46] British losses were limited to two men
killed and twenty-six wounded.[47] Cavalryman Young was in no doubt that
it was British mobility that had proved crucial. 'We have taught the enemy
that distance is no security against antagonists who can march with guns sixty
miles in 24 hours'.[48] Sergeant John Shipp believed that the Marathas' 'want of
vigilance' against night attacks to be attributable to their excessive eating and
smoking of opium such that 'if a gun were fired under a man's nose, he would
scarcely have the power to awake'.[49]

Holkar's horse had been shattered at Furruckabad and his infantry had
already been defeated outside Deig. After splitting from Lake, Fraser went in
search of Holkar's brigades and guns, thought to be in the territories of the
Rajah of Bhurtpore. On 12 November, the British force reached Goverdun,
where the enemy were discovered to have taken up a position between a deep
tank and a morass, their right resting on a fortified village and their left on the
fort of Deig. At three o'clock the next morning Fraser left his camp to make
the necessary detour around the southern extremity of the morass; his force
for the attack consisted of HM 76th Regiment, the First Bengal European
Regiment (101st) and four Bengal native infantry battalions (1/2nd, 1/4th, 1
and 2/15th). The Maratha strength was believed to be twenty-four battalions,
around 14,000 infantry, in addition to considerable horse and 160 guns (see
map 17).[50]

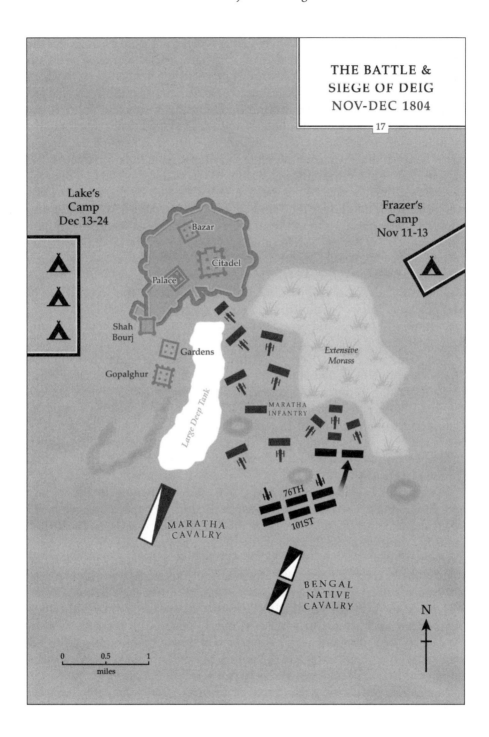

THE BATTLE &
SIEGE OF DEIG
NOV-DEC 1804

17

Lake's
Camp
Dec 13-24

Frazer's
Camp
Nov 11-13

Bazar

Citadel

Palace

Shah
Bourj

Gardens

Gopalghur

Extensive
Morass

Large Deep Tank

MARATHA
INFANTRY

76TH

101ST

MARATHA
CAVALRY

BENGAL
NATIVE
CAVALRY

N

0   0.5   1
miles

By daybreak the advancing army had reached the fortified village on the enemy's right. The troops wheeled into line and Fraser launched the 76th against the village, which was only feebly protected by mud enclosures which crumbled under British fire.[51] The place quickly captured, the 76th charged on down the hill in the face of a furious Maratha cannonade. John Pester describes men being killed not only by round, grape and chain shot, but also by flying stones and bricks.[52] An anonymous British officer of the Bengal Army believed that the enemy attempted to change front to re-form across the neck of land between the tank and swamp. It seems that the Maratha infantry were slow to manoeuvre, the impulsive British assault catching many units still forming the new line.[53] The 76th had soon captured the first line of enemy guns, receiving prompt support from the Bengal European Regiment and the 1/4th and 1/15th Bengal Native Infantry. Major James Hammond, with the 1/2nd and 2/15th Bengal Native Infantry, kept in check outflanking enemy brigades at the southern end of the morass.[54]

The most advanced troops were receiving fire from the second line of Maratha guns. They were now commanded by Monson as Fraser had lost a leg to a cannon shot. A second heroic bayonet charge cleared the enemy not only from their second line of guns, but also from several batteries up to the walls of Deig, two miles distant. Here the British came under fire from the fort itself. The enemy were now 'flying in every direction'. It only remained for a small party of the 76th to rout a body of enemy horse which had transiently retaken the first line of guns, and for the troublesome enemy detachment opposite Hammond to be driven into the morass by artillery fire and the threat of Monson's re-formed infantry. With the captured guns secured, the British encamped on the ground with a cavalry piquet posted to watch the enemy garrison in Deig.[55]

Maratha losses were estimated at 2,000, some drowning in the swamp and ditch. Many survivors took shelter in the fort.[56] British losses were 643 killed and wounded.[57] Fraser died from his wound a few days later. The British casualty figures indicate that the Battle of Deig was no foregone conclusion. Lake described it as the 'hardest fought' in that part of India and he was quick to extol the bravery of Fraser and Monson.[58] In contrast, Maratha contemporary sources decry poor leadership as a major factor in their defeat. Holkar was not on the field. Mohan Singh tells us that the senior commander, Hanah Singh, drew up his force in a manner 'utterly opposed to the rules of war'. He quickly fled from the field, his terror and despair communicated to his soldiers, who soon followed him.[59] Another Maratha account conceded that a number of Holkar's senior officers were 'not warm in the cause'.[60]

Monson immediately undid much of his own good work by making an unnecessary retreat to Agra, thereby greatly exasperating Lake: 'It is somewhat extraordinary that a man brave as a lion, should have no judgement or reflection.'[61] The Commander-in-Chief rushed to rectify the mistake and, on 13 December, the British army was to the west of the fortress of Deig. This was no small encampment. Thorn estimates that there were 60,000 non-combatants, 200 elephants, 2,000 camels and 100,000 bullocks.[62] The fort was powerfully defended and encircled by marshes and lakes. The town was surrounded by a mud wall with round bastions and a deep ditch, the defences culminating in a rocky peak at the southwest corner called the Shah Bourj, in front of which was small castle. Inside the town was a square citadel, while outside there was a redoubt and a dozen batteries defending the open ground between the lake and the swamp (see map 17).[63]

Undaunted, Lake commenced siege operations. The enemy's outlying batteries were engaged, the defences driven in and a practicable breach was made in the Shah Bourj by the British guns. The assault was fixed for the night of 23 December, the attacking force divided into three columns. The right column under Captain Samuel Kelly (four companies of 101st Regiment, five companies of 1/12th Bengal Native Infantry) was to carry the enemy's batteries and trenches on the high ground near the Shah Bourj. The left column, led by Major James Radcliffe (four companies of 101st Regiment, five companies of 1/12th Bengal Native Infantry), was to seize the batteries and trenches on the enemy's right. Finally, the central column under the overall commander Lieutenant-Colonel Kenneth Macrae (flank companies of HM 22nd and 26th, 101st Regiment and 1/8th Bengal Native Infantry) was to be the storming party for the breach.[64]

The whole moved off at 11.30pm. John Pester was in Radcliffe's party.

> Between our batteries and the breach, the ground was very much broken, and in the dark it was utterly impossible to preserve such distance and order as could have been wished; the troops were as silent as death on our approach, but we were no sooner discovered from the works that the whole face was completely illuminated by the enemy's cannon and musketry. The shot flew like hail, and many a gallant fellow dropped; it was, however, no check to us, and instead of returning a single shot we rushed on, with the bayonet, and gained the summit of the breach...[65]

John Shipp, who was with the central column, believed that the storming troops would have been 'annihilated to a man' if the enemy's guns had not been so elevated. The assailants ran down from the breach into the fort where, according to Shipp, the stiff resistance continued.

> Our opponents fought hard to resist our entrance, throwing immense stones, pieces of trees, stink-pots [vessels filled with tar,

brimstone, etc.], bundles of straw set on fire, spears, large shots &c... The streets in the fort were narrow, running across each other, and every ten yards guns were placed, for the purpose of raking the whole streets.[66]

The defenders also fired down from loopholes in the high houses. At 12.30am the moon rose, the improved visibility allowing the British to better coordinate their efforts.[67] By 2am the Shah Bourj and its outworks were captured and the three columns rejoined in carrying the main walls of the town. There only remained the citadel, but this was evacuated the following night. On Christmas Day 1804, the Union flag flew on the walls of Deig.[68]

British losses were perhaps surprisingly light at forty-three killed and 184 wounded.[69] The risks run by individual British officers are well demonstrated by the case of Lieutenant William Forrest of the Pioneers,who had more than twenty wounds and was left for dead on the field, but who ultimately recovered, albeit with the loss of an arm.[70] Most historians make no estimate of Maratha casualties at the fall of Deig. Call believed enemy losses to be around 2,000 judged by the number of bodies in and outside the fort, but this convenient round figure appears all too often in British writings on the battles and sieges of the war.[71]

The Commander-in-Chief's next objective was the reduction of Bhurtpore. The army marched on 28 December and, joined by HM 75th Regiment, reached the capital of the Rajah on the second day of 1805. Duff's introductory words anticipate a turn in British fortunes.

> General Lake being accustomed only to success, without properly reconnoitring the place and with a very inefficient battering train, commenced the siege...[72]

Bhurtpore was a fortified town, six to eight miles in circumference, surrounded by a high mud wall and bastions and a deep unfordable ditch. It was surrounded by jungle and water and strongly garrisoned by 8,000 Jat troops of the Rajah of Bhurtpore and Holkar's remaining infantry (see map 18). A determined resistance should have been expected; the Rajah's 'means of defence were proportionate to his resolution to use them'.[73]

By the afternoon of 9 January, British batteries had created an apparently practicable breach in the wall at the southwest angle of the city. It was resolved to make the attack the same evening, the storming party formed of three columns: Lieutenant-Colonel Edward Ryan with 150 of the Company's Europeans and a battalion of native infantry; Major Walter Hawkes with two companies of HM 75th and a battalion of native infantry; and Lieutenant-Colonel James Maitland with the flank companies of HM 22nd, 75th and 76th Regiments, the

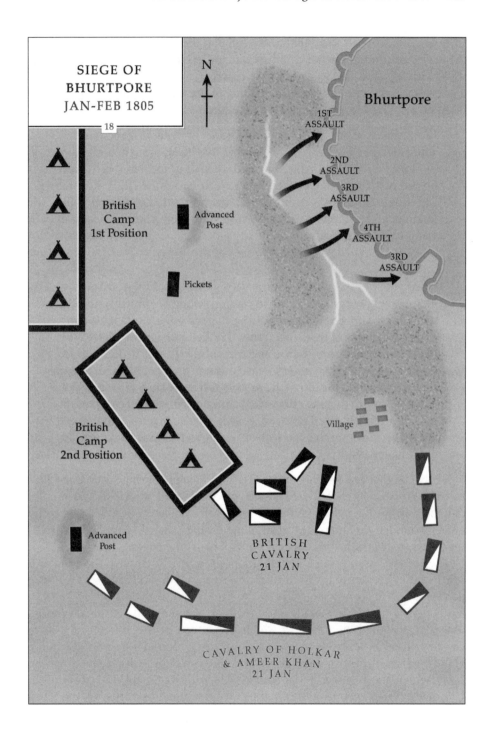

SIEGE OF
BHURTPORE
JAN-FEB 1805

18

N

Bhurtpore

1ST
ASSAULT

2ND
ASSAULT

3RD
ASSAULT

4TH
ASSAULT

3RD
ASSAULT

British
Camp
1st Position

Advanced
Post

Pickets

British
Camp
2nd Position

Village

Advanced
Post

BRITISH
CAVALRY
21 JAN

CAVALRY OF HOLKAR
& AMEER KHAN
21 JAN

Company's European Regiment and a full battalion of sepoys. Maitland's was the centre column; the other columns were ordered to make their way into the town with fugitives and to support the centre.[74]

At 8pm, the three columns moved out of the trenches. John Shipp of the 22nd gives a graphic account of British failure.

> We pushed on at speed; but were soon obliged to halt. A ditch, about twenty yards wide, and four or five deep, branched off from the main trench. This ditch formed a small island, on which were posted a strong party of the enemy, with two guns. Their fire was well directed, and the front of our column suffered severely. The fascines and gabions were thrown in; but they were as a drop of water in the mighty deep...

Shipp and his comrades pressed on towards the breach, becoming increasingly isolated;

> imagine our surprise and consternation, when we found a perpendicular curtain going down to the water's edge, and no footing, except on pieces of trees and stones that had fallen from above. This could not bear more than three men abreast, and if they slipped (which many did), a watery grave awaited them...We had at that moment reached the top of the breach, not more than three a-breast, when we found that the enemy had completely repaired that part, by driving in large pieces of wood, stakes, stones, bushes, and pointed bamboos, through the crevices of which was a mass of spears jabbing diagonally.[75]

Unable to gain any footing, under fire from a neighbouring bastion and harassed by a mixture of spears, darts, stones, pieces of wood, stink-pots and bundles of lighted straw, the party was forced to retreat. Maitland was killed and many others wounded. In Shipp's regiment, none escaped injury.[76] We shall return to the precise nature of British losses at Bhurtpore in later pages.

The second assault was directed at a point a little further to the right and south of the first (see map 18). British progress was slow as the Rajah's working parties toiled to form a stockade in the breach. Nevertheless, by 21 January a practicable breach was made and an attack was planned for the afternoon. This was preceded by a ruse in which the troops of the 3rd Bengal Native Cavalry posed as deserters to make a closer inspection of the size of the ditch. Unfortunately, this extra intelligence proved to be of little use to the storming party, which was formed of 150 men of HM 76th Regiment, 120 of the 75th, 100 of the First European Regiment and fifty remaining men of the 22nd flankers. Once these troops had forced their way in they were to be supported by the same King's regiments and three native battalions. Picked men were to carry portable bamboo bridges to throw over the ditch.[77] John Shipp, whose wounds from the first assault included grape shot in the shoulder, again led the way under heavy fire. It was soon obvious that a serious misjudgement had been made.

> My men kept falling off one by one; and when I arrived at the edge of the ditch, which appeared wide and deep, and was assisting the men with the bridge, I received a matchlock ball, which entered over the right eye, and passed out over the left. This tumbled me, my forehead literally hanging over my nose, and the wound bleeding profusely... I recovered a little from the stun of my wound, when the first thing that met my eye (for I could see with one) was the bamboo bridge quietly gliding down the stream, being some yards too short. Nothing but killed and wounded could be seen, and there was not the most distant chance of getting in.[78]

Retreat was inevitable; many of the wounded were necessarily left behind to be 'mutilated or murdered'.[79] The first failure had been shrugged off, but the men were now shaken at the scale of the casualties and there was resentment at perceived poor planning. James Young questioned the preparations in his journal entry of the 22nd; 'If one ladder was found somewhat too short, why was it not provided with strong hooks and the other instantly attached to it?'[80]

Before describing the final two assaults on Bhurtpore we must move away from its walls to briefly review wider events in the area. In late January, a large British convoy of 12,000 bullocks loaded with grain was attacked by the forces of Ameer Khan at Combir, halfway between Deig and Bhurtpore. The small escort was heavily outnumbered, but it resisted long enough to allow relieving cavalry to come from Bhurtpore and scatter the enemy's horse. A second even larger vital supply convoy from Agra was well enough defended to deter an attack by Ameer Khan, and the Maratha chief instead took his men to Rohilkhand to ravage the country. Lake accordingly sent Major-General Smith with the 8th, 27th and 29th Light Dragoons and three regiments of Bengal native cavalry to hunt him down. The resulting chase was reminiscent of Wellesley's operations against Dhoondiah Waugh. The decisive action occurred at Afzulghur on 2 March, where Smith routed his adversary at the cost of only a handful of casualties.[81] Ameer Khan's biographer blames the catastrophic defeat on the 'impetuosity' of the elite Maratha troops who, contrary to instructions, charged without adequate support.[82] The chief fled, suffering many desertions, while Smith returned to Bhurtpore.

Here, Lake had been reinforced by the Bombay force of General Richard Jones, who had superseded the dithering Murray. This was composed of eight companies of HM 65th Regiment, HM 86th Regiment, five battalions of Bombay native infantry, a troop of Bombay native cavalry and some irregular horse. The siege operations were now being conducted more cautiously by the Bengal Army and it was 20 February before the new breach was deemed suitable for another attempt. In a familiar tactic, three columns were formed. The storming party, under the command of Lieutenant-Colonel Patrick Don, was formed of the available European troops of the Bengal Army and three native battalions. A second column under Captain John Grant of the 86th was deployed to carry the enemy trenches, while a third column, under Colonel Taylor, was to attack the Beem Narain gate, which was reported to be vulnerable to guns and potentially breachable. The attack started inauspiciously. When the storming party arrived at the forward approaches at daybreak on the 20th they were surprised by the enemy who had occupied the vacant trenches the previous night. In the intense skirmishing the British were on the back foot and had suffered significant losses before their artillery dispersed the desperate band of defenders.[83]

The British columns now closed on the fort. Don ordered the storming party to advance into the breach. As John Pester describes, the officers now discovered that they had overestimated their men's morale.

> The Europeans (part of his Majesty's 75th and 76th Regiments) refused positively to quit the trenches. Don harangued them to no purpose, asking them if they wished to bring an everlasting stain upon their country and themselves and telling them that such conduct was unprecedented and such as British soldiers were supposed incapable of; but all to no purpose, and they persisted in their own declaration that 'they would not go to be slaughtered'.[84]

Don was followed by two brave battalions of Bengal native infantry who climbed a bastion known to the British as the Tower. A few clambered to the top and the colours of the 12th Bengal Native Infantry flew at the summit, but it was not possible for sufficient numbers to ascend to maintain any advantage. Some European troops rallied to the cause, but it was too late and the retreat was ordered. The other columns had fared little better, neither Grant nor Taylor able to force the closed Anah and Beem Narain gates.[85]

It might be thought that a third dramatic failure and the collapse of British morale would have deterred further efforts on the place, but Lake was informed that the Tower could be successfully stormed following a further battering. It was decided to renew the storm the following day. The General addressed his men on parade more in sorrow than anger and, overcome with remorse, they volunteered to a man. On this occasion, the storming party was led by Lieutenant Charles Templeton and under the overall command of

William Monson. It was made up of the survivors of HM 26th Regiment, the flank companies of HM 22nd, 65th and 86th Regiments, the flank companies of the Bengal European Regiment (101st), and two battalions of Bengal native infantry.[86] John Shipp, concealing the severity of his wounds from the doctors, led the forlorn hope for the third time.

> We had already experienced three disastrous repulses from this fort, and there now seemed a cloud on every brow, which proceeded, I have no hesitation in asserting, from a well-grounded apprehension that this, our fourth assault, would be concluded by another retreat.[87]

Shipps's pessimism was justified. The damage to the Tower bastion was limited and all attempts to scale it in numbers proved futile. Men driving their bayonets into the ramparts to improvise ladders were forced down by the usual mix of missiles and fire. Shipp himself fell off the bastion and suffered burns. None of his twelve volunteers of the forlorn hope survived to claim their monetary reward.[88] Monson sounded the retreat and the last attack on Bhurtpore was over.[89]

Pester claims that the wounded were 'butchered by the enemy who were thirsting after European blood'.[90] The total British losses in the four assaults on Bhurtpore were in excess of 3,000 men. Some 103 officers were killed or wounded.[91] The losses of the defenders are difficult to formulate. Shipp states that they were 'immense', possibly as many as 5,000 men, women and children.[92] The Jats were fighting not only for political freedom, but also to save their families.[93]

Lake's failure at Bhurtpore can be attributed to inadequate ordnance and men for the task, but it must also be admitted that he was impatient and over-confident. P.E. Roberts concludes that, 'The appalling blunder [was] unpardonable because it was unnecessary'.[94] Arthur Wellesley was no doubt reluctant to criticise his commander-in-chief, but he could not restrain himself from making a judgment.

> They must have blundered that siege terribly, for it is certain that with adequate means every place can be taken and, Lord Lake having been so long before the place, adequate means must have been provided or in his power.

The fault must have been, continued Wellesley, the misuse of resources, either due to the ignorance of the engineers or the 'impetuosity of Lord Lake's temper'.[95]

Fortescue's assertion that Lake was 'unshaken' is not borne out by the General's correspondence. On 8 March, the army's commander wrote to the Governor-General from his camp outside Bhurtpore lamenting the 'late disasters'.[96] He was, however, still resolute and the siege was converted into a blockade while convoys brought battering guns, ammunition and fascines, and damaged guns were repaired.[97] The Governor-General gave conditional approval to Lake's actions; 'I most anxiously hope that you will fix your mind rather upon the certainty than the celerity of your success against Bhurtpore…'.[98]

The Rajah was daunted by the relentless nature of the British preparations and the devastated state of his territories, and he was now expecting little help from Holkar. He opened peace negotiations in mid-March. This development, together with the return of Smith's cavalry from Rohilkhand, gave Lake the opportunity to strike out at Holkar, whose remaining force was camped about eight miles to the west of Bhurtpore. The first attack was made in the early hours of 29 March. Holkar was alert and he fled, albeit with the loss of 200 men in the pursuit. The second British effort, made a few days later, was more successful, with a greater element of surprise. The enemy barely had time to mount their horses. Large numbers were killed on the spot and more fell in a chase of seven or eight miles. Holkar was forced to cross the River Chumbul with a body of about 8,000 horse, 4–5,000 infantry and twenty or thirty guns. News now arrived in the north that 3,000 of Holkar's infantry had been routed near Ahmednuggar by native infantry and irregulars. The chief was seriously weakened, but Thorn's insistence that he was now no more than a 'wandering fugitive' appears an exaggeration. The British continued to underestimate the resilience of their main adversary.[99]

Holkar's reverses encouraged the Rajah of Bhurtpore to sign a peace treaty in mid-April. This was quite favourable to him. He had to pay an indemnity and could not employ Europeans without the Company's permission, but he retained Bhurtpore and much of his realm excepting Deig.[100] On 21 April, the British Army broke up and moved towards the Chumbul. An old threat had re-emerged. Sindia, who had been vacillating as to which side to take, was prompted by the British debacle at Bhurtpore to open communications with Holkar and Ameer Khan. The situation was inflamed by his seizure of the British representative at his court. The Marquess was placatory, the treaty with the Rajah a significant setback to the Maratha cause, but the plotting continued and Holkar, Ameer Khan and Sindia effectively combined forces.[101]

Sindia was a thorn in Lake's side, but also a cause of frustration to his Maratha allies. In Sardesai's words, 'Holkar could not impart his own ardour' to Sindia, 'whose weakness and indolence combined with habits of levity and debauchery' ruined his own cause and that of his nation.[102] When Lake crossed the Chumbul at Dholpore at the end of April, Sindia withdrew up the river towards Kotah. At this time he was abandoned by some of the confederate chiefs who came over to the British camp. Once Lake had concluded a treaty with the ruler of Gohud the army broke up in the third week of May, the Bundelcund detachment marching towards Gwalior and the Bombay division to Tonk. Lake was in headquarters in Muttra with his Bengal Army forces in cantonments at Agra, Secundra and Futtehpore. The whole was ready to move at a moment's notice.[103] Thorn provides a useful return suggesting that Lake's effective force at this time amounted to around 30,000 men (see Appendix VIII).[104]

Military events were now overtaken by political change. Marquess Wellesley's expansive and costly strategy had made him unpopular in both British Government and East India Company circles and the prime minister, William Pitt, and Lord Castlereagh, president of the Board of Control, recalled him. In his place they appointed 66-year-old Lord Cornwallis, who had experience of India but who was in poor health. He was regarded as a 'safe pair of hands', a man who was naturally inclined to appeasement and who would quickly reverse Richard Wellesley's adventurous policies.[105] On his arrival, in July 1805, the new Governor-General summed up his views.

> We are still at war with Holkar and we can hardly be said to be at peace with Sindia… We are now waging war against two chieftains who have neither territory nor army to lose… I deprecate the effects of the almost universal frenzy, which has seized even some of the heads which I thought the soundest in the country, for conquest and victory.[106]

Cornwallis's attempts to end hostilities by conciliation have been widely criticised as a naive attempt to return to the status quo of 1798. Particularly iniquitous was the potential withdrawal of British protection from the Rajput chieftains who had given notable service in the war, a policy that 'would be paid for by the agony of millions of helpless peasants'. Lake protested vehemently at the damage to British honour, but Cornwallis was already failing and he died on 5 October at Ghazipore having held office for little more than two months.[107]

Holkar marched northwards with his remaining troops in early September with the hope of eliciting help from the local Sikh chiefs. Lake, still determined to crush his elusive opponent, put the army in motion, ordering the forces at Agra and Secundra to move to Muttra while a detachment was dispatched to Saharanpoor for the protection of the Doab. At the end of October, the General set off to pursue Holkar in person with the following force.

1st Brigade Cavalry: HM 24th and 25th Light Dragoons; 6th Bengal Native Cavalry

2nd Brigade Cavalry: HM 8th Light Dragoons; 3rd Bengal Native Cavalry
Reserve: HM 22nd Regiment; EIC European Regiment (101st); 1/9th and 1/11th Bengal Native Infantry

Lake arrived at Delhi on 7 November and then followed Holkar north into Sikh territory. Benefiting from reinforcement by four sepoy battalions and some irregular horse, the British detachment reached Ludhiana on 2 December (see map 15). Holkar may have been at the head of, in Thorn's words, a 'numerous rabble', but the Maratha warrior was still difficult to catch. Lake's advanced guard were unable to prevent his men crossing the River Beyah and the enemy were soon at Amritsar. The pursuing British arrived at Jallundar on 9 December, where they were welcomed by Sikh emissaries.[108]

The new Governor-General, Sir George Barlow, was even more determined than Cornwallis to end the fighting by all means. A peace had already been made with Sindia on 28 November, in which Gwalior and Gohud were restored and the defensive alliance abandoned. Barlow next made a pact with Holkar, which was widely regarded as being overly generous. P.E. Roberts asserts that the 'defenceless' chief would have agreed to almost any terms. Signed in early January 1806, the treaty allowed Holkar to retain the bulk of his dominions. Much to the chagrin of Lake, there was to be no British protection for many of the minor Rajput chieftains. 'I am sick to death', he wrote, 'of the present government all over India'. He was not alone in his disillusionment. An envoy of the betrayed Rajah of Jaipur complained that 'this was the first time since Great Britain had been established in India that it had been known to make its faith subservient to its convenience'.[109]

The Anglo-Maratha conflict thus ended. It was, Fortescue believed, typical of many British wars with 'the concession of all that had been gained by great expenditure of blood and treasure…'.[110] Lake embarked for England in February 1807. Holkar's restless spirit was ill-suited to a peaceful life and he was soon to suffer 'a fit of insanity', probably in large part induced by alcohol. He died in 1811, aged 30 years.[111]

III Soldiers

Chapter 9

We dread not the Mahrattas, but the Sun: Voyage and Arrival

Soldiers of the Revolutionary and Napoleonic era had mixed feelings when sent to India. There was likely career advancement and adventure, but also the perceived dangers of what was an obscure and incredibly distant place. That a posting to the tropics engendered fear is undoubted. However, it seems that India was regarded with less foreboding than the pestilential West Indies. In 1796, Ensign Richard Bayly of HM 12th Regiment notes that when reports circulated that they were bound for the Caribbean, several officers tried to resign:

> the Colonel would not accept, as he was determined his officers should accompany their corps to all climates and service to which the government should destine them… Some of them did, however, continue to quit, but to their great regret, when it was made public that the regiment was to hold itself in readiness to embark for the East [Indies] forthwith.[1]

John Blakiston, who was to also fight in the battles of the Anglo-Maratha War, admits to being traumatised at the sudden removal from his family at seventeen years of age in 1802.

> All that I had clung to for support and protection; all that I had ever loved, or that had ever loved me; all that I knew, or that knew me; in a word, all that I cared for, or that cared for me, seemed to sink from my sight with the lessening cliffs of my native land.

He later adds that the 'elasticity of youth' allowed him to quickly recover his spirits.[2] Lieutenant-Colonel Stapleton Cotton, a little older than Blakiston at twenty-three years, was pleased to be despatched to India at the end of 1795, believing that it would be 'advantageous' for the regiment and especially himself. He did, however, have to resist the entreaties of his mother and sisters to exchange into another corps and thereby avoid the risks of the climate.[3]

Most voyages to India departed from the large naval stations of the south of England. Richard Bayly marched from Newport to West Cowes in the summer of 1796;

[we were] accompanied by at least five hundred women, the wives of the soldiers, only sixty of whom were permitted by regulation to embark with their husbands. The lighters [flat-bottomed barges] were all ready for our reception, and we got on board as expeditiously as possible, to be conveyed to the Indiamen, then lying off Portsmouth. The cries and lamentations of the poor women who were destined to separation from their husbands were distressing beyond description; tearing their hair, beating their bosoms, and rolling in the mud and sand on the beach... it must be acknowledged – to the disgrace of our sex – that the husbands of these forlorn creatures were by no means affected with such symptoms of deep distress. They even laughed and joked with imperturbable nonchalance and indifference...[4]

Prior to their embarkation, the soldiers might be held in barracks; for much of the period all King's regiments in India and also the East India Company maintained small depot barracks in Chatham.[5] Others joining their regiments were usually accommodated in local inns. Lieutenant George Elers of HM 12th Regiment, 22 years old, had the dubious pleasure of staying at the appropriately named Indian Arms in Gosport in 1796.

The next morning I was much disgusted at the dirty bed and room I had been put into; the chambermaid, I conclude, saw that I was a young Johnny Raw, and that anything would do for such a young one as me.[6]

Such inconveniences were soon forgotten as the time for embarkation approached. The fleet of men-of-war and Indiamen was waiting off the coast. Bayly believed that the sight 'must impress every mind with the ideas of the power and wealth of the English nation'. Flags and streamers flew from the 100 vessels assembled at Portsmouth.[7] Fleets might be even larger. When Stapleton Cotton left England in 1796, 300 ships started together before parting company in the Channel, some heading for India, some for the West Indies and some for other ports around the world.[8]

The 'Johnny Raws' of the Army did have the benefit of well-meaning advice from India old hands. Some of this was in print. Typical of the genre is the two-volume work, *The East India Vade-Mecum or Complete Guide to gentlemen intended for civil, military or naval service of the Honourable East India Company* by Captain Thomas Williamson (also the author of *The Wild Sports of the East*). First published in 1810, the guide gives copious recommendations for all aspects of life in India, including the voyage out. Williamson stresses the limited space available for an army officer's baggage and he dismisses the use of large sea chests.

> I should strongly recommend four boxes well covered with leather
> and clamped with brass, measuring about 26 or 28 inches in length,
> 18 in breadth, and 18 in depth.

He goes on to specify a labelling system, the optimal packing of clothes and
the storage of the boxes in the hold. Once arriving in India, the boxes were of
a size such that they could be carried in canvas slings on bullocks.[9]

The need for this precise advice is understandable when we consider the
other items which were routinely put on board ships sailing to and from India.
Below is the itinerary for the articles loaded on to the *Fortitude* in 1783 for the
use of Major-General James Stuart and his staff.

Liquors	Dozens
Claret	60
Madeira	60
Arrack, half a league	
Brandy	18
Hock	12
Porter	24

> Bullocks 12, Sheep 60, Fowls and capons 30 dozen, Ducks 12 dozen,
> Turkeys 2 dozen, Geese 3 dozen, Hogs and pigs 30, Sows with young
> 2, Milch goats 6, Hams 15, Tongues 5 casks, Cheeses 6, Fine rice 12
> bags, Fine biscuit 30 bags, Flour 3 casks, 1 Tea chest, Sugar candy 10
> tubs, Candles 8 Mds., Butter 5 firkins.

The list was not comprehensive, it being noted that there were also a great
number of smaller items of provision 'care having been taken that nothing
material should be omitted'.[10] When George Elers boarded the East Indiaman
Rockingham, he was accompanied by his colonel, two flank companies, the
regiment's colours and the band. The embarkation was chaotic.

> The bustle and confusion of getting on board, which was in the first
> week of June [1796], the decks covered with knapsacks, officers'
> baggage, etc., ducks, pigs, poultry, sheep, etc., all quacking, squeak-
> ing, crowing and baaing at the same time, was quite ludicrous.[11]

The route to India was around the Cape of Good Hope and across the
Indian Ocean. There were potential opportunities to get ashore during the
voyage, although some ships made the passage without any stopovers. The
first possible port of call was at the Canary Islands or Cape Verde, where wine
might be taken on board. Here, the ever-vigilant author of the *vade mecum*
gives a warning to the unseasoned traveller;

it may be proper to caution the young adventurer not to ridicule, nor in any way to shew disrespect towards, the religious ceremonies of the Roman Catholics who possess those islands. Under the exercise of prudence and discretion, all persons landing among the Portuguese are certain of receiving every civility and attention; but when insulted, no race of men are more irascible or vindictive: the offender is sure to fall a victim to their unrelenting vengeance![12]

Many vessels proceeded between the Azores and the Canary Islands until they caught the trade winds blowing from the northeast. They then ran along the coast of Brazil, perhaps stopping at Rio de Janeiro or other ports for fresh provisions, before making their course towards the Cape.[13] Ships often touched here, giving passengers the chance to take exercise in a fine climate, although Williamson characteristically warns of the 'offensive avariciousness' of the Dutch inhabitants.[14] Where the Cape was avoided, ships might run south to a latitude of 38 or 40 degrees for more favourable currents. Other stops could be made in the Indian Ocean, for instance at the island of Johanna (Anjouan) for those en route to Bombay.[15]

The duration of the voyage depended on the time of departure from England, the weather conditions, and whether the ships touched land. Vessels leaving Land's End in April might be expected to arrive at Madras in September.[16] Arthur Wellesley left by fast frigate in June 1796, caught up with his regiment at the Cape, and made the remainder of the passage in an Indiaman, arriving at Calcutta in February 1797 'after a most tedious voyage'. On his return home in 1805, Wellesley would have a short sojourn on the small Atlantic island of St Helena, another possible stopover midway between Europe and India.[17] George Carnegie, who was to serve as a British officer in Sindia's army, wrote to his mother in February 1798 from the Madras coastline.

We have been lucky in meeting fine pleasant weather, but in winds quite the reverse. Indeed they seem to have undergone a compleat revolution, and particularly the Trade Winds! For in them we have been much deceived, and the change has seldom been to our advantage.

George's perception that he had been a victim of the elements is exaggerated, as the voyage took only four months and the captain calculated that it would have been three if they had not been slowed by the company of two very heavy sailing ships.[18] George's brother Thomas sailed for Bombay three years later, also to join Sindia's forces. The ship made no stops and completed the uneventful passage in four months.[19]

From the mid-eighteenth century, the voyage was mostly made in East Indiamen. In general, the ships of the East India Company and the Royal Navy were the most seaworthy, Williamson warning of the particular dangers of foreign vessels.[20] Sergeant Robert Butler of HM 26th Regiment sailed from Penang to Madras in 1807 on *La Dedaigneuse*, a French frigate captured by the British. The seas were rough and the ship leaky; 'it was indeed a most disagreeable voyage, for we could not keep our provisions from getting wet by the sea rushing in between every plank!'. On arrival, the ailing vessel was sent straight to the dock.[21] Not all the East Indiamen were of good quality. George Elers left Penang for Madras in 1798 on the 500-ton *Princess Mary*, the crew made up entirely of lascars with the exception of the officers. The ship was small and dirty and the sailors slovenly. The voyage of three weeks was 'long and wretched'.[22]

For those who were not directly employed by the Company, a passage in one of the Company's ships had to be paid for. There was an agreed scale of charges, dependent on military rank. The regulations existed only up to major, as it was assumed that all above that rank would hire a cabin which was extra. The sums paid for the cabins depended on their size and the demand. In 1810, a cabin with a window might cost £200–£300. Homeward-bound prices were usually greater in view of the number of servants and children on board; it was reported that the whole of a great cabin had been let for the astronomical sum of £2,500.[23] When fifteen-year-old Richard Purvis sailed for India as a cadet in the Bengal native infantry in 1804, his costs were incurred by his family.

> I aim to give him [the captain of the ship] £95 for Richard's passage –
> of course he is to be at the Captain's Table…at the third mate's mess
> he could have gone for £35 – but this would not have been looked
> upon as so respectable.[24]

The size of cabins varied considerably. In peacetime they were normally constructed of wooden partitions, but during war it was more usual to divide them by canvas attached to the beams.[25] Sleeping arrangements were either a cot or a fixed bed. The cot was a single oblong of canvas secured by a small cord to strong hooks seven feet apart fore and aft. It was commonly taken down during the day. There was always the risk of being dashed against the ship's sides or bulkheads, but cots were thought to minimise sea-sickness. 'Standing bed-places' were permanent, allowing the occupant to turn in whenever he pleased. Trunks could be stowed underneath.[26] Whatever the arrangement, space was usually very limited. George Elers soon discovered this on the *Rockingham*.

The chief officer showed us to our cabin. Colonel Aston's cabin was divided from ours, and had a quarter gallery. We had the remaining part of the cabin, with a partition for the other part of the quarter gallery, for our own use and that of the officers of the ship. We were eleven officers stowed away in standing berths and cots in a cabin no more than, I should think, ten feet square, besides the rudder-head, which took up very considerable room. I swung in a cot as well as Captain Craigie and the surgeon Dr. Campbell; Meade, Crawford, Robert Nixon, his Lieutenants, lay in the standing berths. Woodall, George Nixon, and Perceval were stowed way in the same manner, and Ensign King in a cot. This was our party.[27]

For most soldiers, the excitement of being on board, destined for a distant land, soon wore thin and they settled into a humdrum daily routine which varied little during the period. Ensign Bayly well expresses the general opinion.

There is no scene so monotonous as a sea voyage, a succession of the rising and the setting of the sun, with no other object to attract the attention than the blue expanse of sea and sky; for a few days only is the novelty entertaining. The fresh, invigorating breezes, or motion of the ship certainly infuse into the human constitution an extraordinary and almost unappeasable appetite; hearty breakfasts at 8 o'clock in the morning, tiffin at 12, dinner at 3, tea at 6, and supper at 8; everyone punctual to the hour and all equally voraciously inclined. Chess, backgammon, cards, fluting, fiddling, and dancing, the principal amusements in the intervals between our meals.[28]

Subalterns and men kept watch on deck from eight till twelve and from twelve till four and then with what were called 'dog watches' extending for two hours from four until six and then six until eight. After breakfast, the men of the regiment were often drilled and parades were held to ensure cleanliness. A subaltern of the day might be appointed to check that all the cots were stowed away, that the decks were swept and that all lights were extinguished at nine o'clock.[29]

For some, the days were too tedious to be worth recording. We have this from East India Company cadet Blakiston.

I shall not dwell upon the manner in which we passed our time on board ship – how we panted under the Line – how we rolled around the Cape, frequently with more soup in our laps than we could keep on our stomachs – how the backgammon board rattled from morning till night – how we paced the quarter-deck...[30]

Under the circumstances, it was important to rub along with fellow officers and civilians. Blakiston overcomes his reticence to inform us of the society he shared: 'Excepting that there was no lady of the party, it was composed of the usual materials to be found at the cuddy-table of an outward bound Indiaman'. There was a judge, a general officer appointed to the staff in India and his aide-de-camp, Indian officers returning to their homeland, officers proceeding to join King's regiments, assistant surgeons, his fellow cadets and a number of civilians. In all, a party of twenty-five dined at the captain's table.[31]

In such small groups, closeted together for months, tempers could be quickly lost. Thomas Carnegie had some quarrelsome shipmates. He resolved to keep his head down, 'I left them to themselves, and steered clear of all scrapes, which is certainly the best plan for everybody, but particularly for me, who was not in the Hon[ora]ble Comp's Service...'.[32] The astute *vade mecum* guide stresses the importance of establishing a good relationship with the captain.

> The captains navigating under the auspices of the India Company, are men who have seen much of the world, and who rarely fail justly to appreciate those marks of attention and respect, which flow voluntarily from those with whom they have dealings.[33]

He also advises as to points of etiquette on board ship. For instance, touching one's hat when ascending from the gun deck to the quarter deck and the importance of strict compliance with the ship's regulations.[34] In such ways, friction between army officers and the ship's crew might be minimised.

Whereas officers at the captain's table were almost always ensured a generous supply of food and water, it was not uncommon for the men to be put on 'short allowances'. When Sergeant Butler rounded the Cape of Good Hope in 1807, the ship was running short of provisions and water was limited to a quart a day and then a pint. It was three weeks before land was reached.

> The reader may be inclined to think that this was no great hardship; but I hope you will not take it amiss, if I say that this shows your entire ignorance of the matter. Only consider for a moment, and you will, I am persuaded, come to a very different conclusion. Take for your dinner a salt herring, or a piece of beef that has been perhaps a twelvemonth in the brine, in a very hot summer day, having ate no breakfast beforehand, and try if you would find an English pint of water sufficient even for the afternoon.

In the extreme heat, some of the men of Butler's regiment were desperate enough to drink seawater. There were soon more than 100 on the sick list, suffering from scurvy and sores. The little 'fresh' water available was so offensive and cloudy that it was impossible to see the bottom of a cup filled with it.[35]

Where conditions were more favourable, some soldiers did experience periods of enjoyment during the voyage. Williamson reassures us that, 'All things considered, the privations experienced by passengers to India are by no means so numerous, nor so severe in their operation, as might at first be apprehended'.[36] George Elers was becalmed for ten days close to the equator and suffering from 'prickly heat', but he was able to appreciate the return of the breeze and the immensity of his surroundings.

> Nothing can possibly be more grand and sublime than the rising and setting of the sun in these latitudes and the moonlight nights are quite delicious. The phosphoric particles in the sea are wonderful, and truly beautiful.[37]

There were sharks and dolphins to be seen and some passed their time fishing. The tedium was also punctuated by the various ceremonies which attended the crossing of the equator. Blakiston judged the visit of 'Father Neptune' to be too stale a subject for recitation, but others regale us with graphic accounts of the crude shaving of blindfolded sailors.[38] The *vade mecum* notes that these amusements are 'filthy in the extreme' but allows that they 'cannot be witnessed without exciting much laughter'.[39]

Of course the greatest novelty was a precious visit ashore en route. In 1797, George Elers spent a very pleasant two months on the Cape, riding and socialising with the locals.[40] Ten years later, Ensign Bayly was fortunate to be one of a selected group of officers allowed to land at the Cape, where he soon found a snug and clean lodging. Life ashore was apparently idyllic, cricket matches being played with the officers of the garrison, but the intimacy and gambling led to frequent duels.[41]

The voyage to India carried real risks, which were well understood by nervous soldiers who dreaded 'one hundred and twenty days in a sea prison, with a plank between one and eternity'.[42] The ship carrying Captain Samuel Rice of the 51st Foot to India in 1799 was struck by a large Indiaman off the Cape, carrying away part of the stern.

> I never was so frightened in my life. I thought that it was certainly all over with us. You can form no idea of the shock. Seamen think nothing of these things, but as for me, who am not a seaman and have no wish to be, I am in constant fear.[43]

The weather could be roughly predicted from the period of sailing. The author of the *vade mecum* complains of the misery of being wind-bound but, perhaps to avoid undue alarm, he makes no mention of the violent storms that might be encountered.[44] John Budgeon, captain in the 84th Regiment, felt the full power of the elements between the Cape and Madras in February 1799.

> Very strong gales with exceptionally heavy squalls and sleet and a heavy sea... Shipped a sea over the starboard gangway which carried away all the iron stantions, sails, hammocks and hammock covers, the calk of wheat was stove and lost on the lower gun deck. A seaman washed overboard but recovered himself. All the tables gave way in the ward room. Several casks broke loose by which several soldiers of the 84th were severely bruised.[45]

Even the shortest voyages transferring troops around India were liable to end precipitately. Arthur Wellesley embarked on the *Fitz-William* at Calcutta in August 1798 to accompany his regiment to Madras. The vessel was soon in trouble and Wellesley later informed his brother Henry that he had been fortunate to survive.

> The ship struck this morning at about five upon which is called Saugor Reef [in the entrance of the Hooghly River], and remained fast until about one, when she was got off, I may almost say, by the bodily strength of the soldiers of the 33rd Regiment. She struck with great violence several times in almost every minute, and now leaks much... If the weather had not been more moderate than it is usually, we must all have been lost.

The resourceful Wellesley jettisoned some of the heavy cargo of saltpetre, ordered his men to start pumping, and proceeded to Madras.[46]

Fire was an ever-present danger, despite regulations limiting smoking to the fore-castle.[47] There was also the constant threat of outbreaks of disease, a subject to which we will return in a later chapter. Ships isolated from the main convoy were vulnerable to attack and capture by foreign privateers. Memoirist William Hickey describes the 'shameful and disgraceful' loss of the *Triton* in the Bay of Bengal in 1800. The outward-bound East Indiaman mistook a French privateer for a friendly vessel and 'In this way did nineteen Frenchmen get possession of a ship having two hundred stout fellows belonging to her, all of whom, as it were, panic-struck, remained cooped up between decks...'. The captain's confusion was understandable as the French pirate, Monsieur Surcouff, had improvised his privateer from a captured British pilot schooner belonging to Bengal.[48]

Not all such encounters ended so ignominiously, but the first instinct of the Indiamen captains was to preserve their ships by avoiding confrontation. In 1797, Roderick Innes embarked at the Cape to join 1,100 men of his regiment making for Bengal. They were forced close to the coast of South America by bad weather and were soon being chased by a French privateer. The captain ran for land at San Salvador. Upon entering the harbour, the privateer made off. When the British left port, it reappeared and now there was little choice but to fight.

Our men then gave three cheers, and the band struck up 'God save the King'. Each of us respectively hoisted French and British colours as we approached one another. At last the roar of his guns whistled in our ears. Our men however, having made themselves visible, so terrified him with their red coats and shining armour, that he put about ship and made off. We gave chase, but were heartily glad to have put to flight one of the best French privateers.[49]

Some soldiers were unimpressed by the first views of India, George Elers declaring that the appearance of Madras from the sea was 'not very interesting'.[50] Others were entranced by the tree-lined coastlines and white buildings. This was an energising sight after the tedium of the voyage. John Blakiston was a little underwhelmed, but he enjoyed the contrast when he neared Madras in 1802.

The most dreary spot in existence will always appear delightful to the eye fatigued with long gazing on the same object. Any novelty must be charming to the mind wearied with a constant repetition of the same scenes; any exercise must be refreshing to the body long pent up within narrow limits. It is not, then, a matter of surprise that almost all navigators should paint the spot at which they first touch, after a long voyage, more in the colours of imagination, than in those of reality; as the *el dorado* of their ideas. Indeed it must require all this, and more, to describe the the approach to the coast of Coromandel as anything strikingly beautiful. A few straggling cocoa-nut trees, rising out of the haze of a tropical horizon, are all that at first strikes the eye, till a closer approximation shows a low line of coast, backed at a considerable distance by a range of mountains of no great height.[51]

Sergeant Butler thought the first view of the polished white buildings of Madras to give 'a very exalted idea of India', but he later added that the city looked best at a distance.[52]

Getting ashore at Madras was not straightforward or without risk. There are several soldier eyewitness accounts, of which Butler's is the most descriptive.

The best boats belonging to his Majesty's navy dare not venture through the prodigious surf that runs every where on the beach, and you may often see the captains of the Indiamen or Men-of-War obliged to leave their elegant boats and fine-dressed crews outside the surf, and get on board of what are called Massulah boats, to be rowed ashore by natives. These boats are constructed nearly like our own, but are considerably deeper. The planks are sewed together by small cocoa-nut ropes, instead of being nailed, and they are caulked by the cocoa-nut hemp (if I may call it so) of which the ropes are made. When the passengers are all seated, the boatmen begin their rowing which they accompany with a kind of song, until they approach the breakers, when the boatswain gives the alarm, and all is activity among the rowers; for if they did not pay great attention to avoid the wave in the act of breaking, the boat would run every risk of being swamped.[53]

The well-tested skills of the boatmen preserved many lives and some were rewarded by grateful officers of the East India Company, allowing them a comfortable retirement.[54] Officers disagree as to the greatest danger. Ensign James Welsh laments that, despite the best efforts of the locals, many drowned in the surf, but George Elers insists that natives rarely drowned ('they float like cork') and that the larger threat was from sharks which frequented the shore.[55]

Once safely on land, the men were marched to barracks and the more senior or fortunate officers were escorted to the mess room of the fort by their new regimental comrades.[56] Other officers had to fend for themselves and for the uninitiated – new arrivals in India were often referred to as 'Griffins' – their first day in the country could be disorientating. James Welsh came ashore at Calcutta in 1790;

whilst everything the stranger meets with on landing, differs so widely from all that he has been accustomed to in Europe, that the mind is lost in surprise: a surprise, not a little increased, on finding that *here* no European uses his own legs; but that all ranks and ages must bend to the custom of the place, and be carried. Here, then, the poor Griffin, once landed, finds himself a man of some consequence; surrounded by hundreds of natives of various castes and costumes, all eagerly pressing on him their proffered services, he is hurried into a palanquin, and borne away as it were in triumph, he knows not whither.[57]

Those landing in Madras or Calcutta with no pre-arranged accommodation were likely to be taken to one of the numerous hotels often named after their owners. These were generally of low quality. John Blakiston commenced his campaigning in India in a hotel in the Black Town suburb of Madras. It was, he says, not frequented by any respectable persons: 'I passed the night in a bed which might be called a chop-house for musquitoes, where fresh tender European flesh was regularly served up to them'.[58] The willing helpers on the beach were often in the employ of the hotel-keepers. An unnamed cadet arriving at Calcutta in 1803 was quickly taken to Parr's Hotel by locals fluent in English, their amicable luggage services later appearing on his bill.[59] For humble cadets the hotel could only be a temporary haven. When David Price stayed at Richard's Hotel in the Black Town it cost him eight shillings a day, far exceeding his pay of 2s 6d.[60] We shall return to soldiers' more permanent accommodation in the next chapter.

Adjusting to the climate was a challenge for all new arrivals from Europe. This was very variable, temperatures ranging from the tropical to the polar.[61] According to Alexander Beatson, the daytime temperatures in the shade in Madras were usually between 73 and 105 degrees Fahrenheit. At Kistnagheri in the Baramaul, the equivalent figures were 70 and 90 degrees, but at sunrise the thermometer might have fallen to a chilly 47.[62] In the sun, temperatures much in excess of 100 degrees were common. Inevitably, most soldiers' accounts focus on the extreme heat, one officer complaining that India was 'as hot as Hades'. Fresh arrivals invariably make reference to the climate in their correspondence. Mornington wrote to Henry Dundas in May 1798, two weeks after his arrival, complaining of the heat in Madras and apprehensive about his imminent move to Calcutta; 'Tomorrow I make my departure for one [city] still more oppressive'. He admitted that during his first week in India he had suffered more than he had expected.[63] Samuel Rice of the 51st, in Madras the following year, believed that the heat precluded any possibility of 'real pleasure', but he also acknowledged that 'this is always the cry of a newcomer; time and necessity may reconcile me to it'.[64]

Veteran James Welsh describes the heat in Masulipatam in the south.

> The land wind, which generally blows here from March till August, and very violently all May, coming over an extensive parched plain, is heated to a degree almost incredible, and positively resembles air passing through a furnace. At this time no European is allowed to stand sentry, and even natives perish by exposure to the blasting influence of this Eastern sirocco; in which birds frequently fall down dead, while passing through it. The greatest heat generally commencing about eight or nine o'clock, A.M., and lasts, sometimes, with increasing force, till noon, or even three, P.M., when a lull is succeeded by a faint sea-breeze, and the poor parched and panting inhabitants begin to revive. In May, 1799, the thermometer within a solid house, with wet tats [flexible blinds] at the doors and windows, rose to 120°; and all the inferior buildings must have had it up to 130°. We were actually in a fever during its continuance...[65]

The nights were close and suffocating. In northern India, John Pester experienced outside temperatures of 115 degrees during the siege of Gwalior in 1804. The wind was 'blowing flames'. In the officers' mess, the temperature reached 120 degrees and the wax candles on the table melted and sank into the cloth.[66]

George Elers comments that in an officer's tent it was routinely 90–100 degrees and that temperatures in the tents of the private soldiers were at least 10 degrees higher.[67] It was widely accepted that such conditions were not only disagreeable, but also unhealthy, Welsh admitting that a sustained period of very hot weather would have 'annihilated' the whole garrison.[68] George Carnegie blithely informs his anxious mother that 'more will fall from the Climate than the sword' and James Young agreed: 'we dread not the Mahrattas but the sun'.[69]

Other extreme weather conditions included the monsoon rains, the rain descending in torrents 'such as no European can form any conception of'.[70] Violent storms and flooding might impair military operations just as much as the heat. Pester witnessed a 'hurricane' near Agra in 1803, all the tents flattened and the surrounding country inundated.[71] As described by Welsh and Pester, the combination of heat and strong winds was especially destructive. In May 1804, Lake's army suffered miserably from the burning wind. Thorn compares the fiery blast to 'the extreme glow of an iron foundry in the height of summer'. Men were suddenly struck down; they 'turned giddy, foamed at the mouth and instantaneously became lifeless'.[72] Of course, there were respites from these life-threatening extremes of climate, particularly at altitude. Blakiston enjoyed the pleasant weather in the Western Ghats of Mysore, the days not hot and the nights only cold enough to require a blanket.[73] The long-suffering Thorn was relieved to find that daytime conditions in the Punjab were delightful.[74]

Soldiers also enjoyed the spectacular scenery. Many accounts of military campaigns are littered with references to the beauty of their surroundings. Approaching Gawilghur in 1803, Mountstuart Elphinstone describes the picturesque country in detail, the fort suddenly coming into view behind a pile of stones: 'There was something of surprise and grandeur in this'. Despite the hardships of campaigning, the sight of soldiers working in the mountains was 'romantic'.[75] Thorn was entranced by the Himalayas.

> Directly before us, at the distance of thirty of forty miles, was a range of hills, rich in verdure, and coveted to their summits with stately forests of saul, sissoo and fir-trees; while far beyond, towered high above the clouds, the gigantic Himalaya mountains, their heads crowned with eternal snow, and glittering with the effulgence of the solar beams, playing on the immense glaciers of these unexplored regions.[76]

Much of India was still uncharted and alien to Europeans. The *vade mecum* warns soldiers and civilians of the dangers that lurked in the ethereal landscape. The author also gives some qualified reassurance;

many may be led to suppose, that, in India, every step is attended with danger; and, that neither the day, nor the night, offers security. This certainly is not always the case; but I should strongly advise every person to act throughout with caution; and to suppose these dangers I have described to be imminent.[77]

Beyond the obvious risks of war, the soldier or civilian traveller faced both human and natural threats. As described in the previous chapters, British control was often fragile and limited to particular territories. An apparently routine journey could end prematurely. John Malcolm, the Governor-General's private secretary, left Poona in October 1802 on the last stage of his transit to Bombay. He was soon fifty miles down the road.

> It was dark before I arrived at Keroli [Karli]. My palanquin was waiting there. I went in to it, and, being fatigued with my ride in a hot sun, I had fallen into a very profound slumber, when I was suddenly awoke by the noise of a number of armed men on foot and horseback, and the light of twenty or thirty flambeaux. Springing out of the palanquin, I demanded to know why I was so surrounded. 'You are our prisoner,' said a man, who appeared to be the leader of two hundred pikemen, who now encircled me.

He was held hostage for two days before the local chief realised that he had seized an English officer who was an ally of the Peshwa. Malcolm was released and the errant chief escaped with a fine.[78]

Natural threats might be on the grandest scale. There are numerous references to a violent earthquake and aftershocks at Alighar in early September 1803. The main event lasted more than two minutes and several buildings were destroyed.[79] John Pester jumped out of bed to hold on to the pole of his tent. He thought he must be dreaming: 'The motion was very like that of a small boat in a moderate sea.'[80] Soldiers rarely suffered from starvation, but they were not immune to the devastation of the famines around them. John Blakiston witnessed events near Poona in August 1803. Cultivations had ceased, villages were deserted and jackals picked over the bodies of the dead. The few local survivors forlornly followed the army, attempting to subsist on the offal of the camp, including the dung of the horses.[81]

Insects and wild animals were other potential dangers. The central role of insects as vectors of disease was not understood (see Chapter 13) but their immediate threat was obvious. Williamson notes that 'with regard to scorpions, centipedes, & c., too much circumspection cannot be used'. Venomous snakes were particularly numerous on jungle paths at night, having left their refuge in the long grass.[82] Arthur Wellesley's correspondence as governor of

Serigapatam in 1802 makes several references to troublesome wildlife. For instance, his General Orders of 23 July:

> It having been reported that several mad dogs have appeared in the fort and upon the island of Seringapatam, and that some accidents have already happened to the inhabitants, all dogs that may be found running loose after 9 o'clock in the morning of the 25th inst., in the fort and upon the island of Seringapatam, are to be killed...

A reward of two fanams was offered for each dead dog.[83] Three years earlier, Wellesley had ordered several tigers close to the city to be shot. They were short of food, untended to, and 'getting violent'.[84] Water brought its own dangers. George Elers enjoyed swimming near Pondicherry despite his constant dread of water-snakes and alligators.[85] On occasion, the latter would leave the rivers and snatch soldiers sleeping on the bank. John Pester saw a *havildar* badly wounded in this way. Starving alligators were deliberately introduced in to the ditches of some native forts.[86]

British soldiers' first reactions to the appearance of the local inhabitants were mostly a mixture of shock and disdain. Roderick Innes marched to the fort at Calcutta with 1,100 men of his regiment, the band playing and colours flying;

> here it astonished us greatly to see the immense number of black people, having no clothes, except a turban for the head, and a piece of cloth tied round the middle...[87]

James Welsh was unimpressed by the crowd of Bengalese who first approached the British ship in their country boats, 'talking a jargon perfectly unintelligible; with their diminutive limbs and shrivelled countenances'. He believed that the natives of India did not deserve to be treated as human beings.[88]

For some, these initial negative perceptions were strengthened by further contact with the local inhabitants. As the historian of the Indian Army, Philip Mason, points out:

> young officers were fair game for everyone from rascally servants to money-lenders, and British troops often saw few civilian Indians except pimps, touts, hawkers and servants of the most degraded kind.[89]

There are anecdotes of exploitation of naive British officers. Griffin John Blakiston was abandoned in the surf by the *massulah* boat boys, only being rescued when he handed over the bribe.[90] Others complain of the bands of thugs who stripped naked and oiled themselves 'so if they are caught they slip through your hands like an eel'.[91] Longer acquaintance brought a softening of attitude for many. Welsh, who was so critical of the feebleness of the locals at first arrival, admitted that he was deluded;

> at Calcutta… men of all sizes, with countenances of the most varied hues and expressions, and limbs of the most perfect symmetry and elegance, are to be met with…[92]

More open-minded officers such as John Blakiston and Roderick Innes, who made efforts to understand the local culture and to engage with civilian Indians, were well rewarded. Blakiston had been encouraged by his parents to familiarise himself with the manners, customs and religions of the people of the countries he visited and he followed this advice. He gives colourful descriptions of meetings with local chiefs and more informal contacts with the natives. Some behaviour puzzled him, but he acknowledged that their manners were generally dignified and polite.[93] Innes found the locals to be 'as conversant a people as any I ever spoke to in all my travels'. He had lively discussions about the relative merits of different religions, an argument he admits that he rarely won, 'for wherever I made a hole they put a nail in'.[94]

George Elers's recollections are of interest as he not only describes his own interactions with the local population, but also those of Arthur Wellesley. Elers objectively portrays both dignitaries and peasants. In 1801, he witnesses Wellesley's skilled negotiations with the local Raja, the young colonel quick enough to seize upon a false relation of his words by the interpreter. The British officer and Indian chief parted on very good terms, Wellesley only refusing an offer of a hunting expedition because he had to rush back to Seringapatam.[95] It seems that, like many educated officers, Wellesley's attitude to Indians gradually changed. A few months after his arrival in Bengal in 1797, he had written to his elder brother.

> The natives as far as I have observed, are much misrepresented. They are the most mischievous, deceitful race of people I have seen or read of. I have not yet met with a Hindoo who had one good quality, even for the state of society for his own country, and the Mussulmans are worse than they are.

Following his later experiences at Madras and in southern India, he lost these prejudices and worked openly and fairly with local rulers and other officials.[96]

In contrast, his elder brother never lost his contempt for the native Indians he dealt with. The Governor-General asserted that 'intrigue, falsehood and collusion' were their common characteristics and that they could only ever be considered for subordinate situations.[97] There is evidence that in the later years of the eighteenth and early years of the nineteenth century the Marquess's patronising vision became more widespread. For much of the previous 100 years, the British had showed relatively little racial prejudice to the people of the subcontinent. They mixed freely with Indians. Historian Channa Wickremesekera well documents the shifting sands.

> Towards the close of the eighteenth century, grim signs of changing attitudes began to appear. In 1789, Governor-General Lord Cornwallis wrote to Sir Robert Yonge at the War Office that Europeans in India generally looked down on Anglo-Indians 'on account of their colour and extraction'.

In the nineteenth century, the growing number of European soldiers, officers and women fostered a sense of exclusivity and the Indian came to be despised.[98] Amiya Barat, in her fine study of the Bengal native infantry, analyses the reasons for this change. As the prestige of the Company increased, memories of 'Maratha hardiness and Mughal splendour faded'. British officers were indoctrinated with a belief in their own superiority.

> A cadet who in 1797 read in Charles Grant's work on 'the Asiatic subjects of Great Britain,' that Indians were 'as a race lamentably degenerate and base' was at least as likely to despise as to pity the villagers of Baraset [the location of the Army's training facility] or the sepoys of his regiment. If he was constantly reminded that everything Indian – religion, law, arts and sciences, habits and manners – was decadent, he was as likely to be filled with contempt as with reforming zeal.

The technological advances in Britain compared with the comparatively static nature of Indian society served to reinforce these opinions.[99] The deterioration in relations was quite rapid, with falling levels of interaction between Europeans and natives. In 1810, Maria Graham, the daughter of a naval officer, regretted that in Calcutta, 'Every Briton appears to pride himself on being outrageously a John Bull'.[100]

Chapter 10

In Slow and Quick Time: Life in the Garrison

John Blakiston interrupted his account of his military adventures to relate the daily routine of the servants of the East India Company. After rising early, a constitutional ride might be taken before dressing for a heavy breakfast, taken at eight o'clock. The morning was mostly passed with the hooka, a newspaper or book before they sauntered to the stable to take a palanquin to the Presidency fort. There they remained, taking a 'slight tiffin', before leaving at 4pm either to return to their family or perhaps enjoying a further ride. Dinner was taken at seven o'clock and the evening was then spent in a manner common to the 'genteel circles in England'.[1]

Blakiston admitted that his own days were 'neither so rational nor so innocent'.[2] The memoirs of British soldiers, mainly officers, reveal that India was bittersweet for many, a country which regularly delivered the extremes of delight and misery. We will address the experience of fighting in the next chapter, here focussing on the mundane hours of life on campaign or in the garrison. The particular perspective of the native Indian soldier of the Company's armies is portrayed in Chapter 12.

British memoirists describe periods of real enjoyment in India. Blakiston's time in Madras was passed 'gaily enough' and he insisted that life in camp was not unpleasant providing that one remained in good health.[3] Captain George Elers gives an account of campaigning in Bengal in 1798.

> Thus I made my debut under canvas in the East. I started with a very modest establishment: a head servant, a second ditto, a boy to carry my chair, and coolies for my cot, table, etc., a Cooderry currah and grass-cutter. These two native servants were for the purpose of attending upon one horse, the only one I had. The novelty of camp life amused me much at first. We were obliged to be up before daylight; the bugle sounded an hour before dawn. The Lascars were then busily at work knocking loose the tent-pegs, the servants packing up the trunks, attending their masters and helping them to

dress, loading the bullocks with trunks, etc. In the course of another hour the second bugle sounds. The regiment is formed in marching order, the drums and fifes begin to play, and the officers are shortly after allowed to mount their horses and ride by the side of their companies. The Quartermaster and his staff precede the regiment, and fix the encampment about nine, ten, or twelve miles from the last ground, according as he finds favourable ground. One thing is indispensable: the vicinity of water, and it should be near a village. We had a fine large mess tent, and our mess man gave us a good dinner every day...[4]

Mountstuart Elphinstone gives a similar view of the routine camp day in Mysore; 'All this is extremely pleasant'.[5]

This was only one side of the burnished Indian coin. Almost all diaries refer to the difficulties of daily existence on the subcontinent. John Pester, at Gwalior in 1804, slept in his clothes for five weeks.[6] Roderick Innes served under the command of Arthur Wellesley for eighteen months, a time during which 'we scarcely ever had our heads under the roof of a house, exposed to hunger and thirst, heat and cold, with little rest night or day'.[7] James Young, writing in October 1804, had been tested by two months in the field: 'No wonder a man's constitution so soon bears out [sic] in India'.[8] Campaign life in any theatre was tough, but India veterans were keen to emphasise the unique challenges of the country. Blakiston again:

> I venture to assert, that no hardships experienced in European warfare, except indeed during a severe winter's campaign, which does not often occur, can be compared with those endured by an Indian army in the field.[9]

Whether on campaign or in garrison, any novelty soon wore thin for many. James Welsh believed an idle life to be always irksome to a soldier and Sergeant Robert Butler agreed.[10]

> I have already said, that upon the march we endured great fatigues, and also many inconveniences; but, when in barracks, a soldier's life in India is commonly very easy. They have not unfrequently eight or nine successive nights in bed; and, as the climate is generally very dry, they are not liable to get their arms or accoutrements often wet; and many of them likewise keep black boys to clean their things, take their victuals upon guard, and relieve them of other labours. They had consequently much spare time which they did not know how to get rid of...[11]

For much of the period, the garrison of one of the Presidency cities would consist of two or three European regiments with support from the native corps. According to Blakiston, everything in the garrison in Madras in 1802 had a feeling of rigidity about it. He describes an air of apprehension among the soldiers who believed that 'they were soon to become the objects if not the victims of its discipline'. He thought it strange that the military formalities in the Presidency fort were greater than he had witnessed in garrisons in England.[12] The authorities were determined to take every step to suppress infractions of the regulations. The Bombay Army orders for garrison duty compiled in 1800 are littered with admonitions, although apparently with some justification. A single entry confers the tone.

> The officers who have been guilty of quitting their guards are desired to discontinue this un-officerlike and un-military practice, or they will take the consequence of disobedience of orders and neglect of duty, as major general Bowles is determined to use the means in his power to enforce obedience. An officer is not to quit his guard either to go to his meals, or for any other purpose unless ordered. – He is to devote his whole attention whilst on duty to a faithful discharge of the trust reposed in him.[13]

Drill was a vital part of the garrison routine. In the late eighteenth century, this was not well defined. Major David Price, serving in Bombay in the late 1780s, admitted that, 'we possessed no established code of discipline to which we could refer; our only system being that which existed separately in the breasts of the separate commanders of battalions…'.[14] This lack of uniformity was addressed by Colonel David Dundas's seminal drill manual, *Principles of Military Movement*, first published in 1788. The primary objective of drill was to prepare for battle. Arthur Wellesley admitted that military operations were more complex, with the interaction of the three arms in variable country, but he emphasised in general orders of February 1803 that 'the mode in which each individual corps is to act will be the same as that which has been practised…'.[15] The following passage from the Bombay Army regulations for July 1802 indicates that there was an expectation that the Presidency armies would conform with the drill regulations of the wider British army.

> The commanding officer of the forces directs that the rules and regulations for the formation, field exercise, and movements of H. M. forces shall be most attentively observed and strictly practised by every corps belonging to this establishment; and as a number of copies of these regulations, carefully prepared, have been received at this presidency with accurate plates, together with Robert's

instructions comprehending the manual and platoon exercise [*Military Instructions including each particular motion of the Manual and Platoon Exercises* by David Roberts, 1798] founded on those regulations with accurate drawings of each motion, the commanding officer of the forces orders that every commanding officer and adjutant of a corps do immediately supply themselves with a set of these useful publications...[16]

Parades of native troops were overseen by European officers. On a field day the men would load arms. Their behaviour did not always meet the expected standards. A Bombay Army directive for December 1800 specifies that all ammunition be expended at the end of the exercise. Otherwise, the soldiers 'immediately begin firing in all parts of the woods and Cumauty village'.[17]

Apart from imposing discipline and preparing for manoeuvres on the battlefield, drill was vital for fitness. The commander of the Bombay garrison did not want to fatigue or harass the men, but he thought moderate exercise to be beneficial for the soldiers' health. We have a number of eyewitness accounts of the relentless nature of drill. Ensign Bayly notes that the 12th Regiment were drilled 'without intermission' in Madras's Fort St George between January and August 1797.[18] This was not always beneficial, Bayly himself being afflicted by sunstroke. George Elers well describes his regiment 'marching round several times both in slow and quick time, saluting etc.' This was followed by practise of the eighteen standard manoeuvres.[19] Parades might be held as a demonstration of British military strength and cohesion. After the capture of Gawilghur, Wellesley formed his men in open order on an extensive plain for inspection by Amrit Rao, the adopted brother of the Peshwa. James Welsh witnessed the scene and believed that the native chief must have been impressed;

> to see twelve fine corps in marching array, at the same moment, with a respectable artillery...no troops in the world could have exhibited a finer line, particularly the cavalry, such a thing never being attempted in any Native service.[20]

Despite all attempts to discipline the Indian army, there were inevitable infractions both by European and native troops. Minor misdemeanours might result in flogging. For the worst crimes, the death sentence was usually enforced. There was a hierarchy of capital punishment, some miscreants being shot while those committing even more shameful acts were hanged or fired from cannon. Wellesley's Indian dispatches contain many examples of the brisk application of military justice. In November 1803, three soldiers were caught plundering cattle from local villages: 'Four drummers of the 78th to attend immediately with their cats at the provost sergeant's tent to inflict 200 lashes'.

Wellesley warned that the next soldier apprehended would be executed.[21] Men deserting from the 84th Regiment in July 1803 were to be hunted down and then shot or hanged according to the decision of the court martial.[22]

Whatever the mode of execution, the sentence was carried out with due ceremony. Wellesley's general orders for 15 October 1803, issued from the camp at Phoolmurry, give details of the execution of a sepoy by firing squad. The following is a short extract.

> The line to be under arms at half past 5 o'clock; the cavalry mounted, and formed on the right of the infantry. A guard of a subaltern officer and 20 men from each corps of infantry in camp (except the 74th), under a captain, will parade at the tent where the prisoners are confined at 4 o'clock, when the provost will deliver them over to the guard, and the captain of it will march them from the right of the cavalry to the left of the infantry in slow time, and back again to the place appointed for the execution of Sheek David, in front of the 1st bat. 10th regt. The music [sic] and drummers and fifes of corps will play the dead march as the prisoners pass.

There is further detail of the make-up of the execution party. The firing of a gun signalled the reading of the sentence passed in general orders and a second gun firing announced the carrying out of the sentence. A third gunshot dismissed the assembled troops.[23]

Mutiny was ruthlessly suppressed. Ensign Bayly remembers a dangerous mutiny among the Company's soldiers marching between Madras and Tanjore in January 1798. He believed that some men from his own regiment, the 12th Foot, were involved. Several European artillerymen were found to be instigators and were sentenced to be blown from the mouth of a cannon. Having witnessed this 'shocking spectacle', the troops returned to camp 'without the slightest indication of any mutinous disposition'.[24]

Mutiny could only result in the most severe punishment, but it is likely that for other crimes the soldier's ethnicity and regiment influenced sentences. In February 1804, Wellesley refers to William Clarke, a private in HM 74th Regiment, who had been sentenced to death by a court martial for the murder of a local inhabitant.

> I have inquired into the character of the prisoner, and I find that he is a notorious thief, that he would have been tried by a regimental court martial for theft if he had not been brought to trial before a general court martial for murder, and that he was in every respect, a man of infamous character. It was, however, desirable not to punish with death a soldier of the 74th regiment...

He was instead transported to Botany Bay for life.[25]

Conditions of service such as pay, leave (furlough) and pensions were subject to change during the period. Efforts to standardise pay rates between the three Presidencies were mostly abortive.[26] The range in pay for different ranks in the Madras Army in 1798 was wide. The monthly wage for general officer on the staff was 1,081 *pagodas*, while an infantry captain drew 76 *pagodas* and a humble assistant surgeon only 45.[27] Payments were often made in the form of silver coins, the *sicca* rupees of Lucknow, Benares and Patna being held as *sonauts* in which the pay of the whole army was calculated.[28]

Pay rates were much complicated by *batta*, an extra allowance given to officers, soldiers and other public servants when in the field or on other special grounds. *Batta* and related incidental allowances could be lucrative and undoubtedly many British officers of the late eighteenth century expected to make their fortune in India. Bengal officers strongly objected to the pay restraints of the 1796 regulations.

> In our early youth we had exiled ourselves from our mother country, bade farewell to our friends not for the mere receipt of the present pay of our respective ranks but for obtaining those high emoluments, bazaar money, revenue commission, double full *batta*, the strong and only inducements which decided our selection of the East India Company's service...

They were concerned that they would become 'grey headed beggars'.[29]

For officers and men serving under Wellesley and Lake, delays in pay were routine and led to much misery. In May 1805, James Young complains of 'pinching poverty' among the officers of the army. Small advances had been made to the men, but officers' remuneration was six months in arrears. The news of the arrival of rupees from Agra sufficient for a month's pay was greeted with great relief.[30] Even when pay was up to date, life in an Indian garrison proved difficult for many officers. In February 1800, Wellesley wrote to the adjutant-general regarding the situation in Seringapatam;

> it will appear that it is impossible for an Ensign to live upon his pay, and that a Lieutenant can barely subsist upon it within this country. This arises from the expense of the European articles which officers must consume...

The General appends *A Monthly Statement of Expenses incurred by Officers at Seringapatam on the most moderate calculation*, the average monthly spend shown as 42 *pagodas*. The European corps messed together, thus pooling resources, but the European officers of the native corps lived separately and were especially vulnerable to local prices.[31]

The 1796 regulations made some sorely needed provisions for leave and retirement. Officers' leave was permitted in each Presidency such that a given proportion of each rank was absent at any time (e.g. a quarter of captains and surgeons). A period of furlough of three years was allowable, but a subaltern would have to have served ten years to be eligible.[32] Exceptions were made for sickness. Officers under the rank of colonel were permitted to retire on the pay of their rank after twenty-five years of service inclusive of the three-year furlough. For the most senior officers, decisions regarding leave and retirement were taken by the commander-in-chief and Government.[33] Many ordinary soldiers were shabbily treated on their return to England, as is related by Sergeant Butler.

> We all got safely ashore at Chelsea, which place was completely crowded with invalids from the Continent, besides those from India; they were in all about four thousand. The Tower and Chelsea being full, some hundreds were billeted in the country. This promised very badly with regard to pension, and upon the 14th of September, 1814, that day on which I passed, there were several hundreds who did not get a penny.

Butler received nine pence, a sum he believed to be small recompense for his fourteen years of Indian service and the damage to his constitution.[34]

The British were increasingly determined to set themselves apart from the perceived slack ways of the country they had invaded and were ultimately to rule. Nowhere was this more obvious than in the choice of a uniform totally unsuited to the climate. In Philip Mason's words, 'they stuck to their woollen clothes, high stiff collars, leather stocks, tight breeches'.[35] In the *vade mecum*, an infantry officer preparing for a campaign is reminded of the need to purchase a few yards of the 'best super-superfine scarlet broad cloth' to make up his regimentals.[36] George Elers was kitted up for a light infantry company in HM 12th Regiment.

> I was obliged to send up to London for a sabre and wings instead of epaulettes, and lots of narrow gold lace for my scarlet waistcoat. We wore blue pantaloons edged with scarlet, hats covered with the finest black ostrich feathers with a stand-up feather composed of red and black.

He admitted that a shower of rain rendered his appearance less impressive.[37]

Once in India, garrison commanders made attempts to maintain sartorial standards. In the Bombay Army orders for 1800, officers of HM 86th Regiment are reprimanded for their slovenly and improper dress. The importance of wearing the established uniform when out of quarters was reiterated the following year;

all shells (except such as are authorised by orders to staff officers) and other fantastical dresses, as well as sleeved waist-coats, are positively forbidden to be worn abroad.[38]

On campaign, officers often took a more pragmatic view of uniform. This was true for Wellesley, whose directives stress the comfort and durability of dress rather than its smartness. At Bombay in May 1804, he demonstrates his usual attention to detail in a letter to General James Stuart.

> As all the corps are in want of clothing… I applied to Mr. Duncan for cloth from the warehouse here, and I have sent up as much as will make a comfortable plain jacket for each man. These will be made before the rains set in… I really could not venture to expose the troops to the rains without clothing.

He explains that many of the men had had no new clothes since 1800. He made no new delivery of cloth to the cavalry as their uniform gave them better protection from the weather that that of the infantry.[39]

The British soldier's diet was dominated by meat. At Seringapatam in 1799, rations included a pound and a half of beef or an eighth of a sheep. This staple was supplemented by allowances of rice, buttermilk, salt and pepper. When supplies ran short, salted beef was substituted for fresh meat and biscuit might replace bread.[40] On campaign, the available bullocks could carry only a maximum of three weeks' supply of food and the quartermasters were continually seeking new stocks.[41] Soldiers rarely starved, although there were instances of serious shortages, especially when the forces were distant from a market or town. Roderick Innes saw men of his regiment almost crushed to death in their attempts to obtain food from a Bombay merchant.[42]

Attitudes to food highlighted the differences between the ranks and the officer class. Most officers expected to eat in some style, particularly when in the regimental mess of the garrison. Elers gives a flavour of this when describing his life in Madras in 1797.

> We had, of course, our own regimental plate. We found two black men, brothers, who agreed to find us an excellent dinner, a dessert, and a pint of madeira each man for ten pagodas a head monthly; also twice a week, Thursday and Sunday, a better dinner, consisting of European articles, such as hams, tongues, cheese, etc..

The mess consisted of forty to fifty of his fellow officers and there were an even greater number of guests.[43] The following year, Arthur Wellesley wrote to his younger brother from Fort St George, informing him that he was obliged to keep a table and requesting that Henry send from Calcutta a soup-tureen and dishes sufficient for twelve people. He only needed to supply eatables and dishes: 'I need not want plates, knives, forks, nor spoons, as everybody in an Indian camp brings these articles for himself...'.[44]

Such elaborate arrangements were difficult to maintain when on campaign. On the march, it was common to combine breakfast and tiffin, often consuming the cold meat of the previous evening's dinner. This meal was eaten as soon as possible after the troops reached their ground. A servant or two would have been earlier dispatched with the mess-trunks and table, carried on the best bullock or camel. As the baggage, including the tents, usually arrived later, the repast was often served under a tree.[45]

Fresh water could be drawn from wells, but for a sizeable army on the march this was too slow and there was much reliance on the water tanks or reservoirs which punctuated the landscape.[46] Engineer officers were given responsibility for their protection as they were liable to run dry and were also easy targets for a retreating enemy.[47] An anonymous officer in the Seringapatam campaign complains of the 'nefarious and fiend-like expedient of poisoning them'.[48] A common method was to throw milkhedge plant into the water, although George Rowley believed its harmful effects to be exaggerated.[49] Wellesley was mindful of the need for adequate water supplies, adopting strategies such as diverting streams to garrisons (as at Ahmednuggar), attaching watermen and bullocks to regiments, and sending trusted subordinates to reconnoitre for natural sources.[50] Most of the anecdotal evidence for water shortages, and men experiencing dehydration, is contained in the literature of the northern campaigns. After the battle of Delhi, a number of witnesses testify to the suffering of both officers and men. John Pester believed that a canteen of muddy water given to him by a drummer had saved his life.

> We were all dreadfully distressed for something to drink. We had been twelve hours in so scorching a sun as ever shone from the heavens, and nearly eighteen hours marching and in action. Our servants, of course, all remained in the rear and the first opportunity the troops had of quenching their thirst was in the Jumnah.[51]

The native troops in British service were astonished at the Europeans' attachment to alcohol. *Subadar* Sita Ram saw them 'worship liquor, give their lives for it, and often lose their lives trying to get it'.[52] This was despite rations containing copious amounts of alcohol. In 1799, the troops received two drams daily allowance; a dram was one fifth of a pint of spirit. At first, this was *arrack* (a coarse spirit distilled from grain, rice or sugar cane) and later, rum.[53] Soldiers were inclined to quickly drain their allowance and then actively seek out more. There were therefore numerous attempts to limit supply and consumption, many iterated in Wellesley's dispatches. The following extract is from a general order of March 1803.

> In future the soldiers are to receive their 2 drams at 2 different times in the day. They will receive the first dram on marching days upon their arrival at the new ground of encampment, and on halting days at daylight in the morning, at the flag of the commissary of provisions, as at present. At the same time the second dram for each man will be delivered to the charge of the quarter masters, who will send the quarter master serjeants, or other trusty persons, to receive it. The commissary of provisions will issue kegs to the quarter masters of regiments in which the arrack is to be kept in the regimental lines, under such a guard as the commanding officers of regiments may think proper to appoint; and the second drams are to be issued to soldiers in their lines at the hours which the commanding officers of regiments may think most proper.[54]

Camp sutlers illegally selling arrack and rum to the troops had their goods confiscated and it was forbidden to sell liquor to European soldiers in the bazaars.[55]

The officers were themselves often consuming enormous amounts of drink. John Pester set out for a march in the summer of 1803 having packed ten dozen bottles of Madeira, four dozen of port and an undisclosed amount of beer.[56] It is a measure of the average alcohol intake that George Elers thought Colonel Arthur Wellesley to be 'very abstemious with wine', despite him routinely drinking four or five glasses with dinner and a pint of claret after.[57] We shall return to the deleterious effects of alcohol on the army's health in a later chapter.

In the early years, British troops were housed in barracks in forts, notably Fort William in Calcutta and Fort St George in Madras. As the British presence and the power of the East India Company grew, barracks were increasingly purpose-built, often grouped together in military cantonments near to towns.[58] These facilities, much preferred by the men to life under canvas, were the responsibility of the quartermaster general. Bombay Army orders for 1800 specify that barrack masters and other officers in immediate charge of all the military quarters, cantonments and barracks, had to make monthly reports to the senior officer regarding their general state.[59] The construction of adequate barracks was often compromised by a lack of organised labour and materials. In September 1799, Arthur Wellesley writes to Colonel John Sherbrooke.

> By the bye, the Scotch brigade have some carpenters and masons, who ought to be made to assist in fitting up their own barracks.

The 33rd Regiment completed theirs with very little or no assistance at all, and if the Scotch brigade do not give their assistance, they must expect that a great length of time will elapse before they will inhabit the Toste Khanah [barracks].[60]

Two years later, Wellesley's efforts to build barracks for 800 European troops at Seringapatam were frustrated by a failure to procure the necessary bricks and *chunam* (cement).[61] The regulations stipulated the space allotted to the men. Wellesley wrote to the ever-demanding Colonel Murray in June 1801 expressing 'astonishment' that the European barracks were insufficient: 'They appear to be to be large enough for a whole regiment'. He conceded that additional buildings could be constructed if it transpired that the regulations were not being complied with.[62]

Some barracks were always intended to be temporary. At Muttra and Agra in 1805, barracks and stables were quickly erected for the native corps with the expectation that they would be soon broken up.[63] The nature of the buildings sometimes suggested a lack of permanency. Roderick Innes was housed in a barracks near Cawnpore which was made of bamboo, covered with banana leaves and fastened together by ropes made of the Cassia plant. It fell down in a gale – 'bedsteads were thrown up in the air and smashed to pieces...'.[64] Other facilities were no doubt much better. Pester was impressed by the accommodation at Berhampore.

The barracks are two storeys, and resemble in front more a superb range of gentlemen's houses, lengthened together, than accommodation for soldiers.[65]

Officers had their own accommodation. At Ponamalee in 1799, Captain John Budgeon was delighted to discover 'commodious and good' officers' quarters.[66] Pester notes that at Berhampore in 1805, their quarters were also 'uncommonly spacious and elegantly built'. Each quarters contained three excellent rooms with verandas.[67] However, there was also much poor-quality provision. In Seringapatam in 1801, the officers' quarters were mostly in ruins, the occupants expected to make repairs at their own expense.[68] In cantonments, many officers lived in their own houses. When George Elers's regiment moved to Warriore there were no formal officers' quarters and the preferred option for him and his fellow officers was detached bungalows.[69] These dwellings might be traded. Captain Philip Le Fevre of the Bengal native infantry records that, in August 1803, he sold a large bungalow with outhouses to Lieutenant-Colonel Robert Dunkley for 400 rupees.[70] Unsurprisingly, the most senior officers could aspire to the most luxurious houses. James Welsh describes his regiment's arrangements at Madurai in 1795.

The commanding officer had an elegant house near the centre, considerably raised from the ground, with a capital garden attached to it; the Paymaster lived in a very roomy building, of eastern architecture... Captain John Bannerman, commanding our corps, resided in a delightful bungalow...[71]

We will consider the army on the march in the next chapter, but here will review the army's accommodation when on active campaign. It was the quartermaster general's duty to find suitable ground for an encampment at the end of the day's march. Pester records these searches in some detail; the ground ideally had to be 'high and dry' to prevent all arms, and particularly the artillery, from getting bogged down.[72] Security was a central concern and, once on the ground, the army took up a prescribed formation. The arrangements in the Mysore campaign are well described by John Malcolm in his journal.

The position of the whole is as follows – the Grand Army [Harris's force] forms one face of an octagon facing the west, the Cavalry form another face of it fronting the NW and the [Nizam's] Contingent form another fronting the SW, and in the Rear of the left of the Contingent is Meer Allum's Camp and the Baggage and the Binjarries and the [space] mentioned in yesterday's journal [possible the heavy park and stores] are in the Rear and covered by the whole Army.[73]

The innumerable camp followers gave this essentially military gathering a unique atmosphere, as is testified by William Thorn.

The power of the imagination can scarcely figure to itself the sudden transformation that takes place on these occasions, when an Indian camp exhibits with the effect of enchantment, the appearance of a lively and populous city amidst the wilds of solitude, and on a dreary plain.[74]

John Blakiston describes his first experience of an Anglo-Indian camp.

The quantity of tents pitched in regular lines, covering a great extent of ground, intermixed with the gay uniforms of the soldiers, and the various flags denoting the stations of the different commanders and departments, had a most brilliant appearance. I had seen camps in England, containing considerable bodies of troops, but nothing on so grand a scale as this. Six tents, considerably larger than the bell-tents used in England, were allowed to each company of Europeans, and three to each company of sepoys. Every officer has a marquee to himself, differing in size according to the rank of the occupier; but the smallest ten feet square, with high walls and a double fly. The whole were pitched in regular order – the private tents in front, the subalterns in a line behind them, the captains next, and the field officers and regimental staff in the rear.

The magnificent tents of the most senior officers were in the 'head-quarter line', which occupied a large area. With the three arms of the army, the ancillary departments and the bazaar, a fighting force of 10,000 soldiers would form a camp two miles wide and half a mile deep. Most of the parallelogram was taken up not by the tents of the army, but by the booths of the bazaar and the smaller tents of the camp followers.[75]

There were precise arrangements for the distribution and carriage of tents. In the Bombay Army of 1803, the European corps was permitted one tent for every eight men and the native corps one tent for every twelve men.[76] Officers received an allowance for the purchase and maintenance of their own tents. The subject crops up often enough in Wellesley's dispatches. In 1800, he advises that officers should carry their tents to spare the bullocks, which were needed to convey grain and stores.[77]

Officers' attitudes to tents varied. In the Mysore campaign, Elphinstone tells us that no expense was spared.

> Everybody tries to get the largest tent he can and nothing but poverty or regulations limit people. They do not talk in camp of the comfort of being snug and compact, with a fine small tent, easily pitched, and nice light baggage, that soon comes up.[78]

Some were more pragmatic. An anonymous officer, writing of the campaign in the north in 1803, admits that his tent did not look much, but he valued its lightness;

> a soldier, when he halts, never knows how soon he may be again called upon to beat a march – so commend to me the tent that travels best![79]

He believed that his tent would last the duration of the war, but many didn't. The cloth tended to rot, particularly when wet for long periods.[80] Tents were also more immediately vulnerable to extreme weather conditions, there being several descriptions of tents being blown away. Blakiston gives an elaborate account of how he secured his tent, but he had to concede that no method protected against heavy rain combined with high winds.[81] Sergeant Butler agrees that 'the pins and cords were no security against the irresistible power of the airy element, but gave way like stubble before the sweeping blast'.[82]

A general order was issued at Seringapatam in December 1802, making reference to accommodation for the families of European and native corps about to leave on active service. Married men were to build new huts.[83] There were only a few European women with the battalions in India. When Richard Bayly's regiment left England in 1796, only sixty of at least 500 women were permitted to embark with their husbands.[84] Eleven years later, the same number of women accompanied a 1,000-strong battalion of the Royals, the selection made by casting lots.[85] The author of the *vade mecum* informs us that, following arrival in India, many European women soon succumbed to the climate, 'which nothing but the most vigorous constitutions, backed by temperance and uncommon prudence can enable the sex to resist'. The survivors were, he said, often of a 'masculine' appearance, their children 'remarkably hardy'.[86] The few fragments of information we have of these women's lives suggest a squalid existence. Roderick Innes was in Calcutta when most of his regiment departed for Egypt, leaving their wives behind.

> The women were put in a bomb-proof by themselves. Our men often paid them visits; and as they loved drink, and consequently were not particular as to what they did, and as our soldiers willingly gave them liquor, scenes not the most moral often were enacted.[87]

At the beginning of the nineteenth century, most officers were not married, very much living the bachelor lifestyle. There were limited opportunities for those who wished to have liaisons and relationships with European women. There were women who visited India to find a husband – later to be known as the 'fishing fleet' – and they tended to gather in Calcutta. They were mostly averse to casual relationships and were not available for sex.[88] John Blakiston gives a cynical account of their aspirations when arriving on the subcontinent;

> the matrimonial market in India is much the same as other markets for live stock… First the young lady is instructed [by her family] to set her cap at a civilian high in office, or at an officer high on the staff. If, in the course of a few months, there is no bidding at that price, then she condescends to cast a smile upon the second rank, and so on to the bottom.

Beauty was so scarce that the possessor was bound to be quickly snapped up.[89] The excess of men encouraged illicit affairs. George Elers noticed that Arthur Wellesley had a 'very susceptible heart', particularly towards married women.[90]

The lives of officers' wives in the upper echelons of Indian European society were far removed from the drudgery suffered by the wives of the men. Much of the advice in the *vade mecum* suggests a cosseted existence.

> Ladies will derive considerable convenience and gratification from having an exterior case made to enclose the pianoforte.[91]

They are rarely glimpsed on campaign, but no doubt there were some who escaped from the music room. John Pester took pity on a British woman who was accompanying an officer of the 15th Light Dragoons in 1805. They had lost their tent and Pester gave them some breakfast. He was impressed by his countrywoman, who was 'remarkably well behaved' with genteel manners.[92]

At this period, the relationship of the British soldier with Indian women was complex, multi-faceted and subject to a change in attitudes. The sexual needs of the ordinary soldiers were catered for by hard-working Indian prostitutes in the 'lal bazaar', an unofficial regimental brothel.[93] The standing orders issued by Wellesley to the 33rd Regiment in 1797 imply a relaxed attitude towards sex.

> The Soldiers are not to bring into Barracks any Common Prostitute, if they do the Sergeant must turn them out and confine the man; however if any man wishes to keep a native woman and obtains his Captain's permission to do so, there is no objection to her being in the Barracks, and the Officer will be cautious not to give permission to any but well-behaved men.[94]

Wellesley was making a distinction between prostitutes and native women who were being 'kept' by the soldier. It was normal for British officers to cohabit with an Indian mistress (*bibi*). In 1800, a third of the Company's servants had Indian wives or mistresses and *Subadar* Sita Ram makes it clear that this extended to the army.[95]

> Most of our officers had Indian women living with them, and these had great influence in the regiment. They always pretended to have more influence than was probably the case in order that they might be bribed to ask the *sahibs* for favours on our behalf… In those days the *sahibs* could speak our language much better than they do now, and they mixed more with us.[96]

The increasing social gulf that developed between the British and the native population in the course of the nineteenth century meant that these Anglo-Indian relationships became less common. The moral climate was to be changed by an influx of European women and the growth of evangelical Christianity.[97] However, at the end of the eighteenth century and the start of the nineteenth, attitudes to religion remained relaxed, with men and officers inclined to base their views on the behaviour of their regimental chaplains. Some of these churchmen were unlikely to inspire agnostic soldiers. Reverend Blunt was chaplain of Wellesley's 33rd Foot in 1796. Three days into an amphibious expedition:

> he got abominably drunk, and in that disgraceful condition exposed himself to both soldiers and sailors, running out of his cabin stark naked into the midst of them, talking all sort of bawdy and ribaldry, and singing scraps of the most blackguard and indecent songs, so as to render himself a common laughing stock.

When the clergyman sobered up he was mortified. Wellesley tried to mollify him but he was inconsolable and died only ten days later.[98] Despite this unfortunate experience, during his later governorship Wellesley made efforts to maintain a religious infrastructure. In 1799, he wrote to Josiah Webbe from Seringapatam asking him to appoint a chaplain to the garrison.[99] These posts were never numerous. Regulations for the Madras Army issued in 1806 increased the number of chaplains from six to nine.[100]

The wider authorities were keen that there should be regular divine service for the troops. In May 1798, the Court of Directors of the East India Company stipulated that a service should be conducted on the Sabbath in all military stations in Bengal, just as would be the case in England.[101] There are similar directives in later Presidency army orders.[102] In practice, there was always a shortage of clergymen and services were sporadic. The religious Sergeant Butler was at Wallajahbad in September 1808.

> We had prayers read for the first time since we came to this country, by the adjutant, who had fifty pagodas a month for doing the duty of chaplain… Oh for an opportunity of hearing a good sermon, from the mouth of a godly minister of Jesus Christ.[103]

John Blakiston found the natives to be surprised and unimpressed by the Europeans' disregard of religious observance.[104]

Between the episodes of marching and fighting, there were many hours to fill. British soldiers' recreations varied according to their predilection, rank and location. In general, many of these pursuits had an Indian flavour, but in the Presidency capitals great efforts were made to recreate the splendours of English high society. This was especially the case in Calcutta under the jurisdiction of the Marquess Wellesley.[105] It was an elitist world well portrayed by the pens of socialites such as the Calcutta lawyer William Hickey, and senior army officers, men such as George Elers and John Malcolm. Hickey regales us with numerous anecdotes of his parties and trips to the hospitable messes of the

10th and 33rd regiments.[106] Elers makes reference to the Governor-General's 'princely style of living'.[107] Judging from Malcolm's description of a grand ball held in Calcutta in January 1803, this was no exaggeration. There were 800 guests.

> The room was not sufficiently lighted up, yet still the effect was beautiful. The row of chunam [stucco] pillars, which supported each side, together with the rest of the room, were of a shining white, that gave a contrast to the different dresses of the company. Lord Wellesley wore the orders of St Patrick and the Crescent in diamond. Many of the European ladies were also richly ornamented with jewels. The black dress of the male Armenians was pleasing from the variety; and the costly, though unbecoming habits of their females, together with the appearance of officers, nabobs, Persians, and natives, resembled a masquerade.[108]

Officers also passed their time playing and watching the popular games and sports of the period, everything from billiards to horseracing. Gambling was commonplace although disapproved of by the military authorities. In his regimental orders for the 33rd, Colonel Arthur Wellesley explicitly forbids it.[109] We must presume that the ordinary soldier whiled away his spare hours in card games and other simple pursuits; as for much of the daily experience of the wars we have few voices from the ranks.

For some officers out in the country, hunting was close to an obsession. Not for nothing did John Pester entitle his memoirs *War and Sport in India*. His campaigning history is interspersed with detailed accounts of his breathless slaughter of wildlife. We find him tracking tigers on elephants, chasing hogs on horseback, pursuing hares with dogs and shooting birds with muskets. One journal entry reports 'a capital day's sport, and killed everything we went after'.[110]

Such vigorous activities were not without risk, but they must have provided a welcome diversion from the horrors of the wars. Many officers were literate, cosmopolitan men and we have allusions to more intellectual interests in their writings. George Elers bought a 'very pretty' portable library from a sick fellow officer. This consisted of sixty or seventy volumes enclosed in a wooden case.[111] Mountstuart Elphinstone's letters from the Indian camps of 1803 contain passages of artistic criticism.

> Much as I like Spenser, I think his Pastorals have been immoderately praised, and that making the crown of eclogue writing pass from Theocritus and Virgil to him was gross profanation.

When later discussing the words of Cicero, he admits that he was seldom in the mood for reading but that he felt it was his duty to study.[112] It is fortunate that eloquent officers such as Elphinstone also made time for the writing of the diaries, journals and memoirs that give us such a vivid insight into army life in India. Some of these have found their way into print but many remain unpublished, lying largely undiscovered and little consulted in the archives of libraries and museums.

Chapter 11

Hand to Hand: In Action

The nature of the King's and East India Company armies has been considered in the first chapter and a chronological account of the wars has followed. In this chapter there will be further discussion of the strategy and tactics adopted by the British commanders and also an elucidation of the particular difficulties they faced, and an exploration of the human dimension of the fighting.

Arthur Wellesley's and Gerard Lake's strategy was based upon mobility and speed. This was to be an audacious war, fought on the front foot. This is explicit in the writings of both men. 'Time is everything in military operations…', Wellesley wrote to John Malcolm in November 1803.[1] The Marathas had to be intimidated by the 'ease and celerity' of movement of the British forces.[2] As we have seen in the Deccan campaign, James Stevenson was continually harangued to 'dash' at the enemy. Lake was even more aggressive in his actions in the north, frequently surprising the Marathas with the rapidity of his response and movement. While Wellesley tempered the risks of this strategy by giving assiduous attention to logistics and supply, Lake was frequently careless in his preparations, a weakness seized upon by his increasingly confident junior colleague. In a letter to Josiah Webbe, Wellesley is openly critical: 'what can have induced the General [Lake] to press for the commencement of the war with Holkar, being entirely unprepared to follow him, or to carry the war beyond the Company's frontier'.[3] Lake often trusted his instinct and left much to chance, whereas Wellesley was the consummate planner.

If Wellesley was the more cautious of the two generals, it can be said that both underestimated their enemy. Wellesley's repeated assertions that the war with Holkar would last only two weeks if Lake 'would only dash at him with his cavalry' seems, at least in retrospect, grossly over-optimistic.[4] Wellesley was frequently to be surprised by the proficiency of his Maratha opponent, but was always able to find a tactical solution. Lake was rewarded for his verve on the battlefield but, as we will later discuss, he was to pay a heavy price in human lives for his complacency in siege operations.

The tactics of the British in the field were broadly similar to those adopted in European campaigns. Infantry manoeuvred and fought in line, transferring their parade ground drill to the battlefield. A two-rank line maximised firepower and the gleaming bayonets considerably increased the psychological threat to an adversary. The Marathas probably underestimated the central role of the bayonet in British tactics. Wellesley's greatest victories in India, Assaye and Argaum, depended on the cohesion of his battalions advancing in line. At Assaye, the British line crossing the river was 1,400 yards long.[5]

King's and East India Company cavalry regiments were effectively used as heavy cavalry on the battlefield, charging at controlled speed with the sabre. Normally these charges were made with squadrons and troops in line, the front and rear ranks of horsemen having an interval of around fifteen yards.[6]

Field artillery tactics employed the two 6-pounder guns routinely attached to each infantry battalion and cavalry regiment. The infantry guns both increased the battalion's firepower and protected the men from the encroachment of enemy cavalry and the close attention of rocketeers. The British were outgunned by the Marathas, but the 'gallopers' (horse-drawn light field guns) of the cavalry proved especially effective, demoralising enemy horsemen. Wellesley was initially sceptical of their use but he eventually admitted that he would only reluctantly part with the flying artillery.[7]

Neither Wellesley nor Lake made any great innovations in tactics. It was the former's objective to always tackle the Maratha foe when they were on the move, avoiding attacking them in a position of their choosing and giving them no opportunity to attack him. Surprise and the relentless grasping of the initiative were key elements. Retreat was not a serious option. At battalion level, Wellesley's tactics at Assaye can be regarded as primitive, the close-quarter use of bayonets and sabres ultimately overcoming the superiority of the Marathas' musketry and artillery fire.[8] There are, however, hints of the future Wellington. His calm order to the distressed sepoys at Argaum to lie down is reminiscent of the tactics he would employ against Napoleon at Waterloo.[9] Lake was more tested in the field than Wellesley, able to draw on his experiences in the American War. He saw no alternative to the orthodox use of musket and bayonet against Sindia's regular battalions.[10] He would also maintain the offensive at almost all cost.

Both Lake and Wellesley have been criticised for their strategy and tactics in India. Any adverse comment must be viewed in the context of British campaigns which were close to being universally successful. There also has to be acknowledgement of the severe challenges of campaigning in the subcontinent. The extremes of climate have been referred to. In addition, there were the difficult terrain and roads, the tenuous nature of supply chains, and the lack of reliable intelligence and maps.

Roads were variable. In late 1802, Wellesley described the roads of the Maratha territories as being excellent, but he was quick to add that heavy rains turned them into a swamp, 'through which it is scarcely practicable for a man to move...'. The wheels of the wagons sank up to their axles in the mud.[11] Writing six months later, and probably having to revise his original optimistic assessment, he complains of the badness of the roads ruining the wagon wheels: 'I shudder when I think of the dreadful destruction of the wheel carriages which there will be, on this day's and to-morrow's march'.[12] Thorn's detailed description of an elephant pulling a cannon from quicksand encapsulates the peculiar difficulties of a campaign in India.[13] River crossings had to be meticulously planned, a procedure well described in Wellesley's dispatches. The General believed this to be an example of superior European knowledge.[14]

The British Army's commissariat and intelligence services have been alluded to in the first chapter. In practice, both depended much on the support of the local population, usually gained by a mixture of charm and coercion. In early 1803, Wellesley and his political agent, John Malcolm, bargained with local chiefs to ensure a constant source of supplies.[15] Ultimately, the army would have struggled to survive on campaign without the entrepreneurial *banjaras*, an itinerant ethnic group who specialised in the trafficking of grain, salt and other commodities.[16] Blakiston describes them continually on the move, living in tents with their families, and armed with a sword. He compares them to 'gypsy muleteers' and freely admits their importance: 'In fact, when I was in India there was no carrying on war without them'.[17] The scale of their operations and interaction with the British is impressive. As early as February 1799, John Malcolm was able to report almost 60,000 *banjaras* accompanying Harris's Grand Army and the Nizam's contingent.[18] Efforts were made not to alienate these vital suppliers, but they were not easy allies. Wellesley's correspondence reveals that they were sometimes reluctant to come forward and then unreliable. In June 1803, they were 'playing tricks as usual' leaving the army with only a third of its anticipated supply of rice.[19]

The British relied on *harkarrahs* to gain intelligence of the country and enemy. These local men were mostly not spies in the modern sense of the word but more messengers relaying information back to advancing armies. Their actions were not necessarily covert.[20] As Blakiston well explains, intelligence was bought and sold much as rice or grain.

> In no country is the system of espionage so well understood as in India. In fact, information is there a regular marketable commodity; and there are professed dealers in it, just as in any other article. The same person, indeed, will often supply different parties with information of each other's movements.[21]

Mountstuart Elphinstone laboured to develop a network of *harkarrahs*, at one time employing 175 at a considerable cost.[22] The enemy were equally vigilant; in September 1803 Elphinstone admitted that one of his informers had been hanged by the Marathas.[23] He describes these men as spies but, as inferred by Blakiston, they probably had fluid loyalties. Prior to Assaye, Wellesley drew on three separate groups of *harkarrahs*. There was always the danger of misinformation and, as has been related, the period before the battle might be regarded as a British intelligence failure.[24]

The nature of India made even internal communications problematic. There was a primitive postal system between the larger Maratha cities, variously known as the *dawk* or the *tappal*, where messages were carried on foot, often over prodigious distances. If speed was essential, camel riders could be employed.[25] Wellesley strove to maintain and improve this system for his own purposes. In July 1801, he writes of the arrangements in Malabar, suggesting an increase in the number of 'runners' at each station from two to three. The work was not without risk, many of the natives avoiding the roads because of the threat from tigers.[26] Despite the best efforts of army administrators, there was a disconnect between the northern and southern theatres of war. Wellesley lamented his 'want of information' regarding Lake's campaigns.[27] The connection with London was even more fragile; overland despatches from Bombay took about four months to reach England.[28] The lack of sophisticated maps was a further headache for Europeans in India, cartography being little advanced. A beginning was made with the establishment of a Department of Survey by the quartermaster general. Senior British officers were mostly expected to research the geography of an area of operations themselves.[29]

To wage a war of aggression in which forward momentum was paramount, the British army had to march often and far. In the southern theatre, we have much detail of the organisation of men on the march in Wellesley's dispatches and general orders. At Khurkha in early September 1803, the General emphasises both the importance of the army being able to move at short notice, and also the need to keep the enemy ignorant of the planned march. The decision to march or halt would not be announced in the orders of the day. The pickets were always to parade at reveille and, when a march was to be made, the *général* was to be beat at 4.30am with assembly at 5am. More specific instructions were issued, for instance for night marches and for several battalions marching in line.[30]

In the north, marches were similarly regulated, there being a need to balance mobility and security. Thorn describes the organisation of the army formed in two columns marching from Agra in December 1804. The columns were parallel to each other, the reserve forming the advance guard and the space of 600 yards between the columns sheltering the artillery, baggage, and provisions train. The union of all the pickets and a cavalry regiment provided the rearguard. The whole was an oblong, designed to prevent incursions by enemy horse.[31]

Rates of march depended on the military imperative and the state of the men. Wellesley expected his force 'in marching trim' to achieve three miles in an hour.[32] A march made in February 1804 was the 'greatest exertion he had ever witnessed', the infantry covering 60 miles in twenty hours.[33] In his valuable account of the Maratha campaigns, Major Helsham-Jones makes a particular study of the British Army's marches and concludes that the three greatest feats were Wellesley's march from Assaye to Argaum in October and November 1803, Lake's pursuit of Holkar in November 1804, and Smith's pursuit of Ameer Khan in early 1805. Calculations of exact distances and routes are frustrated by inexact information and obscure placenames, but Helsham-Jones's estimates are no doubt close to the truth. Leaving Delhi at the end of October 1804, Lake's force of three brigades of cavalry and a reserve brigade of infantry covered 325 miles in eighteen days, an average of 18 miles each day including the halt. Wellesley's achievement was arguably even greater as he was at the head of a whole army with guns and impedimenta.[34]

It is in part the objective of this chapter to give a more personal view of campaigning. Perhaps the most evocative account of life on the march is penned by Sergeant Butler, referring to his exploits is southern India.

> September 22, [1808]… We now presented to the eye a most formidable appearance; and, humanly speaking, it would have taken a considerable force to have opposed our progress, being in all ten thousand King's and Company's Troops. The followers of the army in this country are generally about four to one; so that, in all, we must have been in number about fifty thousand, white and black. Those who follow the army for a living, are washermen, (for it is the men, and not the women, who wash the clothes in this country,) barbers, cooly-boys (that is, bearers of burdens, cooks' assistants, officers' under servants, & c.) dooly-bearers, horse-keepers, grass-cutters, officers' butlers, dubashes [interpreters], and mati-boys, palanquin-bearers, lascars, for pitching the officers' tents, hospital-dressers, elephant-keepers, bandy-men [cart-drivers], camel and bullock drivers, and bazaar people…
>
> September 29 – We were ordered to move forward. Our mode of marching was the following: – If our journey was long, we generally marched about three o'clock A.M., that we might have it over before the heat of the day; and we were allowed just half an hour to put on our clothes, strike our tents, and place them on the elephants, one of which was appointed to each company; and in that space of time our bandies had to be packed, and the army ready to march, – so you may see that we were not idle. We had

mutton and rice twice a-day. The rice was carried upon bullocks, and the sheep driven along with us, and killed when we came to the ground which we were appointed to occupy for a night. We were sometimes nine hours upon the march, although we frequently did not travel above sixteen miles in the course of that time; and this you need not wonder at, for our roads (when we had any) were miserably bad and narrow, being generally confined by jungles on both sides, so that, with such a numerous body, moving forward frequently only two men deep, it was impossible for us to travel otherwise than at a very slow and interrupted pace; yet, although we were thus long upon our journey, we were sometimes two or three hours at our camp ground before we got our breakfast. But this hard marching, (I call it hard, for it was much worse than if we had been moving at an ordinary pace,) I say, this hard marching, and long abstinence, cut off great numbers of men; for we left them upon the road almost daily, both white and black.[35]

Marches might culminate in fighting and we will now turn to eyewitness accounts which illustrate the army's three arms in serious action. The Maratha regular forces were eventually destroyed in three battles; the victories of Wellesley at Assaye, Lake at Laswari, and Fraser at Deig. These were all close-fought affairs with a real possibility of Maratha success. British forces prevailed largely due to better leadership and the tactical superiority of infantry trained to fight autonomously with the bayonet over an enemy tutored by French officers to regard infantry as an adjunct of artillery.[36] John Pester's graphic account of the Battle of Delhi (see map 13) contains the vital elements of officers leading from the front, infantry advancing in a two-deep line in the face of a murderous artillery barrage, a delayed volley of musketry, and a decisive charge with the bayonet.

The reconnoitring party and our advanced picquets were quickly driven in. The drummers on the right of the line now beat to arms, and each brigade took it up in succession. The troops on the right were instantly in motion, and in a few minutes we were all advancing to the attack in excellent order. The rapidity of our advance was so great that our brigade guns and field pieces were obliged to drop in the rear, and we soon found that it was the general's intention to close with the bayonet. The line advanced, silent and determined. Their heavy shot now began to make some havoc among us, and we had yet a full mile to advance under the cannonade of nearly one hundred heavy guns, uncommonly well served, and as their fire seemed every moment to increase, the shot came thicker, and officers and men began to drop fast!

A village on an eminence was immediately in front of our wing, and as we could not pass through it, without throwing the brigade into confusion, Colonel [Robert] Blair ordered them to wheel back by sections on the right, and moved round its flank in column. The enemy's fire was very destructive on us in clearing this village, and while we were forming again after we had passed it, I was with Colonel Blair at the head of the column receiving some orders from him, when a very heavy shot grazed between us, and most completely buried us in the dust it threw up.

The colonel was nearly dismounted by his horse taking fright. We escaped, but the shot plunged directly into the column, and killed and wounded a great many men in the leading company (the Grenadiers of the 14th [Bengal Native Infantry] Regiment). At this moment another cannon shot grazed my horse, and although it touched him, fortunately but very slightly, he dropped on his haunches, but as it was merely the jar of the shot that shook him, he immediately recovered himself, nor did he appear the least intimidated.

We quickly formed our line after we had passed the village, and closed again with the corps on our right. The cannonade at this time to a calm spectator must have seemed tremendous and awful, and the grape came literally in showers. I had the mortification to see poor [Joseph] Aldin and [John] Harriott of our corps fall, while gallantly leading on their respective companies.

A grape shot passed through the housings of my pistols, and shattered the stock of one of them, and I felt my horse staggering under me; another grape had grazed his side, and lodged under the skin; a third went through him. It entered at his near quarter and passed out at the other. He fell on me, and I was a little bruised. General [Frederick] St. John's orderly dragoon (a man of the 27th) by the general's orders rode to the rear to bring up one of his horses, but I mounted one of Colonel Blair's which was immediately at hand. Our troops advanced most gallantly, without taking their muskets from their shoulders, under this galling fire, and such a rattling of shot as we were now exposed to I never witnessed.

At this moment we were within two hundred and fifty paces of the muzzles of their guns. I was the only mounted officer in front of our brigades. I saw the left a little staggered, and was pushing down in front to encourage them, when General Saint John from the rear, who did not observe me, gave the word to 'Fire', and, most miraculous to say, I escaped unhurt, though I was actually within twelve yards of the front rank men, at full speed, when the whole gave their fire. The volley was instantly followed by a cheer, and the drums, striking up, they rushed on with an ardour nothing could resist, closed with the bayonet, when the enemy fled, and the contest with us on the left was now decided. Our troops, after marching eighteen miles, and being so long in action were, of course, much worn and fatigued, and the enemy had greatly the advantage of us in running.

This was a victory won primarily by infantry but not in isolation. The cavalry played an important supportive role, particularly in protecting the flanks. Pester fully acknowledges that the artillery, although in the rear, was also instrumental in the Maratha defeat, keeping up a constant fire.[37]

Cavalry was often held back to be eventually propelled against a discouraged and demoralised enemy. This was certainly the case at Delhi. When its shock action was employed at the height of the battle, for instance at Assaye, the results were mixed. The adrenaline rush of the charge is well conveyed by Mountstuart Elphinstone, who took the opportunity to join the British cavalry in the closing phase of the battle of Argaum. The manuscript account is torn and incomplete.

The balls knocked up the dust under our horses' feet. I had no narrow escapes this time, and I felt quite unconcerned, never winced, nor cared how near the shot came about the worst time; and all the time I was at pains to see how the people looked, and every gentleman seemed at ease as much if he were riding a hunting. The opening of our guns had great effect in encouraging our people.… was shot in passing the village of Argaum. In the charge the [19th Light] Dragoons used their swords for some time, and then drew their pistols. If one cut at a horseman, he would throw himself from his horse… The next man would… or cut him down… I stopped to load my pistols. I saw nobody afterwards but people on foot, whom I did not think it proper to touch. Indeed, there is nothing very gallant in attacking routed and terrified horse, who have not presence of mind either to run or fight.[38]

Blakiston witnessed the charge and was struck by the method of attack employed by the dragoons. The enemy horsemen wore armour or stuffed coats and also turbans. The British cavalrymen first knocked off the turban with the point of their swords before cutting at the head.[39]

Furruckabad was not a major action such as Delhi or Argaum, but James Young's account well illustrates the strengths and weaknesses of the Bengal Horse Artillery, an experimental unit in existence for only a few years. The mobility of the unit – galloping across country with guns and ammunition wagons before unlimbering, firing, limbering, and galloping on again – allowed it to inflict devastating damage on an out-manoeuvred or surprised enemy.[40] On the other hand, the guns were vulnerable when not properly supported by other arms.

> We [the Bengal Horse Artillery] opened a tremendous and quick fire of grape, every shot of which must have told, about thirty or forty rounds were fired when we ceased, and the cavalry followed it up by a rapid charge through our intervals upon the astonished and un-resisting Mahrattas, who fled in terror, screaming and howling, with the utmost precipitations in every direction, leaving their baggage, bazaar, women and children, swords and spears, horses, tattoos, and bullocks on the ground. The scene that ensued an eyewitness alone can believe nor by anyone else can it be conceived. We followed up the cavalry in the rear. They dispersed in troops and squadrons on all sides to cut off the flying enemy. All from this time was a scene of confusion. Daylight which now became stronger, found Lieutenant [Henry] Stark, myself, with two guns and two howitzers, separated from Captain Brown and his two guns, with a squadron of the 8th Dragoons, one of the 6th Native Cavalry along with us. The enemy's horse, were all around in large bodies and infinitely outnumbered our parties, one of these bodies appearing in front. The cavalry along with us instantly charged them, leaving our guns without a man to protect them. A line of conduct almost uniformly observed towards the unfortunate artillery by cavalry and infantry... on this day, had the Mahrattas been so many French dragoons, would have caused every man of us to be cut to pieces and would have deprived the world of the benefit of these memoirs.

The horse artillery covered eight to ten miles in the several hours of fighting. In the previous 24 hours, they had marched 60 miles to reach the action.[41]

Young's observation that his adversaries were so close to his guns that he could 'distinctly see their very features' is a reminder that even on larger fields much fighting was at close quarters, literally hand to hand. There are many anecdotes of such encounters in the literature of the wars, some perhaps exaggerated, but many undoubtedly true. There was heroism on both sides. An anonymous British officer stared into the eyes of his Maratha foe at the battle of Deig;

their brigades, if I may so term them, were so close together, that when we had mastered one, it was only sustaining a round or two of grape from their artillery before we were hand to hand with another. On one of these occasions the Subadar of my company was cut down by one of the enemy, who was about to finish him when I gave the fellow what I thought [was] a huge cut on the shoulder; but I might as well have struck him with a riding whip, my sword made not the smallest impression excepting that of calling the Mahratta's attention to me instead of the poor Subadar, and I should most probably have fared but badly if Captain N-------, my *predestined* friend, had not at that instant come up, and calling to me, 'You should use your point with these fellows, their jackets are quilted an inch thick with cotton,' run my opponent through the body. After this, N------ and I kept close together till the regiment was recalled.[42]

Some personal duels invoked a grim humour, destined to become part of regimental folklore. At Argaum, James Welsh witnessed the wounded Lieutenant George Langlands of the 74th pick up an enemy spear and hurl it back, killing an advancing Arab. A sepoy of a grenadier company was so impressed that he rushed out of the ranks 'and patting the Lieutenant on the back, exclaimed, "Atchah Sahib! bhote atchah keeah!" Well, Sir! very well done!"'. Welsh says that the ludicrous nature of the incident raised laughs even at such a dangerous moment.[43] A few individuals gained fearsome reputations in close-quarter combat. Major George Holmes of the 75th was a man of unusual stature and strength who could boast many successful engagements in which he wielded a 'stout stick'. This could also be used as a shield 'when he condescended to use his sword'.[44]

Much of this hand-to-hand fighting occurred away from the major battles in the innumerable smaller actions which punctuated the conflict. These were the clashes of smaller bodies of troops, the skirmishes around the outposts of armies and the opportunistic attacks on convoys and retreating men. These scenarios have been described in the earlier campaigns section and we will not revisit them all here. However, Captain Henry Anderson's detailed description of the brave resistance of sepoys fighting in square against Maratha attacks during Monson's retreat is of such quality as to merit quoting at length. His diary entry is for August 28, 1804.

One A.M., moved out of the fort [Hindoun], formed the square and marched off – saw nothing of the enemy till daybreak when they made their appearance, but did not attempt anything – They annoyed us a good deal with their Camel pieces carrying from one to two pound balls, with which they killed or wounded a good many camp followers and a few sepoys; they likewise set off some rockets, which never did us any harm, indeed both their Camel pieces and rockets from their bad management had injured themselves more than they did us for they mostly flew over the square and pitched among their own friends on the opposite face.

– 6 am. Entered some ravines whose Banks were so rugged and irregular that it was impossible to keep our order so well as usual, and we did not get clear of them till 7. – As we came out of the ravines with our ranks rather straggling, we perceived the enemy formed into three large Columns, one to the right and left and another in front, on which the square was halted and the ranks closed as quickly as possible, but before we could succeed in getting them quite closed, the enemy charged and came down with such velocity that they overtook the flankers and rode over them – The sepoys on the right face on which the principal charge was made, behaved in the most cool and determined manner that can be imagined, for having wheeled into line and closed their ranks as well as the time would admit, they did not fire a shot till the enemy came within 50 yards, when they commenced full firing, from which the enemy being so near had a wonderful effect; they came down to within ten yards of the Bayonets, when despairing of breaking our line they turned to the left down the line not being able to go directly back because of the numbers which pressed them from behind, at this time being so near, having their broadsides to us and in a manner running the gauntlet of our whole line, almost every shot must have taken effect; at last finding themselves clear of their friends, they galloped off as hard as they could leaving an immense number of dead and wounded men and horses behind them. At the time of their retreat, the sepoys behaved as steadily as they had at the commencement for not a man moved from his rank and the firing instantly ceased when the enemy were out of shot – one or two of their men from their horses having run away with them got in where the ranks were loose but were instantly bayoneted.

The front and left sides of the square resisted less determined attacks despite men leaving the ranks to pursue the enemy. Anderson concludes;

This seemed to be their last effort to cut us up, and from what I have heard from their own men since, they had attacked us so bravely from being persuaded that as soon as our muskets were discharged we should be at their mercy, but they were astonished to find a steady fire kept up so much longer that they had any idea of and no appearance of its being exhausted.[45]

Jungle was the most daunting of the terrains that the Indian army campaigned in. As earlier described by Sergeant Butler, an uncontested march was difficult enough. Fighting in the jungle, such as occurred in the Polygar Wars, was arguably the European soldier's greatest challenge. Arthur Wellesley had definite views on jungle warfare, writing the following to Colonel John Conrad Sartorius in September 1800.

> The result of my observations and considerations upon the mode of carrying on war in jungly countries is just this, that as long as the jungle is thick, as the enemy can conceal himself in it, and from his concealment attack the troops, their followers and their baggage, the operations must be unsuccessful on our side.

He recommended cutting the lower part of the jungle back from the roads. This was tedious but was likely to be ultimately decisive. The alternative was to make 'a great expense of blood and treasure' in desultory and futile operations.[46]

James Welsh's first-hand account of the Polygar Wars gives credence to Wellesley's views. The most minor obstacle in the jungle abruptly halted progress and frustrated the conventional European force. One example will suffice. On 6 August 1801, the enemy raised a high bank at the end of a road the British were cutting through the dense foliage. The bank was reinforced with hedges and armed with four guns. It was successfully stormed but, by the following day, the bank was again defended and had to be assailed once more.

> It was at length taken in flank, but the enemy succeeded in carrying off their guns, and all their killed and wounded. The jungle was so impenetrable, that only one party under Lieutenant King gained their flank in time; another, despatched in the opposite direction, under Major M'Pherson, did not arrive till some time afterwards, or they would have secured the enemy's guns. No further opposition was offered, and the party returned, after having cut about three hundred and fifty yards.
>
> On the 8th, the foraging party under Major Sheppard again brought in a considerable body of straw; and by the covering party under the command of Lieutenant Colonel Dalrymple, the bank was found again raised, hedged, and defended, and was again gallantly taken in flank. The right party alone however, under Lieutenant Fletcher, put the enemy to flight; since the left division did not arrive in time, on account of the thickness of the jungle.

The *polygars* finally scattered into the surrounding vegetation.[47] By using 2,000 pioneers and wood cutters to make broad roads into the jungle, the

British were effectively following Wellesley's dictum and they were to eventually prevail. Welsh makes interesting points regarding jungle warfare. He believed artillery to be far superior to musketry, the latter being of little use in thick jungle. Cavalry often 'served for shew only', the ground preventing their deployment.[48]

British attacks on small to medium-sized forts were a recurring theme of the Polygar Wars and other campaigns in India. Many were built on isolated hills and relied much on the surrounding rocks for protection. According to the historian of the military engineers in India, Lieutenant-Colonel Edward Sandes, they were not really formidable if attacked in the right way. Their design was primitive and their defenders often cowed by a resolute attack.[49] Even the mud forts, such as the unimpressive Panjalamcoorchy, might prove surprisingly resistant, but more often they fell quickly to a determined storm. Captain William Lambton of the 33rd Foot gives a good account of such an operation against insurgents in southern India in August 1799. The *killedar* refused to surrender the fort without orders from Dhoondiah Waugh.

> Colonel [William] Wallace therefore marched early next morning and arrived at the Fort before 6 o'clock quite unexpected by the Enemy, as appeared from their clamours in the fort, signified by shouting and the sounding of horns – Col. Wallace ordered the Europeans and Bengal flankers to advance to the gateway, attended by Pioneers and scaling ladders, preceded by a small party under Lieutenant [H. M'Donnell] Murray 74th Regiment – the Battalion Companies of the Bengal Volunteers were stationed on the right and left of the gateway to cover the flankers and keep up a heavy fire on the parapet while the others were scaling the walls – some shot were fired by the garrison but they were soon silenced by our musketry from the covering companies – In the meantime, Lieut. Murray advanced to the first gateway and perceiving some of the enemy who had been [posted] as a guard on the outside all night, rushing in at the wicket [gate] and endeavouring to shut the gate, but Lt. Murray pushing forward, forced in with a party of the 74th Grenadiers before the wicket could be closed, and at the same instant, the rest of the flank companies advanced after him and by applying the scaling ladders between the 1st and 2nd gateways, soon attained the rampart – The Enemy then gave way and fled in every direction, several jumping over into the ditch – most of those who remained in the Fort were put to the Bayonet.

Other fugitives were hunted down by irregular cavalry.[50] These small forts were taken in such numbers as to become an embarrassment to the

British. Wellesley complained that captured *polygar* hill forts were 'worse than useless'. They were too unhealthy to leave European officers in charge and the small retaining garrisons were liable to be surprised and cut off. He advised abandoning them, but only after destroying both the forts and any local water supplies.[51]

The relative ease with which these smaller objectives were tackled might in part explain British complacency when faced with the reduction of major fortresses such as Alighar, Deig, Gawilghur and Bhurtpore. It can be argued that most British success was due to a combination of heroism and good fortune rather than sound judgment. Lake is particularly vulnerable to this criticism. At Alighar, he made no attempt to breach the walls, but instead blew the gate sustaining significant casualties in the resulting storm. At Agra and Deig, there were obvious technical shortcomings in the siege work. These tactical risks – time was always a factor – paid off, but he gambled once too often at Bhurtpore. Wellesley has emerged relatively unscathed, but he was uncharacteristically cavalier in his approach to sieges. In August 1803, he confidently informed the anxious Colonel Murray at Poona that 12-pound shot would 'break any wall in the country'. This proved to be untrue at Gawilghur four months later. John Pemble suggests that Wellesley's 'freakish' success in capturing Gawilghur was to encourage a subsequent lax attitude to sieges in the Peninsular War.[52]

There is not space here to relate the details of the methodology of siege operations in the early nineteenth century; there are many other works which address this subject. The sequence of events – the isolation of the fortress, the digging of the parallels, the creation of the breach batteries, the establishment of the breach, and a final storm if there was no surrender – were essentially the same in India as in Europe. The expertise was provided by the engineers, but the physical burden of the siege fell upon the infantry, who made up the working parties which dug the trenches and filled the wicker gabions which protected the batteries.[53] This was the application of 'scientific method', but British incursions around the walls of fortresses were often haphazard, especially when parties operated at night. Captain Colin Mackenzie was able to see the comical side of this at Seringapatam; the following is his diary entry for 21 April 1799.

> The disorder of a working party in such a situation in the dark, unarmed, unacquainted with the ground… the scene was now not a little ludicrous notwithstanding the clamours and uncommon cries of the enemy now close to us… their musket shot flying thick over us… Crowds rushing and pressing through the prickly [aloe] hedge at the expense of torn clothes and lacerated limbs.

Sepoys and Pioneers with marmotties [sic] and Pickaxes but many without any, throwing away anything portable... Europeans without shoes or hats; such were some of the Groups that were at intervals exhibited by the glimpses of light which the friendly darkness immediately shrouded, scenes that could not but create a smile in a very serious moment.[54]

Many officers kept the faith until very late in the wars. An anonymous captain in East India Company service wrote his final letter home a day before being killed in the first storming of Bhurtpore. In it, he expresses absolute confidence in Lake, the 'good and heroic' general whose army 'can never be defeated by Native troops'.[55] James Young, writing just after this first failure, voiced an increasingly widespread pessimistic view of British capabilities.

Our regiment has borne the brunt of this cursed business and has suffered in officers out of all proportion to the rest of the army. No wonder indeed for despising our enemies as we do...

Young is very critical of the lack of regularity in the siege preparations at Bhurtpore. He also describes the interminable labour of the officers and ordinary soldiers in the trenches and at the guns, 'for the poor men, who have already been 72 hours on the battery, night and day, there is no hope of relief till the siege is ended'.[56] Ultimately, this frenetic endeavour was not enough. The human cost that resulted from a dearth of proper siege equipment, poor planning and inadequate expertise is captured in John Shipp's account of the dismal final attempt to storm the fortress.

If any sight could be exhibited to the human eye that was calculated to work upon the feelings of men already disappointed and dispirited, it was the scene that was exposed to our view on approaching to this breach; for there lay our poor comrades who had fallen in previous attempts, many of them in a state of nudity; some without heads; some without arms or legs; and others whose bodies exhibited the most barbarous cruelties, for they were literally cut to pieces... Our ascent was found, for the fourth time, to be quite impossible: every man who showed himself was sure of death. The soldiers in the fort were in chain armour. I speak this from positive conviction, for I myself fired at one man three times in the bastion, who was not six yards from me, and he did not even bob his head... I had not been on the breach for more than five minutes, when I was struck with a large shot on my back, thrown down from the top of the bastion, which made me lose my footing, and I was rolling down sideways, when I was brought up by a bayonet of one of our grenadiers passing through the shoe, into the fleshy part of the foot, and under the great toe. My fall carried everything down that was under me. The man who assisted me in getting up, was at that moment shot dead: his name was Courtenay, of the 22nd Light Company. I regained my place [in] time enough to see poor Lieutenant Templer, who had planted the colour on the top, cut to pieces, by one of the enemy rushing out, as he lay flat upon his face on the top of the breach. The man was immediately shot dead, and trotted to the bottom of the ditch. I had not been in my new place long, when a stink-pot, or other earthen pot, containing combustible matter, fell on my pouch, in which were about fifty rounds of ball cartridges. The whole exploded: my pouch I never saw more, and I was precipitated from the top to the bottom of the bastion. How I got there in safety, I know not; but, when I came to myself, I found I was lying under the breach, with my legs in the water. I was much hurt by the fall, my face was severely scorched, my clothes much burnt, and all the hair on the back of my head burnt off.[57]

Another witness describes the incessant fire of grape. The defenders on the walls hurled down pieces of timber, flaming packs of cotton dipped in oil, and pots filled with gunpowder.[58]

When John Shipp crawled away from the breach at Bhurtpore he joined the list of 2,500 British soldiers wounded in the operations against the fort. As has been described in the Campaigns section, several of the battles of the Anglo-Maratha conflict led to significant numbers of British casualties. To understand the medical management of these wounded men, we will focus on the battles of Assaye and Delhi, for which we have the most information. In general, the British medical services in India were organised as in the European campaigns. After a major battle, the bulk of the surgical work fell upon the regimental surgeons. Theoretically, both King's and East India Company regiments had a surgeon and two assistants attached, but a perusal of contemporary army lists for all the Presidencies reveals that in reality most native units had only a surgeon and one assistant.[59] There were also the staff surgeons, but they were in short supply; medical regulations issued from Madras in 1803 stipulated that a European corps on active service was to be accompanied by a field superintending surgeon, two staff surgeons, four assistants, a field apothecary and two sub-assistants.[60]

The medical arrangements at Assaye were improvised and inadequate. The first problem was the lack of a formalised system to remove the wounded from the field. Thomas Swarbrook, who lost his leg in the action, says that each regiment sent out a party to collect its own wounded, but that some lay there for two or three days before being reached.[61] Some immediate surgery was performed in dressing stations in the environs of the field. On the night following the battle, Roderick Innes relates visiting a 'hospital' in a tent two miles away: 'I counted 12 saws cutting as fast as they could drive'.[62] Wellesley struggled to find a location for a proper field hospital, eventually reluctantly opting for Ajanta, twenty miles north of Assaye, a place he believed to be of 'inferior strength' and poorly sited.[63] Doolie bearers took 300 wounded to the hospital on 1 October, eight days after the battle. These were the men who could best tolerate the journey. Other wounded travelled on bullocks or on foot. Some battalions were ordered to provide dressers for the hospital and the staff surgeon was to furnish servants. Pioneers were to assist.[64]

Wellesley's dispatches reveal a man who was genuinely concerned. On 8 October, he visited the wounded at Ajanta: 'I have done the best I can for them, and have secured them as far as in my power'.[65] He ordered extra shades to protect the men from the sun. Eventually the more severely wounded, including those with injuries caused by artillery, were to moved on to Bombay.[66] Allowing for the shortcomings of all the army medical services of the period, it is an exaggeration to describe the aftermath of Asaye as a 'medical disaster',[67] but the lack of a plan for organised casualty evacuation and the delay in establishing a field hospital must have led to unnecessary suffering and fatalities.

Charles Stuart's account of Delhi suggests similar failings in the northern theatre.

> The hospital tents as I have before mentioned were pitched at a considerable distance from the field of action and many men no doubt lost their lives for want of immediate aid for though medical men were present a field of battle is not the place for performing an operation. The Doolee Bearers always kept out of danger which prevented the wounded from being quickly conveyed to the hospitals besides which I imagine the surgeons had more to do than they could well manage. Cornet [Philip] Crowe who had his foot shattered was obliged to go to several places before he could get it taken off.[68]

John Shipp refers to the deliberate mutilation of wounded men in his account of Bhurtpore. Atrocities were carried out by both sides. Holkar's forces were notorious for their cruelty, committing deprivations against friend and foe. A Maratha verse of the period details their excesses.

No Escape! from the wife of the peasant they tear
The pearl-studded jewel that fastens her hair;
From the peasant they wrest all his hoarded rupees,
The grain from his grain-pits, the food off his knees;
If any delays or refuses to give,
He tastes such a beating that scarce he will live.[69]

British army sepoys who fell into Holkar's hands near Agra in October 1804 straggled back into camp with arms, noses or ears cut off.[70] Sen points out that many of these war crimes were very likely committed by the mercenary *pindaris* and Purvias and not by the Marathas.[71]

Arthur Wellesley discouraged mistreatment of the local population by British soldiers. A general order issued from Seringapatam in 1802 notes that some officers, particularly those of junior rank and new to the country, were abusing the natives: 'The practice is very irregular and illegal, and, if not speedily put a stop to, will tend to the material inconvenience and injury of the troops'.[72] In battle it was difficult to control the behaviour of soldiers drunk with victory. A number of contemporary observers believed that, on occasion, a line had been crossed, the legitimate harrying of a beaten enemy descending into a slaughter of innocents. Blakiston witnessed the aftermath of the capture of Gawilghur.

Whether it is owing to the arrack they drink, or some other cause,
I know not; but certainly the European soldiers in India become
very blood-thirsty and ferocious.[73]

Charles Stuart was sickened by the needless killing of civilians after the battle of Delhi. British cavalry caught up with Maratha camp followers trying to swim across the River Jumna.

An old man with a child on his shoulders stood in the water afraid
to proceed. A dragoon, untouched by remorse, shot him, and the
child, I suppose, must have drowned.[74]

Some British atrocities were premeditated. The plundering and burning of Futtypoor in April 1805 was in retaliation for the towns-peoples' previous support of Holkar and their cruelty to the stragglers of Monson's detachment.[75]

There was much looting, but there was also an officially approved route to riches for at least some British soldiers. This was the prize money system. Following the fall of Seringapatam, the treasure and jewels seized were valued at £1,143,216. There were fifteen levels of prize money, the share dependent on the recipient's seniority. A few selected examples, including the two extremes, will serve to illustrate the enormous variation in the amounts of *star pagodas* distributed by the prize agents.

Naicks, sepoys, trumpeters, black doctors, pioneers, gun lascars, and authorised *Puckallies*	12
Private Europeans	18
Havildars	18
Jamadars	36
Subadars	108
Subalterns, assistant surgeons	1,080
Captains, surgeons, aides de camp, chaplains	2,160
Majors, deputy adjutants general	4,320
Lieutenant Colonels	6,480
Colonels	10,800
General officers on the staff	27,000
The commander-in-chief	324,907[76]

At Agra, in October 1804, there was almost as wide a range of payments, Lake receiving close to 10,000 times the amount pocketed by a private soldier.[77] The process was often contentious, the prize agents accused of corruption and the legitimacy of the distribution of the spoils questioned.[78]

Whatever the rights and wrongs, the more senior officers stood to make considerable amounts of money. At Seringapatam, Wellesley received 10,000 *pagodas* in jewels and currency; this was around £4,500 and it allowed the young officer to clear some of his debts.[79] By the time he left India, he was comfortably off. 'I am not rich in comparison with other people, but very much so in comparison with my former poverty... I got a great deal in prize money in the last war...'[80]

For the ordinary soldiers and lower-ranking officers, a campaign in India was rarely the road to wealth. All too often the money slipped through their blackened fingers. Drummer Roderick Innes was among those left with a sense of injustice.

> Prize money resulting from the Mahratta war, was served out to each of us. It only amounted to about 13 rupees, but some of the men declared that it should have been as many pounds. But a report got up, that the white ants, that destructive creature, had eaten all the rest, just as they had done at Madras, after the taking of Seringapatam. I do not know whether they can eat gold...[81]

Chapter 12

Sometimes Bliss and Sometimes Woe: Sepoys

In his fine study of the early British Indian Army, G.J. Bryant asserts that it must be a cause of anguish to modern Indian historians to know that their country was conquered using armies made up mostly of their countrymen.[1] If so, it is a frustration for historians of all nationalities that we lack 'Indian voices' from the wars of the late eighteenth and early nineteenth centuries. Our account is necessarily Anglo-centric, based on the innumerable state papers, contemporary regulations, and soldiers' letters and diaries residing in British archives. Indians were excluded from senior positions in the army and administration, thus further removing their actions and thoughts from the historical record.

Wars are mostly documented by the winners and there were obvious disincentives for sepoys to elaborate their experiences in the armies of the East India Company, an institution which provided their pay and pension. The existence of just one eyewitness account by an Indian soldier of the period would thus be of incalculable historical value. This brings us to the 'memoirs' of Sita Ram Pande, one of the thousands of sepoys who helped the British to dominate nineteenth-century India. Sita Ram enlisted into an infantry regiment of the Bengal Army in 1812 and remained in service until 1860 when he received his pension. He was too late to fight in the Anglo-Maratha Wars of 1803–05, but he saw action in later campaigns, rising in the ranks from sepoy to *subadar*. He was wounded seven times, taken prisoner once and awarded six medals. He was, so the story runs, persuaded to write his memoirs by Lieutenant-Colonel James Thomas Norgate. He completed the manuscript in 1861, shortly after his retirement. The original was written in Hindi, in the Oudh dialect, and Norgate translated it into English with Indian help. It was first published in English in 1880 and was later translated into Urdu by Colonel D.A. Phillott to be used as a standard language examination textbook well known to officers of the British Army in the early twentieth century.[2]

A number of eminent historians have strained to dispel lingering doubts regarding the authenticity of Sita Ram's memoirs. Sir Patrick Cadell spent twenty years researching the military aspects of the text. He acknowledges that the account contains significant omissions (for instance, Sita Ram does not reveal the number of his regiment) and inaccuracies, but he ultimately concludes that the account is believable: 'That the story is absolutely genuine, and Sitaram's own, cannot I think, be doubted'. Philip Mason agrees, arguing that the author's lapses in memory were actually in favour of authenticity. Sita Ram was, he concludes, a 'credible witness'. Saul David was also convinced that only a Bengal sepoy could have provided the rich detail contained in the text.

The most compelling case against authenticity has been constructed by Alison Safadi. Her critique operates at several levels. Firstly, she believes historians to have been overly willing to support authenticity, their arguments subjective, lacking in substance and involving leaps of faith. Secondly, the content of the memoir is dubious, the sepoy's adventures too numerous and 'too good to be true'. Thirdly, and perhaps most tellingly, there are linguistic issues within the text which make Sita Ram an unlikely author.

The historian is left with the dilemma of whether to include Sita Ram's words in any description of sepoy life in the British army of the early nineteenth century, the intention of this chapter. I have used some excerpts from Sita Ram in the following pages and elsewhere. These passages must be treated with a degree of scepticism by the reader. I have chosen to be inclusive as, even if this is not a real voice from the ranks of native Indian soldiers, it is the closest to it that we have. Safadi is unable to prove that the memoirs are fabricated. She decries their use as a reliable historical source but concedes that they are of 'absorbing interest' and that they give 'a useful *reflection* of the events and attitudes of the period they describe'. We will probably never know whether we are reading the words of an Indian soldier of the Bengal native infantry or a British officer's conception of what sepoys thought and felt.[3]

There has been some discussion of general recruitment to the East India Company armies and the distinctive nature of the three Presidency forces in Chapter 1. Here we will further consider the recruitment of native soldiers. In the late eighteenth century, the recruitment of sepoys remained haphazard, there being no special agency to undertake this. At first, there was reliance on Indian officers raising units from the local population. Trustworthy *jamadars* or *havildars* 'with a smart new turban, glaring sword, laced coat and some money' were often successful; '...their fair speeches and tinsel coats [attracted] many followers'.[4] Sepoy officers recruiting well might be rewarded with promotion. Over time, British officers from native battalions took over the responsibility, targeting likely areas such as Buxar on the Bihar-Oudh border in the north. They might tour villages, accompanied by a doctor and interpreter, to seek out suitable young men. Unlike in Britain, the profession of arms was a daily reality for many and there were often willing applicants waiting on the parade ground.[5]

The Presidencies were initially open-minded regarding the nature of their sepoy recruits, but there was an evolving view that the best native soldiers came from the north-west of the country. These men, Rajputs and Pathans, were taller, of paler skin, and of high caste. They were widely believed to be 'natural soldiers'. Thus the Bengal native infantry drew its recruits not from Bengal proper, but from Oudh and the upper provinces of the Bengal Presidency.[6] Arthur Wellesley thought that men from Oudh were chosen because they were of a better size and appearance than others to be found in India. He favoured the Bengal Army native troops over those of other Presidencies, noting that the locals had more respect for them than for sepoys from Madras or Bombay.[7] There was not an inexhaustible supply of such men and the Madras Army often employed the shorter, darker men who predominated in the south. These soldiers had their defenders. General George Harris included the following in a minute of 1798.

> Although the men obtained in the more southern countries are much inferior to the northern recruits in caste, size, and appearance, they are nevertheless hardy and thrifty, and being less subject to local attachments, and little encumbered with religious habits, or prejudices, to interfere with the regular performance of their duty, are found to stand the pressure of military hardships with much fortitude and to manifest, at all times, a firm adherence to the service.[8]

The Bombay Army struggled to recruit quality men and was a necessarily diverse force, recruits being taken from a large number of different races, religions and castes.[9]

All the Presidency armies soon discovered that the best soldiers were often recruited in war zones. Local peasants selected from areas around the Presidency towns were mostly of low calibre, 'absolutely unfit to carry sticks far less firelocks'.[10] The converse of this was that men from martial and politically dominant groups might prove to be of dubious loyalty at best and potential enemies at worst. The Bombay Presidency was suspicious of the nearby Hindu Marathas.[11] One strategy to ensure loyalty and continuity of service was to encourage family links with the Indian Army. Bengal sepoys would commonly recruit their relatives and in the Madras army the sons of sepoys were attached to units with the expectation that they would eventually join the ranks.[12]

There were formal requirements for recruits, although it is likely that these were only loosely applied, especially in times of urgency. In the Bengal Army, the regulations of 1796 stipulate age limits of 16 to 30 years and a minimum height of 5ft 6in. Shorter men were employed if they were healthy and of athletic build. All had to undergo a physical examination by the regimental doctor.[13] The Bombay Army of 1797 permitted a significantly lower height limit of 5ft 2in and again there was flexibility, allowing even shorter recruits if they were of 'robust make' or if there was the prospect of further growth.[14] In Madras, the height limit was 5ft 4in.[15]

Why did young Indian men join the armies of the East India Company? It seems that the major incentives were regular pay, a degree of security, and preferential treatment in civilian life. The Company paid more regularly than many of the Indian powers. This was a powerful draw for men who had families to support and who might be unemployed or in debt. These wages might be supplemented by prize money. There were also the furlough privileges and the boon of a pension, something virtually unknown to soldiers serving under Indian princes. Sepoys were given priority in any civil court of justice case, the Company no doubt keen for them to return to the ranks as quickly as possible. The landed gentry were thus encouraged to have their sons in the Company's armies to gain influence over local administrators and to facilitate their own lawsuits. Native soldiers might also avoid certain taxes and be eligible for free posting of letters home.[16]

Sita Ram claims that he joined the Bengal Army for more romantic reasons. As a child, he imbibed tales of military service from his uncle, a *havildar* in an infantry regiment. He became determined to be a soldier: 'Nothing else could I think of, day or night. The rank of *Jemadar* I looked on as quite equal to that of Ghazidin Hydar, the King of Oudh himself…'. His father had no objection;

> a lawsuit was impending over my father, about his right to a mango grove of some 400 trees, and he thought that having a son in the Company *Bahadur's* service would be the means of getting his case attended to in the law courts of Lucknow.[17]

The young recruit accompanied his uncle to Agra, where the latter's regiment was stationed. He was underwhelmed by his first view of British soldiers (sahibs) who were much shorter and cleaner shaven than he had anticipated. After an introduction to the adjutant, he was taken to the regimental doctor's house. The following passage is typical of Sita Ram's recollections.

> My uncle told me that the Doctor was married and had several children. He was at home and we were ordered into his presence. A chair was provided for my uncle, but no notice was taken of me so I squatted on the ground. My uncle made me stand up, and told me afterwards that it was bad manners to sit down in the presence of a *sahib*. After reading the note, the Doctor ordered me to strip, but I was so ashamed I could not move, for there was a *memsahib* in the room.

Enduring some crude jibes from the doctor and his family, the recruit was eventually pushed into an empty room with reassurance that he would come to no harm;

> [the doctor] examined me, by thrusting his hand against my stom-ach, which nearly made me vomit. Then he opened my eyelids with such violence that tears came into my eyes, and he thumped my chest. After this he pronounced me fit and ceased tormenting me – to my great relief.

A few days later, Sita Ram commenced his drill and, after eight months, he was selected to join the ranks.[18]

Sepoys joining the Bengal Army were expected to take an oath of fidelity binding them to obey their commander, to never abandon the colours, and to faithfully serve the Company. No mention was made of overseas service. Following completion of training, a second oath of allegiance was taken under the colours of the sepoy's new regiment. He was sworn in by the regimental interpreter in front of his comrades before carrying his arms to his company.[19] Many European officers were sceptical of this ceremony, believing that few native soldiers took the oath seriously or fully understood its implications.[20]

The recruit was enlisted for an unlimited period, although there was provi-sion for voluntary discharge after three years if there was no state of war and no shortage of men. The Company could discharge the sepoy at any time.[21] Many native soldiers served for long periods away from their homes. When the men of the 4th Madras Native Cavalry arrived at Arcot in December 1804, they saw their families for the first time since they marched to Seringapatam with the Grand Army in 1799.[22]

Efforts were made to protect native soldiers from being mistreated by Euro-pean officers. General orders and regulations issued in the Madras Army in 1801 included the following directive.

> The attachment of orderly soldiers of officers being solely for the performance of duties purely military, the disgraceful practice of employing Native soldiers in carrying articles of table consumption! in running by the side of palankins! in supplying the place of domes-tics, and horse-keepers behind carriages and bandies! and in follow-ing close at the heels of mounted horses, is to be discontinued...

Although intended to stop abuse, it was later acknowledged that any order distancing sepoys and European officers was double-edged, leading to an ero-sion of the sharing of a common language and an understanding of customs.[23]

Many sepoys were irritated by their new uniform. With the exception of san-dals and turban, the native soldier was kitted out just as his British comrades.

The cost of the turban, waist belt, linen jacket and shoes was deducted from his pay. In the Bengal Army, only two articles of dress, a greatcoat and a pair of cloth pantaloons, were provided by the government.[24] The clothing of both European and native soldiers was ill-designed, uncomfortable, and unsuited to the climate. Sita Ram's reaction was probably typical.

> At first I found it very disagreeable wearing the red coat; although this was open in front, it was very tight under the arms. The shako was very heavy and hurt my head, but of course it was very smart. I grew accustomed to all this after a time, but I always found it a great relief when I could wear my own loose dress. The uniform of the British was always very tight and prevented the free use of arms and legs. I also found the musket very heavy, and for a long time my shoulder ached when carrying it. The pouch-belt and knapsack were a load for a coolie.[25]

The Brown Bess musket weighed nine pounds and the pouch was designed to carry up to sixty rounds of musket ball ammunition.

The military authorities often made little provision for accommodation of native soldiers, the expectation being that sepoys would build their own huts. When in cantonments, ground was dedicated to the sepoy regiments for their construction. In the Madras and Bombay armies there was a 'hutting allowance' but, in the early nineteenth century, the Bengal soldier was expected to fund his own hut. Arthur Wellesley makes reference to huts for the sepoys of the Madras Army, but it is clear from his dispatches that there were also barracks for the native troops. In 1802, there were two such facilities in Seringapatam and smaller similar accommodation at Bangalore.

When in garrison, the native soldier purchased his food from the regimental bazaar. On campaign, there was a general bazaar. The government only provided rations for foreign service. The usual diet of the Bengal soldier consisted of chapatis, dal (split peas or lentils), and rice. Often the sepoy's curry contained only the cheapest vegetables as he could not afford more. Brahmins could not eat meat or fish and Hindu soldiers did not consume beef.[26]

In the mid-eighteenth century, Clive had recommended that native battalions be composed of equal numbers of Muslims and Hindus to ensure that each group effectively checked the other. In practice, Hindus were always recruited in larger numbers. In the Bengal Army of the early nineteenth century only one-tenth of troops were Muslim.[27] This may have been because the Muslims favoured service as cavalry, and also that they preferred to fight for Muslim rulers. British officers debated the relative merits of the two religious groups as soldiers. Warren Hastings expressed a preference for 'tall smooth-faced Hindus', but others argued that the Muslims were less frugal, liable to quickly spend their pay, and therefore more tied to the service. The Bombay Army deliberately targeted Muslims for recruitment into its marine corps as they were more willing to go to sea than Hindus.[28] More perceptive British commanders were prepared to make concessions to religious belief to maintain sepoy spiritual well-being and morale. Lake allowed his Hindu soldiers to visit Mathura to make religious observance between the battles of Delhi and Laswari.[29]

There was a preference for recruits of high caste, although the three Presidency armies differed considerably in their make up.[30] The Hindus of the Bengal Army were mostly of high caste. A tabulation of a regiment raised at Benares in 1814–15 reveals that there were almost 700 men of high caste (Brahmins, Rajputs) compared with just over 100 men of lower caste.[31] The Madras Army was more diverse; in 1759, only eighty men from a 600-strong sepoy battalion were of sufficiently high caste to be allowed to enter a temple they had attacked. The Bombay Army was an even greater mix and more relaxed in its attitude to caste.[32]

In her survey of the Bengal native infantry, Amiya Barat emphasises the profound influence of the Bengal sepoys' 'social and religious prejudices'. Food prepared by a lower caste man was taboo and higher-caste Hindus would rather starve than cook in the pots of others. Sepoys routinely carried their own cooking utensils even when in the field. Such was the significance of caste that a low caste Hindu *subadar* off duty might subjugate himself to a higher caste (Brahmin) non-commissioned officer or private. Colonel Henry Pennington, who served in the Bengal Army between 1783 and 1823, observed that sepoys, if well treated, would show great loyalty.

> But [one] must not interfere in their religion, nor in their prejudice regarding caste. Any wrong done to them on these points [could not] be atoned for by apologies or expressing of regret.[33]

The operational difficulties arising from the mixing of sepoys of different caste were real but mostly soluble. Richard Bayly boarded ship at Madras in August 1797.

> I accompanied two hundred men of the 12th on the 'Ceres', an 1,800-ton Chinaman, and a whole battalion of Rajahpoot Sepoys, consisting of eight hundred, were crowded into the same vessel. No powers of language can describe the scenes of confusion, discontent, and almost mutiny that ensued for several days after each caste, sect, or religion of Sepoys had embarked their own water and provisions, which, according to their prejudices, would have been contaminated if touched by an European or separate sect. Every morning

there was a regular bazaar on the deck, each sect scrupulously and sedulously avoiding contact with the persons or provisions of their fastidious neighbours; but in a short space of time everything was carried on with the most perfect amenity of temper.[34]

James Welsh was impressed that the different castes of the Madras native army – men 'who never unite, even at a meal, or in marriage' – were able to come together to form a disciplined force.[35] An old Madras *subadar* later commented; 'We put our religion into our knapsacks whenever our colours are unfurled.'[36]

In 1779, the commander-in-chief, Sir Eyre Coote, directed that the Company's army perform the same exercises and manoeuvres as practised by the King's regiments. A decade later, the sepoys and Europeans of the Bombay Army were being reviewed together as they followed the routines of Dundas's new drill manual.[37] It is unlikely that there was complete uniformity of drill. When Arthur Wellesley inspected a Madras native infantry regiment in 1800, he was pleased by their appearance, but he noted that 'the system of discipline practised is not that which is general in use at the present days'.[38] Bombay Army orders for native infantry issued in the same year stress the importance of the troops being taught to load and fire with rapidity and to make the manoeuvres most needed on active service.[39] The regulations did not stipulate the period of training of sepoys. Sita Ram states that he was instructed for eight months but this was probably less than average. The drill *havildar* and drill *naick* were immediately responsible for the training and were answerable to the adjutant. Drill instructions were given in English.[40]

Sita Ram's struggles with the language and the alien nature of the manoeuvres were no doubt the common experience of new sepoy recruits.

> In a few days I was sent to begin my drill. It is a day I shall always remember, for is it not impressed for ever on my mind? The parade-ground was covered by parties of six or eight men, performing the most extraordinary movements I had ever seen, and these to orders in a language of which I did not understand a single word. I felt inclined to laugh, and stood astonished at the sight. However, a violent wrench of my ear by the drill *havildar* soon brought me to my senses. I had to attend drill for many months, and one day I happened to forget how to do something and was so severely cuffed on the head by the drill *havildar* that I fell down senseless.

Sita Ram was fortunate that his uncle gave him some protection and he eventually performed his drill expertly enough to convince the regiment's colonel that he was fit for duty, 'I longed to wear a red coat and have a musket of my own.'[41]

As the organisation of the East India Company native battalions became regularised, increasing efforts were made to enforce strict discipline. The emphasis on general obedience of the mid-eighteenth century was replaced by more explicit regulations and an infrastructure for enforcing military law.[42] The reforms of 1796 dictated three types of courts martial for native soldiers; the regimental, the district or garrison, and the general. The general court martial was the only tribunal at which native commissioned officers could be tried; the other courts were only authorised to try sepoys and non-commissioned officers.[43]

Minor infractions would not require a court martial. In the Bengal Army, the commanding officer could punish his men by ordering extra drill or guard duty.[44] It is probable that European officers inflicted informal punishment on sepoys perceived to have stepped out of line. A Bengal sepoy giving evidence to a court martial in 1795 alleged that it was usual for British officers to beat them with sticks. This was not acceptable to the military authorities, but it is likely that most sepoys just accepted the behaviour. They might have experienced worse in other Indian armies of the period.[45]

More serious crimes such as desertion could lead to flogging or dismissal from the service. Mutiny was often punished by death by firing squad or being blown from a canon. However, there is evidence that the British authorities showed empathy towards their native troops. A more flexible discipline was applied where religious beliefs were involved; for instance, travel overseas was repugnant to upper-caste Hindus.[46] Draconian punishments were probably not inflicted disproportionally on native soldiers. Amiya Barat points out the 'negligible' incidence of crime and individual disobedience among the sepoys of the Bengal Army.[47] A veteran British officer of the army, writing in the 1820s, attributed this to the Bengal sepoys' historical deference to authority and their avoidance of alcohol, the nemesis of the European soldier.[48]

Any sepoy could rise from the ranks to the most senior position available to an Indian in the Company's military service. This was different to the European part of the Company's army where officers very rarely came from the ranks, instead being recruited as cadets. The regulations of 1796 stress the centrality of seniority in sepoy promotion, although merit was also to be taken into account.[49] In practice, merit became gradually less important and any promotion by seniority very slow. In the Bengal Army, men often remained as ordinary sepoys for twenty to twenty-five years. A sepoy entering the service at sixteen years of age might expect to be more than fifty years old before he attained the elevated rank of *jamadar* or *subadar*.[50] Sita Ram was a *jamadar* at the age of fifty. Such excruciatingly slow progress was likely to drain enthusiasm, particularly in times of relative peace when the duties were monotonous and irksome.[51]

Disillusionment also arose from the erosion of native officer authority. The increase in the number of European officers attached to native regiments in 1796 inevitably diluted the influence of the native officers with these units.

> From being leaders of their men, the native officers were reduced to playing the role of contact-men between the sepoys and the [European] commanding officers of their regiments.[52]

With the prospect of quick promotion dimmed, sepoys at all grades of seniority were likely to be more motivated by their immediate pay and other incentives such as leave and pensions. Remuneration was made up of ordinary pay and *batta* (see also Chapter 10). Rates were broadly equivalent across the Presidency armies, although there were some differences in allowances.[53] In the Bombay Army of 1801, a *subadar* could expect to receive 42 rupees per month, a *jamadar*, 24 rupees, a *havildar*, 10 rupees, a *naick*, drummer, or fifer, 8 rupees, and the humble private or *puckally*, 7 rupees.[54] The Bengal Army private also received 7 rupees monthly. To discourage desertion, the payment was made in three separate instalments. Out of his pay, the sepoy had to purchase his kit and also the services of a washerman, barber and sweeper.[55] He fed and maintained himself with whatever was left. When pay was increased, other allowances such as house rent or tobacco money were commonly discontinued.[56]

Although the pay of the sepoys of the Presidency armies was not overly generous when compared with that of the soldiers of the native Indian armies or trades-people, serving the Company gave other benefits. The privilege of furlough was introduced into the Bengal Army in 1796. Native soldiers were permitted leave every five to six years providing that no more than 10–15 sepoys and a similar proportion of officers were absent from the regiment at a given time.[57] A pension was allowable to any native soldier who had served the Company for twenty years. Although the amount was relatively small, usually three rupees per month for a private, it was highly valued as it was unknown in the armies of the Indian native princes.[58] Officers were usually pensioned on half pay, but men who had exceptional service records might receive even greater awards.[59] The following letter was written by Arthur Wellesley to the adjutant general in February 1805.

> I beg leave to lay before you the case of Burry Khan, late soubahdar in the 1st battalion 8th regiment, now a pensioner; and I request that you will submit the same to the consideration of the Commander-in-Chief, in the hope that his Excellency will see some grounds for recommending that this soubahdar may have as a pension the full pay of his rank and class, instead of the half-pay to which only he is entitled.

It appears by his certificate that he has served the Company forty years, and that he was a soubahdar of the 1st class. He was also a man of good character, and well connected in his corps; and five of his relations, commissioned and non-commissioned officers in the battalion, were killed in the battle of Assaye, wherein he also received the wound which has occasioned his being transferred to the non-effective establishment.

The wound is in his right shoulder, and has totally disabled that arm, from which splinters of bone continue to come away, and his only chance of relief is said to be in amputation; but from the situation of the wound, the medical gentlemen have not thought proper to attempt that operation.[60]

Provision was also made for the relatives of native troops killed in action. In 1804, an order was issued in the Madras Army directing that the nearest heir of every native officer and soldier who had died in battle or in consequence of wounds received in the war against the Marathas should receive the half pay of his rank. Where the deceased man had left sons, the payment continued for twelve years, but where there were only women or other dependents the arrangement was for the life of the heir.[61]

The Indian native soldier was thus a mercenary soldier who, in large part, had joined the Company's army for monetary and pragmatic reasons. However, there is much evidence that he then served with great loyalty and faithfulness. In the Bombay Army of the late eighteenth century, the behaviour of the sepoys was, according to General Robert Abercromby, 'beyond praise'.[62] The fidelity of the Bengal native soldier was legendary: 'There are no men more patient in submitting to privation than the Bengal sepoys'.[63] Arthur Wellesley, in a typical understatement, noted that they were 'not to be objectionable on the point of discipline'.[64]

Historians have argued that there were deeper reasons for this commitment to the British cause in the face of great hardship, starvation, pay arrears and the resolute resistance of their Indian enemy. Philip Mason stresses the importance of honour, a concept well understood by the Hindu, Muslim and British soldier: 'The oath at enlistment, the sacredness of the colours, the ceremonial of guard-mounting – these rubbed in the point'.[65] There was also the attachment to the regiment. As early as 1797, there is reference to the preference of Bombay recruits for particular units, the regiments becoming increasingly local.[66] At Bhurtpore, the remnants of the ruined colours of the 31st Bengal Native Infantry were secretly preserved by the men who had carried them to the summit of the ramparts.[67] We can only guess the mindset of the Indian soldier marching into battle in the Company's army, but it is obvious that the British eventually became complacent and took this apparent unquestioning loyalty for granted. It is no coincidence that this fracture only occurred after the loss of the aura of invincibility which surrounded the British-led forces in the first years of the century.[68]

We have no sepoy accounts of the battles of Lake and Wellesley. Sita Ram saw action in later years. The following is an excerpt from his description of the storming of the fort of Nala Pani in the Ghurkha War of 1814–16. Although not quite of our period, it is included as the closest we have to a contemporary sepoy's experience of battle.

> The Ghurkhas we always considered to be brave soldiers, and their knives were much dreaded. A touch from them meant certain death. Our force was ordered to march on the fort. The approach road ran through thick jungle and several of my comrades were wounded by arrows. These came from the jungle without making any sound and we saw no-one. Many of the *sepoys* said it was magic and the work of demons. We fired volleys of musketry when the arrows came thick, but the jungle was so dense that we never knew whether any of the enemy were killed.
>
> As we approached the fort, the General *sahib* ordered four columns for the attack. These were to approach the fort from different directions, but the paths were so bad and steep that one column arrived before the others. It was exposed to such heavy fire that it had to retreat, leaving behind many dead. This disheartened the *sepoys* very much, and seeing the European soldiers running back made it worse. At this moment General 'Gilspy' [Rollo Gillespie] led a European regiment to the attack, but despite all his bravery (and he was a veritable lion), he was beaten back two or three times. He was on foot, cheering on his men, when he suddenly fell dead. Then we retreated again, and my regiment covered the withdrawal.
>
> We retreated about one mile, and then halted for four or five days until the big guns could arrive from Delhi under Captain 'Hallow' *sahib* [Lieutenant Hall]. The walls of the fort were not very high, and the officers of my regiment wanted to try scaling ladders which we soon made from the jungle trees. But General 'Maulay' *sahib* [Colonel Mawbey] would not allow the attempt to be made because our losses had already been so terrible. In my regiment forty-eight men had been killed. The British regiment had lost nearly two companies, but they never lost heart and went into the attack again and again. They were like young fighting cocks. The *sepoys* were rather dispirited, but their spirits revived when the guns came up. The walls were battered and breaches were made. Another assault was then mounted, but although we pushed forward as hard as we could,

the British actually running up the breaches, we were still driven back. No-one succeeded in entering the fort. It was the sight of the arrows filling the air which frightened many of the men, rather than the sound of the matchlock balls which we could not see. The Mahommedans in the ranks were the most disheartened; as three attempts had failed, they said that Allah must be against them.

The fort was abandoned on the following day, the defenders escaping into the jungle.[69]

British commentaries of the Anglo-Maratha wars suggest that the Company's sepoy was mostly an effective soldier. Some of these views have been already referred to in the account of the campaigns, but an overview is in order. Very senior British officers praised their native Indian troops, albeit in a qualified manner. Lake was quick to applaud his sepoys, but equally keen to stress that they needed European support. His letter to the Governor-General, written from Agra on 10 October 1803, is in characteristic vein.

> The sepoys have behaved excessively well, but from my observation this day, as well as on every other, it is impossible to do great things in a gallant and quick style without Europeans; therefore, if they do not in England think it necessary to send British troops in the proportion of one to three sepoy regiments, which is in fact as one to six, they will stand a good chance of losing their possessions if a French force once get footing in India.

Lake also made reference to the large number of casualties among the European officers in sepoy regiments, explaining that they had to lead from the front.[70]

Arthur Wellesley wrote to John Malcolm after Assaye, informing him that all the troops had behaved admirably: 'the sepoys astonished me'.[71] Perhaps this was because he had had low expectations of his native battalions. At the end of 1801, he had confided to Major McCauley that he was unhappy with the makeup of his forces: 'I wish that I had a few more English troops and fewer Natives. I don't imagine that the latter are very active in a jungle'.[72] More junior British officers, men such as James Welsh and James Young, pay tribute to the fortitude of sepoy comrades in their memoirs. Welsh relates examples of great individual bravery in the Polygar Wars, while Young pulls no punches in his comparison of the actions of the 'glorious' 12th Bengal Native Infantry Regiment with the disgraced HM 76th Regiment at Bhurtpore in March 1805.[73]

It may be misguided to generalise regarding the competency of the EIC native battalions at this period. G.J. Bryant argues that:

> Although the company had not set out to create a mercenary force of Indian sepoys equivalent in skills and effectiveness to European

troops, this is what they had largely achieved by the end of the eighteenth century.

This was facilitated by the drafting of British officers into both commanding and subordinate roles in these units.[74] Conversely, John Pemble claims that the Company's sepoys were of lower calibre than the native troops of Britain's adversaries, quoting the heavy casualties suffered by the King's regiments which opposed Sindia's regular battalions.

> Why the same class of men should have proved better soldiers on the one side [Sindia] than on the other [Company] it is not easy to determine. Obviously the attractions of service with the British were not all they have been made out to be.[75]

There is evidence that sepoy units were used selectively by the British. Channa Wickremesekera analyses the division of labour in the Company's wars and concludes that:

> despite an increased confidence in their sepoys, the European troops were still treated as the main strength of an attacking party and when, as at Laswari and Assaye, there was a clear point of focus in the attacking formation, European troops were clearly preferred over the native troops.[76]

In the British memoirs of the wars there are many examples of good personal relations between European and Indian soldiers. An anonymous British officer tells the following anecdote in 1803.

> I happened to be present at the meeting between an [British] officer of artillery, lately returned from foreign service, and a Jemadar of the 8th [Bengal native infantry], who had formerly been what was termed Native-Adjutant to the Golundauz; they greeted each other with all the frankness and good humour of old soldiers, meeting upon terms of perfect equality, heartily shaking hands, and inquiring with marks of the greatest interest for mutual friends long since separated from them by the course of the service.[77]

A close relationship between the British and the Company's sepoys, both officers and privates, was in the best interests of the Indian Army. When Colonel David Ochterloney defended Delhi with a small body of sepoys in October 1803, he was able to inspire them to repel an assault and then resist stubbornly despite incessant fatigue. This was, James Grant Duff informs us, because 'He knew them'.[78]

There was overt racism even at the outset of the nineteenth century. Arthur Wellesley penned the following note to the adjutant-general in late 1801.

> I have been informed that two officers, Lieutenant Hook and Lieutenant Stewart, who have lately come out from England to join the 33rd Regiment, are half-caste or men of colour. I do not understand that they were recommended for their commissions in the 33rd Regiment by Colonel Marquess Cornwallis, or that they ever appeared in the War Office or the office of his Royal Highness the Commander-in-Chief, and it is probable that their appearance and the consequent unfitness for the service, particularly in this country, are not known.[79]

Racial stereotyping and British perceptions of racial superiority were to increase in the early 1800s.[80] This was part of the more general hardening of European attitudes towards India alluded to in Chapter 9. There was a deteriorating relationship between European officers and sepoys. Writing of his time in Bangalore in 1810, John Blakiston noted that many European officers 'carried themselves too high with the native officers, and did not encourage their visits, or seem to be so much pleased with their society as they ought to have been'.[81] Forty years later, a British brigadier was more explicit, commenting that there had been 'a great deal too much of the "damned black nigger" style of speaking'.[82] Channa Wickremesekera cogently argues that it was increasingly assumed that Indian soldiers were inferior. They might be 'the best black troops in the world' but they were no more than this. They were regarded by the British as being good *Indian* troops.[83]

Some of the most dismissive opinions were held by inexperienced British officers. Unsurprisingly, sepoys were resentful at being rudely treated by cadets newly arrived in the country and there was a mutual loss of trust and respect. Fighting for the British had never been easy. An old Bombay marching song summed it up.

> Sometimes bliss and sometimes woe,
> Servant of the English![84]

As the century unfolded, there was more woe than bliss and sepoy morale fell. Old Indian soldiers like Sita Ram met to discuss the deterioration of their service conditions and to reminisce about past glories.

> When I was a *sepoy* the Captain of my company would have some of the men at his house all day long and he talked with them. Of course many went with the intention of gaining something – to persuade the company commander to recommend them to the Colonel for

promotion, or to obtain this or that appointment in the regiment – but far more of us went because we liked the *sahib* who always treated us as if we were his children. I am a very old man now and my words are true. I have lived to see great changes in the *sahibs'* attitude towards us. I know that many officers nowadays only speak to their men when obliged to do so, and they show that the business is irksome and try to get rid of the *sepoys* as quickly as possible.[85]

There were multiple causes for unrest among the Company's native soldiers in the first half of the nineteenth century, not least the widening gulf between static pay scales and the cost of living. However, it was largely the combination of British dismissive attitudes and poor man-management that gradually eroded the loyalty of the sepoys and led to large-scale mutiny.[86]

Chapter 13

Scarcely a Good Tempered Man: Doctors, Hospitals and Disease

The medical arrangements for campaigning have been discussed in Chapter 11. Here, we will consider the broader organisation of the medical services, the nature of the doctors who laboured in the hospitals, and the diseases which affected the soldiers. India might not have been as dreaded a posting as the pestilential West Indies, but all the civilian and military men sent there, from the most senior officer to the rawest recruit, knew that their greatest enemy would be disease.

As is detailed in the *Fifth Report of the Commissioners of Military Enquiry*, published in 1808, each Presidency would eventually have its separate medical service directed by a Medical Board made up of senior army doctors.[1] With the arrival of increasing numbers of regimental medical officers from Britain in the second half of the eighteenth century, these surgeons became interchangeable between European and Indian units. The regimental establishments varied. The King's infantry units had their surgeons and two assistant surgeons, as at home. They would also have had attached a steward, a native apothecary and a sizeable number of menial staff.[2] In the Bengal Army in 1803, most of the native regiments had the full complement of three British surgeons and also two native doctors. The same applied in Bombay, but army lists show that the Madras Army had less European surgeons per regiment.[3] The establishment of the Madras force in 1797 gives an overview of how these doctors were employed. Out of a total of 104 surgeons, sixty were full surgeons and the rest assistant surgeons. Of the former, two were posted to the artillery, two to the European infantry and eleven to the native regiments. Of the latter, four were posted to the cavalry, two to the artillery, four to the European infantry and twenty-two to the native regiments, just one assistant surgeon to each battalion. One assistant surgeon was attached to the Madras native battalion and one to the corps of pioneers.[4]

These medical men ran the regiment's own hospital. As we will see, larger and more static general hospitals were also created when the need arose. In addition to the regimental doctors, there were also the 'medical staff' who had no regimental affiliation. There was no such rank as physician in the

Company's service. The staff or superintending surgeons were allocated to divisions and were expected to inspect hospitals and oversee the work of the regimental surgeons, receiving monthly returns of the sick.[5]

What do we know of the doctors who gave the routine medical care to the armies of Lake and Wellesley? They might be educated men, perhaps schooled at Edinburgh University or at a London anatomy institution. For many, their acquisition of a post in the Company's service was very likely not for altruistic reasons. There was the opportunity to earn extra money, not only from the prize funds, but also from the allowances associated with the purchase of drugs and medical supplies. Joseph Hume was appointed as assistant surgeon to the Bengal Army in August 1799, attached to the hospital at Chunar. By the time of his retirement in 1808, he had amassed £40,000. More senior army doctors could also benefit from a lucrative private practice, their patients drawn from the Company's civilian employees.[6]

There are a number of anecdotes of army doctors in the documents and memoirs of the period. Some describe dedicated and competent practitioners. Arthur Wellesley makes several complimentary references to medical officers in his dispatches. In December 1799, he writes to the deputy adjutant general defending his regimental surgeon, Andrew Trevor, against an unreasonable charge of inadequate record-keeping.

> He goes into his [regimental] hospital every morning at 7, and does not quit till 11; he returns to it again at 3, and does not quit till half-past 5. Therefore during the day he has four hours not employed in the hospital. But Dr. Ewart [the accuser] is mistaken if he supposes that the surgeon of the 33rd has not at all times kept a journal…

Wellesley admits that his surgeon's journal was not exactly as prescribed in an earlier order, but it was 'very sufficient' for reporting the care of the patients. Furthermore, the regimental hospital was the best he had ever seen.[7]

In the following year, Wellesley writes directly to Trevor, assuring him that he has his confidence; 'upon all occasions your attention to your duty, your humanity, and your skill, have claimed and received my fullest approbation'. The general had known the surgeon for seven years.[8] It was not usual for a senior officer to mention any doctor in dispatches as they were non-combatants. However, approval might lead to a promotion. Wellesley advises Colonel Barry Close in July 1803 that Staff Surgeon James Gilmour is deserving of military patronage: 'those who do the duty of the army ought to be promoted, and also ought to enjoy its benefits and advantages'. Wellesley also had dealings with doctors who were not a credit to their profession. In 1801, he was exasperated by the 'scandalous' conduct of an assistant surgeon who had tied up and beaten a local inhabitant on the road near Seringapatam.[9]

Ordinary soldiers' views of their doctors reflected the reality of a very wide range of conscientiousness and ability. James Welsh believed his regimental surgeon, John Inglis, to be of the highest calibre;

> he possessed a cheerfulness of disposition, suavity of manners, and benevolence of mind, which endeared him to all who had the pleasure of his acquaintance.[10]

This is in stark contrast to the medical man encountered by the ill George Carnegie.

> The Fever did not annoy me above five days, but the Doctor, a cabbage headed West Country Medicine Pounder, crammed me with such a quantity of Calomel as salivated me completely for 25 days. I had no use of either Gums or Teeth.[11]

Fixed general hospitals were required to manage the more seriously wounded and to cater for the large number of sick.[12] It was normal practice to have separate institutions for British and native troops. For instance, by 1784 there were two large hospitals for the British and one native facility in Bombay.[13] At the outset of campaigns, hospitals were frequently opened in strategic areas where troop concentrations were likely. Hurryhur in Mysore was the site of British and native hospitals at the beginning of 1803.[14] General hospitals in Europe had a poor reputation and, judging from the tone of Wellesley's correspondence, they were regarded by senior officers to be a grim necessity. The following letter is to Colonel James Stevenson and is dated 2 May 1803 at Poona.

> You must immediately establish an hospital, and leave in it all the sick of the Scotch brigade that require carriage. Look for some secure place for this establishment within the Nizam's frontier. If you do not do this, the first action you will have will be ruinous to you. I know that the surgeons will carry about the sick men till they die; although I am aware that, generally speaking, it is best to keep the sick with their corps: but in a case of this kind, where there are so many men sick, and the carriage for the sick is insufficient, and there is every probability that there will be more sick, an hospital must be established…[15]

Unsurprisingly, the locals were not always happy at the prospect of insalubrious hospitals being opened in their towns. After Assaye, the *killadar* at Dowlutabad refused the admission of British sick and wounded.[16] Wellesley was to meet similar opposition in the Peninsular War.

The regulations of all the Presidency armies include directions for the management of general hospitals. There is much emphasis on the level of staffing, the need for cleanliness, and expenditure. Many of the hospitals' 'servants' were drawn from the local population. The following brief excerpt from the Bombay Army regulations of 1800 is typical of the demand for good hygiene.

> Hospitals should be kept very clean, and should be well ventilated. The bedding of the sick should, as often as possible, be exposed to the sun and air, the walls of the hospital be frequently white washed, and if contagious diseases prevail, it is recommended to try the fumigation of doctor Smyth; which is produced by mixing half an ounce of salt petre with half an ounce of vitriolic acid in a sand heat. It is strongly recommended to remove dead bodies from the wards as soon as possible, and to have the cloaths they used well washed, and the straw of their bedding immediately burned.[17]

Where such well-meaning advice was applied by assiduous medical staff, and where suitable buildings were available, general hospitals might be of good quality. John Pester found the hospital at Agra to be 'exceedingly airy and in every respect commodious and well calculated for the purpose'. It had been divided into two halves for natives and Europeans.[18] Overall standards in India were unlikely to have been better than in the despised hospitals of the European campaigns and there are also anecdotes of poor practice. Discipline in the Madras Presidency hospitals of the 1790s was lax, the patients escaping to commit 'every act of enormity'.[19] When George Elers became ill with dysentery in 1798, he was admitted to a hospital converted from one of Tipu Sultan's country palaces. The beautiful gardens were soon full of shallow graves.

> On my arrival sick at the palace I found all the private soldiers lying on the bare ground, some in the agonies of death. It was a shocking sight to behold. The heat and smell were dreadful.

It was normal to accommodate sick or wounded officers separately to the men and in this case the upper rooms were assigned to them. There was, however, no escape from the 'pestiferous air'.[20] After the battle of Delhi, Pester tells us that suitable buildings were converted into general hospitals, but that the wounded officers were admitted to the best situated houses. When he later developed a fever in the city, he was lodged in the quarters of a fellow officer.[21]

Convoys of sick and wounded men moved significant distances across country. The least infirm might walk but there was much reliance on *doolies*. These contraptions, usually constructed of bamboo, are well described by Sergeant Butler.

The [sick] person is put into what is called a doolie, which is nearly in the form of one of the small houses or boxes used in Scotland for watch-dogs, being about six feet long, and three deep. In the middle of each side there is a door to go out and in by, and upon the top, at each end, there is a strong ring, through which a pole is put, and borne by four natives.[22]

Wellesley was determined to ensure adequate provision for the movement of the sick. In February 1802, he acknowledges the shortage of suitable vehicles, particularly in the native corps, but officers are curtly informed that the difficulty, 'like others, can be surmounted'.[23] In a memorandum to the Bombay authorities, probably written in late 1803, he makes recommendations for the number of *doolies* and adds:

wagons should be made in Bombay to carry 20 men from each corps besides those for whom doolies will be provided…if it can be done with convenience and without great expense, the wagons ought to be on springs and…covered from the weather. Their wheels and axles should be strong…

He goes on to suggest that each wagon might carry six men.[24]

It was usual for substantial sick convoys to be accompanied by a regimental doctor to oversee the medical care. When 335 patients were moved from the hospital at Ajanta to Ahmednuggar in February 1804, the convoy was made up of 150 *doolies*, some carts, and also bullocks to carry the tents and provisions. The whole was the responsibility of Assistant Surgeon Alexander Stewart.[25]

The following appeared in the general orders for the Bombay Army in April 1800.

The medical board, in the course of their examination of the number of unfits lately brought before them, have observed that the list of diseases on the return was very incorrect; many of the subjects being afflicted with complaints totally different from those inserted; and one man in particular in the 1st battalion 5th regiment was, in the opinion of the surgeon, unfit from the amputation of a leg, when in fact he had lost an arm.[26]

We can, however, gain some understanding of the army's diseases from the contemporary writings of senior doctors and the cautious interpretation of returns. Inevitably, we have more information for British than native troops.

George Ballingall, assistant surgeon to the 2nd Battalion, 1st Regiment of Foot, was later to become professor of military surgery at Edinburgh. He has left detailed tabulated data pertaining to disease in the men of his own regiment and also in the principal military stations of the Madras establishment between 1807 and 1808. The below figures show the impact of disease on a unit newly arrived in India.

Date	Disease	Admissions	Deaths
December 1807– August 1808	Fevers	239	17
	Flux (dysentery)	541	98
	Hepatitis	20	3
	Other	365	58
Total		**1,165**	**176**

The regiment's effective strength on landing was 1,025 men.[27] This was not as catastrophic a loss as might have been experienced in the West Indies, but disease rates and mortality were much greater than at home. In Bengal, among the least healthy areas of the subcontinent, the risk of death was increased six-fold.[28] About half of the military officers of the East India Company died in India.[29] Only 10% of them lived long enough to collect their pensions.[30] Ballingall's wider figures for the various stations in southern India confirm dysentery as the leading cause of death, although in many places venereal disease was the commonest complaint. For instance, of the 7,668 men documented as being sick in Bangalore during the eighteen-month period, 3,810 had venereal ailments compared with 1,074 with dysentery, 800 with fever, 526 with ulcers, and 226 with hepatitis. The percentage of soldiers dying from their disease varied from only 2% in Nunindroog to more than 11% in Seringapatam and Wallajabad.[31]

Returns from the King's regiments serving in India in 1805 (five cavalry regiments, sixteen infantry regiments, and a Swiss regiment (De Meuron's); see Appendix II) show that out of a total strength of 9,308 men, 1,947 (21%) were sick.[32] The erosive effect of disease was significant. Arthur Wellesley wrote to Major-General John Braithwaite in September 1800 informing him that the 33rd Foot was so sickly that he was unable to take it into the field. Eight months later, his regiment was improved but still unhealthy. The 12th Regiment were worse off, with only 100 men fit for duty.[33]

The human misery and grief caused by these infectious diseases is all too easily lost in formal correspondence and returns. George Ballingall was not constrained by the concept of medical confidentiality and his medical records give us glimpses of the young men of the Royals who never returned from India. Alexander Youll was described as being eighteen years of age, 5ft 3in tall, of stout build with a fair complexion, red hair and grey eyes. He died of dysentery. Sergeant John Douglas was twenty-six years old, 5ft 7in tall, of 'good make', fair complexion, brown hair and grey eyes. He succumbed to a liver disease. We do not know the precise disease which carried off 23-year-old Thomas Pennison, who was described as 'puny' and who presumably had little chance of surviving his Indian adventure.[34] Non-combatants were excluded from returns. Sergeant Butler tells us that of eighty-two women who accompanied his regiment to India, thirty-two died. Fifty-seven children perished during the same period.[35]

We will briefly consider some of the commoner diseases affecting the Indian Army: fevers, dysentery, liver disease, venereal disease, and disorders of the mind. Fever was a term very generally used in the early nineteenth century. It was commonly subdivided into typhus and continued, intermittent, and remittent forms.[36] In India, fevers were often also designated according to their locality; for instance there were hill, jungle, Wynaad and Seringapatam types.[37] There is no doubt that there were many infectious diseases afflicting the troops, but it is likely that a lot of fever cases were malaria, often referred to as 'ague'. This is suggested by the seasonal nature of much of the fever and also its tendency to remit and relapse. While Ballingall is quick to stress that fever was a dangerous disease, he points out that the mortality from the 'bilious remittent' fever seen in the Madras area was relatively low.[38] This is consistent with milder forms of malaria, which were debilitating rather than fatal.

There are a few accounts of fever by soldiers. Twenty-year-old Valentine Blacker very likely contracted malaria while serving in southern India. His illness started in March 1799 and he had several relapses.

> Though I went in a Palanquin it grows so soon hot that I was nearly in the situation of a person in an oven. This with my disorder reduced me to such a situation that I could not lie down or get up without assistance of two or three. My resolution completely failed me and I entreated the Palanquin bearers to lay me down under some trees or water and that all my suffering might be put to an end by Tippoo's Horse. They were deaf to my entreaties and carried me on day after day until we arrived at Seringapatam.

Blacker recovered from the acute episode but was left so thin that he could not sit on a chair without pillows under him. When he had a relapse of his 'ague' in December 1800, he was treated with bark and after this his health much improved.[39] Peruvian bark, the cinchona from which quinine was later to be extracted, was one of the very few potentially effective drugs of the period. Quinine remains important in the management of malaria.

Dysentery, often referred to as the 'flux', was associated with the presence of bloody diarrhoea and was caused by a variety of bacteria.[40] It was a common and frequently fatal disorder, much feared by the soldiers. James Welsh describes it as a 'vile scourge' of the army.[41] Ballingall informs us that, on the first arrival of European troops in India, it was the 'colonitis or inflammation of the large intestine' which proved most destructive.[42] When Arthur Wellesley's 33rd Regiment arrived at Madras in late 1798, many of the men had flux and fifteen of them ('as fine men as any we had...') died.[43] Among Ballingall's detailed case reports is that of 24-year-old James Forum.

> Admitted yesterday, complaining of fixed pain in the lower part of the abdomen, and persisting frequent loose watery stools with blood and mucous...

The patient's treatment is meticulously recorded as he became increasingly distressed with continuous severe diarrhoea. He died two weeks after his admission. The doctor opened the body to find to find the large intestines to be of a 'livid colour' and also evidence of an abscess in the liver.[44]

Sergeant Butler was more fortunate than poor Forum, but dysentery left him permanently debilitated.[45] Ballingall declared that the cause of the disease was obscure (we will return to general theories of disease causation) and soldiers had their own theories. Wellesley believed the travails of the 33rd to be due to the poor quality of water on board. An anonymous eyewitness of the Seringapatam campaign had a more hierarchical theory.

> Bowel disorders were it's true very common but among the higher orders they were occasioned by long [periods] of extreme fatigue and irregular refreshments; among the lower by the greedy and unguarded use of fruit and every vegetable they could find.[46]

Liver disorders were also commonplace and were a mixture of infectious diseases such as hepatitis and more chronic disorders, many of which would have been exacerbated or caused by excessive alcohol consumption. Hepatitis was associated with a much lower mortality rate than dysentery; Mountstuart Elphinstone, John Malcolm and George Elers all suffered from transient liver diseases and made full recoveries despite unhelpful treatments such as mercury and blistering.[47] Conversely, we can only guess at the extent of the damage inflicted on the Indian Army by alcohol. The consumption by Europeans was prodigious. Richard Bayly describes a day's snipe shooting near Wallajabad.

> They are generally attended by black servants carrying water, with several bottles of brandy and Madeira wine, with which they repeatedly quench their insatiable thirst, induced by the intolerable heat and fatigue to which they are exposed for many successive hours; one individual alone has frequently been known to consume the contents of three bottles of brandy in the course of a morning's excursion, independent of repeated tumblers of sangaree (a tumbler of Madeira, sugar and nutmeg, diluted with a wineglass of water).[48]

Some alcoholic drinks were especially toxic. Butler describes the men of his regiment raiding a neighbouring village for *paria arrack*, a beverage that 'made them almost, if not altogether mad'. The word 'paria', he tells us, was applied to anything contemptible or base.[49]

Venereal diseases appear little in the memoirs of the Indian wars, but syphilis and gonorrhoea were very common. It was usual for upwards of 30% of European soldiers to be in hospital with sexually transmitted diseases.[50] Ballingall's data for the fourteen stations of the Madras establishment between January 1807 and October 1808 shows almost 13,000 hospital admissions for venereal disease compared with 9,000 admissions for all forms of fever.[51] Deaths from venereal disease were apparently rare (Ballingall lists only thirty-four) but it is likely that the quoted morbidity and mortality figures are underestimates, as many afflicted soldiers avoided the medical authorities. Venereal disease was probably more prevalent in the British Army in India than in any other part of the world and its ubiquity made it not only of medical but also of strategic concern.[52]

Disorders of the mind also get little attention in the military writings of the period, but we can assume that they occurred in the soldiers of the Indian Army, both native and European, as in all other wars. These afflictions might be only homesickness or mild depression reactive to the sudden change in circumstances. George Elers confesses that he was miserable during his first three years in India, 'my last thought as I lay down to sleep, and the first when I awoke was England'.[53] The brutality of the wars caused more serious problems. John Shipp's reaction to what he had witnessed is compatible with what we would now describe as post-traumatic stress disorder.

> I was visited with the most excruciating headaches and dizziness from the wound in my head; and the terrific spectacle of the last scene at Bhurtpore so affected my mind, that scarcely a night passed in which I did not dream of 'hair-breadth 'scapes i' th' imminent deadly breach,' and fancy I was fighting my battles over again.[54]

Both John Pester and James Young allude to soldiers in Lake's army committing suicide.[55] Mental disease was stigmatised – Mountstuart Elphinstone admitted to a fear of going mad[56] – but it would be wrong to conclude that the provision in India was unusually primitive for the period. In the 1790s, when much management of psychiatric disease in Britain was left to family and community, there were lunatic asylums opened for Indian troops at Monghyr in Bihar and also in the Bombay Presidency.[57]

There were many other diseases which stalked the men of the Indian Army. We will not consider these in any detail, but will simply acknowledge them. In no particular order they included: sunstroke, insect bites, beriberi, guinea worm, scurvy, elephantiasis (filariasis), smallpox, rabies, dropsy, and skin disorders. Doctors and soldiers strained to understand the causes of this almost endless list of ailments. The broad theories of disease aetiology had changed little for 100 years. The Napoleonic Wars pre-dated by a full century the emergence of the science of microbiology and any recognition of the disease-causing organisms carried in water and the role of insects such as mosquitoes. Although there were some 'contagionists', most army doctors believed that 'miasma' or 'miasmata', invisible poisons in the air exuded from rotting animal and vegetative material, the soil and stagnant water, were the primary aetiology.[58] Other more specific factors were often invoked. We have the following from the military author of the *East India Vade Mecum*.

> Under all the circumstances of such a combination of putrid animal and vegetable substance, of mineral adulteration, and of the miasma arising from the almost sudden exposure of an immense residuum of slime, & c.; added to the cessation of the pure sea air, the wind changing after the rains from the southerly to the northerly points, are we to wonder at the malignancy of those fevers prevailing through the province of Bengal Proper, from the end of September to the early part of January, when the swamps are generally brought into narrow limits, and the air is laden with noxious vapours?[59]

Experienced regimental surgeons searched for potentially reversible reasons for the high incidence of disease. James McGrigor, later to be instrumental in the improvement of Wellington's army's medical service in the Peninsula, sought an explanation in environmental factors such as the weather, particularly variations in temperature, and also in the diet of the troops. Heat alone was not the obvious determinant as men were often healthiest in the hottest months.[60] George Ballingall believed fluxes to be caused by the combination of heat and moisture, the excessive consumption of fruit, the abuse of alcohol, and exposure to wind and 'noxious night dews'.[61] Such theories were widespread in other theatres of war, but historian Mark Harrison argues that the view that the liver played a central role in the causation of fever was much more widely held in India than elsewhere. It was thought that the extreme heat induced it to secrete a copious amount of harmful bile.[62]

Ordinary soldiers were bewildered. Richard Bayly appears to support the miasmatic concept of disease, attributing the fever in his regiment to the 'putrescent, unwholesome state of the atmosphere' arising from the rotting carcasses of bullocks. Later, perhaps to reassure himself, he surprisingly states that India was not an inherently unhealthy place.

> I am perfectly persuaded that diseases are neither more numerous nor inveterate than in Europe, provided we pursue that regular course of living generally adopted by our countrymen in England...[63]

British army doctors attacked disease with measures which are usually collectively referred to as 'antiphlogistic' remedies. The combination of bleeding by lancet or other methods, drenching in cold water, and the administration of drugs such as purgatives (designed to induce diarrhoea), emetics (inducing nausea and vomiting), and agents producing profound sweating and salivation formed the mainstays of treatment. In simple terms, the rationale was to remove 'impurities' from the blood.[64]

George Ballingall refers to the components of antiphlogistic therapy in his Indian medical text. For the fevers of the country, purgatives are judged to be 'particularly appropriate' and cold affusions are 'far too sparingly used'.[65] There was, however, a view among doctors that the diseases of India were sufficiently different to those of Europe to warrant a different approach. Treatments were equally 'heroic', no doubt well suited to a military culture, but at the end of the eighteenth century bleeding was used less and mercury more than was the case at home.[66] Ballingall notes that experienced Indian practitioners had 'an extreme aversion to the use of the lancet', the blood-letting being poorly tolerated in a hot climate. Conversely, the liver-based theories of disease causation favoured the extensive use of mercury, administered in the form of calomel pills. This toxic agent largely replaced Peruvian bark and dominated the treatment of fever in British India between 1790 and 1830.[67] Ballingall advocates purgation with mercury in more severe fevers. It was, he says, a remedy in which he had total confidence. He also shares the common view of bark, noting that he not been impressed with the results.[68]

With the benefit of a modern medical perspective, most antiphlogistic strategies adopted by the King's and Company's doctors appear a series of indignities which can only have made sick men more miserable and less likely to survive. Valentine Blacker was probably not the only soldier to take matters into his own hands.

> I am enabled to say that my heath is improving every season and that I believe my constitution is such that having once weathered the grand tryal of the first two years residence it is more congenial to the soil of India than most others. Indeed I have acquired by experience so thorough a knowledge of it that I can in cases of indisposition in general much better prescribe for myself than any medical man and am so well acquainted with the approach of the bile that I am always able to prevent its further progress by the necessary precautions and preventatives.[69]

Medical officers might have disapproved of Blacker's autonomy, but they were also preoccupied with measures that could possibly stem the tide of disease. Ballingall stresses at the outset of his book that prevention rather than cure was the only means of reducing the fatality of tropical maladies.[70] While lacking any real understanding of the causes of disease, doctors still made commonsensical recommendations. These included the optimal recruitment and preparation of men for Indian service, lifestyle changes such as an improved diet, better ventilation and cleanliness of accommodation, and more specific interventions such as quarantine and vaccination. It was widely understood that regiments which had spent considerable time in India were less vulnerable to disease that the newly arrived levies. Thus, in 1798, Harris is loathe to lose the hardened 36th Regiment to be replaced by the untested 33rd.[71] One strategy to ameliorate the heavy losses suffered by the new recruits was a period of 'seasoning' prior to their arrival in the country. Mornington certainly believed this to be advantageous, recommending that regiments en route to India spend a period of time at the Cape;

> the regiments which had passed through the seasoning of the climate, have arrived and continued in much better health, than those which proceeded thither directly from Europe…[72]

It is probable that some soldiers fell victim to their own naivety. John Pester witnessed the newly arrived 53rd Regiment on the Ganges. Many of the officers walked on the shore in the full heat of the day 'by which we concluded that they must have been unacquainted with the nature of this climate.'[73]

There was abundant medical advice available in print. Typical is Surgeon Alexander Stewart's *Medical Discipline or Rules and Regulations for the more effectual preservation of health on board the honourable East India Company's ships in a letter addressed to the Honourable Court of Directors*, published in 1798. His book targets the health of sailors and is organised under subject headings including cleanliness, air, diet, rest, exercise, clothing and general remedies. Most of the advice is prosaic, while being embedded in the prevailing theories of disease causation.

> On leaving England, and in sailing from ports that ships occasionally touch at on the passage, it is customary to keep a part of the live stock (sheep, poultry, and hogs) below on the gun deck, even in midships, or in the very midst of where the men sleep. In such cases, it is evidently almost impossible to keep the deck either sweet or clean; and in so confined and crowded a place (more especially in hot latitudes), the men's breath, mixed with that of those animals, with the effluvia arising from their bodies, and with that of

the different matters they discharge, must highly contaminate and vitiate the surrounding air, and render it very unfit for the purposes of healthful respiration.

Stewart recommends that ships should always anchor far from the shore (to avoid 'land dews'), that men going ashore should avoid getting wet or over-exposed to the sun, and that they should always have a 'warm comfortable breakfast'. He is exasperated by some of the sailors. Outbreaks of disease, he explains, most often occur among:

> prefect lubbers, the meanest and most profligate of mankind; the very scum of the earth and outcasts of society, who, in reality, are an utter disgrace to the jacket they wear.[74]

On occasion, the only apparent solution to epidemics of disease was to move bodies of troops to a healthier area. Some parts of the country were notoriously sickly, the area around the Jumna River being styled the 'St Domingo of the East'.[75] When fever broke out in the 65th Regiment stationed in Bengal in 1815, a third of the men were soon in hospital and the patients began to die. The fever was so violent that the sufferers' heads were too hot to touch. The regiment's colonel ordered several marches to try to escape the disease. Eventually, a camp was established on high ground near the sea and the epidemic subsided.[76]

The need for selective use of quarantining was understood. When the Indian Army returned from Egypt in 1802, there was concern that troops of the Bombay native infantry might be infected by plague. James McGrigor was on board and was subsequently appointed superintendant of the quarantine station on Butcher's Island near Bombay. On the arrival of new ships, he inspected the soldiers and disembarked any men about whom he had suspicions. There was no outbreak of disease and troops were allowed to re-embark to proceed to their destination.[77]

Vaccination against smallpox had been pioneered in the 1790s by Edward Jenner and from 1802 it was used extensively in India. Troops were vaccinated with a dose of cowpox virus, which provided immunity against the more serious disease. Earlier attempts at inoculation with smallpox had proved less successful.[78] Bombay Army orders for 1803 direct that the officers of corps vaccinate all the native troops who carried no signs of having previously had smallpox.[79] Such medical interventions were often embraced in India, where the Company's doctors, so distant from home, were willing to adapt their medical practice to the local environment. This enthusiasm for innovation and experimentation was perhaps due to the nature of these medical men, who were not of the military medical elite and therefore more likely to be open-minded and even dissenting.[80] They were an early part of the British Army's considerable role in the development of the speciality of 'tropical medicine'.[81]

Intelligent military officers fully appreciated the erosive effect of sickness on their men and they took deliberate actions to minimise the impact of the protean infectious diseases that threatened the army. Arthur Wellesley wrote to Colonel Murray from Seringapatam in August 1803.

> Every attention must be paid to economy, but I consider nothing in this country so valuable as the life and health of the British soldier, and nothing so expensive as soldiers in hospital.

Wellesley concludes that it was worth almost any expense to preserve the health of the men.[82] There are many examples of his pro-activity in his dispatches. In 1801, he orders that the inner ditch at Seringapatam, a likely cause of disease in the 12th and 33rd Regiments, should be filled in.[83] The following year, he supports the recommendations of the Medical Board in ordering that the men should not be drilled too early in the morning when it was cold and damp.[84] In 1804, he emphasises the need for cleanliness in the camp at Chinchore.[85]

Arthur also made efforts to protect his own health. This was another subject on which he held definite views, which he shared with his brother Henry.

> I know but one receipt for good health in this country, and that is to live moderately, to drink little or no wine, to use exercise, to keep the mind employed, and, if possible, to keep in good humour with the world. The last is the most difficult, for, as you have often observed, there is scarcely a good tempered man in India.[86]

Despite such precautions and his usually robust constitution, he became ill, suffering from a fungal skin infection, an intermittent fever which was very likely malaria, and troublesome low back pain. Sickness prevented him accompanying the Indian Army in the Egyptian campaign. The loss of this command to David Baird mortified him.[87] Others noted the deterioration in his health. George Elers was concerned that his senior officer was subject to 'fever and ague'. This followed a 'violent eruption' over his whole body, a reference to the skin disorder.[88] John Malcolm describes him suffering from fever and being fretful and anxious.[89] There are frequent allusions to the fever in Wellesley's correspondence. In April 1801, he tells Henry that his fever was in a remission but that it had left him feeling weak. He was receiving nitrous baths for the skin affliction.[90] The recrudescence of the fever documented in May underlines its intermittent nature.[91]

Wellesley's poor health undoubtedly contributed to his decision to return home in the summer of 1804. He informs the Governor-General's military secretary, Major Shawe, that he had served as long in India 'as any man ought, who can serve any where else'.[92] A year later, writing from St Helena, he admits to John Malcolm that he feared that if he had stayed longer he would have become seriously ill.[93] His very senior rank was no protection from the hardships of campaigning and from tropical disease. Of 353 officers in the Bengal Army who were promoted to lieutenant colonel by 1820, 40% died in India, elsewhere in the East, or in transit. As only three were known to have been killed in action, the overwhelming majority of the deaths can be attributed to disease.[94] The future Duke of Wellington was fortunate to survive his eight years in India.

More of the Oak than the Willow

Three men whose efforts were vital for British success in India between 1798 and 1805 were introduced in the first chapter.

Richard Wellesley appears an isolated and unhappy character despite his undoubted successes as Governor-General. As early as 1800, he informed Dundas that his health was poor due to the 'vexation and mortification which I suffered in consequence of the unaccountable conduct of my friends in England...'.[1] Three years later, he was 44 years old and was toiling through his seventh monsoon season.[2] He intended to resign the following year, but he was forced out. He had finally paid the price for his contempt of the Directors and his failure to retain political support at home. His Indian regime divided opinion in Britain, being, in Penderel Moon's words, both 'brilliant' and 'despotic'. He was coolly received and also investigated in parliament, the charges against him lingering on until 1808. It was another twenty-eight years before the Company finally recognised his contribution, expressing their 'admiration and gratitude' with a gift of £20,000 and a marble statue in India House.[3]

Gerard Lake did not long survive his exertions in Hindustan, dying after a short illness in February 1808.[4] He was a great fighting general, enormously popular with his men, and his current obscurity is undeserved. He was tainted by poor political and military judgements and his damaging failure at Bhurtpore. Despite his notable victories, he was compared adversely with Arthur Wellesley. In December 1803, Mountstuart Elphinstone, writing from Wellesley's camp, admitted that Lake's campaigns were brilliant. However:

> if any one considers the difficulties occasioned by distance from home, difficulty of supplies, narrow resources, and insecure rear, doubtful allies, and an enemy well provided with cavalry and headed by chiefs, I think he will allow most merit to our General.[5]

Arthur Wellesley, the man who overcame these challenges, already had many of the character traits which he later displayed as the Duke of Wellington. When, in May 1803, he portrayed a fellow officer as being excellent but with 'more of the oak than the willow in his disposition' he might have been describing himself.[6] Captain George Elers saw a young man who could laugh and joke, but who was unforgiving of mediocrity: '[he] openly declared that, if he commanded an army, he should not hesitate to hang a *Commissary* for any dereliction of duty'.[7] He appeared unafraid of unpopularity and the memoirs of officers such as Richard Bayly and William Harness suggest that he was not universally liked.[8]

Wellesley was not a great innovator, something he acknowledged and chose to justify in a communication to the Bombay Government in 1803;

> it has been my constant wish to conform to existing rules and establishments, and to introduce no innovations; so that at the conclusion of the war, when my duties would cease, every thing might go on in its accustomed channel.[9]

Within this normal framework, he laboured endlessly, displaying the common sense and phenomenal attention to detail which were to permeate his entire military career. His *Indian Dispatches* are a testimony to his dynamism and staying power. When later in life he was asked how a sickly child had developed such stamina, he answered 'Ah, that was all in India'.[10]

A meaningful assessment of the contribution of Wellesley's Indian experience to his later campaigns and political life would require a more wide-ranging and comparative study than has been attempted in this book. However, it is of interest to consider the conclusions of several modern historians. Arthur Bennell emphasises the political dimension of Wellesley's Indian years. The general had learnt the basic trade of warfare, but more than that:

> because he had carried together political and military authority, he had come to appreciate the contrast between potential political power and the often very different and enfeebled reality.[11]

Wellesley had analysed the letters of Residents and negotiated with Indian agents. He was, according to the Prussian general von Gneisenau, on the eve of Waterloo, a man who could 'outwit the Nabobs themselves'.[12] He was sceptical of politicians, complaining to the Governor-General in 1804 of the Government's 'breach of faith' and of ministers' failure to understand the situation in India.[13]

Edward Ingram sees echoes of India and particularly the subsidiary alliance system in the Wellesleys' approach to the Iberian Peninsula. They attempted to treat the Kingdom of Portugal 'as if it were Hyderabad'.[14] He also detects elements of the Duke of Wellington's later battles in Arthur Wellesley's battlefield tactics. At Assaye, he instructed the sepoys to lie down, an order he was to repeat to the allied army at Waterloo.[15]

Rory Muir, in his magisterial biography of Wellington, also interprets the Indian years as being a seminal experience for an evolving soldier. He was already an excellent general who attributed his success to pragmatism and graft rather than to any inherent genius.

> As a soldier, he had not merely seen action, but learnt to command an army on campaign and in battle. He had shown boldness, daring and courage, but also meticulous planning and preparation, and great care for the welfare and discipline of his troops.

He met adversity with patience, he was flexible, and he was ruthless.[16]

Huw Davies makes interesting observations and poses questions relating to Wellesley's use of tactics in India and in the Peninsular War. They were superficially different, the aggression of South India apparently replaced by a more conservative, defensive form of warfare. Was the narrow escape at Assaye the reason for this? Alternatively, was he innately cautious, his Indian recklessness a desperate reaction of the moment? Davies concludes that, in reality, Wellesley and Wellington were not so far apart, Indian tactics being evolved and adapted to a new setting. There were no fundamentally different Indian and European doctrines.[17] Davies is surprisingly harsh on his subject.

> Rather than a flowering military genius, the Wellesley of the Deccan campaign was manifestly incompetent in the organisation of his intelligence collection; and arrogant to the point of imbecility in the analysis of that intelligence and in his interpretation of the nature of his enemy. From these errors stemmed most of the problems that Wellesley encountered in 1803. Despite these errors, he still won.[18]

Davies accepts that Wellesley learn from his mistakes. In later years, the Duke was to tell Lord Stanhope that at the time of his departure from India he had 'understood as much of military matters as I have ever done since or do now'.[19] He remained loyal to India throughout his life. In 1810, he advised his quartermaster general, George Murray, that the East India Company was still the most promising route for young men without much money or patronage.[20] He was repaying a debt. India had been the making of him.

Appendix I

General Lake's Army at Secundra, 26 August 1803 (from Thorn, Maj W., *Memoir of the War in India*, p. 88).

Infantry	
1st Brigade (Lt-Col Monson)	2/4th Bengal Native Infantry (BNI)
	4 companies 17th BNI
	HM 76th Regiment
	1/4th BNI
2nd Brigade (Col Clarke)	2/8th BNI
	1/12th BNI
	2/9th BNI
	6 companies 16th BNI
3rd Brigade (Col McDonald)	1/15th BNI
	2/15th BNI
	2/12th BNI
4th Brigade (Lt-Col Powell)	1/2nd BNI
	1/14th BNI
	2/2nd BNI
Cavalry	
1st Brigade (Lt-Col Vandeleur)	1st Bengal Native Cavalry (BNC)
	HM 6th Light Dragoons
	3rd BNC
2nd Brigade (Col St Leger)	2nd BNC
	HM 27th Light Dragoons
	6th BNC
3rd Brigade (Col Macan)	3rd BNC
	4th BNC
	HM 29th Light Dragoons
Artillery	
2 battalion guns attached to each battalion of infantry (28 guns)	
2 galloper guns attached to each regiment of cavalry (16)	
1 Brigade of Horse Artillery (6)	
12 six-pounders, 4 twelve-pounders (16)	
3 5½ inch howitzers (3)	

Appendix II

Effective Strength of his Majesty's Regiments serving in India, taken from the latest returns, 1 April 1805 (from Wellesley, R., *The Dispatches*, Vol. IV, p. 670).

Cavalry	Present for Duty	Sick	On Command	Total	Wanting to complete
8th Dragoons	362	152	..	514	59
19th do.	245	49	56	350	198
22nd do.	324	86	1	411	133
27th do.	218	56	2	276	199
29th do.	219	63	1	283	183
Total Cavalry	1368	406	60	1834	772
Infantry					
12th Foot	552	61	23	636	556
17th do.	1322	115	3	1140	..
22nd do.	560	165	86	811	172
33rd do.	278	74	221	573	550
34th do.	944	76	3	1023	..
65th do.	61	61	437	559	448
73rd do.	587	52	2	641	489
74th do.	127	92	6	225	848
75th do.	397	127	..	524	399
76th do.	581	199	..	780	250
77th do.	426	58	40	524	325
78th do.	380	51	104	535	529
80th do.	409	36	316	761	213
84th do.	444	67	73	584	318
94th do.	357	193	4	554	548
Swiss	422	50	1	473	387
Total infantry	7940	1541	1463	10944	6625
Total infantry and cavalry	9308	1947	1523	12778	7397

Appendix III

Ordnance to accompany the Troops in the Field according to a Letter from Lieutenant-General Stuart of the 26th November [1803], and Bullocks required to draw them (from Wellington, The Duke of, *Supplementary Despatches*, Vol. IV, pp. 5–6).

Ordnance Carriages		Number of bullocks in each carriage	Total bullocks
4 brass 18-pounders		35	140
2 8-inch howitzers		28	56
2 5½-inch howitzers		14	28
4 iron 12-pounders		47	188
6 brass 12-pounders		14	84
36 brass 6-pounders		10	36
Tumbrils	Number of tumbrils		
4 18-pounders	4 each = 16	12	192
2 8-inch howitzers	2 each = 4	12	48
2 5½ -inch howitzers	2 each = 4	12	48
4 iron 12-pounders	1 each = 4	12	48
6 brass 12-pounders	2 each = 12	12	144
Ditto with shells	1 each = 6	12	72
36 brass 6-pounders	1 each = 36	12	432
Spare in Mysore for 6-pounders	10	12	120
Store in Mysore	4	12	48
For 4 gallopers, 6-pounders	2	12	24
Spare Carriages			
1 5½-inch howitzer		10	10
1 8-inch howitzer		20	20
5 6-pounders		6	30

Appendix IV

Return of Tippoo Sultaun's Army at the Commencement of the Campaign of 1799 (from Wellington, The Duke of, *Supplementary Despatches*, Vol. I, p.205).

Names	Number of fighting men
Meer Meerans (Generals)	26
Meer Suddoors (Officers in general superintending of forts)	9
Buckshees, or Commanders of Brigades	101
Stable Horse	3,503
Silladar Horse (a horse the property of the rider)	9,392
Infantry, Regulars	23,483
Geish (Armed Militia)	6,209
Ashaam	4,747
Total Fighting Men	47,470
Mootsuddies, Lascars, Pioneers, Artificers, Establishments, &c.	22,392
Total of every description of persons attached to the Army	69,8621

Appendix V

State of the Force composing the Grand Army under the Command of Lieutenant General Harris, February, 1799 (from Wellesley, R., *The Dispatches*, Vol. I, p.700).

Corps	Non Commissioned Drums Rank and File
Cavalry	
19th Regiment Light Dragoons	447
25th Do. Do.	465
1st Regiment Native Cavalry	443
2nd Do. Do.	443
3rd Do. Do.	443
4th Do. Do.	437
Total Cavalry	2678
Artillery	
2 Companies Bengal Artillery	148
1st Battalion Artillery	128
2nd Do. Do.	300
Total Artillery	576
Infantry	
12th Regiment of Foot	773
33rd Do. Do.	869
73rd Do. Do.	851
74th Do. Do.	801
Scotch Brigade	500
Swiss Regiment	814
Total European Infantry	4608
1st Battalion 1st Regiment	1077
2nd Do. 3rd Do.	1022
2nd Do. 5th Do.	1086
1st Do. 6th Do.	1012

Corps	Non Commissioned Drums Rank and File
1st Do. 8th Do.	1101
2nd Do. 9th Do.	857
1st Do. 12th Do.	838
2nd Do. 12th Do.	1068
Three Battalions Bengal Volunteers	3000
Total Native Infantry	11061
Gun Lascars	1726
Pioneers	1000
Grand Total	21649

Appendix VI

Abstract Statement showing the Strength in Non Commissioned Rank and File and distribution of Forces in the Field under Lieutenant-General Stuart; Detachment with the Honourable Major-General Wellesley; the Subsidiary Force under Colonel Stevenson; the Detachment at Hyderabad commanded by Major Irton and of the Troops stationed under Colonel Montresor in Malabar and Canara [August/September 1803] (Adapted from Wellesley, R., *The Dispatches*, Vol. III. pp.665–6).

State of the Army in the Doab under Lieutenant-General Stuart			
Corps	**Europeans**	**Natives**	**Total**
Cavalry	431	846	1277
Artillery	251		251
Infantry	1529	4769	6298
Total (sick and well)	2211	5615	7826

State of Forces detached under Major-General the Honourable A. Wellesley (with Colonel Murray's Force)			
Corps	**Europeans**	**Natives**	**Total**
Cavalry	384	1347	1731
Artillery	266		266
Infantry	1838	6666	8504
Total (sick and well)	2488	8013	10501

State of the Force subsidised by his Highness the Nizam under Colonel Stevenson (in the field)			
Corps	**Europeans**	**Natives**	**Total**
Cavalry	4	905	909
Artillery	120		120
Infantry	778	6113	6891
Total (sick and well)	902	7018	7920

State of Major Irton's Detachment now stationed at Hyderabad			
Corps	**Europeans**	**Natives**	**Total**
Artillery	28		28
Infantry	3	1966	1969
Total (sick and well)	31	1966	1997
State of Forces under Colonel Montresor in Provinces of Malabar and Canara			
Corps	**Europeans**	**Natives**	**Total**
Artillery	156		156
Infantry	1367	7926	9293
Total (sick and well)	1523	7926	9449

Appendix VII

Review of Perron's Force [1803] (adapted from Thorn, Maj W., *Memoir of the War in India*, p.78).

Corps	Where Stationed	Battalions in each Brigade	Regular Infantry in the Battalions	Aly Gools	Total in each Brigade	Number of Guns
1st Brigade (Bourquien)	Delhi	8	6000	1000	7000	50
2nd Brigade (Hessing)	Secundra	7	4000	1600	5600	50
3rd Brigade (Pohlam)	Deccan	8	5000	1000	6000	80
4th Brigade (Dudernaigue)	Deccan	7	4000	1000	5000	70
5th Brigade	Coel, Alyghur, Delhi, Agra	7	4000	NK	4000	
Corps under M. Dupont	Deccan	4	2000	NK	200	NK (c.20)
Major Brownrigg's Corps	Deccan	5	2250	NK	2250	30
Begum Sumroo's Corps	Deccan	4	2400	NK	2400	20
Late Filoze's Brigade (Baptiste)	Ougein and vicinity	6	3000	NK	3000	60
Ambajee Inglia's Brigade	Deccan	16 (stated to be)	6400	NK	6400	84
Grand Total		72	39050	4600	43650	464

NK: Not Known

Appendix VIII

Strength, in round Numbers, of the effective fighting men present with the Army [of Lake] at the above period [April 1805] (adapted from Thorn, Maj W., *Memoir of the War in India*, p. 469).

Corps	Europeans	Natives	Total
Bengal Army			
Infantry			
1st Brigade	250	500	750
2nd Brigade	400	1400	1800
3rd Brigade	190	1100	1290
4th Brigade		1200	1200
Reserve	50	1550	1600
Artillery	150	350	450
Cavalry			
1st Brigade	450	1100	1550
2nd Brigade	520	780	1300
Horse Artillery	50		
Bombay Division			
Infantry and Artillery	600	4200	4800
Troop Of Cavalry		120	120
Guzerat Horse			1000

Glossary

A number of these words have more than one meaning or interpretation. The definition given is that most pertinent to the text.

Arrack	–	Term used to describe a wide variety of Indian alcoholic drinks variably distilled from palm, cane-molasses and rice.
Banjaras	–	Itinerant group trafficking in grain and salt.
Bargir	–	A Maratha cavalryman who did not own his own horse.
Batta	–	An extra allowance allotted to EIC officers, soldiers, or other public servants when in the field or in other special circumstances.
Begum	–	Wife of a Muslim ruler.
Bibi	–	An Indian mistress, common law wife, or long-term consort of a European.
Chunam	–	A type of cement or plaster.
Coss (Kos)	–	A unit of distance. Approximately two miles in the Bengal Presidency.
Dawk	–	Indian postal system of runners.
Deccanis	–	Small resilient horses widely used by the Marathas.
Doab	–	The land between two rivers, especially the Ganges and the Jumna.
Doolie	–	A simple litter used to carry wounded or sick men.
Durbar	–	A court.
Ekas (Ekandas)	–	Horsemen who voluntarily joined the Maratha Army bringing their own horses and accoutrements.
Gaekwar	–	Ruler of Baroda.
Ghat	–	A pass through the hills or a river crossing point.
Golundaz (Golumdauze)	–	An Indian gunner.
Harkarrahs	–	Messengers providing intelligence for armies in the field. Not spies in the modern sense as their operations were non-covert.
Havildar	–	Indian infantry officer in an EIC unit with rank equivalent to sergeant.

Howdah	–	Box-like structure used for riding elephants.
Jagirdar *(Jaghirdar)*	–	Holder of a *jagir*, a revenue-producing estate.
Jamadar	–	Indian infantry officer in an EIC unit with rank equivalent to lieutenant.
Janbaz	–	Mysore suicide troops.
Jasud	–	A spy.
Jowk	–	A Mysorean 100-man unit of infantry equivalent to a company.
Jowkdar	–	A Mysorean officer in command of a *jowk*: equivalent rank to captain.
Kazzak	–	A Mysorean irregular cavalryman; often predatory and similar to the *pindaris* of the Maratha Confederacy.
Khijmatgar	–	A servant.
Killadar *(Killedar)*	–	Commandant of a fort.
Kutcheri	–	A Mysore infantry or cavalry unit equivalent to a division.
Kushun	–	A Mysore infantry unit equivalent to a brigade.
Lakh	–	One hundred thousand. Often applied to *rupees*.
Lascar	–	An Indian artilleryman tasked with moving the guns.
Massulah	–	Indian boat designed to bring ships' passengers ashore.
Matross	–	An artilleryman subordinate to the gunner.
Mokub	–	A unit of Mysorean cavalry equivalent to a regiment.
Naick	–	Indian infantry soldier in an EIC unit with rank equivalent to corporal.
Naqib	–	Mysorean officer with rank equivalent to adjutant.
Nullah	–	A water-course or other feature connected with water.
Pagoda	–	The currency of South India.
Parbias	–	Men from Eastern India (Oudh, Doab, Rohilkhand).
Peshwa	–	Hereditary Prime Minister of the Maratha King and later the nominal head of the Maratha Confederacy.
Pettah	–	A town adjacent to a fort.
Pindaris *(Pendharis)*	–	Irregular Maratha light horse paid only by plunder.
Polygars	–	Subordinate chiefs of South India.
Potdar	–	A treasurer.
Puckally	–	Water-carrier.
Purvia	–	One belonging to the eastern provinces (e.g. Oudh).
Rajput	–	A Hindu warrior caste of northern India.
Risala	–	A Mysore infantry unit equivalent to a battalion.
Risaladar	–	Mysorean officer with rank equivalent to colonel.

Sardar	–	A Maratha military officer or politician.
Sepoy	–	An Indian soldier in the service of the British or another European power.
Serang	–	A native boatswain or head of a body of lascars.
Shutarnal (Zumburak, Shahin)	–	Maratha artillery-piece sometimes fired from the back of a camel.
Sicca	–	Silver coin of Mughal origin used in the Maratha Confederacy. The *sicca rupee* was worth 2s 4d in 1805.
Siladar (Silahdar)	–	Maratha or Mysorean horseman who owned their own horse and weapons.
Sipahdar	–	Mysorean officer commanding a *kushun*.
Sirdar	–	A soldier of high rank.
Sonaut	–	A Maratha silver coin of lower worth than the *sicca rupee*.
Subadar	–	Indian infantry officer in an EIC unit with rank equivalent to captain.
Tappal	–	An Indian postal system.
Tindal	–	An Indian artillery officer in charge of lascars or a boatswain aboard ship.
Tulwar	–	A curved sword.
Vakil	–	An agent or messenger.

Notes

Preface

1. Longford, E., *Wellington: The Years of the Sword.*
2. Muir, R., *Wellington: The Path to Victory 1769–1814.*
3. Cooper, R.G.S., *The Anglo-Maratha Campaigns and the Contest for India.*
4. Bennell, A.S., *The Making of Arthur Wellesley.*
5. Forrest, D., *Tiger of Mysore: The Life and Death of Tipu Sultan.*
6. Weller, J., *Wellington in India.*
7. Muir, p. 677.
8. Brett-James, A., *Life in Wellington's Army.*
9. Howard, M.R., *Death Before Glory.*

Chapter 1

1. Robson, B., *The Organisation and Command Structure of the Indian Army*, p. 10.
2. Heathcote, T.A., *The Indian Army and the Grand Strategy of Empire*, p. 21.
3. Robson, p. 10.
4. Heathcote, pp. 21–2; Bryant, G.J., *The Early Years of the East India Company's Armies*, p. 36.
5. Holmes, R., *Sahib: The British Soldier in India 1750–1914*, p. 216.
6. Wellington, The Duke of, *Supplementary Despatches*, Vol. IV, pp. 524–5.
7. Blakiston, J., *Twelve Years' Military Adventure*, Vol. I, p. 234.
8. Bryant, G.J., *Imperial Mercenaries in the Service of European Imperialists*, p. 28.
9. Collins, B., *Effectiveness and the British Officer Corps*, p. 69.
10. Wellesley, R., *The Dispatches*, Vol. IV, p. 225.
11. Thorn, W., *Memoir of the War in India*, p. 469.
12. Wellesley, Vol. I, pp. 700–702.
13. Wellesley, Vol. IV, p. 597.
14. Wellington, The Duke of, *The Dispatches*, Vol. I, p. 631: Millar, S., *Assaye 1803*, p. 27.
15. Wellington, *Supplementary Despatches*, Vol. IV, pp. 308–9.
16. Ingram, E., *Two Views of British India*, p. 10.
17. Roberts, P.E., *India under Wellesley*, pp. 260–1.
18. Wellesley, Vol. IV, p. 670.
19. ibid., p. 670.
20. Lushington, S.R., *The Life and Services of General Lord Harris*, p. 194.
21. Wellington, *The Dispatches*, Vol. II, p. 1424.
22. Wellington, *Supplementary Despatches*, Vol. IV, p. 629.
23. Wickremesekera, C., *The Best Black Troops in the World*, pp. 154–7.
24. Wellesley, Vol. IV, p. 670.
25. Pemble, J., *Resources and Techniques in the Second Maratha War*, p. 402.
26. Cooper, R.G.S., *The Anglo-Maratha Campaigns and the Contest for India*, p. 144.
27. Pemble, p. 402.
28. Holmes, p. 220.
29. Biddulph, Col J., *The Nineteenth and Their Times*, pp. 101–102.
30. Ingram, E., *Wellington and India*, pp. 11–12.
31. Bayly, R., *Diary of Colonel Bayly*, p. 105.

32. Harness, W., *Trusty and Well Beloved*, pp. 148–50.
33. Cooper, pp. 163–4, 167, 206.
34. Blakiston, Vol. I, p. 233.
35. Wellington, *Supplementary Despatches*, Vol. I, pp. 136–7; Wellington, *The Dispatches*, Vol. I. p. 665.
36. Pitre, Brig K.G., *The Second Anglo-Maratha War*, p. 24; Wellington, *The Dispatches*, Vol. I, p. 480.
37. Pitre, p. 23.
38. Wellington, *Supplementary Despatches*, Vol. I, p. 491.
39. Bennell, A.S., *The Making of Arthur Wellesley*, pp. 82–3.
40. Cantlie, Lt Gen Sir N., *A History of the Army Medical Department*, Vol. I, pp. 410–16.
41. Bryant, *The Early Years of the East India Company's Armies*, pp. 36–7.
42. Reid, S., *Armies of the East India Company*, p. 13; Mason, P., *A Matter of Honour*, p. 139.
43. Holmes, pp. Xxvii, 233.
44. Pitre, p. 19.
45. Heathcote, T.A., *The Military in British India*, pp. 47–9.
46. Barat, A., *The Bengal Native Infantry*, p. 188.
47. *New Regulations for the Bengal Army*, p. 3.
48. Barat, p. 188.
49. Wickremesekera, p. 114.
50. *East-India Register and Directory for 1803*, pp. 34–75.
51. Barat, p. 91.
52. *East-India Register and Directory for 1803*, pp. 158–97.
53. Moor, Capt E., *A Compilation of all the Orders and Regulations of the Bombay Army*, pp. 15–17; *East India Register and Directory for 1803*, pp. 232–49.
54. Mason, pp. 140–1; Reid, p. 23.
55. *New Regulations for the Bengal Army*, p. 3.
56. *East-India Register and Directory for 1803*, pp. 27–32, 151–7; Wilson, Lt-Col W.J., *History of the Madras Army*, Vol. II, p. 288.
57. Pemble, p. 400.
58. ibid., p. 401.
59. Thorn, p. 447.
60. Pemble, p. 386.
61. Weller, J., *Wellington in India*, pp. 290, 295.
62. *New Regulations for the Bengal Army*, p. 2.
63. Pemble, p. 387.
64. Pemble, pp. 386–7; *East-India Register and Directory for 1803*, pp. 76–8.
65. *East-India Register and Directory for 1803*, pp. 198–204, 251–2.
66. Millar, p. 25.
67. Wellington, *Supplementary Despatches*, Vol. IV, pp. 5–6.
68. Pemble, p. 403; Mason, pp. 145–6.
69. *East-India Register and Directory for 1803*, pp. 79, 200, 253.
70. Vibart, Maj H.M., *The Military History of the Madras Engineers*, Vol. I, pp. 391–2.
71. Philippart, J., *The East India Military Calendar*, Vol. I, pp. 132–4.
72. Collins, pp. 69–70; Holmes, p. 53.
73. Purvis, R., *Soldier of the Raj*, p. 63.
74. Collins, pp. 69–70.
75. Gilmour, D., *The British in India*, p. 78.
76. Barat, pp. 73–5, 78–9.
77. Blakiston, Vol. I, pp. 9–10.
78. Purvis, p. 39.
79. Barat, pp. 81–2; Heathcote, *The Military in British India*, p. 47.
80. Barat, p. 56.
81. Reid, p. 9; Barat, pp. 54–7; Malcolm, J., *Malcolm: Soldier, Diplomat, Ideologue of British India*, p. 36.
82. Barat, p. 57.
83. Mason, p. 122.
84. Bayly, p. 105.
85. Blakiston, Vol. I, p. 10.
86. Young, J., *Galloping Guns*, pp. 139–40.

87. Blacker, Lt-Col V., *War without Pity*, p. 134.
88. Barat, pp. 116–117.
89. Pemble, pp. 390–1.
90. Reid, p. 39.
91. *New Regulations for the Bengal Army*, p. 3.
92. Malcolm, BL Add Ms 13664.
93. Pemble, p. 401.
94. Bennell, p. 77.
95. Wellington, *The Dispatches*, Vol. II, p. 1371.
96. Pemble, p. 401.
97. Young, p. 221.
98. Welsh, Col J., *Military Reminiscences*, Vol. I, pp. 204–5.
99. Holmes, pp. 216–17.
100. Wellington, *Supplementary Despatches*, Vol. IV, p. 526.
101. Bennell, pp. 1–2; Roberts, pp. vi–vii; Malcolm, *Malcolm: Soldier, Diplomat, Ideologue*, pp. 4–5.
102. Holmes, pp. 183, 186.
103. *East-India Register and Directory for 1803*, pp. 20–1, 145, 228.
104. Roberts, pp. 9–12, 175–6; Ingram, *Wellington and India*, p. 19.
105. Ingram, *Two Views of British India*, pp.12–13; Moon, Sir P., *The British Conquest and Dominion of India*, p. 295.
106. Bennell, pp. 2–3.
107. Roberts, p. 29.
108. Moon, p. 323; Fortescue, J.W., *A History of the British Army*, Vol. V, pp. 136–7; Bennell, pp. 168–9.
109. Muir, R., *Wellington: The Path to Victory 1769–1814*, p. 99.
110. Wellington, *The Dispatches*, Vol. I, p. 563.
111. Roberts, p. 2.
112. Ingram, *Wellington and India*, p. 12.

Chapter 2

1. Roberts, P.E., *India under Wellesley*, p. 41.
2. Wellesley, R., *The Dispatches*, Vol. I, p. 669.
3. Roy, K., *War,Culture and Society in Early Modern South Asia*, pp. 77–8, 93.
4. Forrest, D., *Tiger of Mysore*, pp. 140–1.
5. Roberts, p. 59.
6. Wilks, Col M., *Historical Sketches of South India*, Vol. III, p. 463.
7. Wellesley, Vol. I, p. 442.
8. Roy, p. 81.
9. ibid., p. 79.
10. Wellesley, Vol. I, pp. 652–3.
11. Wellington, The Duke of, *Supplementary Despatches*, Vol. I, p. 205.
12. Forrest, p. 138.
13. Wellington, *Supplementary Despatches*, Vol. I, p. 205.
14. ibid., Vol. I, p. 208.
15. Malcolm, BL Add Ms 13664.
16. Roy, p. 80.
17. ibid., p. 80.
18. Roy, p. 80; Forrest, p. 139.
19. Roy, p. 80.
20. Bayly, R., *Diary of Colonel Bayly*, p. 74.
21. Roy, p. 80; Forrest, p. 140.
22. Muir, R., *Wellington: The Path to Victory 1769–1814*, p. 76.
23. Forrest, p. 139.
24. Holmes, R., *Sahib: The British Soldier in India 1750–1914*, p. 333.
25. Roy, pp. 78–9; Forrest, p. 139.
26. Roy, p. 81.

27. Rowley, Ensign G., *Journal of the Siege of Seringapatam*, p. 126; Forrest, p. 140.
28. Bayly, pp. 82–3.
29. Rowley, p. 126.
30. Roy, p. 81.
31. Wellington, *Supplementary Despatches*, Vol. I, p. 208.
32. Wilks, Vol. III, p. 463; Roberts, p. 59; Roy, pp. 80–1, 94.
33. Malcolm, J., *Malcolm: Soldier, Diplomat, Ideologue of British India*, p. 159.
34. Sen, S.N., *The Military System of the Marathas*, p. Xiii.
35. Muir, p. 106; Malcolm, *Malcolm: Soldier, Diplomat, Ideologue of British India*, p. 160.
36. Muir, p. 106; Malcolm, *Soldier, Diplomat, Ideologue of British India*, p. 161; Roberts, p. 26; Wellington, *The Dispatches*, Vol. II, p. 1441.
37. Muir, p.106; Malcolm, *Soldier, Diplomat, Ideologue of British India*, p. 161; Roberts, p. 27.
38. Muir, pp. 106–7.
39. Wellington, *The Dispatches*, Vol. II, p. 1449.
40. Sen, p. 77; Duff, J.G., *A History of the Mahrattas*, Vol. III, p. 320; Moon, Sir P., *The British Conquest and Dominion of India*, p. 331; Roberts, p. 27.
41. Sen, p. 78.
42. Pemble, J., *Resources and Techniques in the Second Maratha War*, p. 404; Bennel, A.S., *The Making of Arthur Wellesley*, p. 196.
43. Bennell, pp. 6–7; Sen, p. xviii; Cooper, R.G.S., *The Anglo-Maratha Campaigns and the Contest for India*, p. 240.
44. Sen, pp. 235–6.
45. Duff, Vol. III, p. 238.
46. Sen, p. 241.
47. Smith, L., F., *A Sketch of the Rise, Progress and Termination of the Regular Corps*, p. 61; Sen, p. 117.
48. Pemble, p. 382.
49. ibid., p. 382.
50. ibid., p. 383.
51. ibid., p. 383.
52. Wellesley, A., *The Maratha War Papers of Arthur Wellesley*, p. 26
53. Pemble, p. 384.
54. Sen, pp. 62–3, 66–7, 120.
55. Sen, pp. 62–3; Pemble, p. 392.
56. Sen, pp. 66–7.
57. Roberts, pp. 221–2.
58. ibid., pp. 223–4.
59. Pitre, Brig K.G., *The Second Anglo-Maratha War*, pp. 26–7.
60. Sen, p. 118.
61. Wickremesekera, C., *The Best Black Troops in the World*, p. 61.
62. Sen, p. 118.
63. Cooper, p. 195.
64. Sen, p. 118.
65. Young, J., *Galloping Guns*, p. 108.
66. Sen, p. 118.
67. Wellington, *The Dispatches*, Vol. I, p. 755.
68. Pemble, pp. 379–80.
69. Carnegie, G., *The Mahratta Wars 1797–1805*, p. 35.
70. Pemble, p. 383.
71. Sen, p. xvii.
72. ibid, pp. 67–8.
73. ibid., pp. 5, 68–9.
74. ibid., pp. 69–70.
75. ibid., pp. 69–70.
76. ibid., p. 75.
77. Shipp, J. *Memoirs of the Extraordinary Military Career of John Shipp*, Vol. I, p. 122.
78. Sen, p. 76.
79. Carnegie, p. 35.

80. Pemble, p. 398.
81. Sen, p. 52.
82. Pemble, p. 399.
83. Carnegie, p. 35.
84. Sen, pp. 76–7.
85. Pemble, p. 385.
86. Sen, p. 108.
87. Pemble, pp. 384–6.
88. ibid., pp. 384–5.
89. Wellington, *The Dispatches*, Vol. I. p. 755.
90. Blakiston, J., *Twelve Years' Military Adventure*, Vol. I, p. 176.
91. Wellesley, R., *The Dispatches*, Vol. III, p. 668.
92. Pemble, p. 385.
93. Sen, pp. 71–2.
94. Wellington, *The Dispatches*, Vol. II, pp. 825–6.
95. Wickremesekera, pp. 78–9.
96. Sandes, Lt-Col E.W.C., *The Military Engineer in India*, Vol. I, p. 203.
97. Sen, pp. 92–5.
98. ibid., p. 130.
99. ibid., p. 68.
100. ibid., p. 133.
101. Carnegie, p. 43.
102. Sen, pp. 134–5; Pemble, pp. 399–400.
103. Sen, p. 138.
104. Pemble, p. 375.
105. Sen, p. xvii.
106. Wellington, *The Dispatches*, Vol. II, p. 868.
107. Mason, P., *A Matter of Honour*, p. 54.
108. Pemble, p. 403.
109. ibid., p. 378.
110. ibid., pp. 392–3.
111. Sen, pp. 120–2.
112. Carnegie, pp. 43–4.
113. Cooper, pp. 229–30.
114. Sen, pp. 121–2.
115. Wickremesekera, p. 74.
116. Pemble, pp. 394–5.
117. Cooper, pp. 304–6.
118. Carnegie, p. 49.
119. Welsh, Col J., *Military Reminiscences*, Vol. I, pp. 103, 112.
120. ibid., Vol. I, p. 126.
121. Sen, p. 75.
122. Muir, p. 93; Sardesai, G.S., New History of the Marathas, Vol. III, p. 361.
123. Thorn, Maj W., *Memoir of the War in India*, p. 123.

Chapter 3

1. Holmes, R., *Sahib: The British Soldier in India 1750–1914*, pp. 41–2; Mason, P., *A Matter of Honour*, pp. 17–18.
2. Roberts, P.E., *India under Wellesley*, pp. 22–3.
3. Bennell, A.S., *The Making of Arthur Wellesley*, pp. 1–2; Ingram, E., *Two Views of British India*, pp. 1–4.
4. Wilks, Col M., *Historical Sketches of the South of India*, Vol. III, p. 463.
5. Roberts, pp. 57–8.
6. Forrest, D., *Tiger of Mysore*, pp. 247–0, 253–6, 277–9.
7. Ingram, p. 5.
8. Moon, Sir P., *The British Conquest and Dominion of India*, p. 280.

9. Forrest, pp. 259–60; *Muir, R., Wellington: The Path to Victory 1769–1814*, p. 63; Ingram, p. 5.
10. Forrest, pp. 266–7.
11. Wilson, Lt-Col W.J., *History of the Madras Army*, Vol. II, pp. 309–10.
12. Wellesley, R., *The Dispatches*, Vol. I, p. 357.
13. Beatson, Lt-Col A., *A view of the origin and conduct of the War with Tippoo Sultan*, p. 50.
14. Duff, J.G., *A History of the Mahrattas*, Vol. III, p. 176.
15. Fortescue, J.W., *A History of the British Army*, Vol. IV (II), p. 722.
16. Moon, pp. 282–5; Forrest, pp. 269–76.
17. Wellesley, Vol. I, p. 127.
18. ibid., Vol. I, p. 383
19. ibid., Vol. I, p. 400.
20. Fortescue, Vol. IV (II), p. 724.
21. Forrest, pp. 269–75; Moon, pp. 282–5.
22. Roberts, pp. 50–1.
23. Lushington, S.R., *The Life and Services of General Lord Harris G.C.B.*, p. 260.
24. Muir, pp. 70–3.
25. Moon, p. 280; Lushington, p. 171; Forrest, pp. 264–5.
26. Lushington, pp. 259–60.
27. Fortescue, Vol. IV (II), p. 724.
28. Wellesley, Vol. I, p. 700; Beatson, pp. 54–6.
29. Malcolm, BL Add Ms 13664.
30. Wilson, Vol. III, p. 313; Wellesley, Vol. I, p. 701.
31. Muir, pp. 73–4; Moon, p. 286; Malcolm, J., *Malcolm: Soldier, Diplomat, Ideologue of British India*, p. 83.
32. Wellesley, Vol. I, p. 703.
33. Wellington, The Duke of, *Supplementary Despatches*, Vol. I, p. 205.
34. Beatson, appendix XXX.
35. Muir, p. 75.
36. Beatson, p. 52.
37. Moon, p. 287.
38. Cadell, Sir P., *History of the Bombay Army*, pp. 127–8; Fortescue, Vol. IV (II), p. 727.
39. Beatson, p. 77.
40. Wellesley, Vol. I, pp. 482–4.
41. Price, D., *Memoirs of the Early Life and Services of a Field Officer*, p. 373.
42. Wellesley, Vol. I, p. 485.
43. Price, p. 43.
44. Cadell, p. 128.
45. Wellesley, Vol. I, p. 704.
46. Fortescue, Vol. IV (II), p. 728.
47. Malcolm, *Malcolm: Soldier, Diplomat, Ideologue of British India*, p. 82.
48. *Journal of the Campaign of 1799 in India by an Officer of the 25th Light Dragoons*, pp. 19–20.
49. Wilks, Vol. III, p. 407.
50. Fortescue, Vol. IV (II), pp. 730–1.
51. Beatson, p. 70.
52. *Journal*, p. 21
53. Muir, p. 77.
54. Wellesley, Vol. I, pp, 505, 515.
55. Fortescue, Vol. IV (II), p. 732.
56. Mackenzie, BL Add Ms 13663.
57. Beatson, p. 81.
58. Bayly, R., *Diary of Colonel Bayly*, pp. 73–4.
59. Wellesley, Vol. I, pp. 505, 515.
60. Fortescue, Vol. IV (II), p. 732.
61. Rowley, Ensign G., *Journal of the Siege of Seringapatam*, p. 122.
62. See *Journal*, Lushington, Beatson, Fortescue Vol. IV (II), Wilks, Vol. III, and Roberts.
63. Beatson, p. 82.
64. Forrest, p. 281.
65. Journal, p. 24.

66. Wilks, Vol. III, p. 416.
67. Beatson, pp. 138–9; Forrest, pp. 282–3.
68. Beatson, pp, 138–9, appendix XXX.
69. Fortescue, Vol. IV (II), p. 735.
70. Wellington, The Duke of, *The Dispatches*, Vol. I, p. 28.
71. Muir, p. 80.
72. Forrest, pp. 284–5.
73. Beatson, pp. 89–90.
74. Lushington, pp. 294–5.
75. Rowley, pp. 123–4; Bayly, p. 88.
76. Bayly, p. 89; Elers, G., *Memoirs of George Elers*, pp. 100–101.
77. Muir, pp. 81–3.
78. Lushington, p. 315; Muir, pp. 83–4.
79. Sandes, Lt-Col E.W.C., *The Military Engineer in India*, Vol. I, p. 176.
80. Beatson, p. 108.
81. Lushington, p. 319; Beatson, p. 115; Fortescue, Vol. IV (II), p. 738.
82. Sandes, Vol. I, p. 177; Macquarie, BL IOR/H/814.
83. Vibart, Maj H.M., *The Military History of the Madras Engineers and Pioneers*, Vol. I., pp. 324–5.
84. Forrest, pp. 285–6.
85. Stubbs, Maj F.W., *History of the Bengal Artillery*, Vol. I, p. 182.
86. Wellesley, Vol. I, pp. 569–70; Vibart, Vol. I, pp. 316–17; Beatson, p. 127.
87. Wellesley, Vol. I, pp. 697–8.
88. Rowley, p. 129.
89. ibid., p. 129.
90. Price, p. 427.
91. Rowley, pp. 129–30.
92. Beatson, p. 128.
93. Vibart, Vol. I, pp. 319–20.
94. Rowley, p. 130.
95. Lushington, p. 343.
96. Rowley, p. 130; Vibart, Vol. I, p. 320; Roy, K., *War, Colture and Society in Early Modern South Asia 1740–1849*, p. 93.
97. Wellesley, Vol. I, p. 707; Wellington, *The Dispatches*, Vol. I, p. 28.
98. Vibart, Vol. I, pp. 320–1.
99. Wellington, *The Dispatches*, Vol. I, p. 27.
100. Moon, p. 289
101. Wellington, *The Dispatches*, Vol. I, p. 28.
102. Fortescue, Vol. IV (II), pp. 746–7; Beatson, p. 203.
103. Beatson, p. 151.
104. Muir, p. 76.
105. Wellington, *The Dispatches*, Vol. I, p. 208.
106. Fortescue, Vol. IV (II), p. 745.
107. Forrest, pp. 294–6.
108. Moon, pp. 292–3; Malcolm, *Malcolm: Soldier, Diplomat and Ideologue of British India*, p. 87.
109. Macquarie, BL IOR/H/814.
110. Malcolm, BL Add Ms 13664.
111. Roberts, p. 70.
112. Wellesley, Vol. II, p. 131.
113. Wilson, J., India Conquered, pp. 165–6.

Chapter 4

1. Fortescue, J.W. *A History of the British Army*, Vol. IV (II). pp. 748–9, 767–8.
2. Wellesley, R., *The Dispatches*, Vol. III, p. 53.
3. Sardesai, G.S., *New History of the Marathas*, Vol. III, p. 361; Biddulph, Col J., *The Nineteenth and Their Times*, p. 115.

4. Harness, W., *Trusty and Well Beloved*, p. 143.
5. Wilson, Lt-Col W.J., *History of the Madras Army*, Vol. III, pp. 1–5.
6. Wellington, The Duke of, *Supplementary Despatches*, Vol. I, pp. 341–2; Wilson, Vol. III, pp. 6–7; Fortescue, Vol. IV (II), pp. 751–2.
7. Wellington, *Supplementary Despatches*, Vol. I, p. 486.
8. Wilson, Vol. III, pp. 12–14; Fortescue, Vol. IV (II), p. 752; Wellington, *Supplementary Despatches*, Vol. I, pp. 533, 557.
9. Wellington, The Duke of, *The Dispatches*, Vol. I, p. 105; Muir, R., *Wellington: The Path to Victory 1769–1814*, pp. 94–5.
10. Biddulph, p. 118.
11. Wellington, *Supplementary Despatches*, Vol. II, p. 140.
12. Vibart, Maj H.M., *The Military History of the Madras Engineers and Pioneers*, Vol. I, p. 337; Wilson, Vol. III, p. 14; Wellington, *The Dispatches*, Vol. I, p. 117.
13. Wellington, *The Dispatches*, Vol. I, p. 141.
14. Wellington, *Supplementary Despatches*, Vol. II, p. 61.
15. Wellington, *The Dispatches*, Vol. I, p. 156.
16. Wellington, *Supplementary Despatches*, p. 148.
17. Wellington, *The Dispatches*, Vol. I, p. 162.
18. Ibid., Vol. I, p. 167.
19. Ibid., Vol. I, p. 168.
20. Biddulph, pp. 121–2.
21. Wellington, The Dispatches, Vol. I, p. 178.
22. Muir, p. 94.
23. Fortescue, Vol. IV (II), p. 759.
24. Sardesai, Vol. III, pp. 362–3.
25. Biddulph, p. 122.
26. Moon, Sir P., *The British Conquest and Dominion of India*, p. 295.
27. Roberts, P.E., *India under Wellesley*, p. 131.
28. Moon, pp. 209–306.
29. Roberts, p. 131.
30. Wellington, *Supplementary Despatches*, Vol. II, pp. 438–9.
31. Wilson, Vol. III, pp. 7–10.
32. Wellington, *Supplementary Despatches*, Vol. II, pp. 310–3; Wilson, Vol. III, pp. 28–30.
33. Wilson, Vol. III, pp. 30–32.
34. ibid., Vol. III, p. 37.
35. ibid., Vol. III, pp. 37–9.
36. Welsh, Col J., *Military Reminiscences*, Vol. I, pp. 65–6.
37. Wilson, Vol. III, pp. 40–2; Vibart, Vol. I, pp. 345–6.
38. Welsh, Vol. I, pp. 75–6.
39. Wilson, Vol. III, pp. 43–4; Vibart, Vol. I, p. 347.
40. Wellington, *Supplementary Despatches*, Vol. II, p. 461.
41. Welsh, Vol. I, p. 126.
42. Wilson, Vol. III, pp. 45–8.
43. Welsh, Vol. I, p. 128.
44. Wilson, Vol. III, pp. 49–51; Vibart, Vol. I, p. 352.
45. Wellington, *Supplementary Despatches*, Vol. II, pp. 607–8.
46. ibid., Vol. III, pp. 29–30, 33–4.
47. ibid., Vol. III, pp. 33–4.
48. Wilson, Vol. III, pp. 53–4.
49. Wellington, *Supplementary Despatches*, Vol. III, p. 342.
50. Wilson, Vol. III, p. 55.
51. Wilson, Vol. III, p. 57; Wellington, *Supplementary Despatches*, Vol. III, p. 542.
52. Wellington, *Supplementary Despatches*, Vol. III, pp. 570–1.
53. Cadell, Sir P., *History of the Bombay Army*, pp. 135–8; Duff, J.G., *A History of the Mahrattas*, Vol. III, pp. 218–21.
54. Fortescue, Vol. V, pp. 3–5; Fregosi, P., *Dream of Empire*, pp. 229–31.
55. Roberts, p. 189; Muir pp. 111–12.

56. Bennell, A.S., *The Making of Arthur Wellesley*, pp. 7–8.
57. Roberts, pp. 192–3; Bennell, pp. 22–3.
58. Roberts, pp. 190–2.
59. ibid., p. 194.
60. Bennell, p. 23.
61. Moon, p. 317.
62. Sardesai, Vol. III, p. 402.
63. Wellington, *Supplementary Despatches*, Vol. III, p. 461.
64. Roberts, pp. 199–203.
65. Wellington, *Supplementary Despatches*, Vol. III, p. 395.
66. Muir, pp. 118–19.
67. Wellington, *The Dispatches*, Vol. I, pp. 342–3.
68. Muir, pp. 119–20.
69. Wellington, *The Dispatches*, Vol. I, pp. 345–6.
70. Bennell, p. 38.
71. Wellington, *The Dispatches*, Vol. I, p. 382.
72. Fortescue, Vol. V, p. 9.
73. Wellington, *The Dispatches*, Vol. I, p. 406.
74. Malcolm, *Malcolm: Soldier, Diplomat and Ideologue of British India*, p. 167.
75. Bennell, p. 42.
76. Wellington, *The Dispatches*, Vol. I, p. 76.

Chapter 5

1. Fortescue, J.W., *A History of the British Army*, Vol. V, pp. 9–11; Sardesai, G.S., *New History of the Marathas*, Vol. III, pp. 399–0.
2. Thorn, Maj W., *Memoir of the War in India*, pp. 65–7.
3. Wellesley, A., *The Maratha War Papers of Arthur Wellesley*, p. 152.
4. Muir, R., *Wellington: The Path to Victory 1769–1814*, pp. 126–7.
5. Sardesai, Vol. III, pp. 403–4.
6. Wellesley, *The Maratha War Papers*, p. 159.
7. Wellington, The Duke of, *The Dispatches*, Vol. I, p. 555.
8. ibid., Vol. I, p. 560.
9. Wellesley, R., *The Dispatches*, Vol. III, pp. 165–6.
10. Roberts, P.E., *India under Wellesley*, p. 211.
11. Bennell, A.S., *The Making of Arthur Wellesley*, pp. 25–6, 65; Bennell, A.S., *Arthur Wellesley: The Sepoy General*, pp. 75–6.
12. Muir, p. 130; Bennell, *The Making of Arthur Wellesley*, p. 65.
13. Malcolm, J., *Malcolm: Soldier, Diplomat and Ideologue of British India*, p. 169.
14. Roberts, p. 213.
15. Wellington, *The Dispatches*, Vol. P. 617.
16. ibid., Vol. I, p. 520.
17. Sardesai, Vol. III, pp. 398–9.
18. Fortescue, Vol. V, pp. 11–12.
19. Wellington, *The Dispatches*, Vol. I, p. 595.
20. Wellesley, *The Dispatches*, Vol. III, pp. 154–5.
21. Bennell, *The Making of Arthur Wellesley*, p. 70.
22. ibid., pp. 71–2.
23. Wellington, *The Dispatches*, Vol. I, p. 613.
24. Wellington, *The Dispatches*, Vol. I, pp. 594–5, 631; Wellesley, *The Dispatches*, Vol. III, pp. 665–6; Fortescue, Vol. V, pp. 14–15; Muir, p. 130; Bennell, *The Making of Arthur Wellesley*, pp. 67–70, 77.
25. Wellington, *The Dispatches*, Vol. I, p. 595.
26. Wellington, *The Dispatches*, Vol. I, pp. 586–7; Wellesley, *The Maratha Papers*, pp. 181–3.
27. Duff, J.G. *A History of the Mahrattas*, Vol. III, p. 235.
28. Wellington, *The Dispatches*, Vol. I, p. 595.
29. Muir, pp. 131–2.
30. Wellington, The Duke of, *Supplementary Despatches*, Vol. IV, pp. 100–101.

31. Pitre, Brig K.G., *The Second Anglo-Maratha War*, p. 53; Wellington, *Supplementary Despatches*, Vol. IV, p. 100; Millar, S., *Assaye 1803*, pp. 40–1.
32. Millar, p. 41.
33. Blakiston, J., *Twelve Years Military Adventure*, Vol. I, p. 128.
34. Davidson, Maj H., *History and Services of the 78th Highlanders*, Vol. II, p. 144.
35. Wellington, *The Dispatches*, p. 625.
36. Davidson, Vol. II, pp. 144–5.
37. Welsh, J., Col J., *Military Reminiscences*, Vol. I, pp. 157–8.
38. Millar, p. 44.
39. Davidson, Vol. II, p. 147.
40. Wellington, *The Dispatches*, Vol. I, p. 625.
41. ibid., Vol. I, p. 625.
42. Sardesai, Vol. III, p. 410; Cooper, R.G.S., *The Anglo-Maratha Campaigns and the Contest for India*, p. 92.
43. Wellington, *The Dispatches*, Vol. I, p. 626.
44. Welsh, Vol. I, p. 158.
45. Davidson, Vol. II, p. 145.
46. Welsh, Vol. I, p. 164.
47. Cooper, p. 93.
48. Ingram, E., *Wellington and India*, p. 16.
49. Wellington, *The Dispatches*, Vol. I, p. 646.
50. Fortescue, Vol. V, pp. 19–21; Millar, pp. 46–9.
51. Wellington, *The Dispatches*, Vol. I, p. 686.
52. Harness, W., *Trusty and Well Beloved*, p. 182.
53. Cooper, pp. 95–7.
54. Bennell, *The Making of Arthur Wellesley*, p. 77.
55. Duff, Vol. III, p. 238.
56. Wellington, *The Dispatches*, Vol. I, p. 724.
57. Wellington, *Supplementary Despatches*, Vol. IV, p. 210.
58. Muir, p. 136.
59. Wellington, *Supplementary Despatches*, Vol. IV, p. 210.
60. Elphinstone, M., *Life of the Honourable Mountstuart Elphinstone*, Vol. I, p. 62; Cooper, pp. 98–9.
61. Millar, p. 52.
62. Muir, p. 136; Fortescue, Vol. V, pp. 23–4.
63. Welsh, Vol. I, p. 174.
64. Fortescue, Vol. V, pp23–5; Millar, p. 27.
65. Fortescue, Vol. V, p. 23; Millar, pp. 27, 49; Cooper, pp. 101–2; Bennell, *The Making of Arthur Wellesley*, p. 90; Pitre, pp. 62–4.
66. Wellington, *The Dispatches*, Vol. I, p. 724.
67. Millar, p. 54; Fortescue, Vol. V, p. 25.
68. Elphinstone, Vol. I, p. 87.
69. Swarbrook, NAM 1982-07-64.
70. Elphinstone, Vol. I, p. 87.
71. Blakiston, Vol. I, pp. 169–60.
72. ibid., Vol. I, pp. 160–1.
73. Cooper, p. 106.
74. Frazer, BL Add Ms 13857.
75. Millar, p. 57; Fortescue, Vol. V, p. 26.
76. Blakiston, Vol. I, pp. 161–2.
77. Millar, p. 61.
78. Cooper, pp. 106–8; Millar, pp. 57–8.
79. Wellington, *Supplementary Despatches*, Vol. IV, p. 185.
80. Fortescue, Vol. V, p. 28.
81. Blakiston, Vol. I, p. 164.
82. Elphinstone, Vol. I, p. 66.
83. Fortescue, Vol. V, p. 29.
84. Cooper, pp. 110–11; Millar, pp. 61–2.

85. Wellington, *Supplementary Despatches*, Vol. IV, p. 211.
86. ibid., Vol. IV, pp. 185–6.
87. Blakiston, Vol. I, p. 165.
88. Frazer, BL Add Ms 13857.
89. Millar, pp. 64–5; Muir, pp. 139–40.
90. Millar, p. 69.
91. Wellington, *Supplementary Despatches*, Vol. IV, p. 186.
92. Swarbrook, NAM 1982-07-64.
93. Wellington, *The Dispatches*, Vol. I, p. 729.
94. Swarbrook, NAM 1982-07-64.
95. Blakiston, Vol. I, p. 167.
96. Millar, p. 73; Cooper, p. 114.
97. Elphinstone, Vol. I, p. 68.
98. Frazer, BL Add Ms 13857.
99. Millar, pp. 73–7; Cooper, p. 115; Muir, p. 140.
100. Millar, p. 77.
101. Blakiston, Vol. I, pp. 170–1.
102. Fortescue, Vol. V, p. 31; Millar, p. 81.
103. Blakiston, Vol. I, p. 169.
104. Wellington, *Supplementary Despatches*, Vol. IV, p. 186.
105. Singh, M., *Waqai-Holkar*, p. 105.
106. Wellington, *The Dispatches*, Vol. I, p. 741.
107. Wellington, *The Dispatches*, Vol. I, p. 725; Muir, p. 141; Fortescue, Vol. V, pp. 33–4.
108. Swarbrook, NAM 1982-07-64.
109. Wellington, *The Dispatches*, Vol. I, pp. 187–8.
110. Sardesai, Vol. III, p. 410; Cooper, pp. 104–5; Ingram, E., *Wellington and India*, p. 16.
111. Roy, K., *War, Culture and Society in Early Modern South Asia 1740–1849*, p. 120.
112. Khan, A., *Memoirs of the Puthan Soldier of Fortune*, pp. 194–5.
113. Wellington, *Supplementary Despatches*, Vol. IV, p. 186.
114. Elphinstone, Vol. I, p. 71.
115. Fortescue, Vol. V. P. 32; Cooper, pp. 115–15.
116. Roberts, p. 116.
117. Bennell, *The Making of Arthur Wellesley*, p. 85.
118. Mill, J., *The History of British India*, Vol. VI, p. 367; Fortescue, Vol. V. P. 22.
119. Fuhr, E., *Strategy and Diplomacy in British India*, pp. 128, 133.
120. Davies, H.J., *Moving Forward in the Old Style*, pp. 10–11.
121. Ingram, p. 121.
122. Roberts, p. 216.
123. Bennell, *The Making of Arthur Wellesley*, p. 85.
124. Mason, P., *A Matter of Honour*, p. 161.
125. Muir, pp. 142–3.
126. Roberts, p. 217.
127. Elphinstone, Vol. I, p. 72.
128. Wellington, *Supplementary Despatches*, Vol. IV, p. 186.
129. Muir, p. 140.
130. Wellington, *The Dispatches*, Vol. I, p. 755.
131. ibid., Vol. I, p. 776.
132. ibid., Vol. I, p. 768.
133. ibid., Vol. I, p. 776.
134. Elphinstone, Vol. I, p. 80.

Chapter 6

1. Wellington, The Duke of, *The Dispatches*, Vol. I, p. 767.
2. Bennell, A.S., *The Making of Arthur Wellesley*, p. 92; Muir, R., *Wellington: The Path to Victory 1769–1814*, pp. 143–4.

3. Cooper, R.G.S., *The Anglo-Maratha Campaigns and the Contest for India*, p. 121.
4. Wellington, *The Dispatches*, Vol. I, p. 799.
5. Millar, S., *Assaye 1803*, p. 83.
6. Cooper, p. 123; Millar, p. 84.
7. Muir, p. 143.
8. Wellington, *The Dispatches*, Vol. II, p. 837.
9. ibid., Vol. I, p. 805.
10. Millar, p. 85.
11. Wellington, *The Dispatches*, p. 887.
12. ibid., Vol. II, p. 888.
13. Cooper, p. 125.
14. Welsh, Col J., *Military Reminiscences*, Vol. I, p. 188.
15. Wellington, *The Dispatches*, Vol. II, pp. 893–4.
16. Blakiston, J., *Twelve Years' Military Adventure*, Vol. I, p. 195.
17. Welsh, Vol. I, p. 189.
18. Fortescue, J.W., *A History of the British Army*, Vol. V, p. 39.
19. Fortescue, Vol. V, pp. 39–40; Cooper, p. 126.
20. Pitre, Brig K.G., *The Second Anglo-Maratha War*, pp. 90–1.
21. Cooper, p. 127.
22. Blakiston, Vol. I, pp. 198–9.
23. ibid., Vol. I, pp. 200–1.
24. Fortescue, Vol. V, p. 39.
25. Welsh, Vol. I, p. 192.
26. Cooper, p. 127; Fortescue, Vol. V, pp. 39–40.
27. Wellington, *The Dispatches*, Vol. II, p. 894.
28. Welsh, Vol. I, p. 190.
29. Blakiston, vol. I, pp. 202–3.
30. Innes, R., *The Life of Roderick Innes*, p. 129.
31. Blakiston, Vol. I, p. 203.
32. Welsh, Vol. I, pp. 190–1.
33. Innes, p. 130.
34. Wellington, *The Dispatches*, Vol. II, p. 895.
35. Pitre, p. 90.
36. Elphinstone, M., *Life of the Honourable Mountstuart Elphinstone*, Vol. I, p. 90.
37. Wellington, *The Dispatches*, Vol. II, p. 895.
38. ibid., Vol. II, p. 895.
39. Fortescue, Vol. V, p. 41.
40. Welsh, Vol. I, p. 198.
41. Blakiston, Vol. I, p. 207.
42. Wellington, *The Dispatches*, Vol. II, p. 913.
43. Welsh, Vol. I, p. 195; Vibart, Maj H.M., *The Military History of the Madras Engineers and Pioneers*, Vol. I, p. 381; Fortescue, Vol. V, p. 41.
44. Innes, p. 132.
45. Cooper, p. 133.
46. Muir, p. 146.
47. Wellington, *The Dispatches*, Vol. II, p. 913.
48. Pitre, pp. 99–100; Wellington, *The Dispatches*, Vol. II, p. 915.
49. Wellington, *The Dispatches*, Vol. II, pp. 913–4.
50. Blakiston, Vol. I, p. 220.
51. Wellington, *The Dispatches*, Vol. II, p. 903.
52. Fortescue, Vol. V, p. 42.
53. Wellington, *The Dispatches*, Vol. II, p. 914.
54. Elphinstone, Vol. I, p. 95.
55. Wellesley, A., *The Maratha War Papers*, p. 411.
56. Wellington, *The Dispatches*, Vol. II, p. 914; Sandes, Lt-Col E.W.C., *The Military Engineer in India*, Vol. I, p. 212; Vibart, Vol. I, p. 884; Welsh, Vol. I, p. 196.
57. Blakiston, Vol. I, pp. 222–3.

58. Wellington, *The Dispatches*, Vol. II, p. 909; Vibart, Vol. I, p. 384.
59. Wellington, *The Dispatches*, Vol. II, pp. 914–15; Fortescue, Vol. V, pp. 43–4.
60. Elphinstone, Vol. I, pp. 103–6.
61. Blakiston, Vol. I, pp. 228–30.
62. Innes, pp. 136–7.
63. Wellington, *The Dispatches*, Vol. II, p. 915.
64. Wellesley, R., *The Dispatches*, Vol. III, pp. 673–4.
65. Wilson, Lt-Col W.J., *History of the Madras Army*, Vol. III, pp. 129–30; Vibart, Vol. I, pp. 389–91; Wellesley, *The Dispatches*, Vol. III, p. 671.

Chapter 7

1.   Wellesley, R., *The Dispatches*, Vol. III, pp. 597–8.
2.   Thorn, Maj W., *Memoir of the War in India*, pp. 88–9; Fortescue, J.W. *A History of the British Army*, Vol. V, pp. 47–8.
3.   Thorn, pp. 77–8.
4.   Duff, J.G., *A History of the Mahrattas*, Vol. III, pp. 235–6.
5.   Fortescue, Vol. V, p. 13.
6.   Cooper, R.G.S., *The Anglo-Maratha Campaigns and the Contest for India*, pp. 78–9; Thorn, pp. 75–6.
7.   Wellesley, R., *The Dispatches*, Vol. III, pp. 189–90.
8.   Cooper, pp. 145–7; Stubbs, Maj F.W., *History of the Bengal Artillery*, Vol. I, pp. 200–203.
9.   Pester, J., *To Fight the Marathas*, p. 139.
10. Thorn, pp. 91–2; Stuart, NAM 1992-04-121.
11. Wellesley, *The Dispatches*, Vol. III, p. 283; Thorn, p. 92.
12. Stuart, NAM 1992-04-121.
13. Pester, p. 139.
14. Thorn, pp. 92–3; Cooper, pp. 154–5.
15. Call, NAM 1968-07-150.
16. Wellesley, *The Dispatches*, Vol. III, pp. 284–5.
17. Pester, p. 140; Cooper, p. 156; Wellesley, *The Dispatches*, Vol. III, p. 284.
18. Fortescue, Vol. V, p. 49.
19. Helsham Jones, Maj H., *The Campaigns of Lord Lake against the Marathas 1804–6*, p. 65.
20. Thorn, p.95.
21. Wellesley, *The Dispatches*, Vol. III, p. 287.
22. Thorn, p. 95; Cooper, pp. 159–61.
23. Thorn, pp. 96–7.
24. Pester, pp. 143–4.
25. Thorn, p. 47; Pester, p. 144.
26. Thorn, pp. 98–9.
27. Call, NAM 1968-07-150.
28. Thorn, p. 99.
29. Fortescue, Vol. V, pp. 51–2.
30. Pester, p. 145; Stuart, NAM 1992-04-121.
31. Cooper, p. 165.
32. Wellesley, *The Dispatches*, Vol. III, pp. 666–7; Thorn, p. 100.
33. Wellesley, *The Dispatches*, vol. III, p. 294.
34. Cooper, pp. 166–7.
35. Wellington, The Duke of, *The Dispatches*, Vol. II, p. 783.
36. Singh, M., *Waqai-Holkar*, p. 144.
37. Call, NAM 1968-07-150.
38. Thorn, pp. 105–7; Fortescue, Vol. V, p. 52; Cooper, pp. 168–70.
39. Sardesai, G.S., *New History of the Marathas*, Vol. III, p. 414.
40. Cooper, pp. 171–2; Thorn, p. 108; Fortescue, Vol. V, p. 53.
41. Pester, p. 157.
42. ibid., p. 153.

43. Thorn, pp. 110–11; Duff (Vol. III, p. 250) states 12 battalions of regular infantry amounting to 8–9,000 men, besides 5,000 cavalry, and 70 pieces of cannon.
44. Thorn, pp. 110–11, Fortescue, Vol. V, pp. 53–4; Duff, Vol. III, p. 250.
45. Thorn, p. 111.
46. Thorn, p. 112; Fortescue, Vol. V, p. 54; Duff, Vol. III, p. 251.
47. Stuart, NAM 1992-04-121.
48. Call, NAM 1968-07-150.
49. Thorn, p. 112.
50. ibid., pp. 112–13.
51. Wellesley, *The Dispatches*, Vol. III, p. 308.
52. Pester, p. 155.
53. Thorn, p. 113; Cooper, p. 177.
54. Call, NAM 1968-07-150.
55. Pester, p. 155.
56. Stuart, NAM 1992-04-121; Cooper, p. 182.
57. Call, NAM 1968-07-150.
58. Stuart, NAM 1992-04-121.
59. Wellesley, *The Dispatches*, Vol. III, pp. 667–8.
60. ibid., Vol. III, p. 309.
61. ibid., Vol. III, p. 668.
62. Cooper, pp. 190–1.
63. Singh, p. 144.
64. Call, NAM 1968-07-150.
65. Roberts, P.E., *India under Wellesley*, p. 226.
66. Pester, p. 167; Cooper, p. 190.
67. Fortescue, Vol. V, p. 57.
68. Thorn, pp. 176–7; Cooper, p. 192.
69. Wellesley, *The Dispatches*, Vol. III, p. 312.
70. ibid., Vol. III, p. 395.
71. ibid., Vol. III, p. 395.
72. Thorn, pp. 181–2; Cooper, pp. 194–6.
73. Wellesley, *The Dispatches*, Vol. III, pp. 408–9; Thorn, pp. 184–8; Cooper, pp. 196–8.
74. Pester, p. 191.
75. Wellesley, *The Dispatches*, Vol. III, p. 670.
76. ibid., Vol. III, pp. 408–9.
77. Thorn, pp. 211–12; Duff, Vol. III, pp. 252–3; Fortescue, Vol. V, pp. 58–.
78. Wellesley, Vol. III, p. 440.
79. Thorn, pp. 212–13; Duff, Vol. III, p. 254.
80. Cooper, p. 200.
81. ibid., p. 201.
82. Thorn, pp. 213–14.
83. ibid., pp. 214–15.
84. Thorn, p. 215; Call, NAM 1968-07-150.
85. Wellesley, *The Dispatches*, Vol. III, pp. 442.
86. Hickey, W., *Memoirs of William Hickey*, Vol. IV, pp. 277–8.
87. Fortescue, Vol. V, p. 61; Thorn, p. 230.
88. Fortescue, Vol. V, p. 61.
89. Wellesley, *The Dispatches*, Vol. III, p. 442.
90. Wellesley, *The Dispatches*, Vol. III, p. 442; Cooper, p. 205.
91. Thorn, pp. 217–18; Fortescue, Vol. V, p. 62.
92. Hickey, Vol. IV, p. 278.
93. Thorn, p. 218; Cooper, p. 205.
94. Hickey, Vol. IV, p. 278.
95. Thorn, p. 219.
96. Ibid., pp. 219–21.
97. Wellesley, *The Dispatches*, Vol. III, p. 443.
98. Thorn, pp. 221–2.

99. Hickey, Vol. IV, p. 279.
100. ibid., Vol. IV, p. 279.
101. Thorn, p. 222.
102. Call, NAM 1968-07-150.
103. Wellesley, *The Dispatches*, Vol. III, p. 444.
104. Thorn, p. 230.
105. Fortescue, Vol. V, p. 67.
106. Thorn, p. 224.
107. Wellesley, *The Dispatches*, Vol. III, p. 446.
108. ibid., Vol. III, p. 445.
109. Thorn, p. 222.
110. ibid., pp.233–4.
111. ibid., p. 236.
112. Thorn, pp. 288–90; Fortescue, Vol. V, pp. 68–9.
113. Thorn, pp. 239–46; Duff, Vol. III, pp. 257–9.
114. Moon, Sir P., *The British Conquest and Dominion of India*, pp. 318–19.
115. Thorn, p. 314.
116. Moon, pp. 329–30.
117. Roberts, p. 232.

Chapter 8

1. Bennell, A.S., *The Making of Arthur Wellesley*, pp. 124–5; Thorn, Maj W., *Memoir of the War in India*, pp. 246–9; Pester, J., *To Fight the Marathas*, pp. 251–2.
2. Roberts, P.E. *India under Wellesley*, p. 239.
3. Duff, J.G., *A History of the Mahrattas*, Vol. III, pp. 272–3.
4. Sardesai, G.S., *New History of the Marathas*, Vol. III, pp. 423–4.
5. Roberts, pp. 240–1; Bennell, pp. 151–2.
6. Pitre, Brig K.G., *The Second Anglo-Maratha War*, p. 146.
7. Wellington, The Duke of, *The Dispatches*, Vol. II, p. 1023.
8. ibid., Vol. II, p. 1023.
9. Muir, R., *Wellington: The Path to Victory 1769–1814*, pp. 156–7.
10. Wellington, The Duke of, *Supplementary Despatches*, Vol. IV, p. 373.
11. Wellington, *The Dispatches*, Vol. II, p. 1193; Bennell, p. 154, Fortescue, J.W., *A History of the British Army*, Vol. V, p. 75.
12. Muir, p. 159; Fortescue, Vol. V, pp. 75–6.
13. Duff, Vol. III, p. 276; Fortescue, Vol. V, p. 76.
14. Thorn, pp. 340–2.
15. Roberts, pp. 242–3.
16. Roberts, pp. 242–4; Fortescue, Vol. V, pp. 77–8; Bennell, pp. 157–9.
17. Thorn, p. 344; Fortescue, Vol. V, pp. 78–9.
18. Khan, A., *Memoirs of the Puthan soldier of Fortune*, pp. 205–6.
19. Thorn, p. 344; Fortescue, Vol. V, p. 79.
20. Wellesley, R., *The Dispatches*, Vol. IV, p. 80.
21. Williams, Capt, *A Historical Account of the Rise and Progress of the Bengal Native Infantry*, pp. 298–300.
22. Fortescue, Vol. V, pp. 80–1.
23. Wellington, *The Dispatches*, Vol. II, p. 1252.
24. Bennell, pp. 170–1; Roberts, p. 245.
25. Khan, p. 217.
26. Good accounts of Monson's retreat are found in Bennell, pp. 172–5; Roberts, pp. 246–51; Thorn, pp. 357–67; Fortescue, Vol. V, pp. 85–92; Duff, Vol. III, pp. 277–85.
27. Anderson, BL Mss Eur C626.
28. Singh, M., *Waqai-Holkar*, pp. 159–60.
29. Wellesley, *The Dispatches*, Vol. IV, p. 197.
30. Roberts, pp. 247–9.
31. Roberts, pp. 247–51; Wellesley, *The Dispatches*, Vol. IV, p. 242.
32. Thorn, pp. 367–8; Fortescue, Vol. V, p. 93.

33. Duff, Vol. III, p. 285.
34. Wellesley, *The Dispatches*, Vol. IV, p. 214.
35. Bennell, p. 192.
36. Young, J., *Galloping Guns*, p. 64.
37. Thorn, p. 372.
38. Wellesley, *The Dispatches*, Vol. IV, pp. 346–7.
39. Carnegie, G., *The Mahratta Wars 1797–1805*, p. 57.
40. Thorn, pp. 382–3.
41. ibid., pp. 383–5.
42. Fortescue, Vol. V, p. 97.
43. Thorn, p. 389.
44. Singh, p. 178.
45. Call, NAM 1968-07-150.
46. Young, p. 93.
47. Fortescue, Vo. V, p. 99.
48. Young, p. 93.
49. Shipp, J., *Memoirs of the Extraordinary Military Career*, Vol. I, p. 131.
50. Thorn, p. 394; Wellesley, *The Dispatches*, Vol. IV, p. 234.
51. *The Old Field Officer*, Vol. I, p. 137.
52. Pester, p. 316.
53. *The Old Field Officer*, Vol. I, pp. 137–8.
54. Thorn, p. 395.
55. Wellesely, *The Dispatches*, Vol. IV, p. 234; Thorn, pp. 395–6.
56. Wellesely, *The Dispatches*, Vol. IV, p. 234.
57. Fortescue, Vol. V, p. 104.
58. Wellesley, *The Dispatches*, Vol. IV, p. 245.
59. Singh, pp. 180–1.
60. Khan, p. 229.
61. Wellesley, *The Dispatches*, vol. IV, p. 246.
62. Thorn, p. 407.
63. Sandes, Lt-Col E.W.C., *The Military Engineer in India*, Vol. I, p. 218.
64. Thorn, pp. 407–9.
65. Pester, pp. 335–6.
66. Shipp, Vol. I, pp. 140–1.
67. Call, NAM 1968-07-150.
68. Thorn, pp. 410–11; Fortescue, Vol. V, p. 108.
69. Thorn, pp. 412–13.
70. ibid., p. 412.
71. Call, NAM 1968-07-150.
72. Duff, Vol. III, p. 293.
73. Duff, Vol. III, pp. 293–4; Pitre, p. 188.
74. Thorn, pp. 416–17; Wellesley, *The Dispatches*, pp. 264–5.
75. Shipp, Vol. I, 168–9.
76. ibid., Vol. I, p. 170.
77. Thorn, pp. 419–23; Wellesley, *The Dispatches*, Vol. IV, p. 265.
78. Shipp, Vol. I, pp. 187–8.
79. Pester, p. 350.
80. Young, p. 161.
81. Fortescue, Vol. V, pp. 116–20; Duff, Vol. III, pp. 293–4.
82. Khan, pp. 256–8.
83. Thorn, pp. 449–51; Fortescue, Vol. V, pp. 122–3.
84. Pester, p. 353.
85. Wellesley, *The Dispatches*, Vol. IV, pp. 292–3; Thorn, pp. 452–4; Creighton, J.N., *Narrative of the Siege and Capture of Bhurtpore*, p. 161.
86. Thorn, pp. 454–6.
87. Shipp, Vol. I, pp. 199–200.
88. Ibid., p. 204.

89. Thorn, pp. 456–7; Wellesley, *The Dispatches*, Vol. IV, pp. 293–5; Creighton, p. 163.
90. Pester, p. 356.
91. Thorn, p. 458; Fortescue, Vol. V, pp. 112–27.
92. Shipp, Vol. I, p. 205.
93. Pitre, pp. 202–3.
94. Roberts, p. 253.
95. Fortescue, Vol. V, pp. 127–8.
96. Wellesley, *The Dispatches*, Vol. IV, p. 301.
97. Thorn, p. 459.
98. Wellesley, *The Dispatches*, Vol. IV, p. 310.
99. Thorn, pp. 459–62; Fortescue, Vol. V, pp. 128–9.
100. Wellesley, *The Dispatches*, Vol. IV, pp. 523–4; Moon, Sir P. *The British Conquest and Dominion of India*, pp. 337–8.
101. Fortescue, Vol. V, pp. 129–30.
102. Sardesai, Vol. III, p. 431.
103. Thorn, pp. 468–72.
104. Ibid., p. 469.
105. Moon, p. 345; Malcolm, J., *Malcolm: Soldier, Diplomat, Ideologue of British India*, p. 209.
106. Roberts, pp. 290–1.
107. Roberts, pp. 291–2; Fortescue, Vol. V, p. 132; Moon, p. 346.
108. Thorn, pp. 478–88; Fortescue, Vol. V, p. 133.
109. Roberts, pp. 292–4.
110. Fortescue, Vol. V, p. 134.
111. Sardesai, Vol. III, p. 437.

Chapter 9

1. Bayly, R., *Diary of Colonel Bayly*, p. 24.
2. Blakiston, J., *Twelve Years' Military Adventure*, Vol. I, pp. 17–18.
3. Cotton, S., *Memoirs and Correspondence of Field –Marshal Viscount Combermere*, Vol. I, pp. 51–2.
4. Bayly, p. 27.
5. Holmes, R., *Sahib: The British Soldier in India 1750–1914*, p. 93.
6. Elers, G., *Memoirs of George Elers*, pp. 39–40.
7. Bayly, p. 30.
8. Cotton, Vol. I, p. 52.
9. Williamson, Capt T., *The East India Vade Mecum*, Vol. I, pp. 18–20.
10. Wilson, Lt-Col W.J., *History of the Madras Army*, Vol. Ii, p. 360.
11. Elers, p. 45.
12. Williamson, Vol. I, p. 62.
13. ibid., Vol. I, p. 62.
14. ibid., Vol. I, pp. 72–3.
15. ibid., Vol. I, pp. 109–.
16. ibid., Vol. I, p. 38.
17. Muir, R., *Wellington: The Path to Victory 1769–1814*, pp. 45–7, 166.
18. Carnegie, G., *The Mahratta Wars 1797–1805*, pp. 18–19.
19. ibid., p. 100.
20. Williamson, Vol. I, pp. 23–4.
21. Butler, R., *Narrative of the Life and Travels*, pp. 68–70.
22. Elers, pp. 70–71.
23. Williamson, Vol. I, pp. 20–21, 28–9.
24. Purvis, R., *Soldier of the Raj*, p. 51.
25. Williamson, Vol. I, p. 25.
26. ibid., Vol. I, pp. 29–31.
27. Elers, pp. 45–6.
28. Bayly, p. 32.
29. Elers, p. 46.

30. Blakiston, J., *Twelve Years' Military Adventure*, Vol. I, pp. 23–4.
31. ibid., Vol. I, pp. 19–21.
32. Carnegie, p. 102.
33. Williamson, Vol. I, p. 23.
34. ibid., Vol. I, p. 33.
35. Butler, pp. 46–8.
36. Williamson, Vol. I, p. 46.
37. Elers, pp.51–2.
38. Blakiston, Vol. I, p. 24.
39. Williamson, Vol. I, p. 66.
40. Elers, pp. 52–8.
41. Bayly, pp. 34–5.
42. Holmes, p. 97.
43. Rice, S., *The Life of a Regimental Officer during the Great War 1793–1815*, pp. 89–90.
44. Williamson, Vol. I, pp. 38–40.
45. Budgeon, BL Mss Eur A103.
46. Wellington, The Duke of, *Supplementary Despatches*, Vol. I, p. 84.
47. Williamson, Vol. I, p. 42.
48. Hickey, W., *Memoirs of William Hickey*, Vol. IV, pp. 223–5.
49. Innes, R., *The Life of Roderick Innes*, pp. 38–9.
50. Elers, p. 58.
51. Blakiston, Vol. I, pp. 27–8.
52. Butler, pp. 73–4.
53. ibid., pp. 70–72.
54. Williamson, Vol., p. 130.
55. Welsh, Col J., *Military Reminiscences*, Vol. I, p. 6; Elers, p. 59.
56. ibid., p. 59.
57. Welsh, Vol. I, p. 3.
58. Blakiston, Vol. I, p. 34.
59. *The Old Field Officer*, Vol. I, pp. 26–7.
60. Price, D., *Memoirs of the Early Life and Services of a Field Officer*, p. 28.
61. Holmes, pp. 30–31.
62. Beatson, Lt-Col A., *A view of the origin and conduct of the War with Tippoo Sultan*, p. 258.
63. Ingram E., *Two Views of British India*, pp. 46, 52.
64. Rice, p. 93.
65. Welsh, Vol. I, p. 44.
66. Pester, J., *To Fight the Mahrattas*, pp. 268–70.
67. Elers, p. 63.
68. Welsh, Vol. I, p. 45.
69. Carnegie, p. 54; Young, J., *Galloping Guns*, p. 251.
70. Blakiston, Vol. I, p. 60.
71. Pester, p. 200.
72. Thorn, Maj W., *Memoir of the War in India*, pp. 345–6.
73. Blakiston, Vol. I, pp. 72–3.
74. Thorn, p. 501.
75. Elphinstone, M., *Life of the Honourable Mountstuart Elphinstone*, Vol. I, p. 95.
76. Thorn, p. 437.
77. Williamson, Vol. II, p. 193.
78. Malcolm, J., *Malcolm: Soldier, Diplomat, Ideologue of British India*, pp. 147–8.
79. Cooper, R.G.S., *The Anglo-Maratha Campaigns and the Contest for India*, p. 159.
80. Pester, p. 142.
81. Blakiston, Vol. I, pp. 145–9.
82. Williamson, Vol. II, p. 193.
83. Wellington, The Duke of, *The Dispatches*, Vol. I, p. 290.
84. ibid., Vol. I, p. 27.
85. Elers, pp. 74–5.
86. Pester, p. 196.

87. Innes, p. 42.
88. Welsh, Vol. I, p. 2.
89. Mason, P., *A Matter of Honour*, p. 164.
90. Blakiston, Vol. I, pp. 35–6.
91. Elers, p. 145.
92. Welsh, Vol. I, p. 2.
93. Blakiston, Vol. I, pp. 52, 90.
94. Innes, pp. 79–81.
95. Elers, pp. 118–20.
96. Muir, p. 49.
97. Wellesley, R., *The Dispatches*, Vol. II, p. 580.
98. Wickremesekera, C., *The Best Black Troops in the World*, pp. 18–20.
99. Barat, A., *The Bengal Native Infantry*, pp. 76–7, 112–14.
100. Kincaid, D., *British Social Life in India 1608–1937*, pp. 128–9.

Chapter 10

1. Blakiston, J., *Twelve Years' Military Adventure*, Vol. I, pp. 273–5.
2. ibid., Vol. I, p. 275.
3. ibid., Vol. I, pp. 39, 120.
4. Elers, G., *Memoirs of George Elers*, pp. 73–4.
5. Elphinstone, M., *Life of the Honourable Mountstuart Elphinstone*, Vol. I, pp. 84–5.
6. Pester, J., *To Fight the Mahrattas*, pp. 257–8.
7. Innes, R., *The Life of Roderick Innes*, p. 142.
8. Young, J., *Galloping Guns*, p. 98.
9. Blakiston, Vol. I, pp. 118–19.
10. Welsh, Col J., *Military Reminiscences*, Vol. I, p. 156.
11. Butler, R., *Narrative of the Life and Travels*, pp. 141
12. Blakiston, Vol. I, pp. 31–2.
13. Moor, Capt E., *A Compilation of all the Orders and Regulations of the Bombay Army: Garrison Duties*, p. 189.
14. Price, D., *Memoirs of the Early Life and Services of a Field Officer*, pp. 124–5.
15. Wellington, The Duke of, *The Dispatches*, Vol. I, p. 330.
16. Moor, *A Compilation of all the Orders and Regulations of the Bombay Army: Discipline*, p. 70.
17. ibid., p. 54.
18. Bayly, R., *Diary of Colonel Bayly*, p. 44.
19. Elers, p. 61.
20. Welsh, Vol. I, p. 198.
21. Wellington, *The Dispatches*, Vol. II, p. 839.
22. ibid., Vol. I, pp. 566, 568.
23. ibid, Vol. I, p. 787.
24. Bayly, pp. 57–8.
25. Wellington, The Duke of, *Supplementary Despatches*, Vol. IV, p. 341.
26. Barat, A., *The Bengal Native Infantry*, p. 81.
27. Wilson, Lt-Col W.J., *History of the Madras Army*, Vol. II, pp. 378–9.
28. Williamson, Capt T., *The East India Vade-Mecum*, Vol. II, pp. 227–8.
29. Barat, pp. 66–7.
30. Young, p. 253.
31. Wellington, *Supplementary Despatches*, Vol. I, pp. 451–5.
32. Wilson, Vol. II, p. 292; *New Regulations for the Bengal Army*, pp. 7–8.
33. Moor, *A Compilation of all the Orders and Regulations of the Bombay Army: Retiring*, p. 1; Wilson, Vol. II, pp. 292–3.
34. Butler, p. 276–7.
35. Mason, P., *A Matter of Honour*, pp. 62–3.
36. Williamson, Vol. I, p. 17.
37. Elers, pp. 41–2.

38. Moor, *A Compilation of all the Orders and Regulations of the Bombay Army: Dress*, pp. 37, 43.
39. Wellington, *The Dispatches*, Vol. II, pp. 1173.
40. Mason, p. 139.
41. Malcolm, J., *Malcolm: Soldier, Diplomat, Ideologue of British India*, p. 80.
42. Innes, p. 90.
43. Elers, pp. 60–1.
44. Wellington, *Supplementary Despatches*, Vol. I, p. 107.
45. Blakiston, Vol. I, p. 72.
46. Malcolm, p. 80.
47. Blakiston, Vol. I, p. 61.
48. BL Mss Eur B276.
49. Rowley, Ensign G., *Journal of the Siege of Seringapatam*, p. 121.
50. Wellington, *The Dispatches*, Vol. II, pp. 1076, 1238; Wellington, *Supplementary Despatches*, Vol. IV, p. 92.
51. Pester, p. 156.
52. Ram, S., *From Sepoy to Subidar*, p. 38.
53. Mason, p. 139.
54. Wellington, *The Dispatches*, Vol. I, p. 356.
55. Wellington, *The Dispatches*, Vol. I, p. 171; Wellington, *Supplementary Despatches*, pp. 143–4.
56. Pester, p. 125.
57. Elers, p. 121.
58. Holmes, R., *Sahib: The British Soldier in India 1750–1914*, p. 138.
59. Moor, *A Compilation of all the Orders and Regulations of the Bombay Army: Barracks*, p. 28.
60. Wellington, *Supplementary Despatches*, Vol. I, p. 315.
61. ibid., Vol. II, p. 414.
62. Wellington, *The Dispatches*, Vol. I, p. 489.
63. Young, pp. 255–6.
64. Innes, pp. 54–5.
65. Pester, p. 407.
66. Budgeon, BL Mss Eur A103.
67. Pester, p. 407.
68. Wellington, Supplementary Despatches, Vol. II, p. 415.
69. Elers, p. 133.
70. Le Fevre, NAM 1981-06-10.
71. Welsh, Vol. I, pp. 23–4.
72. Pester, pp. 170–1.
73. Malcolm, BL Add Ms 13664.
74. Thorn, Maj W., *Memoir of the War in India*, pp. 88–9. See also plan of camp.
75. Blakiston, Vol. I, pp. 62–3.
76. Moor, *A Compilation of all the Orders and Regulations of the Bombay Army: Independent Corps*, p. 28.
77. Wellington, *The Dispatches*, Vol. II, pp. 1606–7.
78. Elphinstone, Vol. I, p. 53.
79. *The Old Field Officer*, Vol. I, pp. 71–2.
80. Wellington, *Supplementary Despatches*, Vol. II, p. 203.
81. Blakiston, Vol. I, pp. 114–18.
82. Butler, pp. 169–70.
83. Wellington, *The Dispatches*, Vol. I, pp. 316–17.
84. Bayly, p. 27.
85. Butler, p. 36.
86. Williamson, Vol. I, p. 458.
87. Innes, pp. 66–7.
88. Malcolm, *Malcolm: Soldier, Diplomat, Ideologue of British India*, p. 51.
89. Blakiston, Vol. I, pp. 49–1.
90. Elers, pp. 125–6.
91. Williamson, Vol. I, p. 47.
92. Pester, pp. 378–9.
93. Malcolm, *Malcolm: Soldier, Diplomat, Ideologue of British India*, p. 49.

94. Muir, R., *Wellington: The Path to Victory 1769–1814*, p. 53.
95. Malcolm, *Malcolm: Soldier, Diplomat, Ideologue of British India*, p. 49.
96. Ram, p. 24.
97. Mason, p. 176.
98. Hickey, W., *Memoirs of William Hickey*, Vol. IV, pp. 170–2.
99. Wellington, *Supplementary Despatches*, Vol. I, p. 403.
100. Wilson, Vol. III, p. 163.
101. Wellesley, R., *A Selection of the Despatches*, p. 753.
102. Moor, *A Compilation of all the Orders and Regulations of the Bombay Army: Miscellaneous*, p. 26.
103. Butler, p. 87.
104. Blakiston, Vol. I, p. 276.
105. Mason, p. 175.
106. Hickey, Vol. IV, pp. 251–2.
107. Elers, p. 152.
108. Malcolm, *Malcolm: Soldier, Diplomat, Ideologue of British India*, p. 151.
109. Muir, p. 53.
110. Pester, pp,. 121–3, 203–4, 208.
111. Elers, pp. 133–4.
112. Elphinstone, Vol. I, pp. 57–8, 78–9.

Chapter 11

1. Wellington, The Duke of, *The Dispatches*, Vol. II, p. 865.
2. Fortescue, J.W., *A History of the British Army*, Vol. V, p. 8.
3. Bennell, A. S., *The Making of Arthur Wellesley*, pp. 162–3.
4. Wellington, The Duke of, *Supplementary Despatches*, Vol. IV, pp. 395, 397.
5. Weller, J., *Wellington in India*, pp. 290–3; Pemble, J., *Resources and Techniques in the Second Maratha War*, p. 404.
6. Weller, pp. 292–3.
7. Weller, pp. 295–6; Pemble, p. 403; Mason, P., *A Matter of Honour*, pp. 145–6.
8. Ingram, E., *Wellington and India*, p. 17.
9. ibid., p. 18.
10. Cooper, R.G.S., *The Anglo-Maratha Campaigns and the Contest for India*, p. 148.
11. Wellington, *The Dispatches*, Vol. I, p. 296.
12. ibid., pp. 394, 403.
13. Thorn, Maj W., *Memoir of the War in India*, pp. 433–4.
14. Wellington, *The Dispatches*, Vol. I, p. 390.
15. Wilson, J., *India Conquered*, pp. 171–2.
16. Cooper, p. 335.
17. Blakiston, J., *Twelve Years' Military Adventure*, Vol. I, pp. 191–2.
18. Malcolm, BL Add Ms 13664.
19. Wellington, *The Dispatches*, Vol. I, pp. 495, 519.
20. Cooper, p. 337.
21. Blakiston, Vol. I, pp. 107–8.
22. Pitre, Brig K.G., *The Second Anglo-Maratha War*, p. 23.
23. Elphinstone, M., *Life of the Honourable Mountstuart Elphinstone*, Vol. I., p. 62.
24. Bennell, pp. 82–3.
25. Stanhope, P.H., *Notes of Conversations with the Duke of Wellington 1831–1851*, p. 181; Pitre, p. 22.
26. Wellington, *The Supplementary Despatches*, Vol. II, p. 509.
27. Bennell, p. 108.
28. ibid., p. 188.
29. Pitre, p. 22.
30. Wellington, *The Dispatches*, Vol. I, p. 691; Wellington, *Supplementary Despatches*, Vol. IV, p. 429–30.
31. Thorn, p. 407.
32. Wellington, *The Dispatches*, Vol. I, p. 686.
33. Wellington, *Supplementary Despatches*, Vol. IV, p. 342.

34. Helsham Jones, Maj H., *The Campaigns of Lord Lake against the Marathas 1804–6*, pp. 117–21.
35. Butler, R., *Narrative of the Life and Travels*, pp. 97–9.
36. Pemble, p. 404.
37. Pester, J., *To Fight the Mahrattas*, pp. 153–6.
38. Elphinstone, Vol. I, p. 89.
39. Blakiston, Vol. I, pp. 207–8.
40. Mason, pp. 145–6.
41. Young, J., *Galloping Guns*, pp. 91–3.
42. *The Old Field Officer*, Vol. I, pp. 140–1.
43. Welsh, Col J., *Military Reminiscences*, Vol. I, pp. 194–5.
44. Duff, J.G., *A History of the Mahrattas*, Vol. III, p. 221.
45. Anderson, BL Mss Eur C626.
46. Wellington, *The Dispatches*, Vol. II, p. 1615.
47. Welsh, Vol. I, pp. 98–100.
48. ibid., Vol. I, pp. 97, 101.
49. Sandes, Lt-Col E.W.C., *The Military Engineer in India*, Vol. I, p. 202.
50. Lambton, BL Add Ms 13664.
51. Wellington, *Supplementary Despatches*, Vol. II, p. 10.
52. Pemble, pp. 388–9.
53. Holmes, R., *Sahib: The British Soldier in India 1750–1914*, pp. 380–1.
54. Mackenzie, BL Add Ms 13663.
55. Hickey, W., *Memoirs of William Hickey*, Vol. IV, p. 308.
56. Young, pp. 140–1; 152–3.
57. Shipp, J., *Memoirs of the Extraordinary Military Career*, Vol. I, pp. 200–3.
58. Creighton, J.N., *Narrative of the Siege and Capture of Bhurtpore*, p. 163.
59. *East-India Register and Directory for 1803*, p. 59.
60. *Compilation of Medical Regulations* (Madras, 1803), BL IOR/F/4/155/2723.
61. Swarbrook, NAM 1982-07-64.
62. Innes, R., *The Life of Roderick Innes*, pp. 132–4.
63. Wellington, *The Dispatches*, Vol. I, p. 764.
64. ibid, Vol. I, pp. 740, 747.
65. ibid., Vol. I, p. 765.
66. Wellington, *The Dispatches*, Vol. I. 735; Wellington, *Supplementary Despatches*, Vol. IV, p. 195.
67. Cooper, p. 119. The conclusion is debatable but Cooper provides an excellent account of the aftermath of Assaye.
68. Stuart, NAM 1992-04-121.
69. Sen, S.N., *The Military System of the Marathas*, p. 139.
70. Young, p. 56.
71. Sen, p. 140.
72. Wellington, *The Dispatches*, Vol. I, p. 291.
73. Blakiston, Vol. I, p. 229.
74. Cooper, p. 182.
75. Young, p. 246.
76. Wellington, *Supplementary Despatches*, p. 223.
77. Call, NAM 1968-07-150.
78. Moon, Sir P., *The British Conquest and Dominion of India*, p. 289.
79. Wellington, *Supplementary Despatches*, Vol. I, p. 245.
80. Muir, R., *Wellington: The Path to Victory 1769–1814*, p. 164.
81. Innes, p. 147.

Chapter 12

1. Bryant, G.J., *Indigenous Mercenaries in the Service of European Imperialists*, p. 2.
2. Ram, S., *From Sepoy to Subidar*, pp. xv–xvii.
3. For the debate regarding the authenticity of Sita Ram's memoirs, see Ram, S., pp. xvi–xvii; Cadell, P., *The Autobiography of an Indian Soldier*; Mason, P., *A Matter of Honour*, pp. 207–10; Safadi, A., *From Sepoy to Subadar*.

4. Barat, A., *The Bengal Native Infantry*, p. 49.
5. Bryant, p. 11; Wickremesekera, C., *The Best Black Troops in the World*, pp. 97–9.
6. Bryant, pp. 11–12; Barat, p. 118.
7. Barat, p. 120; Wellington, The Duke of, *The Dispatches*, Vol. II, p. 1046.
8. Wilson, Lt-Col W.J., *History of the Madras Army*, Vol. II, p. 350.
9. Cadell, Sir P., *History of the Bombay Army*, pp. 12–14.
10. Bryant, p. 13.
11. ibid., pp. 13–14.
12. ibid., p. 14.
13. ibid., p. 129.
14. Moor, Capt E., *A Compilation of all the Orders and Regulations of the Bombay Army: Recruiting*, p. 12.
15. Wickremesekera, p. 99.
16. Barat, pp. 127, 139, 150–1; Bryant, pp. 15–16.
17. Ram, pp. 4–5.
18. ibid., pp. 12–16.
19. Barat, pp. 129–32.
20. ibid., p. 157.
21. ibid., pp. 129–30.
22. Murland, Lt-Col H.F., *Baillie-Ki-Paltan*, p. 125.
23. ibid., pp. 283–4.
24. Barat, pp. 130–1, 136, 166. For a full description of uniforms, see Reid, S., *Armies of the East India Company 1750–1850*.
25. Ram., p. 23.
26. Barat, pp. 130, 168, 173; Wellington, The Duke of, *Supplementary Dispatches*, Vol. III, pp. 198, 213.
27. Barat, p. 121.
28. Bryant, p. 14.
29. Cooper, R.G.S., *The Anglo-Maratha Campaigns and the Contest for India*, p. 192.
30. Wickremesekera, p. 105.
31. Barat, pp. 121–2.
32. Bryant, pp. 16–17.
33. Barat, pp. 174–5.
34. Bayly, R., *Diary of Colonel Bayly*, pp. 51–2.
35. Welsh, Col J., *Military Reminiscences*, Vol. I, p. 14.
36. Mason, P., A Matter of Honour, p. 23.
37. Wickremesekera, p. 123.
38. Wellington, The Duke of, *Supplementary Despatches*, Vol. I, p. 450.
39. Moor, *A Compilation of all the Orders and Regulations of the Bombay Army:Native Infantry*, p. 31.
40. Barat, p. 31.
41. Ram, p.15.
42. Wickremesekera, p. 125.
43. Barat, pp. 160–1.
44. ibid., p. 160.
45. Wickremesekera, p. 165.
46. ibid., pp. 126–6.
47. Barat, p. 158.
48. Badenach, W., *Inquiry into the State of the Indian Army*, p. 107.
49. Barat, pp. 151–2.
50. ibid., p. 154.
51. ibid., pp. 154–5.
52. ibid., p. 182.
53. Wilson, Vol. II, p. 296.
54. Moor, *A Compilation of all the Orders and Regulations of the Bombay Army:Pay*, p. 170.
55. Barat, pp. 130–1.
56. Moor, *A Compilation of all the Orders and Regulations of the Bombay Army:Pay*, p. 170.
57. Barat, p. 141.
58. ibid, pp. 139, 142–3.
59. Moor, *A Compilation of all the Orders and Regulations of the Bombay Army: Pensions*, p. 15.

60. Wellington, *Supplementary Despatches*, Vol. IV, p. 495.
61. Murland, 284.
62. Cadell, *History of the Bombay Army*, p. 114.
63. Barat, p. 176.
64. ibid., p. 176.
65. Mason, pp. 126–7.
66. Cadell, *History of the Bombay Army*, p. 114.
67. Mason, p. 130.
68. ibid., pp. 198–9.
69. Ram, pp. 26–8.
70. Wellesley, R., *The Dispatches*, Vol. III, p. 396.
71. Wellington, *The Dispatches*, Vol. I, p. 739.
72. Wellington, *The Supplementary Despatches*, Vol. III, p. 15.
73. Welsh, Vol. I, p. 79; Young, J., *Galloping Guns*, pp. 207–8.
74. Bryant, pp. 27–8.
75. Pemble, J., *Resources and Techniques in the Second Maratha War*, p. 397.
76. Wickremesekera, pp. 154–7.
77. *The Old Field Officer*, Vol. I, pp. 103–4.
78. Duff, J.G., *A History of the Mahrattas*, Vol. III, p. 287.
79. Wellington, *Supplementary Despatches*, Vol. III, pp. 567–8.
80. Wickremesekera, pp. 25–6.
81. Blakiston, J., *Twelve Years' Military Adventure*, Vol. I, p. 325.
82. Barat, p. 186.
83. Wickremesekera, p. 180.
84. Mason, p. 214.
85. Ram, pp. 24–5.
86. Barat, pp. 297, 304; Bryant, p. 28.

Chapter 13

1. *Fifth Report of the Commissioners of Military Enquiry: Army Medical Department*, pp. 37–8.
2. Cantlie, Lt Gen Sir N., *A History of the Army Medical Department*, Vol. I, pp. 411–13.
3. *East India Register and Directory for 1803*, pp. 83–7, 206–9, 257–9.
4. Wilson, Lt-Col W.J., *History of the Madras Army*, Vol. II, pp. 296–7.
5. *Fifth Report of the Commissioners of Military Enquiry: Army Medical Department*, p. 38.
6. Harrison, M., *Disease and Medicine in the Armies of British India 1750–1830*, p. 88.
7. Wellington, The Duke of, *Supplementary Despatches*, Vol. I, pp. 406–8.
8. ibid., Vol. I, p. 455.
9. Wellington, The Duke of, *The Dispatches*, Vol. I, p. 539.
10. Welsh, Col J., *Military Reminiscences*, Vol. I, p. 125.
11. Carnegie, G., *The Mahratta Wars 1797–1805*, p. 57.
12. See Howard, M.R., *Wellington's Doctors*, pp. 91–123, for a wider discussion of military hospitals during this period.
13. Harrison, M., *Public Health and Medicine in British India*.
14. Cantlie, Vol. I, p. 414.
15. Wellington, *The Dispatches*, Vol. I, p. 422.
16. ibid., Vol. I, p. 734.
17. Moor, Capt E., *A Compilation of all the Orders and Regulations of the Bombay Army: Medical Department*, p. 19.
18. Pester, J., *To Fight the Mahrattas*, pp. 195–6.
19. Kincaid, D., *British Social Life in India 1608–1937*, p. 78.
20. Elers, G., *Memoirs of George Elers*, pp. 92–3.
21. Pester, pp. 166, 310–11.
22. Butler, R., *Narrative of the Life and Travels*, pp. 54–5.
23. Wellington, *The Dispatches*, p. 282.
24. *Arthur Wellesley's Order Book 1803–1804*, NAM 1963-08-11.

25. Wellington, *The Dispatches*, Vol. II, pp. 1055–6.
26. Moor, *A Compilation of all the Orders and Regulations of the Bombay Army: Medical Department*, p. 20.
27. Ballingall, G., *Practical Observations on Fever, Dysentery and Liver Complaints*, pp. 163–4.
28. Harrison, *Disease and Medicine in the Armies of British India 1750–1830*, p. 90.
29. Collins, B., *Effectiveness and the British Officer Corps 1793–1815*, p. 70.
30. Holmes, R., *Sahib: The British Soldier in India 1750–1914*, p. 474.
31. Ballingall, p. 306 (appendix V).
32. Wellesley, R., *The Dispatches*, Vol. IV, p. 670.
33. Wellington, *The Dispatches*, Vol. II, p. 1627; Wellington, *Supplementary Despatches*, Vol. II, p. 377.
34. Ballingall, p. 153 (appendix I).
35. Butler, pp. 184–5.
36. Howard, p. 170.
37. Ballingall, p. 22.
38. ibid., pp. 23–4.
39. Blacker, Lt-Col V., *War without Pity*, pp. 70, 72, 88, 97.
40. Howard, p. 168.
41. Welsh, Vol. P. 110.
42. Ballingall, pp. 46–7.
43. Wellington, *Supplementary Despatches*, pp. 96, 103.
44. Ballingall, pp. 238–42.
45. Butler, pp. 65–7.
46. *Letter from an officer in the Seringapatam Campaign*, BL Mss Eur B276.
47. Elphinstone, M., *Life of the Honourable Mountstuart Elphinstone*, Vol. I, p. 58; Malcolm, J., *Malcolm: Soldier, Diplomat, Ideologue of British India*, p. 171; Elers, p. 71.
48. Bayly, R., *Diary of Colonel Bayly*, p. 101.
49. Butler, pp. 121–2.
50. Peers, D., *The Indian Army and the British Garrison Sate in India c1800–1858*, pp. 137–8.
51. Ballingall, appendix V.
52. Peers, pp. 139–40.
53. Elers, p. 63.
54. Shipp, J., *Memoirs of the Extraordinary Military Career*, Vol. I, p. 214.
55. Pester, p. 369; Young, J., *Galloping Guns*, pp. 218, 251.
56. Elphinstone, Vol. I, p. 54.
57. Harrison, *Public Health and Medicine in British India*; Moor, *A Compilation of all the Orders and Regulations of the Bombay Army: Medical Department*, p. 35.
58. Howard, pp. 182–3.
59. Williamson, Capt T. *The East-India Vade Mecum*, Vol. II, p. 262.
60. Blanco, R.L., *Wellington's Surgeon General: Sir James McGrigor*, pp. 68–9.
61. Ballingall, pp. 47–8.
62. Harrison, *Disease and Medicine in the Armies of British India 1750–1830*, p. 94.
63. Bayly, pp. 97, 101.
64. Howard, pp. 162–3.
65. Ballingall, pp. 30, 36.
66. Harrison, *Disease and Medicine in the Armies of British India 1750–1830*, pp. 94–107.
67. ibid., p.98.
68. Ballingall, p. 41.
69. Blacker, p. 128.
70. Ballingall, p. 1.
71. Wellesley, *The Dispatches*, Vol. I, p. 238.
72. Ingram, E., *Two Views of British India*, pp. 41–2.
73. Pester, pp. 402–3.
74. Stewart, A., *Medical Discipline*, pp. 12, 32–5, 80–1.
75. Philippart, J., *The East India Military Calendar*, Vol. I, p. 327.
76. Wallace, R.G., *Fifteen Years in India*, pp. 325–6.
77. McGrigor, J., *The Autobiography and Services of James McGrigor Bart.*, pp. 135–7.
78. Harrison, *Public Health and Medicine in British India*.
79. Moor, *A Compilation of all the Orders and Regulations of the Bombay Army: Native Infantry*, p. 39.

80. Harrison, *Disease and Medicine in the Armies of British India 1750–1830,* pp. 109–10.
81. Herron, J.B.T. and Dunbar, J.A.T., *The British Army's Contribution to Tropical Medicine.*
82. Wellington, *The Dispatches,* Vol. I, p. 648.
83. Wellington, *Supplementary Despatches,* Vol. II p. 377.
84. Wellington, *The Dispatches,* Vol. I, p. 316.
85. ibid., Vol. II, p. 1216.
86. Wellington, *Supplementary Despatches,* Vol. II, p. 501.
87. Muir, R., *Wellington: The Path to Victory 1769–1814,* pp. 98–9.
88. Elers, p. 116.
89. Muir, p. 163.
90. Wellington, *The Dispatches,* Vol. I, p. 252.
91. Wellington, *Supplementary Despatches,* Vol. II, p. 382.
92. Wellington, *The Dispatches,* Vol. II, p. 1216.
93. ibid., Vol. II, p. 1456.
94. Collins, pp. 70, 75.

Epilogue

1. Ingram, E., *Two Views of British India,* p. 311.
2. Bennell, A.S., *The Making of Arthur Wellesley,* p. 224.
3. Moon, Sir P., *The British Conquest and Dominion of India,* pp. 339–44.
4. Philippart, J., *The East India Military Calendar,* Vol. III, p. 518.
5. Elphinstone, M., *Life of the Honourable Mountstuart Elphinstone,* Vol. I, p. 97.
6. Wellington, The Duke of, *The Dispatches,* Vol. I, p. 462.
7. Elers, G., *Memoirs of George Elers,* pp. 120–1.
8. Bayly, R., *Diary of Colonel Bayly,* pp. 87–91; Harness, W., *Trusty and Well Beloved,* p. 154.
9. Wellington, *The Dispatches,* Vol. II, p. 902.
10. Malcolm, J., *Malcolm: Soldier, Diplomat, Ideologue of British India,* p. 203.
11. Bennell, pp. 224–5.
12. James, L., *Raj: The Making and Unmaking of British India,* pp. 70–1.
13. Wellington, The Duke of, *Supplementary Despatches,* Vol. IV, pp. 347–8, 358.
14. Ingram, E., *Wellington and India,* pp. 20–1.
15. ibid., p. 18.
16. Muir, R., *Wellington: The Path to Victory 1796–1814,* pp. 165–6.
17. Davies, H.J., *Wellington's Wars: The Making of a Military Genius,* p. 74.
18. ibid., p. 73.
19. Stanhope, P.H. Earl, *Notes of Conversations with the Duke of Wellington 1831–1851,* p. 130.
20. Harding-Edgar, J., *Next to Wellington: General Sir John Murray,* p. 166.

Bibliography

Manuscripts

British Library (BL), London
Add Ms 13663: Captain Colin Mackenzie's Journal
Add Ms 13664: Captain John Malcolm's Journal
Mss Eur A103: Captain John Budgeon's Journal
Mss Eur C626: Captain Henry Anderson's Diary
Mss Eur 128/168: Strachey's description of Assaye
Mss Eur B276: Letter from an officer in the Seringapatam Campaign
Mss Eur F175/7: Jasper Nicoll's Journal
Add Ms 13857: Captain Frazer's account of Assaye
IOR/H/814: Major Macquarie's account of Seringapatam
Add Ms 13664: Captain Lambton's Journal
IOR/F/4/155/2723: Compilation of Medical Regulations (Madras, 1803)

National Army Museum (NAM), London
1992-04-121: Charles Stuart's Diary
1968-07-150: George Isaac Call's Journal
1982-07-64: Swarbrook's account of Assaye
1963-08-11: Arthur Wellesley's Order Book 1803–1804
1981-06-10: Captain Philip Le Fevre's Diary

Primary printed sources

Anonymous, Journal *of the Campaign of 1799 in India by an Officer of the 25th Light Dragoons*, United Service Journal (1838), Vol. 3, pp. 15–31.

Anonymous, (ed. Stocqueler, J.H.), *The Old Field Officer*, 2 Vols., Edinburgh, 1853.

Badenach, W., *Inquiry into the State of the Indian Army*, London, 1826.

Ballingall, G., *Practical Observations on Fever, Dysentery and Liver Complaints*, Edinburgh, 1823.

Bayly, R., *Diary of Colonel Bayly, 12th Regiment 1796–1830*, London, 1896.

Beatson, Lt-Col A., *A view of the origin and conduct of the War with Tippoo Sultan*, London, 1800.

Blacker, Lt-Col V., (ed. Howell, D.C.J.), *War without Pity in the South Indian Peninsula 1798–1813: The Letter Book of Lieutenant-Colonel Valentine Blacker*, Warwick, 2018.

Blakiston, J., *Twelve Years' Military Adventure*, 2 Vols., London, 1829.

Bulletins of the Campaign, London, 1804.

Butler, R., *Narrative of the Life and Travels of Serjeant B -----*, Edinburgh, 1823.

Call, G.I., (ed. McGuffie, T.H.), *Lake's Mahratta War Campaigns; Report on the Call Journals, 1803 to 1805, now in the Royal United Service Institution*, Journal of the Society for Army Historical Research (1951), Vol. XXIX, pp. 55–62.

Carnegie, G., (ed. Cormack A.A.), *The Mahratta Wars 1797–1805: Letters from the Front*, Banff, 1971.

Copies and Extracts of such parts of the Correspondence between the Governor General and the Governments of India respectively with the Court of Directors and the Secret Committee thereof as relate to Hostilities with the late Tippoo Sultan, London, 1799.

Cotton, S., (ed. Combermere, Viscountess M. and Knollys, Capt W.W.), *Memoirs and Correspondence of Field-Marshal Viscount Combermere*, 2 Vols., London, 1866.

Creighton, J.N., *Narrative of the Siege and Capture of Bhurtpore*, London, 1830.

Crowe, P., (ed. Glover, G.), *The Indian Diary of Lieutenant Philip Crowe 2nd Bengal Native Cavalry 1799–1812*, Huntington, 2014.

East- India Register and Directory for 1803, London, 1803.

Elers, G., (ed. Lord Monson and Gower, G.L.), *Memoirs of George Elers*, London, 1903.

Elphinstone, M., (ed. Colebrooke, T.E.), *Life of the Honourable Mountstuart Elphinstone*, 2 Vols., Cambridge, 2011.

Fifth Report of the Commissioners of Military Enquiry: Army Medical Department, London, 1808.

Harness, W., (ed. Duncan-Jones, C.M.), *Trusty and Well Beloved; The letters home of William Harness*, London, 1957.

Hickey, W., (ed. Spencer, A.), *Memoirs of William Hickey*, 4 Vols., London, 1925.

Hunter, W., *An Essay on Diseases incident to Indian Seamen or Lascars on long voyages*, Calcutta, 1804.

Innes, R., *The Life of Roderick Innes lately of the Seventy-Eighth Regiment*, Stonehaven, 1844.

Kenward, W., (ed. Kenward, D. and Nesbitt-Dufort, R.), *A Sussex Highlander: The Memoirs of Sergeant William Kenward 1767–1828*, Sedlescombe, 2005.

Khan, A., *Memoirs of the Puthan Soldier of Fortune*, Calcutta, 1832.

Malcolm, J., *The Political History of India*, 2 Vols., London, 1826.

McGrigor, J., *The Autobiography and Services of Sir James McGrigor Bart.*, London, 1861.

Moor, Capt E., *A Compilation of all the Orders and Regulations of the Bombay Army*, Bombay, 1801.

New Regulations for the Bengal Army, Calcutta, 1796.

Orrok, J., (ed. McBrayne, A.), *The Letters of Captain John Orrok*, Leicester, 2008.

Pester, J., *To Fight the Mahrattas. The Journal of an Officer of the Bengal Native Infantry 1802–1806*, 2009.

Price, D., *Memoirs of the Early Life and Services of a Field Officer*, London, 1839.

Purvis, R., (ed. Gordon, I.), *Soldier of the Raj*, Barnsley, 2001.

Ram, Sita, (ed. Lunt J.), *From Sepoy to Subidar*, London, 1970.

Rice, S., (ed. Mockler-Ferryman, A.F.), *The Life of a Regimental Officer during the Great War 1793–1815*, Edinburgh, 1913.

Rowley, Ensign G., *Journal of the Siege of Seringapatam*, Reports… of the Corps of Engineers, Madras Presidency (1856), Vol. 4, pp. 119–130.

Shipp, J., *Memoirs of the Extraordinary Military Career of John Shipp*, 2 Vols., London, 1829.

Singh, Mohan, (ed. Sinh, R.), *Waqai-Holkar*, Jaipur, 1998.

Smith, L.F., *A Sketch of the Rise, Progress and Termination of the Regular Corps*, Calcutta, 1805.

Stanhope, P.H. Earl, *Notes of Conversations with the Duke of Wellington 1831–1851*, London, 1888.

Stewart, A., *Medical Discipline or Rules and Regulations for the more Effective Preservation of Health on board the East India Company's Ships*, London, 1798.

Thorn, Maj W., *Memoir of the War in India*, London, 1818.

Wallace, R.G., *Fifteen Years in India or Sketches of a Soldier's Life*, London, 1823.

Watt, A.G., (ed. Hewison, W.S.), *Not Born to be Drowned: An Orkney Soldier in the Napoleonic Wars*, Kirkwall, 2001.

Wellesley, A., (ed. Bennell, A.S.), *The Maratha War Papers of Arthur Wellesley*, Stroud, 1998.

Wellesley, R., (ed. Owen, S.J.), *A Selection of the Despatches, Treaties and other Papers of the Marquess Wellesley K.G. during his government in India*, Oxford, 1877.

Wellesley, R., *History of all the Events and Transactions which have taken place in India*, London, 1805.

Wellesley, R., (ed. Martin, M.), *The Dispatches, Minutes, and Correspondence of the Marquess Wellesley during his administration in India*, 5 Vols., London, 1886–1887.

Wellington, The Duke of, (ed. Gurwood, Col), *The Dispatches of Field Marshal The Duke of Wellington*, 8 Vols., London, 1844–1852.

Wellington, The Duke of, (ed. Wellington, Duke of), *Supplementary Despatches and Memoranda of Field Marshal Arthur Duke of Wellington K.G.*, 15 Vols. London, 1858–1872.

Welsh, Col James, *Military Reminiscences*, 2 Vols., London, 1830.

Williamson, Capt T., *The East India Vade-Mecum*, 2 Vols., London, 1810.

Young, James, *Galloping Guns: The Experiences of an Officer of the Bengal Horse Artillery during the Second Maratha War 1804–1805*, 2008.

Secondary printed sources

Atkinson, C.T., *A Cavalry Regiment of the Mahratta Wars*, Journal of the Society for Army Historical Research (1955), Vol. 33, pp. 80–87.

Barat, A., *The Bengal Native Infantry: Its Organisation and Discipline 1796–1852*, Calcutta, 1962.

Bennell, A.S., *Arthur Wellesley: The Sepoy General*, in Guy, A.J., *The Road to Waterloo*, London, 1990.

Bennell, A.S., *The Making of Arthur Wellesley*, Hyderabad, 1997.

Biddulph, Col J., *The Nineteenth and Their Times*, London, 1899.

Blanco, R.L., *Wellington's Surgeon General: Sir James McGrigor*, Durham, 1974.

Brett-James, A., *Life in Wellington's Army*, London, 1994.

Bryant, G.J., *Indigenous Mercenaries in the Service of European Imperialists: The Case of the Sepoys in the Early British Indian Army 1750–1800*, War in History (2000), Vol. 7, pp. 2–28.

Bryant G.J., *The Early Years of the East India Company's Armies to c1800*, in Guy A.J. and Boyden, P.B, *Soldiers of the Raj*, London, 1997.

Cadell, Sir P., *History of the Bombay Army*, London, 1938.

Cadell, P., *The Autobiography of an Indian Soldier*, Journal of the Society for Army Historical Research (1959), Vol. 37, pp. 49–56.

Cadell, P., *The Dress of the Bombay Soldier*, Journal of the Society for Army Historical Research (1948), Vol. 26, pp. 143–6.

Cantlie, Lt Gen Sir N., *A History of the Army Medical Department*, Vol. I, Edinburgh, 1974.

Collins, B., *Effectiveness and the British Officer Corps 1793–1815*, in Linch, K. and McCormack, M., *Britain's Soldiers: Rethinking War and Society `1715–1815*, Liverpool, 2014.

Cooper, R.G.S., *Logistics in India 1757–1857: The Achievement of Arthur Wellesley Reconsidered*, in Guy, A.J. and Boyden, P.B., *Soldiers of the Raj*, London, 1997.

Cooper, R.G.S., *The Anglo-Maratha Campaigns and the Contest for India*, Cambridge, 2007.

Crawford, Lt-Col D.G., *A History of the Indian Medical Service 1600–1913*, 2 Vols., London, 1914.

Creese, M., *Swords Trembling in their Scabbards*, Solihull, 2015.

Davidson, Maj H., *History and Services of the 78th Highlanders*, 2 Vols., Edinburgh, 1901.

Davies, H.J., *'Moving Forward in the Old Style': Revisiting Wellington's Greatest Battles from Assaye to Waterloo*, British Journal for Military History (2015), Vol. 1, pp. 2–23.

Davies, H.J., *Wellington's Wars: The Making of a Military Genius*, New Haven 2012.

Dodwell, E. and Miles, J.S., *Alphabetical List of the Officers of the Indian Army*, London, 1838.

Duff, J.G., *A History of the Mahrattas*, 3 Vols., Calcutta, 1918.

Forrest, D., *Tiger of Mysore: The Life and Death of Tipu Sultan*, London, 1970.

Fortescue, J.W., *A History of the British Army*, Vol. IV (II), London 1910–1915.

Fregosi, P., *Dreams of Empire*, London, 1989.

Fuhr, E.M., *Strategy and Diplomacy in British India under Marquis Wellesley; The Second Maratha War 1802–1806*, (PhD Thesis, Simon Fraser University, 1994).

Gilmour, D., *The British in India*, London, 2018.

Gleig, G.R., *The Life of Major-General Sir Thomas Munro*, 3 Vols. London, 1830.

Guy, A.J. and Boyden, P.B., *Soldiers of the Raj*, London, 1997.

Harding-Edgar, J., *Next to Wellington: General Sir John Murray*, Warwick, 2018.

Harrison, M., *Disease and Medicine in the Armies of British India 1750–1830*, in Hudson, G.L., *British Military and Naval Medicine 1600–1830*, Amsterdam, 2007.

Harrison, M., *Public Health and Medicine in British India*, at https://pdfs.semanticscholar.org/bc7b/49774183d5b55e9dcfeac690d9417955f112.pdf

Heathcote, T.A., *The Indian Army and the Grand Strategy of Empire to 1913*, in Guy, A.J. and Boyden, P.B., *Soldiers of the Raj*, London, 1997.

Heathcote, T.A., *The Military in British India*, Barnsley, 2013.

Helsham Jones, Maj H., *The Campaigns of Lord Lake against the Marathas 1804–6*, in Professional Papers of the Corps of Royal Engineers (1882), Vol. 8, pp. 33–111.

Herron, J.B.T. and Dunbar, J.A.T., *The British Army's Contribution to Tropical Medicine*, Clinical Medicine (2018), Vol. 18, pp. 380–3.

Holmes, R., *Sahib: The British Soldier in India 1750–1914*, London, 2006.

Howard, M.R., *Death Before Glory. The British Soldier in the West Indies in the French Revolutionary and Napoleonic Wars, 1793–1815*, Barnsley, 2015.

Howard, M.R., *Red Jackets and Red Noses. Alcohol and the British Napoleonic Soldier*, Journal of the Royal Society of Medicine (2000), Vol. 93, pp. 38–41.

Howard, M.R., *Wellington's Doctors: The British Army Medical Services in the Napoleonic Wars*, Staplehurst, 2002.

Ingram, E., *Two Views of British India*, Bath, 1969.

Ingram, E., *Wellington and India*, in Gash, N., *Wellington: Studies in the Military and Political Career of the First Duke of Wellington*, Manchester, 1990.

James, L., *Raj: The Making and Unmaking of British India*, London, 1997.

Kaye, J.W., *The Life and Correspondence of Sir John Malcolm G.C.B.*, 2 Vols. London, 1856.

Khanna, D.D., *Monson's Retreat in Anglo-Maratha War*, Allahabad, 1981.

Kincaid, D., *British Social life in India 1608–1937*, London, 1973.

Longford, E., *Wellington: The Years of the Sword*, London, 1969.

Lushington, S.R., *The Life and Services of General Lord Harris G.C.B.*, London, 1840.

Malcolm, J., *Malcolm: Soldier, Diplomat, Ideologue of British India*, Edinburgh, 2014.

Martin, Sir J.R., *The Sanitary History of the British Army in India*, London, 1868.

Mason, P., *A Matter of Honour*, London, 1974.

Mill, J., *The History of British India*, 3 Vols., London, 1817.

Millar, S., *Assaye 1803*, Oxford, 2006.

Moon, Sir P., *The British Conquest and Dominion of India*, London, 1990.

Muir, R., *Wellington: The Path to Victory 1769–1814*, New Haven, 2013.

Murland, Lt-Col H.F., *Baillie-Ki-Paltan being a History of the 2nd Battalion Madras Pioneers 1759–1930*, Uckfield, 2005.

Pearse, H.W., *Memoir of the Life and Military Services of Viscount Lake*, Edinburgh, 1908.

Peers, D., *The Indian Army and the British Garrison State in India c1800–1858*, in Guy, A.J. and Boyden, P.B., *Soldiers of the Raj*, London, 1997.

Peers, D.M., *Soldiers, Surgeons and the Campaigns to Combat Sexually Transmitted Diseases in Colonial India 1805–1860*, Medical History (1998), Vol. 42, pp. 137–160.

Pemble, J., *Resources and Techniques in the Second Maratha War*, The Historical Journal (1976), Vol. 19, pp. 375–404.

Philippart, J., *The East India Military Calendar*, 3 Vols., London, 1823–26.

Pitre, Brig K.G., *The Second Anglo-Maratha War*, Poona, 1990.

Reid, S., *Armies of the East India Company 1750–1850*, Oxford, 2014.

Roberts, P.E., *India under Wellesley*, Gorakhpur, 1961.

Robson, B., *The Organisation and Command Structure of the Indian Army from its Origins to 1947*, in Guy, A.J. and Boyden, P.B., *Soldiers of the Raj*, London, 1997.

Roy, K., *War, Culture and Society in Early Modern South Asia 1740–1849*, Abingdon, 2011.

Safadi, A., *From Sepoy to Subadar / Khvab-o-Khayal and Douglas Craven Phillott*, The Annual of Urdu Studies (2010), Vol. 25, pp. 42–65.

Sandes, Lt-Col E.W.C., *The Military Engineer in India*, 2 Vols., Chatham, 1933.

Sardesai, G.S., *New History of the Marathas*, 3 Vols., 1948.

Sen, S.N., *The Military System of the Marathas*, Bombay, 1958.

Stubbs, Maj F.W., *History of the Bengal Artillery*, 3 Vols., London, 1877–95.

Thompson, E., *The Making of the Indian Princes*, Oxford, 1943.

Vibart, Maj H.M., *The Military History of the Madras Engineers and Pioneers*, 2 Vols., London, 1881.

Weller, J., *Wellington in India*, London, 1972.

Wickremesekera, C., *The Best Black Troops in the World*, New Delhi, 2002.

Williams, Capt, *An Historical Account of the Rise and Progress of the Bengal Native Infantry*, London, 1817.

Wilks, Col M., *Historical Sketches of the South of India*, 3 Vols., London, 1817.

Wilson, J., *India Conquered*, London, 2016.

Wilson, Lt-Col W.J., *History of the Madras Army*, 5 Vols., London, 1882–89.

Index

G

Gawilghur, 108; fortress of, 115–16; march on, 116–18; siege and storm, 118–20; casualties, 120
Gilmour, Surgeon James, 242
Gujars, 134
Gwalior, 145

H

Haliburton, Colonel John, 115
Harcourt, Lt-Col. 121
Harkarrahs, 18, 95, 208
Harness, Colonel William, 8, 66–7, 90, 94
Harris, Lt-Gen George, 5–6, 45, 59, 227; character of, 47–8; relationship with Arthur Wellesley, 48; competence of, 47
Hartley, Maj-Gen, 51
Hickey, William, 179, 203–4
Holkar, Jaswant Rao, 28, 79, 82; character of, 28, 145, 222–3; strengths, 28; weaknesses, 29, 156; relationship with other Maratha princes, 79, 85; campaigns against Lake 1804–1805, 145–8; relationship with British, 145; objectives, 147; treaty with British, 168; death, 168
Holmes, Major George, 215
Hospitals, 9, 243–4; general, 222, 243–4; field, 222; regimental, 241
Hume, Joseph, 242
Hyderabad Contingent, 48

I

India, Warfare, British Eyewitness Accounts: looting, 63, 120, 223; atrocities, 120, 133, 222–3; attitudes to Indian service, 171–2; voyage, 172–80; women, 172, 201–2; alcohol, 173, 196–7, 248–9; water, 177, 196; arrival, 180–2; scenery, 180, 183–4; climate, 182–3; natural events, 184; wild animals, 185; locals, 185–7; garrison, 188–90; views on sepoys, 186–7; hardships on campaign, 189; drill, 190–1; discipline and punishment, 191–3, 223; mutiny, 192; pay and prize money, 193–4, 223–4; uniform, 194–5; diet, 195–6; leave, 194; pensions, 194; insects, 194; camps and tents, 199–201; religion, 202–3; leisure, 203–4; reading and writing, 204–5; marching, 209–11; fighting, general, 211–13; fighting, hand to hand, 214–16; bravery, 214 15; jungle fighting, 217–18; attacks on forts, 218–19; sieges, 219–21; wounded, 221–2
India, Warfare, General: history of, 4; transport and supply, 8–9; intelligence, 9, 208–9; strategy, 80, 206; marching, 82, 109–10; campaigns in 1803, 86; climate, 126, 34, 149, 182–3; public reaction to in Britain, 144; limited British control, 184; tactics, 206–7, 211, 13; roads, 207–8; communications, 209; maps, 209; sieges, 219
Inglia, Ambaji, 136–43, 145
Inglis, Surgeon John, 243
Innes, Drummer Roderick, 113–15, 120, 179–80, 185–6, 189, 19, 198, 210, 222, 224

K

Kenny, Lt-Col William, 119–20
Khan, Ameer, 39, 149–52, 163, 210
Kirkpatrick, Captain James, 45
Koonch, 149–50

L

Lake, General Gerard (Commander-in-Chief): character of, 21–2, 129, 165–6; strengths, 21, 132, 256; weaknesses, 22, 256; tactics, 22, 132, 134, 206–7, 211; strategy, 123, 136, 145–7, 149, 206; relationship with Governor-General, 123; objectives, 123, 142; bravery, 132, 139; views on native troops, 133, 135, 237; views on Maratha troops, 143, 154; popularity, 143; honours, 144; approach to sieges, 160, 165, 219; views on India and EIC, 168; return to England, 168; relationship with British Government, 168; comparison with Arthur Wellesley, 206–7, 256; prize money received, 224; death, 256
Lalley's Corps, 59
Lambton, Captain William, 218
Langlands, Lt George, 215
Laswari, Battle of: battle, 136–42; Lake's tactics, 137, 140; casualties, 142